The Other I

(From My Diaries)

Zohra Zoberi

To order additional copies of this book, contact:
Xlibris
844-714-8691
www.Xlibris.com
Orders@Xlibris.com
739205

Oceans Apart, Close to Our Hearts

A Star Is Born!

The Train Journey

'From a Widow's Closet' (play #4)

Literally Gala at the Embassy

PART FOUR

Challenges, and . . . Creative Escapes!

The Iron Man

The Internal Flame

Mind Battle

The Rock Guard

PART FIVE
Sunset…and…Sunrise

Family Is Family
Coping with Covid
Our Connection with a Genius

The End

This book is dedicated to*:*
My late husband Dr. Mujeeb Zoberi, and…
My children Dr. Kashif Zoberi and Shireen Kashif

The Second Journey

With a handful of precious values
to the East I bid farewell
to adopt, adapt, submerge, and
emerge in the West—inquisitive, passionate
From deep down arose my quest
Where did this journey begin?
How did I come this far?
Where will I be tomorrow?

To befriend my inner self, I decided
to take the adventurous journey again
to visit the special places I once did
> *Rekindle my romance and,*
> *rest on the sweet memories of those*
> *who reside in my soul!*

To spend time to cherish those
who had positive impact upon my life
Along this journey, how could I ignore . . .
those who gave me heartaches
yet invoked my strength and wisdom
Hindsight, my best friend, is now holding my hand
to rejoice over the hurdles overcome.

This second journey
may provide me with an insight
Where do I go next?
.....

Zohra Zoberi

"If words come from the heart, they will enter the heart."

—Rumi

PREFACE

At age ten, fascinated by a young lady who was travelling off to Canada alone, I rush into my father's room, and swirl his globe around upon its axis with a flick of my fingers, to see how far Canada was . . . *ouff*—all the way on the other side of the world! The impossibility eventually became a possibility.

Six years later, a high school girl in 1963, my life takes a sudden turn when I finally fly alone from Pakistan, but to an unknown destination in Africa, to spend my life with a scholar who promised to take me around the world. My long detour involved no less than twelve years of fascinating travels, travails, and tumultuous experiences in three dozen countries spanning East and West Africa, Europe, and the Middle East. The Canadian Dream was finally realized in 1976.

Upon arrival, a major hurdle stares me in the face, but when my unfettered panoramic vision recognizes the potential over here, as I explore away from off the beaten track, opportunities abound. My story is about embracing surprises, overcoming hurdles, celebrating successes. It's an attempt to achieve the 'best of both worlds' melding values from the East and the West and adapting without losing my core values.

Fortunately, I already had exposure to people of many cultures, faiths, colors, and creeds that blessed me with a bird's-eye view. Having observed the lifestyle of the filthy rich as well as the marginalized poor along the way, kept me grounded. Through my writer's lens I was able to decipher societies' failures and successes. Much of it reflects in my eclectic poetry book *True Colours—from the Universe to the Inner Mind*. I wholeheartedly embraced the multicultural aspects of Canadian society in the **True North** as it is known. This enabled me to avail many careers as well as socio-cultural opportunities.

In order to give back to the community, I have attempted to harness the power of the literary arts to raise intercultural awareness. However, my focus has been upon South Asians who comprise over half the population of Mississauga and the region of Peel.

Since my life has straddled two cultures simultaneously, the need to remain connected with blood relatives in the land of my birth, 'Indo-Pakistan', has beckoned me to travel back and forth frequently. The reader may empathize with the initial restlessness of my spirit, but also accompany me on a journey of gradual change, taking place within my psyche. Moreover, I invite the *Western* readers to travel with me and take a glimpse into the lives and experiences of everyday people in Pakistan and extend a warm invitation to the *Eastern* readers to travel with me to Canada. Through my eyes, witness a colorful and compelling story of migration, highlighting our struggles as newcomers, our desire to fulfill purposeful roles and contribute to the vibrant multicultural mosaic. Mississauga is a perfect example which has evolved as the hub of art and culture over four decades or longer—right before my eyes!

The story of migration is universal, as our ancestors too embraced the unknown, travelling and settling in faraway lands since time immemorial. Through my personal voyage of self-discovery, my hope is to inspire the readers, from younger to the more mature in years, to employ the power and passion of the human spirit within their own lives, to effect change, and to affect the lives of themselves and others in a positive manner.

Sprinkled with some 'juicy', some 'scary' episodes, as well as many unexpected twists and turns, this story showcases the potential for *'Enlightenment through Entertainment'* and raises numerous serious, real-life social dilemmas and mental health issues we must reflect upon, debate, and learn from, *together.*

****

*The city I have joyfully resided in for 46 years is the traditional territory of the Mississauga Anishinaabeg. Therefore, I express my heartfelt gratitude to the First Nations, the original owners of this precious land they nurtured.

Acknowledgments

First and foremost, I am grateful to the **Mississauga Arts Council** for continued support over seventeen years in the field of Literary Arts, and now by way of their Matchmaker MicroGrant Program. Special thanks to the Executive Director Mike Douglas for his keen interest.

Rodica Albu: My immense gratitude to Ms. Albu (*Professor Emerita of English Language, Linguistics and Canadian Studies*). Almost two decades back during her visit to Canada, we made literary/spiritual connection. I feel honored that this scholar has taken keen interest in my story and provided the back cover review.

Reva Stern: A heartfelt appreciation to my friend, Author/Director who has been closely involved in several of my literary arts projects detailed in this book. She edited a few excerpts finalized as stand-alone stories for publications, included in this memoir. Reva has also been a pillar of support during my challenging times. I appreciate her back cover comments.

Dr. Khalid Sohail: Psychotherapist by profession, a prolific author with numerous publications and extensive outreach from West to East. I thank him for his back cover comments which 'fit like a glove' as he has captured all five aspects of my memoir. He is the only local author I know who also writes prose, poetry, and plays, both in English and Urdu.

Linda Thomas: Previously the Executive Director of the Mississauga Arts Council, who has supported me in my past projects, as well as this one.

Nathan Medcalf: I thank him for reviewing my poems, intended to add flavor to this memoir.

Dr. Kashif Zoberi: Thanks to my son for providing me his loving support whenever I felt 'overwhelmed' with this task.

My grand daughters, Elina, Marzia, and Daania: Thank you for inspiring me by reading some excerpts from my book with interest. I'm thankful to Shireen Hasan, my 'daughter-in-love' for taking the cover page photo in color. Thanks to my talented niece Zainab Mansoor for designing the cover page (using my 1963 bridal picture).

Writers and Editors Network: Thanks to Maria Marchelletta, Jasmine Jackman, and other authors for their support, many of whom participated in my innovative literary projects (stage shows). I also thank other Artists and volunteers from the community for participating in my stage productions. Thank you all for giving me the permission to use your real names in this story.

Courtney Park Authors Club: I am grateful to Cheryl Xavier of IOW, Mary Ellen Korosil, and others who have patiently listened to the excerpts from these memoirs.

Zehra Naqvi: My friend, whose gourmet-style home cooking and her immense fascination for my life stories encouraged me to entertain her with my *animated recitals*. Many evenings were spent in inspirational literary discourse as she proffered her honest critique of my work.

****

Recipient of previous MARTY's Awards, I am grateful to the Mississauga Arts Council for supporting me in my life's most significant literary endeavor by way of a recent Matchmaker MicroGrant.

PART ONE

Uncharted Territory

A Turning Point

1 Everyone's life is a journey. Some travel the direct path, while others wander off on to side roads. My voyage began in 1963, on the day I returned from school.

The *Tangay Waala* pulled up in front of my house as usual. I jumped out of the carriage, gave a friendly yank at the horses' tail, straightened out my form-fitting *Shalwaar Kameez* and as I turned to say goodbye, I noticed the driver eyeing my school uniform from behind, with more than tasteful curiosity. However, this was routine, so I waved a curt goodbye and skipped my way through the front door of my house.

Ammi (my mom) called from the drawing room, "Shadan, come in and join everyone for tea."

I wondered why we were having tea in the formal drawing room instead of the usual TV lounge! But my confusion was clarified when I saw a tall, slim stranger sitting comfortably in my father's favorite chair, while my father was seated, quite stiffly, on the sofa beside my mother. Across from them sat my favorite aunt, my dad's only sister Rasheeda.

My mother cooed like one of our pet budgies.

"Shadan, come and meet Muzaffar Bhai, your father's cousin from Karachi."

There was always a new relative coming to visit our home.

We had such an enormous family. I could probably live to be one hundred and still never meet them all. But I smiled politely and greeted him, "*Salam Alaikum, Uncle*," and that was just about all I had to say.

I sat quietly while the conversation went on all around me.

"How does the weather differ between Karachi and Rawalpindi?" "How green is Rawalpindi compared to the brown sand of Karachi?" "How is it that the people look more vibrant and healthier in Pindi than the leaner folks of Karachi?" Frankly, I was bored. All I wanted was to have another piece of *gulab jaman* (a popular sweet).

Luckily as I reached out for a second helping, the gentleman rose to his feet saying, "This has been pleasant, but I must leave now. I don't want to miss my plane."

My parents got up to walk him to the door, but my aunt Rasheeda remained behind.

As I stuffed the *gulab jaman* in my mouth, she cleared her throat as if to begin a conversation. "Shadan, the gentleman that was just here, has come to bring us good news,"

"Muzaffar Bhai and his two brothers live in Karachi. The fourth and youngest brother lives in London England and…the good news is…he is quite a catch. He is a University Professor with more degrees than I ever knew existed. Shadan, we know how much you admire the educated, so that alone should perk your interest."

What was she telling me? Of course, I was now struggling to swallow the *gulab jaman* without choking. Surely this was not a marriage proposal? I was only sixteen, and my dream was not to be the wife of a doctor, but to be a doctor myself. I was stunned in silence.

"I see that you are overwhelmed by such an incredible surprise," said my aunt. "All you have to do is to meet him and decide. That is, of course, if his brother has approved of you. If so, then the gentleman will fly in as early as tomorrow to meet you."

When my parents returned, my mother asked Aunt Rasheeda, "I can tell by the dumbfounded look on Shadan's face, that you've already explained everything to her."

Abbaji (my father) excused himself. "I'll leave you ladies to take care of women's business. I have to attend to my *budgies*."

I'm sure that no one would ever imagine that such a decision would be simple for an undersized, underweight sixteen-year-old who could almost pass for twelve, but my intense curiosity challenged me, so it was difficult to resist at least 'toying' with the idea.

Of course, there was one glaring concern that had not yet been raised. What did this suitor look like? Could he be Waheed Murad, or Paul Newman? Or more like 'Frankenstein' or the 'Hunch back of Notre Dame'? I had to ask.

"Does anyone by any chance have a photo of this prospect?"

The two ladies chuckled, and Aunt Rasheeda said, "Well, I do have a photo he left with us." She casually handed it over.

"*Aray wah, such mouch?* He does look almost like Paul Newman." The two women sat on either side of me and squinted as I pointed.

"Oh my God, he has such gorgeous green eyes!" Both chuckled and said, "No, no, not Mr. Green Eyes, it's the other one." Unfortunately, the other gentleman in the photo was out of focus, so I wasn't able to make a comparison.

"Let's just say, if it is 'Mr. Green Eyes,' I'm willing to say yes right now, but…if it's the other one, since I can't see him clearly, I'm willing to meet him, but no commitment."

Ammi cut me down to size.

"How do you know you've been approved? What you don't know, my dear, is that he stopped by this morning, and saw you at your *Janamaz*, saying your morning prayers. You were all covered up, praying with fervor, looking like a saint. And then you wiggled in this afternoon, with your tight-fitting *shalwar kameez* and your shiny stilettos.

"I tell you, he seemed very uncomfortable with the way you were dressed. Before he left, your father and I made every attempt to convince Muzaffar Bhai that you are a proper and obedient young lady."

"Well, I guess I'll never get to find out if the other guy was almost Paul Newman."

The scales of negotiation were already tilted in his favor. I was given a faded 3 x 5 fuzzy photo of my suitor, while he got to judge *my* qualifications by viewing an 8 x 10 full color glossy that was willingly given by my family to Muzaffar Bhai.

He must have headed to the post office the minute he stepped off the plane in Karachi, because within days, the gentleman had left London, bypassed Karachi, and was seated in my drawing room, waiting for the big reveal.

I, on the other hand, was in my room, being fluffed, puffed, brushed, and exquisitely dressed for the occasion.

Now my entourage of cousins and aunts had to face a serious problem. I looked ready, but I was not prepared to budge. For the first time in my memory, I was overcome with a paralyzing shyness.

Tea and refreshments were served in the finest bone china. The conversation went on, while I remained determinedly in my room, easing my tension by cutting out red paper hearts. Time passed slowly for the visitor, but the lack of an appearance by his potential fiancée made him so uncomfortable, he finally rose to his feet, smiled, and announced his departure.

My cousin took him aside and whispered, "Mujeeb Bhai, I would like to show you something amazing."

He thought it was going to be *me*, but he was in for a big surprise.

My cousin led him down the hall, past my room, across the back verandah, to my father's pride and joy: a caged-off room that was filled with many rainbow-hued magnificent budgies! It was my dad's hobby, and amongst our circle of friends, every infant on their first birthday, received a gift from my father, of a beautiful bird cage with a pair of his very special pets inside.

He was utterly confused; he had come to view a potential wife and instead he was staring at dozens of budgies. My cousin *Shahida* confessed to me later that the trip to 'bird-land' was simply to sneak him away from the family and bring him to meet me.

Shahida led him back down the hall, opening the door to my room, and cheekily proffered, "Perhaps you prefer this budgie?"

That was how Dr. Mujeeb Zoberi and I first laid eyes on each other. My cousin slipped away, closing the door behind her, and left us to navigate our own way through a conversation.

For several minutes, we sat in silence. I continued to cut out paper hearts, and he continued to watch. I sneaked a peek or two. I was curious. He finally began the conversation.

"Do you want to continue cutting out those hearts, or do you want to take advantage of this opportunity your cousin has given us? Please, let's talk about *our* hearts. Do you like me?"

I was silent.

"Would you like to travel to exotic places?" My silence continued.

"Do you realize I could give you everything?" I still didn't break my silence.

"You and I, no third life between us"

Always having to change diapers of my little siblings or cousins, the idea excited me, but I didn't let on. Then he said, "Are you at least considering giving me your consent?"

I put down my scissors and paper and turned to look directly at him.

"But I don't even know you."

He didn't seem the least bit shaken by my claim. Instead, he nodded and suggested, "Fair enough. How about you and I go for a picnic and get to know each other?"

I said doubtfully, "Just the two of us?"

He replied without a second thought, "Just the two of us."

The next morning, my mother came running into my room.

"Wake up, Shadan! Come, you must look out the window."

"Why, have the guavas turned to gold, overnight?"

"Better than that, it's the day of your picnic...and it's raining. This is such a good omen. You know that day after day, we have endured scorching sun, and we always pray for even a little rain. Well, today is the day. Now get up, everybody is waiting for you for breakfast, and Taaj Bibi has made your favorite *parathas.*" (Flat bread fried on a griddle)

Ammi always knew that she could lead me anywhere with the promise of a tasty *paratha.*

Everyone in the house eagerly helped to prepare for the picnic. Our maid was preparing the food, my mother was making tea, and my cousin had already laid out my freshly ironed *shalwar kameez.* This truly was to be a special day.

Within an hour of breakfast, the sun had also awoken and was scorching Rawalpindi. I couldn't resist teasing my mother, "So, Ammi, is this ball of fire a bad omen, so we should cancel the picnic?"

"Just go and get dressed," she ordered, then muttered, "*Hamari hi billi hami se meow*" (my own cat is meowing at me).

By one in the afternoon, our *Tangay Wala*, Aziz, had already picked up Dr. Mujeeb Hasan Zoberi from his hotel, and had arrived in front of our door. My father had thought that instead of his old Mazda why not treat the 'foreigner' to ride in one of our special carriages.

We were particularly fond of our driver Aziz, who was always impeccably dressed all in white from top to toe. His elegant horse *Masthi* sported a towering red plume on top of its head, and the *Tanga* (carriage) was hand painted in vibrant colors with matching seat covers.

Mujeeb was a perfect gentleman. He came to the door and escorted me swiftly to the Tanga. As I began to step up to the carriage I realized that we had not picked up the picnic basket from the veranda. When I turned around, I saw my cousin coming toward us, carrying the basket. Behind her, another cousin, with an armful of mats! And behind her, yet another cousin, carrying a sun umbrella.

I turned to Mujeeb and spoke my first words of the day, "Just the two of us, huh?"

I took my seat beside him, at the front of the Tanga, and the three cousins sat back-to-back with us, closely conspiring together, like the three witches of Macbeth. It was now clear, that they were to be our chaperones. Our challenge for the day would be to avoid them.

Our Only Date…

We arrived at our destination and began to unload.

The picnic spot, formerly known as Topi Park, had been upgraded, and renamed Ayyub National Park after President Ayyub Khan who was extremely popular.

Mujeeb was impressed with the wonder of it all.

As we headed toward the stream, two dozen hands were waving at us and cheering.

Mujeeb must have thought as though we were at a cricket game. As we got closer, I realized about a dozen other relatives had arrived ahead of us to secure a spot for us. One of the three witches shouted, "Your cars may be faster, but we prefer to ride in a first-class carriage." Again, all I could think of was, *Just the two of us, huh?* But I said nothing.

The family quickly laid out the picnic lunch, and we all gathered around to eat our fill of *Shami kebabs*, sandwiches, and mangoes. When everyone was satisfied and sleepy, Mujeeb whispered, "Come with me, please."

I got up and cautiously obeyed him, and within minutes we were seated in a rowboat, facing a slender young oarsman who was getting ready to leave the pier.

Suddenly, I felt a rumble inside the boat. I turned around and saw the three witches comfortably seated behind us. Mujeeb shrugged, looking quite helpless. He had tried. As we pulled away, another boat loaded down with relatives of various shapes and sizes sailed parallel to us for the rest of the ride.

There was little conversation that day, but there was a running monologue from Mujeeb.

Upon return, I nodded my shy polite goodbye to him, he was returning to his hotel.

I went inside with my cousins. Soon after, Aunt Rasheeda sneaked into my room, and the cousins disappeared. She asked me, "Did you enjoy yourself today?"

"It was okay."

"Are you attracted to him?"

"Um kind of okay,"

"Do you like him?"

"He's okay."

"Isn't there anything about him that's better than okay?"

"Well, he has a PhD, and a bunch of other degrees. I sure like that."

"That's it? What's wrong with you? Don't you realize this man can give you everything? He has money, power, position, what more could you want?"

I candidly asked, "Tell me honestly, Auntie. Is he really that perfect?"

"To be honest …"

"To be honest what, please, be honest. What is it?" I asked.

"Look, I heard from Fareeda, his cousin's mother that he is planning to become a visiting professor and travel the world. That he's not interested in having children. Shadan *Beti,* the other thing is that both his parents are gone. Other than his brothers, there are no in-laws to interfere." It took all my inner strength to control the faint smile that threatened to give me away. How could I tell my aunt that all I wanted was to travel the world, be exposed to education, never have to change any diapers . . . and most of all, I would have no in-laws to control me. I had heard so many horror stories about that. So this was the best news she could have delivered.

I could tell by the look in her eyes that she felt she had just betrayed the entire family by pointing out those *liabilities*. Little did she know those were the very assets that prompted me to speak up and say, "Auntie, my answer is YES."

Opposition to Love by Arrangement…

It was a surprise to discover how far one could travel in just three days.

I had gone from a picnic in Ayub Park, to accepting a marriage proposal, and I was now amidst the chaos of wedding plans activated by our friends, family, and neighbors.

It all seemed like a great adventure. I was surrounded by the most splendiferous scents coming from the kitchen; and the most magnificent jewelry, shoes, bangles, and other accessories being brought in for my approval. After inspecting several fabric samples that Aunt Rasheeda had rushed out to select for my bridal gown, my grandmother *Ammajan* settled on rich-crimson brocade, laden with silver roses. To my delight, it was my choice as well.

During the flurry the doorbell rang. Grandma didn't waver in her duty, and I remained motionless on the step stool, as she tucked, pinned, cut, and even stitched my wedding gown (*Gharara*) right onto my body.

My father answered the door and accepted the telegrams from the courier.

In those mere hours since the word had spread that there was to be a wedding, there had been no end to the phone calls, the gifts, and the well-wishers who came bearing sweets and flowers. My father's routine had been disrupted enough. He handed the telegrams to my aunt with this proclamation, "You open them, you read them I'm too busy."

My mother stepped in and said, "We've got a hundred things on our to-do list, and you don't have time to open two envelopes? Maybe a little less attention on the budgies and a little more on this wedding would be a good idea."

My father mumbled, "Budgies don't talk back" and he headed to the cage room.

I became more and more excited, waiting for my aunt to open the first telegram.

"Please Aunt Rasheeda, read it, read it, maybe it's from the President,"

"Oh, you've become very self-important,"

"Only when it comes to President Ayyub Khan," I put my hand on my heart and feigned a deep sigh. *Ammajan* protested, "Stop moving, do you want to have a *Gharara* (gown) shorter on one side than the other?"

I put my hand down at my side and again asked my aunt to read the telegram.

The first telegram was from Zubaida Auntie who had always hoped that I would become their daughter-in-law.

"We are surprised to hear of the forthcoming wedding. Our son was particularly upset since he believed that he might be the groom one day. In any case, we offer our congratulations."

I said, "Did they really think that the most appropriate husband for me, in all of Pakistan, was their son?"

"This only proves that love is supposed to be blind," Aunt Rasheeda chuckled.

"Why would you say such a thing?" grandma asked.

"Have you seen Abid? He's twenty and already bald, buck-toothed, and was bounced out of school by the time he was sixteen? Is this the prize catch they had in mind for our Shadan?"

I suggested to Aunt Rasheeda, "Let's get on to the next telegram." And that she did.

"I am most upset to hear the news of Shadan's marriage. Why would you do such a stupid thing to a bright young girl with a promising future?

Mujeeb may be a fine gentleman, but he's old enough to be her father. If you needed a replacement father for Shadan because

you couldn't afford to keep her, why didn't you ask me? I would have stepped up. I'm sorry, Hameed, I won't attend this wedding. And I sincerely hope that you change your heart and cancel it before it's too late."

The impact of those words coming from my father's dearest friend *Asad,* managed to suck the oxygen out of the room. Everyone within earshot was breathless. My grandmother, immobilized, sat back on the floor with pins still in her hands and tears in her eyes.

I teetered on the stool, nearly tumbling off. Aunt Rasheeda exhaled and whispered, "How could Asad Bhai write such a letter, at such a time?"

I could hear my own voice speaking without thought, "We mustn't tell Abbaji."

Ammajan stood up as tall as her five feet would allow, pointed her finger at me, and said, "You will not make that decision, your father has a right to know, it's for **him** to decide. Now stand straight and let's get on with this fitting."

For the next two days, that telegram became the center of our universe. There were defenders who agreed that this marriage was not the right match; and there were those who agreed that this was a match made in the 'skies'.

Being a teenager I began to feel more and more convinced that this was absolutely the *right* decision. I felt secure and determined to marry Dr. Mujeeb Zoberi and begin my Life of Adventure *'Just the two of us!*

With all the activity monopolizing my thoughts and my time, I had overlooked a very important factor. I was to be married in two days, on Wednesday, which was the same day as I was to be honored by the Education Minister for first prize achievements in sports, drama, public speaking, and other activities which included a gold medal as the 'All-Round Best Student.'

Until just a few days prior, the Prize Distribution Day had been the only event around which my thoughts revolved. Wedding proposals and preparations had been the farthest thing from my mind. Now they had clouded my rational thought, and were bound to prevent me from receiving the honors that I had worked so hard to achieve. Unbeknownst to me, my parents had already called the school to explain my situation. We realized later that my high school principal, Mrs. Masood, must've given serious consideration to my concerns because she accepted the invitation to my wedding, and changed the date of the awards to Friday, so I might still be able to attend.

The marriage proposal had been accepted on Saturday, the invitations were printed on Sunday, and hand delivered on Monday.

My school friends on receiving the notice giggled in disbelief, thinking that it must be some kind of practical joke. To their credit, they did arrive at my house on the day of the wedding; but each one was casually dressed and carried a shopping bag that contained their dazzling wedding outfits…just in case it was not a joke.

The wedding ceremony and reception was a High Tea. There was no time to arrange a proper banquet for 250 guests. In the presence of three witnesses, I signed the Nikah (wedding document) and didn't shed a tear. I was becoming an independent woman.

Outside the room I could hear my Aunt *Haseen Fatima* sobbing and saying, "She's too young to understand what she's getting into."

What my aunt didn't know was that I was more certain on that day than any of my family…***that I was absolutely sure.***

The signing of the Nikah is only one phase in a Muslim marriage. The first phase we had already skipped, the formal engagement. The second phase would have been the traditional Henna party. There was no time, we had to skip the party, but they managed to decorate my hands with ornate henna designs. After the Nikah, there would normally be the send-off (*Rukhsati*) prior to the consummation of the marriage; but my groom's time in Pakistan was limited. He was scheduled almost immediately to return to England, where I would be joining him later. There was no send-off and no consummation. Being sixteen and naïve, the only thing I can say for certain is that we were never undressed.

I do recall however, a moment after the Nikah, when we were left completely alone in a private room. And for the first time, Dr. Mujeeb Zoberi hugged me. It was the first contact of that sort with a man I had ever known. In retrospect, I think the hug took longer than a hug should probably take; and the relief he seemed to feel at the end of the hug.

Inch by inch, he was winning my heart. He won an added fraction when he changed his flight in order to attend my awards ceremony. What a powerful message that sent to me.

......

On the day of the awards ceremony, the front rows were reserved for my Rawalpindi friends and family… and my *new* Karachi family. I felt elated, as if I had just been awarded the Nobel Peace Prize.

On the stage, I overheard the Education Minister whisper to our principal,

"This young girl's hands look like a bride's!"

The principal whispered back, "She is a bride. And I'll bet you thought that only illiterate families would do such a thing."

I heard it, and interpreted it to mean that I was from a highly educated family. I was on the road to rationalizing my way through this new life.

So my last vivid memory of high school, where my journey began, has accompanied me through all the destinations in my life. It is a photograph that was published on the front page of a very popular Urdu newspaper, *Jang*. It was me, extending my Henna decorated hand toward the Minister, exposing my wrist that was adorned with a dozen gold and red bangles; and a wedding ring saucily encircling my middle finger. It was the only finger it would fit, but it also gave me secret pleasure that it was pointed toward the ample belly of the opinionated Minister.

I looked down into the audience, and the only face I focused on was that of my husband who looked up at me with an overwhelming sense of pride. I pressed my thumb under the beautiful gold medal they had just pinned on me, and I directed it toward him. He smiled and I wondered if he could see the engraving of three female hands lighting a candle that signified the supreme importance of education and enlightenment; or was he simply admiring the warm glow cast by my joy?

I woke up the next morning in my own bed, when the reality of all that had happened over the past week struck me. I had met, become engaged, married, and received accolades for my high school achievement in a matter of days; and now here I was, a married woman whose husband was in a hotel several blocks away, packing to return to England without his wife.

I was to stay behind and wait for my signal to join him. I got dressed in my finest shalwar kameez and silver stilettos, and sat patiently waiting for my family to join me.

We picked up my husband at the hotel, and drove to the airport in a strange silence. I didn't know how long it would be before I saw him again, and *I was confused as to why it left me with such hollowness as I had never felt before.*

When we said goodbye at the airport, surrounded by family and friends, he handed me a small portfolio and whispered, "Make good use of it, please."

I nodded and accepted the gift not knowing what was inside. Frankly I didn't care. I had this strange, sad feeling that this man who had just given me the most exciting week of my life was now boarding a plane to return to a place I had never been, and in that moment, I thought I may never hear from him again.

When we returned home my mother asked, "What's in that case?"

As though I had been squeezing the black out of the leather for the longest time! Ammi gently took it from my hands, unzipped it, and looking closely, sighed. By then my curiosity was awakened, I slid in beside her and discovered dozens of self-addressed stamped envelopes and matching writing pad. There was an accompanying note that said,

I chose pale blue vellum because I know it's your favorite color. And I took the liberty of addressing and stamping all the envelopes, so that all your time can be used in writing to me, and none of it spent searching for stamps.

And that was how we communicated for the next six months. Despite negative comments by many relatives who came to not only congratulate me, but also to express their surprise, I looked forward to my reunion. With every letter I received, I searched to the end to see when I was to join him. Finally, I received the following:

"My darling Shadan, I have news. I've been offered a professorship at the University of Ife in Nigeria, to head up the Botany Department. I'm writing to ask, if you are prepared to begin our travels together in Nigeria instead of England. If you agree, we can be together within weeks. I hope you will see this as an opportunity for both of us to

expand our horizons. I miss you and can't wait to see you and hold you. I await your reply."

I felt no hesitation in saying yes.

Saying Goodbye…

Seven cars screeched to a halt at Pindi train station. It looked like a scene out of a James Bond movie, the Interpol chasing a villain. In this case there was no villain—it was just me travelling to Karachi to catch my plane to Nigeria, and half of Rawalpindi coming to see me off.

Of course, my husband had sent two emissaries to protect me en route. One was his new sister in-law *Haseena* older than my mom, the other, his frail and ancient cousin. I had a feeling that if danger approached, it would be I who would be doing the rescuing.

There were just minutes left to say goodbye. My religious uncle Professor Haroon sent his son to a nearby bookstore to purchase *Bahishti Zewar* (The Jewels for Heaven), a comprehensive guide for a Muslim woman. My entourage followed me to the platform. It was a hive of activity, crying babies, frantic mothers, and coolies in red uniforms, bearing multiple trunks on their turbaned heads, while following closely behind. The kaleidoscope of colors that rushed by resembled a Bollywood movie on fast forward.

As I was saying my last goodbyes, my maternal grandmother *Nani Jaan*, who had been standing off to one side, began to sway like a pendulum, and then in slow motion, began to crumple to the ground. Everyone rushed to her rescue, Ammi quickly sprinkled water on her face. Her eyes fluttered open, and a family vacated a nearby bench so we could sit her down. I settled in next to her and asked, "Are you missing me already?" She smiled back and said, "No."

"Then what is it?" She was unresponsive.

"Nani Jaan, please. Whatever it is, I promise, I won't get upset… come on … please."

Slowly and quietly she unfolded the tale, "This morning, my friend told me that she knows of a young girl, just like you, who was sent abroad to meet her husband. She was picked up by a stranger at the airport, and they never saw her again."

I looked my grandmother in the eyes, my nose almost pressed to hers, and I made a vow. "Nani Jaan, no matter what nightmares you dream up, you cannot get rid of me that easily. You will hear from me. I will arrive safely, and I *will* make you proud."

I kissed her on top of her head, and as I rose from the bench, the Conductor waved at me and said, "Young lady, if you're getting on board, do it now. The train is about to leave the station." That's when suddenly I heard a voice cry out.

"Wait. Wait." Uncle Haroon had arrived, weighed down by the burden of a book the size of a mini-suitcase. I stood on the train steps, and he pushed the book into my hands, almost toppling me over. I handed the book off to one of my emissaries.

As I turned again, Ammi and Abbaji reached for my hands and clasped on to them. The train slowly began to rumble along, but my parents refused to let go. They walked, then jogged, then ran alongside the train, still holding on to their last memories of their little girl, Shadan. They knew, as I did, that the next time we saw each other, I would be a woman. Suddenly the train lurched ahead. I remained on that step until they were out of sight.

Our grasp was broken but our bond was ensured.

For the first time since this whirlwind began, I found myself floating in my own tears. It wasn't fear of where I was going … it was just the melancholy of what I had left behind. I hadn't really faced the fact that I would miss my family so deeply. Startled, just as I was wiping my tears, a gentle hand on my shoulder pulled me back to reality and escorted me to my seat.

A glass of water and a few kind words worked wonders. I was glad for the time we spent together, I got to know and respect these mature women who were going to be in my life, in some way. They were wise and modern, unlike the rest of my husband's family who seemed more traditional. The first lesson they taught me, was to leave the cumbersome 'Guide' behind. "I'm sure your mother taught you all you'll ever need to know about being a good Muslim wife."

They assured me that I was a beautiful young lady and said, "We heard that there were many disappointed young men in Rawalpindi on your wedding day. One of them even said, 'Change the groom.'" Though I was aware of boys and their attraction to me, I remained naïve.

"Not just your uncle but other family members probably feel you will need some guidance." I didn't think that my secular and modern-thinking father would have ever chosen the controversial *Bahishti Zewar* (Jewel for Heaven) as my guide.

The trip from Rawalpindi to Karachi afforded me time to adjust to the distance that now lay between me and my family. It also gave me an opportunity to speak openly to my new family, and to uncover some minor secrets about my husband.

The 'transition' days that I spent in Karachi before leaving for Nigeria were unforgettable. Mujeeb's family embraced me as if I had hatched from their very own egg. I was the youngest member of his family, and I think I may have added a refreshing and humorous new element to their lives, while they offered acceptance, respect, and wisdom to mine. It seemed as if there was a never-ending stream of parties, high teas, and luncheons, to ensure that I met and charmed every single person in Karachi. When I did finally leave for Nigeria, it seemed as if half the population of Karachi was at the airport to see me off.

· ·

A Flight of Fury and Fancy

2 My first sensation of independence was while boarding the Japanese Airlines flight to Rome en route to Nigeria … and I loved it.

I stored my silk shawl, vanity case, British umbrella, and fake fur coat in the overhead bin. I settled into my seat and gazed out the window with a sense of excitement.

I was soon joined by my seatmate, a pale-skinned European lady. Since I didn't speak German and she didn't speak Urdu, we settled on bits and pieces of English. I was frustrated to have only a handful of English words at my disposal, while she had an enviably full arsenal of vocabulary from the dictionary at her disposal. But as our flight continued, so did our conversation. She had a lengthy list of questions about my Henna designs, my bangles, and then of course the ultimate, "You're married, and you're how old?"

She was the first non-Pakistani person I'd ever had a real conversation with.

The whole flight experience was fascinating to me: the Japanese doll-like air hostesses, the delicate food trays with exotic cuisine that I couldn't eat but loved to admire. It looked to me like a modern art exhibit. The blend of experiences I was encountering made for an intoxicating cocktail. There were so many new faces, new languages, new sensations, all contained within one flying tube. How many more adventures would I encounter when I arrived at my destination? The thought made me quiver with excitement.

In the instant the plane rolled to a halt, I was dwarfed by the male passengers reaching over me to rescue their briefcases from the overhead bins while my possessions slowly tumbled from above. First my fake fur, which my European seatmate managed to intercept; then my vanity case which barely missed her well-coiffed head. My silk shawl floated gently into my hands, but now I had this gripping fear that my spear-like umbrella could pierce some unsuspecting victim, for which I would be arrested and would never reach Nigeria.

I needed to rein in my imagination.

A gentleman handed me my umbrella, along with a wink and his calling card. In fact, by the time I exited the plane, I had collected five calling cards and several more winks. I wasn't sure exactly what it all meant, but it somehow felt pleasantly embarrassing.

I had arrived at the first stopover of my journey in the exotic city of Rome.

Traditional Indian and Pakistani girls don't wear a *saree** until they are older, or married (whichever comes first). My cousins wanted to present me in Nigeria as a well-dressed married woman. Amongst many outfits my parents gifted me was a beautiful pink silk saree, so they proudly dressed me in it for the trip. As I stood in the terminal holding on to my carry-on's, I could feel six yards of Chinese silk slipping away, and I knew if I didn't find a lady's washroom immediately, my profound embarrassment would prevent me from ever getting on that plane. I spotted the universal sign for the ladies' washroom and scurried along, grasping tightly to the fabric with one hand, and my luggage with the other. Once inside, I double knotted the *Petticoat* and tucked in the saree, so tightly I feared I would need a surgeon to liberate me.

*(Six yards of fabric pleated and tucked around the waist, draped on one shoulder)

My father had used his best connections to make sure that I wasn't left alone during my six hour stopover in Rome, so I was to be met at the airport by the wife of the Pakistani ambassador to Italy. Although I saw no sign of such a person, I was strangely calm. I even managed to find a money exchange where I was ecstatic to see how my relatively small pile of US dollars had morphed into a huge stack of Italian liras. This was a great thrill for a sixteen-year-old girl. I ran from gift shop to gift shop, spending with abandon. I was now the proud owner of a decidedly *hand-painted* Michelangelo souvenir cigarette case, a miniature guitar, and a 'priceless original' replica of Venus de Milo. The bonus was that all these items fit neatly into my vanity case.

I'm not certain how this stately diplomat's wife identified me. But I suspect it was the sight of a bewildered young Pakistani girl in a saree, with a fake fur draped over her shoulder.

My sophisticated chaperone escorted me to an elegant Italian dining room for lunch, which she ordered in perfect Italian. I watched in awe as she adeptly spun the lengthy strings of spaghetti bolognaise around her fork without a splatter or a splash. I had never seen such a dish in my life. I wondered how in the world I would transport this unusual spicy-scented delicacy to my own mouth. I tried lifting. I tried twirling. And finally I picked up a knife, preparing to slice it all into small pieces. My gracious hostess gently placed her hand on mine, directing the knife safely back on to the table. Then she patiently taught me how to twirl and transport the pasta to my mouth without an embarrassing mishap. I was Eliza Doolittle to Professor Higgins, and I sensed that there would be many more similar scenarios to come.

Flying over the Sahara Desert…

Switching from Japanese Airlines to Nigeria Airways en route to Lagos, I noticed a stark contrast; the dainty Japanese girls wore silken hand-painted kimonos in pastel colors. But the Nigerian air hostesses wore huge head scarves in sharp colors, and African-style wraparound skirts, made from tie-dye cotton materials. Some were 'pleasantly plump' their thick gear magnified the effect. For the first time I realized that having been raised in a society plagued with color prejudice, even I was somewhat impacted. Unaware that someday I'd begin to appreciate, not only like but *love* the 'African look' and treasure friendship bonds with them.

In an attempt to educate myself about my future home, I read that Nigeria achieved independence from the British in 1960. That the impact of the British influence was evident in many aspects of academic life, the kind of housing for expatriates, even the food served in their guest houses around the country, such as the *West African Curry.* I was curious.

Soon my attention was drawn to a fascinating aerial view of the sand dunes. I recalled my geography lesson.

'This non-Arctic 'Greatest Desert' covers most of Northern Africa—over 9000,000 square kilometers, and stretches from the Red Sea, including parts of the Mediterranean coasts, to the outskirts of the Atlantic Ocean.' Now I was actually flying above it!

How fondly I used to draw maps of Africa in color to delight my geography teacher. Luckily, I had the window seat, so I clung to the glass, captivated by the vast expanse of dunes and ripples. *'Some of the sand dunes can reach as high as 180 meters.'*

Fatigued from looking down, my neck stiffened. Leaning back on the headrest, I tried but couldn't fall asleep. A diarist from age thirteen, I requested the hostess for stationery to make notes for my travelogue. I didn't know those notes would transform into a fourteen-page letter to my aunt Haseen Fatima. (Excerpts of which were later published in *Akhbar-e-Jahan*)

Finally, the announcement was made. "Ladies and gentlemen, please fasten your seat belts as we will soon be landing in Lagos." Just as the plane descended, my excitement also took a dive into a sinking feeling, mixed emotions intensified. It was to be my first-ever 'one-on-one encounter' with my life partner. My gut was apprehensive.

Landing in Lagos…

Lagos Airport was a drastic contrast from the fancy Rome Airport, reflecting the image of a third world country. I wondered if I had done the right thing to opt for Nigeria over England.

In the arrivals lounge, at Passport Control, I was struggling to bring out my passport and the landing card. While trying to tuck in my slippery saree, protecting my Vanity Case (a bride's cosmetic/jewelry box), I held on to the fur coat. I had already lost the umbrella and symbolically, my precious, antique, hand-woven silken shawl was left on the plane too. *Nothing compares to all else I have left behind,* I thought.

As I anxiously turned my head toward the reception lounge, I saw dozens of Nigerian faces pasted onto the glass window, but no brown face? Only a white guy gleefully peeking at me! Fear crept in my veins. *Could my grandma be right? Is it possible that a stranger has come to pick me up?* In panic, I dropped the vanity case, my gold jewelry and cosmetics were scattered. Two or three Nigerians rushed to help me pick them up. Just then a young man delivered a note, "Don't worry, darling, I'm here to pick you up." What a relief!

After the customs clearance, we were chauffeured into a Mercedes Benz. "It belongs to the University," Mujeeb clarified. In the back seat, his arms around me, I was feeling ecstatic. Passing through miles and miles of lush greenery of the Tropical rainforest also fascinated me.

"Darling, Ibadan is the largest town in Africa, South of the Sahara, it's less than 100 miles north from the capital city of Lagos." I remained silent, but he went on,

"The population is about 600,000* (now 3.8 million)."

"Our University of Ife Campus is temporary, adjacent to Ibadan University but the final site is to be built on a grand scale in a *Yoruba* heritage town Ile-Ife." Secretly scratching my waist, I tried to listen. "Most of the professors are Europeans or Americans, and the entire establishment was originally set up by the British,"

I finally spoke, "I know Nigeria became independent in 1960."

As a compliment he pulled me closer. I felt a strange sensation, somewhat pleasant.

......

Our Honeymoon…

As the Mercedes pulled into the driveway, my excitement began with the sight of an impressive modern bungalow—our new abode.

"Sweetheart, the good news is that the University is closed for Christmas. With all the festivities, no one will bother us, so we get to relish our honeymoon."

The wedding night in Pakistan is so different. The bride is escorted to the groom's family first for 'after party' fun-filled rituals with the immediate family. The honeymoon comes later.

That luxury three-bedroom bungalow allotted to us was fully furnished with imported modern Italian furniture. He was showing off all the rooms to me, the kitchen, the servants' quarters, and the huge backyard where the tall trees known as the *Flame of the Forest* wore a canopy of bright red blooms at the top. The floor-to-ceiling louvre (glass shutters) fascinated me, wall-to-wall windows overlooking the backyard, and a plush fence. As a newlywed couple we were overjoyed with all those luxuries presented to us on a platter.

Soon he drove me down to his office on the campus.

It wasn't until I changed into my nightclothes that I felt physically at ease. I had been promised I would be spared the first night, thank God.

Mujeeb now boasted, "Many girls were lined up for me, but I chose you."

"So why did you choose me if you were such a hotshot in demand?"

"I was looking for a mature girl," he replied.

"How could you tell in two days that I was that *mature girl*?"

"I am a scientist, I have keen observation."

"Okay, stop impressing me Professor. Just tell me what you observed."

"When your little brother Shahid was up to mischief, they called *you* to discipline him."

"That's it?" I felt flattered once he related more examples, and I remained upbeat with my wisecracks, in a leg pulling mood. Maybe it was my attempt to distract him from…?

"By the way, our conversation has been recorded, by … Mr. Philips,"

"What!" My heart skipped a beat. His mischievous smile gave it away.

"But I have been taught … that all our deeds are being recorded by *Munkar Nakeer*, supposedly the two angels are appointed just for that."

"Do you really believe that?" he asked but I didn't respond. In our case it happened to be Philips—the reel-to-reel tape deck Mujeeb had hidden under our bed! So, my spontaneous asides were preserved on a brown plastic tape around a stainless-steel spool that played for two hours.

I pleaded, "Promise you'll never share this with anyone,"

"Of course not, but you must promise never to erase it," he insisted.

We listened to it over and over, it was unbelievably hilarious. But I was surprised at Myself—how I teased him about his language, his accent, and even the letters he wrote to me.

"You must've been upset with my rude comments about your first letter."

"What comments?"

"That your writing style reminds me of my grandmother's?"

"I wasn't upset. Incidentally that was my Second letter. I never sent you my First letter."

"Really! Why not? What did you hold back from me?" My curiosity peaked, I kept asking, but unfazed he changed the subject.

As promised, I was spared the first night, mission accomplished. Nonetheless, I kept wondering about the unsent letter, *what... did... he ... hold back?*

Unfortunately, the tape recording of our honeymoon night was accidentally erased—that innocent precious spontaneity was lost forever!

The next day, we were eager to exchange gifts. Amongst the many gifts he showered me with were low-neck skintight blouses, slacks, gorgeous lingerie, even a swimsuit—I had never worn one before. Trying on those outfits excited me, not to mention the glow on his face. I had mixed feelings…the excitement of a teenager bursting with desires to try on all things new, and that of a sheltered traditional Muslim girl. I didn't want to disappoint anyone, especially my in-laws. His religious brother had brought my proposal, after he found me sitting on the prayer rug with a head scarf, which incidentally, I only used while praying. Wouldn't he be shocked to see this side of me? *But it doesn't mean I'll give up my prayers,* I secretly resolved.

Trying on my *first* swimsuit I felt a tinge of 'ticklish guilt.'

"We will soon make a trip to Lagos. You would love the sandy beach at *Tarkway Bay.*"

"What! Wear this in front of other people?" No way.

"By the way, these are just small presents. I still owe you the special gift."

"What special gift?" He must be talking about **Meher** (after the marriage is consummated, the groom gives a valuable present to the bride, precious jewelry or a generous cash gift).

Then, it was my turn to bring out the presents I bought at Rome Airport.

"Okay, here is a miniature guitar, hand-painted. Here is the replica of Venus de Milo for which I paid thousands of liras," I boasted. "And now, my favorite special gift for you," I pulled out a souvenir cigarette case I had carefully tucked in my vanity case.

"It's Michelangelo hand-painted on silk,"

"Not bad." His response was enough to burst my bubble of excitement. That must mean not good either? Noticing my sinking voice, he clarified, "The British expression 'not bad' means 'quite good.'" Nonetheless I did observe his *changing facial expressions.*

Christmas holidays allowed us uninterrupted time together. The cook brought us breakfast, and later knocked to pick up the tray. Breakfast, lunch, and dinner provided in the bedroom…with each knock it felt as though we were in a five-star hotel. Trained by his previous *Master* (employer) an English family, our chef's cooking was mostly bland. I sprinkled lots of salt and pepper over it, and pretended to like it.

Soon I learned that the gentleman I had married was nothing like the rest of his family, or mine. He no longer appreciated Urdu music nor mingled with Indo-Pakistanis, and had given up on spicy food. In short, he had abandoned a big chunk of our culture I so cherished. He mostly spoke English, with a lousy accent I might add, enjoyed western music, and had taken ballroom dancing classes in England. Regardless, he was a PhD and I … just a high school girl.

Most people take baby steps when it comes to adapting to other cultures. I had to be adept to adopt and adapt in leaps and bounds. Thank God for my innate desire to try anything new. I was excited and determined to catch up, and match up with the 'Brown Englishman.'

…………………………

Mixed Emotions

3 Adventurous and excited, yet deep down, a part of me felt sad … something didn't feel right. I was unsure if I was influenced by the opinions of my elders? I recalled Asad Bhai's telegram with a stern warning to my father. Other relatives also expressed surprises. "Shadan is into her studies, what was such a rush? Did you even find out his background, his age?"

'Am I now feeling the impact of those comments, which sounded like condolences?'

'He was a distant relative, highly regarded by many elders in the family.' With those thoughts I alluded it was the sudden alienation from my entire family. There was no one my age, my race, or who spoke my language. I relived vivid memories of my departure to Karachi. During those few days in transit, I had received the photos of my *Rukhsati* (send-off party), along with a handwritten note in my dad's beautiful writing.

"Pyari Bacchi (dear little girl) *Shadan: When we said goodbye to you at the railway station, how you were sobbing on the footsteps of the moving train! As though we had cut a piece of our flesh off, we returned home feeling wounded. Our lives without you have instantly become meaningless. Now we keep staring at your wedding pictures which I'm sending by urgent mail. See how innocent and beautiful you look! All we can do now is to wish and pray that you have a good life."*

Smudged with my teardrops, each time I'd secretly pull out that piece of paper it invoked sadness! I kept my husband in the dark about how lonely I felt. He once said, "Darling, I've put my past behind in my own interest, and I think you should do the same." He continued to smother me with love and affection but ... would he ever understand I was of a very different nature? I silently conceded to assume my new role.

I often reflected upon the two names given to me. On my passport I was registered under my official name **Zohra** (Arabic meaning morning light, planet Venus, or the dawn). Grandma said, "When God took my mother away, he replaced her with you. I'm giving you her name Zohra, so you have to be a good girl like her." But my dad gave me the nickname **Shadan** (Persian word for cheerful). While friends and family called me Shadan (more poetic), *Ammajan* would often say, "Meri Zohra Bano" (My Zohra). *Bano* means princess or a gentle woman. A friend commented, "What a huge burden she put upon your little shoulders."

In our culture it's generally perceived that names have an impact on one's personality. Some people live their entire life with a name they can't stand. Fortunately, I loved both these meaningful names. How would these two names divide my personality or impact upon me socially, culturally, and spiritually?

In short, sometimes it felt as though Zohra had landed on a different planet; Shadan in a way had been unintentionally left behind, or submerged to take a secondary position?

A New Reality…

Like an alien landed onto a new planet, where no one spoke my language or even had my color of skin—they were either whites or blacks. The only exception being the brown Englishman, twice my age!

Suddenly separated from all my loved ones, no direct telephone connection, and no email back then. To establish contact with my parents, a letter from Ibadan, Nigeria, to Rawalpindi, Pakistan, would take a minimum of three months to arrive. That is, if they replied the same day they received it. I tried to cling to my husband by making surprise visits to his Biology Department on the campus. He smothered me with affection I couldn't ignore.

One afternoon Mujeeb returned from work excited, with an invitation in his hand.

'You are cordially invited for a dinner reception to welcome The Young Bride who has recently arrived on our Campus.' Hosted by Jeoffrey and Rolly Smith

Mujeeb had known this English couple from his days in London.

………………………………..

The Deadly Exhale

4 Geoffrey was a tall blond Englishman. His wife Rolly's red hair and freckles, which their daughters Sarah and Fiona had also inherited, caught my attention. I found their Oxford English accent adorable. After the formal introduction, Mujeeb whispered,

"My wife is too shy to speak English."

That I would turn out to be such a *novelty* to this multinational community of mostly elderly Professors and their wives, was a surprise gift for me. Many had left their children behind in their respective countries in order to continue their education. They only visited their parents in Nigeria during summer vacations. I was therefore the youngest one around, and available to be pampered at will. Youth is so attractive to the elderly. In any case, it felt great to be the guest of honor where everyone else was at least twice my age! I vowed to be on my best behavior for the occasion.

My taste buds were trained for *achar and chutney* (spicy and sweet pickles)—flavors I hungered for. The aroma of the delectable *Qorma* (fancy beef curry, with delicate herbs) or fragrant *Basmati* rice suffused with aromas of saffron and cinnamon, were now just a dream. The four-course dinner menu that evening included green pea soup and liver pate instead. Though I can handle it now, but back then that thick green soup reminded me of my little siblings' baby poop and the liver pate more like ... eh ... dare I describe? Nonetheless I took on this challenge wholeheartedly; and despite the urge to throw up, I managed to competently gulp it down. I even mimicked everyone else by saying, "It's so delicious."

From the corner of my eye, I secretly observed everyone else in order to choose the right fork and the appropriate knife for each course. I found it impossible to balance those miserable little slippery peas at the back of my fork. My husband, having lived in England for a decade, could do it quite comfortably. Uh-huh, so he did have an edge over me! My main agenda was to impress him as much as possible ... to show him that I wasn't just a sheltered teenager from the little town of Rawalpindi ... that I knew it all.

Throughout dinner I felt self-conscious about my limited vocabulary. Other than *yes* and *no* and 'it's delicious,' I hardly conversed; I was afraid to make any mistake in front of Mujeeb. It was his ten years in London and the PhD rubbed in so often, it gave me a complex.

After dinner, our host presented a cigarette to a smartly dressed European lady who was sitting beside me, and whose mannerisms I had found highly impressive and worthy of emulating. Gracefully accepting the cigarette offered to her, she bent forward with a noticeable style. The host lit her cigarette, and she leaned back with a relaxing inhale, followed a few seconds later by a gentle exhale—wow! I observed it all. I felt a cold shiver up my spine, but it disappeared in seconds. The host then offered me a cigarette. I gracefully bent forward, copying each and every motion of that stylish lady I had carefully noted, including the way I crossed my legs and tilted my head ... and I **inhaled!**

Surprisingly enough, I didn't cough even once. How I felt was a different matter. In spite of the dizziness and nausea, I was so proud of myself, ever more determined to never let my partner down.

I noticed that Mujeeb remained silent throughout the evening—that being one of his positive traits, initially I ignored it. Once I glimpsed the sadness on his face, I became concerned that he might in fact not be feeling well. It was only on the way home, when he would hardly even answer me that I realized there was a good possibility that he was upset with me, which came as a shock in itself. How could anyone be upset with me? I had never perceived myself as a spoiled brat. After my repeated requests, he reluctantly uttered a few words.

"Do you really have no idea what's bothering me?"

"I don't, really I don't." I vehemently pleaded my innocence.

He then told me how disappointed he was that I hadn't even noticed his disapproval of my smoking that cigarette.

I vowed, "I swear to God that it is the first cigarette I have ever smoked in my entire life." I finally convinced him of my innocent and sincere intentions to please him—for that I was willing to go to any length. For my skillful participation in the smoking event, in my mind I had deserved a *pat on the back* instead! He told me he had left some gorgeous English girl behind in order to marry an Eastern traditional girl from Pakistan ... only to find out she's a 'chain-smoker.' I swallowed my pride, pleading for forgiveness, "I did it to please you. I hope you at least appreciate my adaptable nature." He finally forgave me, and the issue was resolved.

But I started dwelling on who this gorgeous English girl was that he had sacrificed over me? I pulled out his photo album in which there was a pretty lady with curly locks and a frilly frock. *What an old-fashioned woman,* I consoled myself with that observation. But... what was she holding in her right hand? A cigarette!

I then recalled Mujeeb's initial reaction to my gift of cigarette case. *So that's why he had a long face.* In any case, I concluded that even though my one-time-only act of 'Inhale-exhale' displeased my hubby, it seemed to have entertained the old folks at the party.

......

Nostalgic Memory Surge

How long could our honeymoon last? Professor Zoberi had to prepare lectures and carry on his research. After a luxurious breakfast served by our cook, Mujeeb would drive off to his office, leaving me alone in that strange new world. On those lonely mornings, daydreaming became my escape.

I would transport myself back to Rawalpindi, where I grew up as one of five siblings, with nine cousins across the street, and our next-door neighbor's four children, all together making eighteen of us. We were one big happy family, always up to fun and mischief. On weekends and evenings we enjoyed picnics at Ayyub National Park and late-night walks, joking and teasing one another.

During *Basant* (rainy season), they hung swings, using the steel beams reinforcing the high ceiling of the veranda. My cousins would push me on the swing and I would scream, "Higher... higher... higher!" until my feet would touch the top.

Our three seemingly 'posh' houses were originally built by the **Sikh** families, who were forced to flee to India during the Partition of 1947, just as my parents had to flee from India to Pakistan, leaving behind all their belongings as well as their luxurious houses. So we initially resided right in the midst of a very poor neighborhood. Scantily dressed children and their mothers in old, wrinkled clothing, lined up as our spectators, when we decked up for a social evening and passed through that *galee* (narrow brick-paved alley). Little did we realize the true value of streets paved with hand-laid bricks!

During the Partition of the subcontinent, one million lives were lost! "Heavy price for freedom from the British rule for two centuries," my grandma used to say with a sigh.

"So, Ammajan, why did they fight?"

I would ask and she would fill me with stories about the Hindu caste system. "*Brahmins* were the most superior, *Shudras* and *Achooth* were untouchables. *Muslims* were considered the lowest caste. Hindus wouldn't even drink water from the same glass used by a Muslim.

"But don't we treat Basheerun, our *Jamadar* (Toilet Cleaner) the same way?" I asked. "Everybody makes her feel as though she's untouchable, that's why I like to give her hugs."

Other family members would weigh in, "We did live in harmony for more than a thousand years when the *Mughal Emperors ruled India." But the cynics would enter the discussion by saying, "It was the '**Divide and Rule'** policy of the British, when they ruled the subcontinent for two hundred years. The *Ghadar Movement* to free India from the British led to the partition tragedy." Others offered a more simplistic theory. "The Hindus are vegetarians, the cow is their sacred animal, and Muslims are meat-eaters, and that sums up the story." However, behind that massive tragedy was 'the complex political manoeuvring by the politicians from three sides', I'd only learn in later years.

Growing up I found those discussions boring, especially when I saw Ammi become emotional I avoided asking questions. She had to leave her parents and a brother behind; one other brother (blonde and blue eyed) had been murdered!

"You will see that the ripple effects of this travesty will continue for generations to come," was my father's conclusion.

But now... my thoughts drifted between the two continents, Asia to Africa. I started comparing the old, with my new lifestyle.

*The Muslim Mughal Empire ruled the subcontinent from 1536-1761

......

The Starlit Night...

Nigerian weather was mild and has two rainy seasons, so they had slanted roofs. But in Pindi we had flat rooftops. Summer temperatures could soar to 135 F. On a very hot night it wasn't an uncommon practice to sleep on the rooftop *(chath or kotha)*. Tall boundary walls created privacy. We sometimes coaxed our parents to let us sleep under the canopy of a starlit sky, a privilege to be enjoyed only once in a while. "If it rains, you will have to rush indoors in the middle of the night," my parents would caution.

For sleeping on the roof, lightweight portable hand-woven *Nivaar* beds were used, with fancy wooden legs hand-painted in bright colors. Crisp white bed sheets frosted with a bit of evening dew felt nice and cool. Our parents insisted we use *Macchar daanee* (a white net canopy over the bed) to protect us from nasty mosquito bites. "You don't want to get malaria, do you?"

I recalled how we were mesmerized by the beauty of the galaxy— clusters of stars in the pitch-dark night when we tried to spot *Dubb-e-Akbar* (Ursa Major or the Big Dipper).

In Nigeria, I felt deprived of all that.

The next-door neighbors were like family. Ubaida, Moonis, and two other brothers often resorted to sleeping on their fancier rooftop.

It being a semi-detached home, we could easily cross over each other's roof. During the day, my male cousins flew colorful kites. I was content just carrying their *Manjha* (extra-strong thread roll) and enjoyed friendly kite fights.

How much fun our three families had, telling jokes, reciting poetry, singing songs, sharing our unique talents on our rooftops. My father mimicked cat fights—making sounds from his throat and hand movements. When not looking at him, one would easily believe that two angry cats were growling at each other. Ammi was often persuaded to recite love poems she wrote for Abbaji or sing her favorite song:

"Yaad na kar dil-e-hazeeN bhoolee huiee kahaanyaN"
(Oh my heart, do not dwell upon forgotten tales)

Sadly it was mainly through the old songs she relived her memories of growing up in the pre-partitioned India— her coping mechanism.

A Memory in my Hard Drive…
On one moonlit night my sister and I had obtained permission to sleep on the roof.

"Hello, would you like to join our party up here?" I heard a soft whisper.

Our parents were asleep downstairs, so no permission seemed necessary. Moonis was only two years older than me and his sister Ubaida, two years his senior, a role model for me. So, feeling perfectly justified, I climbed over through the small entrance gate to join them.

They were sharing with their house guest Uncle Imtiaz how both our families were fond of a popular radio program, *Binaka Geet Mala,* broadcast from Radio Ceylon! Every Wednesday evening, my parents, siblings, Moonis, and Ubaida religiously gathered around the radio. There was a weekly countdown of thirteen top songs from Urdu and Hindi cinema. Moonis memorized some songs and I kept track of the winning numbers each week, even recorded the score in my fancy diary. The losers had to treat the winner.

That evening, under the spell of the full moon, Moonis and I were persuaded to sing the winning number of the week, a duet:

"Jaane na nazar pehchane jigar
Yeh kaun jo dil per chaya
Mera ung ... ung ... muskaya"

(Sensual expression of falling in love)

We had barely started singing when we heard an angry voice holler:

"Where are you? **Get back here...right now**! Who gave you permission to go over?"

My heart racing with fear, I ran for the door. My father had come to check up on us and was shocked to discover I was missing from my bed. I couldn't believe my soft-spoken loving father could scream so loudly. His green eyes glowed in the dark, like a feral cat.

The painful memory was tattooed on my mind. But I felt innocent.

What about when our parents slept upstairs and I caught them red-handed, in bed, but stepped right back? Never asked them what *they* were up to, just shared it with my school friend Shahida Shaikh. She hushed me, "All parents do that, that's how babies are made."

The morning after I had been scolded, Abbaji offered to take me to watch a documentary. "I have a lot of homework!" was my feeble excuse to refuse.

Abbaji had completed his Masters in English Literature. He now translated sensitive documents at GHQ—General Army Head

Quarters, where the staff and family members received courtesy invitations to watch English films or documentaries. Ammi wasn't interested in movies, but I loved to accompany him and he translated for me.

The following week he asked me, but I refused again. Concerned with my unexpected anger toward my father, cousin Shahida took me aside for a heart-to-heart talk. "Shadan, do you remember the guest at their house, Uncle Imtiaz?" I nodded as she shifted in her seat.

"Well, um, let me just say that he is not the sort of person who should be around young girls. Do you understand what I'm telling you?"

Innocent as I was (at fifteen), I finally realized that Abbaji was simply protecting me.

After that incident, I banned myself from going to Ubaida's house, even when my parents insisted that I come along. I was sure they heard the anger-fueled fiasco, so how could I ever face them? But worse than that, my singing duet with Moonis was left incomplete.

Finally, one day Abbaji managed to tempt me. "Shadan, it's a documentary about K2, so I know this will interest you,"

"Yes, Abbaji, I do want to go." He looked euphoric.

K2 is the highest mountain peak in Pakistan, the second highest in the world, approximately 28,251 feet. I was fascinated to view it on the large screen. After the movie, over ice cream, we reconciled.

. . . . . .

Only a year later, my becoming a married lady was a surprise to everyone including Moonis and Obaida's family.

After my *Nikah* (legal marriage), during the interim months before my *Rukhsati* (send-off), I continued my education. Every single morning, on my way to school, I found Moonis sitting on one of the marble posts in front of his house, scowling at me as I passed by. Upon my return, he would be there again sitting and glaring. His angry stare was unnerving, yet I had no choice but to pass by his house to reach mine. I would simply look down and walk faster.

Many nights he would sit upon the ledge of the dividing gate between our rooftops, singing love songs. One evening, I was sitting out in our courtyard under the stars with *Nani Jaan* (maternal grandmother) who was visiting from India.

"Aa laut key aja meray meeth
Tujhay meray geeth bulathay hein"
(My lyrics are calling you back)

Both of us equally enchanted by those lyrics, Grandma knew nothing of my Moonis issue and yet, as we listened to his lovely refrain, suddenly she turned toward me, smiled softly, and whispered, "This boy sings just like **Mukesh**, and I think he's singing for you."

· · · · · ·

As usual, after the memory surge, I got up to play a cassette of Urdu songs. Like a teenager enters a fantasy world while watching a romantic film, then she forgets all about it. I returned to the real world. Now it was Nigeria, even the very sound of a doorbell excited me.

………………………..

STRANGERS AT MY DOOR

5 One morning as I answered the doorbell, it turned out to be a Nigerian trader. "Call your mommy," he said. I was taken aback, almost offended. "I am the lady of the house," I retaliated, but he didn't seem to buy it. I did not look my age –barely five feet in height, weighing 90 lbs, and scrawny. He gave me a long second glance before reluctantly displaying his handicrafts. He himself was a skinny, tall teenager. While showing me his collection of carved ivory tusks, thorn carvings, leather *poufs,* he stealthily glanced at me as if in disbelief, looking at the entrance door as though an older lady would soon pop-up.

The miniature figurines of ***Thorn Carvings**** depicting Nigerian lifestyles fascinated me the most—tradesmen carrying fruits and vegetables in miniature boats, women with babies tied to their backs, pounding yams, etc. Dark chocolate-color thorns were used for faces and limbs, and light cream color ones used for clothing. I picked up two pieces, but when I paid him he hiked the price. I later learned about their unique 'bargaining' style, being an integral part of Nigerian culture.

I was relieved to get rid of the Trader but not without a desire for him to return with more carvings. "Please come back in a few weeks." I later learned about these fascinating creatures. Made principally by the Yoruba people since the 1930s, these miniature folk art pieces referred to as Tourist Art usually featured aspects of everyday Nigerian life.

The thorns used for these carvings come from two varieties of trees: the Ata tree and the Egungun tree. The thorns grow up to five inches in length, and their relative suppleness makes for easier carving. They come in three colors: cream, rose, and brown.

......

Fiasco in our Neighborhood

One morning, alone in my new Nigerian home, I heard someone screaming outside.

"Help, please help ... Pleeease!" In a panic, I raced out the door without my shoes.

There, lying on the grass was a young man with blood spurting from a deep gash in his throat. I stood stock-still in horror. At the scene were three elderly white women I recognized as fellow professors' wives. They were clearly not EMS, but they were desperately trying to save his life.

One expatriate lady was attempting to hold together his slit throat with both hands, while the other two were trying their best to contain his violent shaking. I was about to make a feeble attempt to step up to help, but backed off when a fountain of blood surged in my direction.

The young man, who had slit his own throat with a machete, was a servant in the compound. His pregnant wife, with another baby in a sling on her back, was pounding on her thighs with both hands and wailing in Yoruba. Unfortunately, by the time the ambulance arrived, he was gone!

As the ambulance pulled away en route to the morgue, the gossip began.

"I heard the couple fighting,"

"Me too, I heard him threaten that he would kill himself and his wife told him to go ahead,"

I volunteered that, "Perhaps the poor woman thought he was joking," Another offered something more realistic, "His mother said she was sure he was suffering from malaria because he was burning up with fever since yesterday ... and that could cause delirium."

As we were leaving, the crowd was building up to join the bereaved. They were most likely wives of servants from the neighboring bungalows. They took the young widow inside, but we could hear the conversation in Yoruba increase in volume. My heart was still racing.

We later researched about that horrifying disease.

'Malaria can be "a chronic cognitive dysfunction risk of subclinical depressive and anxiety symptoms, as well as altered executive functioning, particularly following severe malaria infection." This disorder (PMNS) is post-malaria neurological syndrome.'

Perhaps the young man suffered from that?

From then on, Mujeeb and I took our anti-malarial pills regularly... until the day we both forgot! We were attacked by this hideous disease, running a temperature of over 105 degrees. In one week, we each lost ten pounds. Once recovered, we were religiously committed to taking the pills.

Reflecting upon my Upbringing...

While growing up, my parents did not pray, but I prayed five times a day. My *Humanist* father had no objection, "As long as it teaches you the love of humanity."

Back then my dreams were influenced by religious uncle Masood's teachings. I recalled one:

'Prophets Muhammad, Moosa (Moses) and Isa (Jesus Christ) PBU them, visited our home. Awestruck, I stood by the doorstep of our drawing room, envious of my uncle, seated beside them, conversing.'

Seeing all of them 'together' reflected my father's humanist influence of inclusivity, "Regardless of your faith, race, color or creed, you have to be a good ***Insaan*** (human) first."

Fortunately I had a happy childhood. I was my grandmothers' favorite, my aunts *Zakia* and *Haseen Fatima*, and my teachers adored me as well. Being their firstborn I got my parents' full attention, always asking my opinion about different situations, which made me feel grown up and important. Now I found out that sadly, Mujeeb's childhood experience was just the opposite!

He confessed that, "After my mother passed away I was totally neglected, but you have been a lucky girl."

Although I drew strength from old memories, I had no news of my parents' well-being, or how my siblings were doing? I wondered if anyone missed me ... or was I just a *Good riddance?* Cut off from everyone I had ever known in life, I took solace in those precious gifts of love, so my ***Pilot Light*** (Shadan) would forever remain ignited. Abbaji told me that he gave me that name for a reason.

With the flashbacks of Mukesh songs Moonis sang every night, now my anger toward him magically transformed into sweet memories like a precious gift: *"Laut ke Aa"* rang in my ears. I was once humming that song when our steward Nyang entered the room.

"Madamme, *lonch* is at the table, the *Docto* (Doctor) *jost* arrived." In seconds I travelled back from Pakistan to Nigeria. So now for me the pattern was set.

Western music while in the company of the brown Englishman. I also liked his golden collection on our reel-to-reel tape deck, and even started enjoying the popular African *High Life* played on the radio. Any music made me *shadan* (cheerful).

Sometimes I welcomed hubby at the door, humming one of the sixties tunes:

"Honey in the morning, honey in the evening, honey at supper time
Be my little honey and love me all the time!
Sugar in the morning, sugar in the evening . . ."
Or...
"Zooby Zooby Zoo, means that I love you"
His face would light up each time he heard his new nickname, **Zooby.** He promised me a trip to Europe which I looked forward to.

……

A Toddler comes to see a Bride…

Nyang brought for us afternoon tea and snacks then suddenly rushed to close the glass shutters one by one, expecting a heavy downpour. "How can the Nigerians predict the rainfall in advance?" I wondered. Lounging in our family room, sipping Jasmine Delight we were admiring the view of lush greenery through floor-to-ceiling glass windows when my thoughts drifted,

"I wish there were some people from our own background." I rarely voiced my deep-down emotions, or even expressed how the suicide incident behind our backyard had affected me. But that day was exceptional. Just then we heard the doorbell, Nyang swiftly reached for the front door and returned surprised.

"There's a strange lady at the door, with a little boy. She says she is a doctor's wife from downtown Ibadan. Should I let her in?" Getting up swiftly I looked at Mujeeb with a smile.

"See the magic, how God has granted my wish instantly?"

"May I come in?"

"Yes, yes of course," Mujeeb also got up to receive her, she introduced herself.

"I'm Shehnaz Khan and this is my son Moony." She was a pretty young lady, barely five feet tall, with fair skin and exceptionally long, silky hair. Two more inches of it would have touched the ground. She wore a fancy shalwar suit, but I was dressed western.

"In downtown Ibadan, we got the news that a bride from Pakistan has arrived Ife campus." We cast warm smiles at each other.

"You see, my son has never seen an Indian or Pakistani bride, so I've brought him along…but … but… eh," she seemed taken aback, looking at me from top to bottom. She least expected to find a bride in a mini dress, so she candidly asked, "But…what do I tell him now?"

Feeling embarrassed, I escorted her to our living room. Nyang was trained to automatically get the tea tray ready with a variety of refreshments.

Surprisingly, within thirty minutes of our conversation, it was as though we had known each other forever. A young Muslim woman from Lucknow, India, married to a Pakistani doctor—we were birds of the same feather, in a way.

"*Chalo,* let's go see your *Jahaiz* wardrobe (fancy outfits gifted to the bride by her parents)." My suitcase that had remained locked thus far was now being unpacked by a total stranger, in my bedroom, how bizarre!

"No, not that blue satin, it's raining, take out that multicolored *Gharara.*"

In no time she assumed an advisory role like an older sister, ordering me what to wear.

We looked outside, and as usual, after a ten-minute heavy downpour, the sun was already shining in its full glory. So she settled for my pale pink taffeta *lehnga,* and almost demanded: "Take out your bridal jewelry set, and give me the pink lipstick."

Full make-up was applied—matching bangles and all.

Transformed like a chameleon, I emerged from the bedroom feeling like a princess. Mujeeb rose from his chair as if to welcome royalty. Nyang had already signaled our Gardener's wife *Tambara* who was peeking through the door. *(Tambara means A Girl at Ease, from Hausa tribe)

"Turn around, let them see how beautiful you look," said Mrs. Khan with a sense of accomplishment. I myself became a '*Tambara'* in that moment and started cat-walking. Everyone enjoyed my performance. Her face glowing with delight, she told her son, "See Moony, this is how Pakistani brides are *supposed* to look."

The chubby little enchanted toddler staring at me, was speechless, maybe a little nervous?

It's a small world, unions and reunions take place when least expected. Who knew that decades later that toddler would re-appear in my life, in a different continent!

The hour of bonding flew by. On her way out, Shehnaz assured me, "I will introduce you to a few South Asian Doctors and Teachers who live downtown."

I could hardly wait to get back into my comfortable lounging gown. In my green room I heard Mujeeb call out, "By the way, I'll take you downtown for that special gift I promised."

Mrs. Khan had already filled me in about different stores, exclusive for us expatriates.

My Prized Possession…

The following week we ventured out for my special gift Mujeeb had promised.

Downtown Ibadan was a drastically different world—rattling old beeping cars on semi-paved roads, crying babies with pot bellies and runny noses, children playing with old tires. Men and women clad in colorful Nigerian tie-dyed *Agbadas* and wraparound skirts.

"Why do the Nigerian babies have such protruding belly buttons?" I asked.

"It is called Umbilical Hernia, it goes away by itself."

I was fascinated to see women pounding yams in large wooden barrels, with babies tied to their backs. "Zooby, I just saw two women wearing skirts but no blouses, only fancy bras!"

"It's common for older women, but I wish ...," Mujeeb paused with a mischievous look.

As we drove zigzagging through avoiding potholes, he said, "This is the real Nigeria, not that bubble of mini 'Great Britain' we get to enjoy."

Beep, beep. There were goats crossing the roads, driving the drivers round the bend.

"Thank God we don't live downtown. But we should revisit, it's fascinating, full of life!"

After our grand tour of the stores exclusive for us expatriates—Kingsway and Leventis, I stopped and spontaneously declared, "Oh my God, this is it, darling,"

"What! Are you telling me this is the Bridal Gift you had in mind, a sewing machine?"

"Yes ... look, it has the capacity to create 200 different stitches."

Surprised by my choice, he took out his wallet—the price was of no concern. After all, fifty percent of his salary was deposited in Barclays Bank, Switzerland. Soon, the top-of-the-line Singer Machine became my prized possession. I could hardly hold back my excitement.

The sales lady asked, "Will you be making dresses for yourself? Here are some patterns."

"A predesigned dress pattern on paper... already marked and cut?" I had never seen one. In Pakistan, the male Tailors just took measurements and invented their own, or skilfully copied intricate designs. I bought a few patterns and proceeded to the fabric section right away. A bright yellow embossed self- pattern I fancied. On the way back, in excitement I blabbered on, "I once copied my grandma and stitched a tiny *muslin* bras for my doll when I was young."

But now, it was merely my desperate need to invent a new pastime.

Strangely, my dress-making experiments became such a passion that I started stitching all types of complicated garments. How proud I felt with my first dress, a double-breast design in vogue. Bright yellow self-embossed sunflowers that still brighten up my memories. I later learned to stitch shorts for my husband, complete with buckles, and intricate pockets.

Mujeeb was delighted to wear his grey silken pyjamas. "This is the best gift you have given me." How proud would Haseen khala be (my blue-eyed blonde aunt).

If only I could show her my latest creations. *IF Only, If Only* became my inner secret.

It was my desire to get admission to the American International School on the campus. But my English was still a 'work in progress.' My secret strategy to improve English was to silently repeat every single word other people spoke.

. . . .

ENTERTAINMENT UNDER THE STARS

6 One Friday evening, my husband and I drove downtown to watch an Indian movie *Janglee* (Wild) in a large private courtyard that had been converted into the Nigerian version of a drive-in theatre. But instead of the comfort of our own cars, we sat on rough wooden chairs, under the open sky. Local Nigerians were crazy about Bollywood films, even though they didn't understand a word of Urdu or Hindi. Most of them didn't even follow the subtitles, they were so mesmerized by the fantasy world of Indian girls singing and dancing in parks.

"Zooby, just look around … we are the only foreigners in this crowd."

"You mean the only *Oebos?*" he joked. Suddenly, the entire theatre broke into a loud musical frenzy. I too joined the chorus.

"Chahay mujhe koi janglee kahay

Kehnay do jee kehta rahay"

(Let them call me Wild, I don't care)

What an experience …the Nigerians singing a famous Urdu song, even though they didn't understand a word! Jubilant, I sang along as we all became **Janglee** (Wild/from the jungle).

As if I was back home. Mujeeb didn't share my sentiments, but he was delighted.

"I haven't seen you in such a good mood for a long time."

The *Mini Minor Horror...

After the movie ended, we zoomed along carefree in our little Mini Minor on the pitch-dark road toward the Campus. It was past midnight, and in our haste to reach the campus, we failed to notice a railway crossing sign. A freight train was storming toward us at full speed. Mujeeb slammed on his brakes, stopping a hair's breadth away from the tracks. Fear took my mind to hell, and back to heaven, within seconds. Scared stiff, we held hands and I prayed:

"*Rabbana aathainaa fiddunya...*" (Arabic prayer)

Mujeeb repeatedly tried to start the car, but it wouldn't even offer up a gasp. Of course, there was no telephone booth in that vast, deserted no-man's land.

"So are we left to pray that some other crazy expatriate will pass by?" I begrudgingly snapped, before I returned to quiet prayer once more. He turned the key again and magically the engine began to purr like a contented tiger. Off we drove, shifting instantly, from fear to laughter.

"Imagine if someone made a video of this episode, what an ad it would be for our Mini Minor!" (*A British icon of the sixties)

"Yes, but please don't relate this story to anyone," Mujeeb sheepishly pleaded.

"Oh no, sir, you cannot ask that of me," I replied through torrents of giggles. "I'll never ever be able to hold this one back."

"Oh, you are such a devil …but didn't you say you wanted me to teach you to drive?"

I was desperate to share the crazy fiasco with anyone who would listen … but I also wanted to learn to drive, so I always began the tale with: "One of our friends did the craziest thing …"

…......

Shehnaz later introduced us to a circle of Indian and Pakistanis in Ibadan. Soon we were invited to a dinner with 'pick-and-drop' service. Our host Dr. Dastoor's driver pulled in our semi-lit driveway and got out of the shiny black Cadillac. As he greeted us with a smile I noticed his pearl white teeth sparkle. He opened the door for us and I asked,

"Was it difficult to find our place?"

"No, I just asked at the gate, 'which house belongs to the people with the car plate WAL 162,' and they directed me here." The Nigerians have a vivid memory for license plates!

That South Asian circle later included us in their lively parties. No lack of activities in that 'Tropical Oasis'. The following week a staff dinner dance was scheduled.

......

My First Evers...

After a heavy downpour, the clouds had cleared and the air was blossoming with the sweet aroma of the moist earth. As we drove through the plush, freshly bathed greenery, we could hear the Nigerian *High Life* music blaring up ahead. We parked the car and headed into the gala. I was feeling very grown-up in my elegant maroon silk evening gown that I had stitched myself. But as the entrance loomed closer, I began to feel anxious. I slowed down and requested my husband, "Zooby, please don't ask me to dance with those hungry old professors. I hate the way they ogle me while I'm dancing with you."

"Respect them. They are old enough to be your grandfathers."

"Exactly," I agreed.

"But darling, sometimes you have to oblige out of politeness."

As soon as we made our grand entrance, a few friends got up to receive us; they had reserved our spot.

Mujeeb and I were dancing to a *High Life* number when the music suddenly switched to Western songs: waltz, tango, and other music that was strange to me. My hubby had taken dancing classes in London, even knew Scottish dancing, so he was only too eager to join in. "Come on let me teach you a few steps." He pulled me to the dance floor. With one swift twirl I tripped, but managed to stay upright, then quickly retired to my table.

In Pakistan, I only danced at all-female gatherings or with my brothers or cousins at weddings, I used to be the life of the party. Sadness struck me at the realization that over here I'm just a party pooper. Still, I concluded that it shouldn't affect my husband's good time.

"Go ahead, Zooby, please have fun. I'm fine here chatting with our friends."

I was sipping my third tumbler of *Fanta,* rather than the prescribed tulip glass of Chablis, and feeling ever more out of place, when I heard a soft voice, "Steve Bentley here. May I?"

I looked up…for once, he was not an *old* man—older than me but not *ancient*. He bowed politely. Despite my shyness, I easily rose from my chair. In his mid-twenties, he was an average-looking tall blond fellow with sparkling blue eyes. He was the new doctor from England that everyone had been talking about. It was the first dance with a stranger that I didn't have to pretend to be enjoying. I was happy he kept a respectable distance.

Upon my return to our table, Mujeeb gave me an odd look that I had never seen before.

"What happened, are you okay?" I asked.

"We'll talk later. Let's have some food." He rose abruptly and headed for the buffet table. I followed, like a lamb. Could my two minutes of dancing pleasure have dampened the entire evening? "Why did you agree to dance with him?" he whispered.

"You said I have to be polite and oblige … so I did."

"But I didn't say you can dance with some young stud."

"But he's not a stud, he's Dr. Bentley. The poor guy is new on the campus, and doesn't know anyone."

"Well, now he certainly knows you." Sarcasm dripped from his lips.

"Alright, Zooby, I promise, I will not dance with him or with anyone else, ever?"

"Not even with me?" His voice had clearly sweetened.

"Of course I'll dance with *you* but I want to know…" I paused.

"You look beautiful when you are angry." He picked up his camera. "What do you want to know sweetheart?"

"Nothing," I said. But what I really wanted to understand was why it was okay for him to be twirling a variety of beautiful and not-so-beautiful women all over the dance floor, but it was not acceptable for me to have one dance, with one almost handsome man who asked?

Later that night, in the safety of our bed, as sleep hovered, I thought about Pakistan when I had performed a *snake dance* on the school stage and won first prize for it. They had dressed me in a tight-fitting snakeskin costume and placed a snake head replica over mine. As the *Sapaira* (snake man) played on his **Been**, I emerged from a huge cane basket, swirling, and undulating to the music. As the dance ended, I could hear the audience's wild applause.

Lying there, drifting into sleep, I could feel my teachers wrapping me in hugs and kisses.

"Mun dolay mera tun dolay
Mere dil ka gya qarar ray
Yeh kaun bajai bansurya"
(My restless heart starts dancing at the sound of flute)

This was the lullaby of my first dance that finally allayed my anxiety and sent me peacefully off to sleep.

The Tarkwa Bay, a tourist attraction in Lagos Nigeria, was packed with tourists. A vast expanse of powdery white sand, clear turquoise water, swaying palm trees, and surging waves captivated me. From one end to the other, colorful umbrellas, printed towels, plastic balls, and rubber rafts added the 'urban' vitality to the serenity of vast stretch of virgin sand by the ocean. A variety of languages mingled with surging waves, echoing like music in my ears. In that brilliant sunshine the water was warm, but I barely wet my feet, and retreated.

Too shy to remove my towel gown, I wondered 'W*hy am I the only one with hang-ups?'*

International tourists from various racial and cultural backgrounds, slim or plump, black or white, how freely they were enjoying themselves. Cloaked in my cultural inhibitions I felt envious.

On our honeymoon night I had gladly modelled my powder-blue swimsuit Mujeeb brought from London. But now I was feeling uncomfortable exhibiting myself in broad daylight.

"No one is looking at you,"

"I'll join you as soon as I'm ready," I replied.

"Are you worried about getting a tan?" he asked.

We brown folks deprive ourselves of vitamin D by avoiding the Sun, just so we don't get any darker. I observed a few white women in bikinis, basking under the sun, just to get a tan. In Pakistan my siblings were complimented for their light complexion and green eyes, only after I came to Nigeria, I met Europeans who appreciated my natural tan... so that was the least of my concerns.

Splashing about, playing with surging waves, Mujeeb kept giving me inviting looks, but I was procrastinating. I said, "Can we wait until some people leave, and it's not as bright?"

"Don't create such drama,"

I pleaded, "Few more minutes please."

Right around dusk, as the sky turned pink and peach, he made the final call. "Are you coming or not? The water is starting to get cold."

Looking side to side, the crowd now scanty, I summoned up the courage. "Take my towel gown when I ask you to." A big wave surged, I rushed forward casting my towel away, and quickly submerged myself in the water so no one could see me.

"Wow, you've finally taken the plunge into the..."

"The Atlantic Ocean," I said gleefully.

Against the sunset, Mujeeb snapped over a dozen shots of me in various poses. I was shocked and upset to find out that he later mailed the duplicate prints to his brother.

"Remember your brother chose me for you because he saw me on a *janamaz* (prayer rug)? Now, they'll think it is **me** who has corrupted **you**."

"But he also saw you in your tight-fitting clothes and stilettos, my dear. I heard in Pindi they called you a *Teddy Girl*."

"True, in Karachi they said if you want to see fashion, go to Pindi and meet *Shadan*," I boasted.

As for my swimsuit photos mailed without my knowledge, it was too late to protest.

……

Back to School...

Returning from downtown one afternoon, we passed by the *American International School* on the campus. I said, "Imagine if I took admission in this school?"

"Imagine? Why just imagine?" Mujeeb swerved the steering, turned the car toward the gate. Before we came out of the school, we had completed my application.

"See you at ten tomorrow. You'll be interviewed by Mr. Gillespie," said the admission clerk. I requested, "Please don't share it with the staff."

"Of course not," he assured me.

On the first day, a girl named *Abigail* approached me and offered, "You can sit with me in class, and I'll introduce you to other friends." She was a lovely Jewish girl from Israel, my first-ever non-Muslim friend. From amongst students from all over the world; Belgian, Danish, French, German, and the Nigerians, we two found most in common.

"Are you two sisters or cousins?" Some people asked about Abigail and me. Perhaps our identical uniforms created a visual delusion.

It was embarrassing that I had to carry an Urdu/English dictionary in order to study Geography, a subject I once excelled in, but was now struggling with. Understanding Chaucer and Shakespeare for an Urdu medium student was 'astronomical.' Thanks to Mr. Gillespie who was a patient teacher as well as *Philipa Wyld* an Australian Professor's daughter, for her helping hand.

Eventually I pulled through. Mujeeb was pleased but was surprised that I enjoyed Joseph Conrad's **'Lord Jim'** which he thought was a difficult read!

I was thrilled to also join the basketball team. By then, my sewing machine was put to rest as a new world had opened up to me. Meeting others of my own age was almost like you water a parched plant and it starts blooming.

We were given the choice to opt out of the morning assembly of Christian Service, but I decided to join. I was surprised to find that as a Muslim, I was taught more about Christianity, the prophets Moses and Jesus, than the rest of my classmates!

Abigail became curious, "How do you know so much about Moses?"

"We say *Prophet* Moses, *Peace be upon Him.* Calling him just by his name shows disrespect!" Abigail was wide-eyed surprised. The Morning Choir reminded me of the *Milad* get-togethers in Pakistan, when women gathered to sing religious songs in Urdu, followed by prayers.

But now in Nigeria, in an American school, I was joyfully singing hymns with the international youth. Christmas carols bring sweet memories to this day.

'On the first day of Christmas my true love sent to me ...' was my favorite tune.

Thanks to my 'nonreligious humanist' father who taught me to be accepting of all people. Muslims were not stereotyped at that time and in Nigeria the Christian/Muslim population ratio was almost 50:50. We met a Muslim husband with a Christian wife, who willingly shared with us,

"My wife became a Christian just so she would qualify for a scholarship."

Once I cleared my Advanced Level exam (conducted via London, England) I asked Mujeeb, "When will you enrol me in the University?"

He pulled me closer and replied, "Let's wait for a while," then he went on…

"Remember you promised to start cooking on the weekends, I'll help you."

Though we were still discovering each other's quirks, likes, and dislikes, my cooking skills were yet to be tested.

……

Me... A Home-maker!

Sunday came too soon. Wearing my fancy apron, I entered the kitchen as if I was about to do the world a favor. "What's your specialty darling?" Mujeeb asked.

"What specialty?" My only cooking experience was in Grade 10 Home Economics class when we learned how to make *Matar Pulao* and *Zeera Aloo*. I didn't even know where the ingredients were kept? So, I posed the same question to him, "What's *your* specialty, Zooby?"

"I can make many dishes. I spent ten years in London on my own."

"I have a great idea. First Sunday when Simon is away, you cook, and I'll do the dishes. The following week I will cook and you …"

"Your wish is my command," he said even before I finished my sentence.

He then reminded me, "It's time for us to reciprocate all those dinner invitations."

My first experiment with roast chicken was a disaster—a solid rock announced its arrival on our platter. "Jeoffery and Rolly said 'it's delicious but we are dying for a Pakistani curry meal!"

So … together we began our cooking experiments, some of which were total disasters!

I phoned Shehnaz Khan, "Our curries look anaemic. I'm used to colorful **salans** (gravy)."

After her suggestion to add tomato paste, from a local store I grabbed two cans with a picture of tomatoes marked 'Tomapep.'

Soon we invited two couples over for dinner, to show off our culinary skills.

"Wow! Your *Aloo gosht looks so good." Mujeeb came to the kitchen.

Rolly and Geoffrey arrived with a bouquet. Dinner table adorned with our finest bone china, starched napkins, etc. From the kitchen I overheard them remark, "It smells delicious."

Back in the kitchen, as I dished out the curry in a serving bowl, I took a little taste. "Oh my God"! My mouth was on fire, eyes teary, in panic I called Mujeeb.

"What's wrong?" I gulped down cold water then signalled at the pot.

Mujeeb took a taste. "Oh no," He then checked the second can from the cabinet. Beside the picture of a tomato, there were red chillies too. That fiery blend was more Pep less Toma!

"Wash the meat, quickly make new *masala*."

"What! Wash the meat?" We had no other choice.

Our guests enjoyed the meal so much they requested, "You must tell us the recipe."

"This is my wife's speciality, and she is keeping it a secret even from me," Mujeeb replied sheepishly. We chuckled the next day repeating our innovative recipe,

"Wash up cooked meat and then dip it in a mild sauce."

Eventually we did master curry meals that attracted many.

*Aloo gosht is beef and potato curry, eaten with naan or chapatee (flat bread)

Touring Europe

7 Holding the itinerary I cheered, "Oh wow, are we going to all those places? How much did our tickets cost?"

"That's not your headache, darling." First-class fare was paid by the university.

We flew with Swiss Air from Lagos to Rome, our first stopover as tourists.

I strived to impress my hubby with the fact that I was well informed. I often carried the brochures with me. "Of all the places we visited in Rome, I found the **Colosseum** most impressive. Did you know it can accommodate fifty to eighty thousand spectators?" I asked.

Mujeeb added, "And... did you know that unlike other amphitheaters, it is **Oval**?"

"I thought you were going crazy taking pictures at **Piazza Navona**."

"That's where I got rid of my Nigerian change, in the wish fountain."

"By the way, we are off to see *your* favorite statue of Michelangelo."

From his tone I sensed maybe he hadn't forgotten my one-time smoking impulse?

At times the pedestrians asked me for directions ... in Italian.

"Sorry, *Ne Parla Italiano*" was all I could say.

"You seem flattered to be mistaken for an Italian."

"Yes, a tanned Italian, but I'd love to learn Italian, it's so expressive …"

Our Playful Pilot...

The one-hour special flight from Rome to Geneva on a day of brilliant sunshine will remain etched in my mind. What a captivating aerial view of the deep-blue Mediterranean Sea and the European coastline! Mujeeb's Cannon camcorder managed to zoom in and videotape the entire flight. Our Swiss Air pilot took immense delight in entertaining his passengers—flying at an angle, tilting and swaying the wings, he gave us a perfect view of the **Mont Blanc**.

"Oh wow Zooby, we are actually flying over the Alps," I could hardly keep myself strapped into my seat so I wobbled. "Sit down, please,"

I replied, "Should I start calling you daddy?"

"Look over there, Lake Geneva and the giant water fountain they call **Jet D'Eu**. I read about this landmark in a postcard." Watching it from the air was a rare opportunity.

The next morning before breakfast at the hotel, I picked up a brochures from the kiosk to plan our day when a voice addressed us, "*Ho na ho*, you two are from Karachi, right?"

I turned back and said with pride, "My husband is, but I'm from Rawalpindi."

This young tourist, a *Karachiite* desperate for company, introduced himself as *Saleem*.

"We came to Switzerland to cool off but... there's a heat wave all over Europe,"

"May I join you?" he asked.

Before we could give our consent, the well-groomed, slender young man was already comfortably seated on the third vacant chair.

I noticed his shiny black hair and seemingly generous application of *Brylcreem* Pakistani style. It's strange how easily you can spot your own countryman, which class they belong to. So … we snobs felt comfortable with him.

"Let's forget about a conducted tour by professional guides, it's too expensive."

"For that price, we could have three luxury meals in a five-star restaurant," he said.

"A trip to the mountains on our own would be cooler and cheaper." We made spur-of-the-moment plans to combat the weather.

"Birds of the same feather tour together," I said, and Saleem was quick to compliment,

"Well said, *bhabi,"* Bhabi means sister-in-law, how our people form instant relationships.

Saleem got up to pour himself coffee, and Mujeeb whispered to me, "Don't get too friendly with him,"

"Are you being protective or possessive?" I whispered back.

"Bit of both, it's a sign of love."

Our journey by electric train to the Chamonix Mountains in the Swiss Alps was my 'dream come true.' As the bright red train curved uphill, against the backdrop of the captivating Alps, I almost had the full view of the engine and the train as well. I captured it on our camcorder.

"Aren't we lucky to get the cabin at the tail end?" I gloated.

"And you were disappointed we missed the front most."

After spending the day in those alluring hills and at other tourist attractions, we were bone-weary. Having lost the directions to the train station at the time, we were fed up of asking everyone over and over, "Ou est la gare? (Where is the railway station).

*__Gare__ d'Agen Aigle railway station (Switzerland).

We kept mispronouncing, repeating the phrase till our throats dried. Lost in the mountains, neither of us could understand the replies in French: '**tout droit**'

Near a parking lot, we sat on a bench to catch a breath. Looking at a sparkling gray Mercedes Benz, I joked, "Imagine if I had the keys to this, I'd drive off to Geneva,"

"Here are the keys, be my guest, *Bhabi.*" My 'pretend brother-in-law' Saleem playfully put his hand in his pocket. I cast a fatigued smile of indifference.

Meeting them in the Mountains...

We forced ourselves to get up and move on. Down the road I spotted an elderly couple meandering. I sped up to catch up with them, "Excusez-moi, Monsieur... o*u est la Gare?*"

"Are you folks from Pack-is- taan?" (Pakistan over-stretched in American accent).

"Yes, we are," I was energized with my least expected discovery.

They too were equally excited to *discover* us—of all the places in the Chamonix Mountains, in Switzerland! What a stimulus, it instantly cured the feeling of fatigue.

Mr. and Mrs. Hansen had spent five memorable years of their life in Lahore, a historical city of Pakistan, employed by the United Nations World Health Organization.

"We are also heading to Geneva. So forget about the Railway Station, we'd be delighted to give you folks a ride." On the way Mr. Hansen shared, "Two of my favorite things in life are—the Azalea flower and …" he paused.

We were all ears. "...the young women of *Pack-is-taan.*"

"You mean Pakistan?" I pronounced it my way.

Mrs. Hansen then added, "He fell in love with one, and I had a hard time holding him back."

Unsure of the intended pun, we refrained from laughing.

We, the three small-size young stooges from Pakistan, followed the tall elderly American couple. As they made a turn toward the parking lot, Mr. Hansen took out his keys and headed for the **same ... gray ... Mercedes** that I had jokingly wished to ride in! No less than a God-sent miracle. As they opened the doors of their car ... and their hearts for us, I said, "Do I have a story to share with you?" Getting into the back seat, I couldn't resist reciting my pet verse in Urdu:

"Dil se jo baat nikaltee hai asar rakhtee hai
Per nahin, Taqat-e-pervaaz magar rakhtee hai"
(A sincere wish has the power to fly)

"Wow, Dr. Zoberi, your wife has a song or a verse for every situation," Saleem said and Mujeeb nudged me once again. I welcomed Mr. Hansen's diversion: "You'll have to translate that for us, Urdu is such a poetic language, but we barely managed to learn a few phrases."

On the way back to Geneva, we were given a guided tour, priceless! Hansen made brief stop over's in various small villages, allowing us to take pictures. He parked at an exclusive spot saying, "There's something you just cannot miss." What a perfect view of the **Mon Blanc**—breath-taking!

"This is the **Matterhorn Peak** at the border of Switzerland and Italy. It is 14,692 feet high."

"I've heard about the four faces but... eh..." I was reluctant to answer.

While Mujeeb's camera was on endless rampage of *click, click, click,* Hansen explained, "The four faces of the Matterhorn are the Four Cardinal Directions—north, east, south, and west." We still possess that precious shot, preserved in our albums and in our minds.

As we approached the city of Geneva he asked, "We have a swimming pool on the rooftop of our building, would you accept our invitation?"

Mrs Hansen added, "You'll get a perfect view of Lake Geneva, the jet fountain."

What more could we want? They went out of their way to stop at our hotel, so we could pick up our bathing suits. Thankfully, Saleem exercised wisdom and stayed back.

Their multi-story apartment building sat on top of a hill. We were spellbound at the sight.

After the swim they treated us to a simple American meal my taste buds had already adapted to. Their immaculately furnished apartment was also adorned with paintings and pictures of the **Shalimar Gardens** and **Badshahi Masjid**—the Royal Mosque in Lahore (historical remnants of the Mughal Empire). "I'd never have imagined we would find **Lahore in Geneva**!"

At that note, Mr. Hansen got up to switch the music from jazz to *Sitar and Tabla.*

"Just for you young lady," he charmed me.

As they dropped us to our hotel, they advised, "Don't forget to see ***Parc La Grange,*** Geneva's world-famous Rose Garden."

The next morning, my whimsical mood prompted me to wear my chiffon *saree*—forest green with pink roses. Mujeeb was surprised, "Going site-seeing dressed like this?"

"Yup, I know your candid camera and the urge to send pictures abroad," I said, then took out the brochure and read,

'The Parc La Grange is the single largest green space in Geneva also the most beautiful. Two theatre scenes offer plays and gigs from June to September It is famous for its biggest rose garden in Geneva.10,000 roses from 200 different species. It was granted the Award of Garden excellence by the World Federation of Roses Societies. It is celebrated for its great care and preservation of rose species.'

Saved in the hard drive of my mind, I can retrieve at a moment's notice the images of the **Parc La Grange**—roses of all sizes and colors, simply bedazzling! I thought of my father's mini rose garden, how delighted he would be to see perfectly trimmed rose bushes; vines tied to posts to appear as the 'Rose Trees.' My loved ones always travelled with me. How could I put my past behind?

Mujeeb's Leica urged me to stop and pose. "Did you notice how men were staring at your exposed tanned midriff?"

"Not really, but I did notice how both of you have been ogling at lovely white long legs of Swiss girls," he changed the subject, "Next time we'll allow more time for Geneva."

Germany...

After landing at Flughaafan, the Frankfurt Airport, we were driven straight to the showroom, what a surprise! An *Opel Rekord* hubby had booked from Nigeria, a top-of-the-line model with turquoise-blue leather seats and other upgrades.

"How did you know it was my dream to see Europe by car?"

"Well my darling, you no longer have to drive the Mini Minor with a silencer, not so silent."

Zooming along the German Autobahns felt like sailing on calm waters.

"What a difference from the potholes of Ibadan roads!"

We were invited by Uncle Saeed who was the Vice Counsellor-General in the Pakistani Consulate located in the neighboring municipal city **Bad Godesberg**. Before meeting him in Bonn, we took a scenic boat cruise that blew my mind. The Tour Guide announced:

"River Danube journeys through the heart of Europe, passes through some of the world's most elegant, vibrant cities. Multiple capital cities—including Budapest, Vienna, and more, along the course of this beautiful waterway, we provide our guests with an insight into the history of the continent."

Sailing through different countries, I heard the guide inform, "It's the second largest river in Europe." I remained spellbound, but at times felt irritated with Mujeeb's best friend snapping away.

"You keep missing lovely views. Remember I *live* with you."

......

Once we drove down to my uncle *Saeed Chacha's* place, our Opel got to rest, and he became our chauffeur and chaperone.

Although there's distinct cultural divide from province to province, the Embassy staff flocked together like 'Pakistanis of the same feather'. Back home, they may never have associated with one another. Observing the unity between the *Bengali* speaking; *Punjabi* speaking; *Urdu* speaking and even *Pukhtoons,* I commented, "I'm so happy to see such interprovincial harmony." Saeed Chacha took the compliment as though it was to his credit.

Of the various tourist sites he took us to, **Rheinaue Park** which was extraordinary.

Before our departure, the Embassy staff gave us a farewell dinner. My thoughtful uncle also invited the Biology Professor from the University of Bonn. He spoke English with a strong German accent: *"Rheinische Friedrich-Wilhelms-Universität Bonn was founded by*

Frederick William, also known as the Rhine University, in October 1818."

I jotted down the grand finale in my travel diary. Our next destination was Austria.

"For your love of music darling, we can't bypass Vienna."

Reading the brochure, I was blown away, realizing I had entered a Tourists' Paradise.

"The expense part is not your headache," Mujeeb assured me and arranged a conducted tour for one day; the rest we explored ourselves.

I was happy to pose beside Beethoven's magnanimous statue—one of 18th century's top Composers. We recalled our classical collection of music: The 9th symphony Choral.

"What about *'Ode to Joy'*?"

"Oh...you remember that?" he said in a teacher-like manner.

"Just for the Violin Concerto in the Concert Hall, and the Live Orchestras in perfectly manicured parks, I think Vienna tops Geneva." I had changed my mind.

"So now you know why it's called the City of Music, because of its musical legacy." "**The City of Dreams**—home to the world's first Psychoanalyst." Mujeeb smiled back.

"It's the city of Sigmund Freud, right?"

"By the way, did you know it was my dream to become a Psychiatrist?" "Yes."

"Next time we must meet my brother's Viennese ex-girlfriend." That was news to me...

......

For our onward journey Mujeeb had planned to drive through Belgium and Holland, after that we would take a boat across the channel for the UK.

"The English Channel …" I paused, Mujeeb interjected, "Sweetheart, this time *I* have picked up a brochure."

At night I expressed my wish, "Aren't we going to visit Paris?"

"For Paris we need a separate trip. Now go to sleep, I have a lot of driving to do."

……

Showcased in London...

For Mujeeb it was a homecoming—where the *East was to meet the West.*

We reached the Isle of Whyte in England via ferry. Our Opel Rekord was transported along with us. Upon arrival we could just turn the ignition on, and drive off to London. A friend had booked temporary accommodations at the Imperial College, one of the College dorms of London University.

By now Mujeeb expected me to read the pamphlet:

'Some of the richest cliffs and quarries for dinosaur fossils in Europe are right here. This is the Island which has been home to the poets Swinburne and Tennyson and . . . eh . . . and its Queen Victoria's summer residence, the Osborne House.'

"I get the hint, but now I can hardly wait for you to meet my friends."

"You mean friends who said don't make a mistake to marry a **Desi Girl*?" (Indian or Pakistani)

Ten years was a long time for him to bond with the place, the culture, and good friends.

"My best friends are Mukhtar and Kerstine, they live in the suburb Enfield. We will go there also but first we are meeting the group in Central London. Just remember they've all married European women—Italian, German, Spanish, British, you name it, but you would be the *only* Pakistani wife."

"Oh wow!" I felt a surge of excitement.

Mukhtar's wife Kerstin, a pretty blonde lady, greeted us in her sweet Swedish accent. Seven other couples were brown-and-white combinations. During the late fifties and early sixties, amongst Indian and Pakistani men, to marry white women was 'fashionable.'

I felt self-conscious, feeling like an *object,* being scrutinized by an observation panel. It was hard to tell if they were surprised to see me dressed Western. Once we got past the formalities of how was our trip to Europe, which country I liked best, the conversation kept shifting into **Urdu.**

I was trying to stick to English, but they replied in Urdu. Ladies decided to help the hostess.

I felt it was rude to communicate in a language they didn't follow, so I reluctantly hinted,

"Any of your wives speak Urdu?" They looked at each other and one of them spontaneously replied, *"Kitnee sikha deingay?"* (How much Urdu can we teach them?)

Another one candidly clarified, "It may sound rude to you, but it's been so long since we all conversed in Urdu."

"Please let us indulge for a few hours, in our *Mother Tongue.*"

"Our jaws are aching, having to speak a foreign language all the time."

I wondered whether to feel sorry for these men or their wives?

They started asking me for favors, "Zohra, please show us how to make *Pakoray.*"

"Could you teach my wife *Kashmiri Murgh?*" Maybe I should've surprised them and confessed that I'm fond of lamb chops, mashed potatoes, and green peas!

One of them suggested, "Let's have a feast. You decide the menu we'll follow your directions and help out." Anita, the German lady retaliated,

"So the saying is true...that the way to a man's heart is through his stomach."

As for Mujeeb I noticed his chest swelling with pride. Before we left, they were already planning our next visit to another friend's house. Someone whispered to Mujeeb, "Lucky you!"

I overheard his reply, "I have groomed her *yaar." (Buddy)

On the way back I retorted, "Why do men like to take all the credit?"

"Protesting, are you?" I secretly thought, *not all girls are able to adapt like I did.*

"Our educated men from good families are attracted to white complexions and... easy... you know... they can get … eh … you know what I mean? But when European *men* marry into our culture, they fall for our classy girls from educated families with *Eastern values.*"

"There are exceptions," said the man of few words.

A distant relative *Taj* (our third or fourth cousin) helped us book a decent accommodation at the Imperial College residences. Craving for company he often visited us as well.

Mujeeb had a project to complete at the University, so I became an *African Alice in the British Wonderland!* I walked and walked on Oxford Street, from one end to the other. I visited the dream department stores such as *Selfridges; Marks and Spencer's; John Lewis;* and the *Harrods.* No comparison with Nigeria's *Kingsway* and *Leventis* with scanty supplies.

Excited to sit in the upper deck of the red double-decker buses, we visited tourist attractions—fed pigeons at Trafalgar Square, how they sat on my arms and across my shoulders! I was tickled in more ways than one.

One day I picked up a surprise call:

"Salah-uddin Zuberi here, you must've heard my name I'm related to you." I placed my hand on the phone, "Zooby, a stranger is claiming to be our relative!" Mujeeb shrugged his shoulders, "The Zuberi clan is scattered all over the world."

With a pale complexion and blond hair, I would have thought he was an Englishman. In isolation, obsessed with family, carrying the **Zuberi Shajra** (family tree) in his head, he mentioned names of relatives I hadn't heard. With our history of marrying first cousins, many are related.

Since he had the same passion and taste for music, such as classic Urdu songs, we hit it off. Soon he gifted me a ghetto-blaster and brought dozens of music cassettes—I was all set.

He readily accepted *Sal* as his nickname. His marriage was arranged to a Hyderabadi girl named Sadiqa. He explained, "Not from Hyderabad Pakistan." (During the 1947 Partition, some provinces were also split in two! Hence there are two Punjabs, two Bengals, and two Hyderabads.)

On weekends we visited the British Museum, dedicated to human history, art, and culture. "It has one of the largest comprehensive collections." Now I had two tourist guides explaining it all. The National Art Gallery and Museum in Trafalgar Square *'Founded in 1824, houses a collection of over 2,300 paintings dating from the mid-13th century to 1900.'*

I could spend hours admiring the works of legendary masters like Van Gogh, Da Vinci, Botticelli, and Renoir. So I made a second visit on my own. It was quite an experience to also watch the Premier Show of 'The Sound of Music' at Piccadilly Circus in central London!

"What a contrast from the old house in Ibadan converted into a Drive-in theatre!" Nonetheless, singing along with the local Nigerians under the starlit sky, had its own charm. But Now I hummed, *'How do you like to solve a problem like Maria?'* and *'The hills are alive ..."*

Time flew by. Sal made a heartfelt offer, "Next time you visit London, you must stay with us" as though we had known each other forever.

Mujeeb caught me off-guard and cast a mysterious smile creating suspense …

"I've noticed that in your dreams you've been conversing with your parents. So here's a special gift for you." Handing me a British Airways open ticket to Rawalpindi he promised, "Next year, we'll go together."

....

Reuniting with my Family

8 My entire family including my cousins were at the airport to welcome me with flowers, smiles, and tears of joy. On the way back, I noticed how jam-packed the three cars were. My younger siblings ducked to dodge the police at every stoplight.

Upon arrival, I toured the house room to room, touching the walls, opening the cupboards to check if my stuff was still there. Familiarity now *Unfamiliar*—so strange!

Ammi couldn't get enough of me and kept asking, "Are you happily married? Is Mujeeb good to you? Just tell me the truth." I assured her I was a pampered wife. But I did create drama: "Ammi, in Nigeria I felt like an alien landed on another planet. No one looked like me, nor spoke my language, Ma." Everyone tuned in as I went on. "It's all black, white, or green" my statement confused them. "White Professors and black students on the campus, but in downtown Ibadan *everyone* is black."

"Who is green?" my nine-year old brother Shahid innocently asked.

"The forest is deep green and except for the roads, the entire earth is covered with thick tropical forest." I went on. "The Nigerians are really nice people, especially when I say a few words in their language." They listened on, my parents' arms around me, their faces radiant with affection. Tea and snacks were brought. Mom put something so tasty in my mouth that I mumbled, "I'm talking too much, so I better shut up."

"No, no we miss our chatterbox." Abbaji added, "Your siblings don't talk as much."

My sister Nigma two years younger, my brother Sikandar, Rubeena then Shahid my youngest brother—their gaze was so intent, I reacted. "Don't look at me like I'm a stranger over here too." Everyone burst out laughing.

"How come they all have green eyes, and I don't?" I grumbled.

"They inherited eyes from your father but you..." Ammi held my hand and kissed it.

Abbaji added, "She is happy you inherited her brown eyes."

I replied, "But not her complexion ... but Ma, guess what, the expatriate Professors on the campus –Europeans and the Americans actually admire my brown complexion!" Indo-Pakistanis unfortunately suffer from a *complexion complex*. "Over here, everyone used to compare me with my siblings."

Ammi reassured me, "But Ammajan (grandma) always defended your wheat complexion as *Gandumi* rang being her favorite." I caressed her face with affection. Looking into her eyes, I started humming:

"Beautiful beautiful brown eyes
I'll never love blue eyes again"

"Aray wah, now you're singing English songs too?" My siblings exchanged funny looks, I stopped ... but Abbaji added, "That's Mujeeb's song for her I think, right?" But I teased him back, "I remember you used to hum the lyrics to Ammi.

"Neend mein doobee huee hein Sharbatee Aankhein" (Sleepy eyes, intoxicating)

Everyone went to bed, but Ammi sat by my bedside, gently combing my hair with her fingers. "Every relative who visited us criticized, *'What a gamble we played to send you away with someone we hardly knew'* I worried if it was our blunder."

"But Ammi, *I* said yes, so why should *you* feel guilty?"

My mom continued, "When we let go of your hand at the railway station, I was so shaken up that even my jaw line started hurting. My dentist has warned me that if I continue to grind my teeth, I'll soon end up with a denture."

"Relax, Ma. I am a pampered wife and everyone on the campus adores me too, though I don't know why?"

It was obvious my mother had bottled up her emotions and concerns. "I had apprehensions, what if he mistreated you, and there would be no one to turn to?"

I wondered if she was recalling how *she* felt when they risked their lives to flee from Delhi, India to Rawalpindi, Pakistan. My migration wasn't nearly as challenging as hers.

"Ammi, it's not as though you pushed me against my will." I reiterated.

"Still, what does a sixteen-year-old know?"

"Look who is talking, you had to flee your country with a small baby, leaving behind your parents, your brother and all your belongings, with no hope of ever returning!"

"It's only your father who kept reassuring me 'Shadan is more mature than other girls her age' he was right." Ammi exhaled a sigh of relief, cast her *Mona Lisa* smile and left the room.

The next morning at the breakfast table, fresh *parathas* with delectable omelette and other goodies were made by ***Sarvar***. "His name is Server?" I asked jokingly.

"Not the English spelling" one of my siblings cheekily replied.

"It's such a joy to have a full dining table. In Nigeria it's only the two of us."

Our organized father brought out the list of all the places we could visit: a trip to **Muree** and **Nathya Galee** (foothills of the Himalayas), a visit to Taxila (ancient historical site). Dinner invitations at family and friends' homes occupied most evenings. Women from poor neighborhoods brought food, and innocently gifted me small amounts of money.

Operation Gibraltar (1965)

The news of cross-border skirmishes between India and Pakistan were becoming serious.

Subsequently, our social plans got cancelled.

The excitement of gift exchanges and warm hugs didn't last long. There was a barrage of warnings broadcast all day long, and instructions to dig trenches and how to take cover.

'During the air raids, at the sound of the sirens, turn off all lights and take cover. Do not even light a match stick.'

We decided that during the air raids we would all gather at my uncle's house, across the street, in one room that had three exits.

No one expected it, but an all-out war started on August 5th (1965). Petrified, I used to be the first one to wake up at the ominous sound of the sirens warning of air raids. One by one I'd holler names in the dark. "Hurry up Nigma, Sikandar, Ammi, please wake up!"

One night as I helped everyone cross the street in the pitch dark, the door closed, I was left outside and the shelling began! When names were called, I was missing...the door opened, everyone hollered in panic, "Hurry up, Shadan, get in quick." During the air raid my heartbeat raced; to witness shelling was one of the scariest episodes I've relived each time there's a war. *How do the innocent children endure all-out bombings and the loss of their loved ones?*

They named it 'Operation Gibraltar'— designed to liberate the Kashmiris from Indian occupation. India had retaliated by launching a full-scale military attack on West Pakistan. The seventeen-day war caused thousands of casualties on both sides. They say it was the largest engagement of armored vehicles and the largest tank battle since World War II.

Mujeeb took emergency leave to come so I wouldn't travel alone. Worrying if I would ever see him again, I counted down the hours. Once he arrived, I experienced intense emotions like never before... that's when I realized that,

I had fallen in love with him! Romance overpowered all my fears.

Diplomatic intervention by the Soviet Union and the United States resulted in what they termed as the 'Tashkent Declaration.' The United Nations-mandated ceasefire was declared. I hated how each side boasted about the bravery of their own soldiers and their military might.

Mujeeb and I celebrated our escape half-heartedly, as our loved ones were left behind.

Relief came with the news that:

A peace agreement between India and Pakistan was finally signed on January 10, 1966 that resolved the Indo-Pakistani War of 1965.

I worried about our relatives in Pakistan and my uncle in India; no direct contact possible with either of them. We reached to safety and the comforts of our home on the Ife campus—our own comfort zone ... now in Africa!

....

OIL BOOM AND THE MILITARY COUP

9 It was now a mini-America planted in the middle of Africa. What a transformation!

When Mujeeb had first taken me on a tour to view the future site, all we saw were vast stretches of lush tropical rain forest. To construct a new learning center at that location, almost thirteen thousand acres of the forest had been methodically sawed, burned, and cleared. Animals, insects, and reptiles had to abandon their homeland and search for refuge in the receding forest.

Ile- Ife (pronounced as Eee lay Eee fay) means the **Hub of the Universe**. The pagans in Nigeria believed that this was the place from where mankind had originated.

'Ile- Ife is the city where the Yoruba believe their civilization began as well as the location where the Gods descended to earth. The name Ile- Ife literally means place of dispersion. According to Yoruba tradition, Ife was founded by the deities Oduduwa and Obatala when they created the world.'

It was a long time dream of the *Yoruba* (Western Nigerian tribe) to finally build a permanent site that had now been fulfilled. In the heart of this primitive locale, modern buildings seemed to instantly appear. The new university campus was designed by top-notch Italian architects, and it soon became the main center of learning and culture in Nigeria.

The Temporary Campus established by the British was in the city of Ibadan, but now mass movement of the entire teaching staff as well as the students had taken place. From all over the world, expatriates were being enticed back to Nigeria, with handsome salaries, paid vacations, and other luxurious fringe benefits. Exclusive bungalows allocated to the Professors were adorned with imported Scandinavian furniture and European appliances. All they had to do was come and impart their knowledge to the African youth.

Social life of the expatriate staff on the campus included bridge games, potluck dinners, and dance parties. Amongst our close circle were some twenty-three nationalities, we counted one day. The Ibadan Indian families were left behind, we now made friends with the Lebanese* families in downtown Ife, mostly business owners. With them we enjoyed outdoor BBQs on the rooftops, under the starlit sky. Life was great.

*The Lebanese businessmen were amongst the earliest settlers in Nigeria.

The Military Coup...

Barely a few months had passed since my return from Pakistan when an incident shook Nigeria to the core.

It was in January 1966, one morning I had driven to the Humanities Centre to read my western newspapers. The building was referred to as the Tenth Anniversary Cake because it was shaped like an enormous layer cake. The top floor of the structure had a huge library where I went twice a week to read the London Observer and New York Times.

I was surprised to notice that mine was the only car in the entire parking lot. When I parked and got out of the car I heard a loud holler, "Halt!"

As I looked up, I was shocked to see dozens of Nigerian soldiers posted on different floors of the Humanities building.

I was confronted by a horde of armed soldiers, with guns pointed directly toward me!

My incredulous and immediate reaction was to burst out laughing, which confounded the soldiers, but actually eased the tension somewhat.

"Aa Aa! Aren't you scared, Madame?" One of them asked.

"Should I be scared? But I haven't done anything wrong," After a stressful moment, the guns were lowered.

"Don't you know many leaders have been killed, and there's a curfew on the campus? You are not supposed to be on the road," said a soldier with authority. I needed time to absorb the shocking news.

One of the soldiers offered, "I will escort Madame to her house." A chubby gentleman in military uniform, wearing numerous badges looking like their Senior General came forward.

Soon I found myself being escorted home by him. Scared, yet feeling adventurous, I experienced mixed emotions. Charity and Pious received me in the driveway … scared to see the army jeep, their faces changing colors, so I assured them, "Don't worry, I'm safe."

In that bloody coup of 1966, *Abubakar Tafawa Balewa, Sir Alhaji Ahmadu Bello*, and other high-ranking leaders as well as some of the wives, altogether twenty-two people, were murdered in cold blood. *General Yakubu Gowan* became the head of the government; thus, Nigeria entered a spell of military rule. It was also the start of the civil war, struggle for the Cessation of Biafra (Eastern Nigeria).

Now in an African country, fear spread amongst the expatriates on the campus; however, within a few days, life on the campus got back to normal as if nothing had happened. The only noticeable changes were the checkpoints and random searches at the roadblocks.

......

The Oil Boom Impact...

The new Generals established a committee made up of the fifty-one most intelligent men in the country, to serve as the advisory board to the military government. Our Vice Chancellor, Professor Oluwasami, a PhD in agriculture from Harvard, was made a key member of this 'Think Tank' for the country. At almost seven feet tall, in his crisp white Agbada (flowing wide- sleeved robe), his appearance was befitting his status, as he stood well above the staff. His multimillion-dollar four-acre estate, designed by the Italian architects, stood magnificently on top of the beautiful rolling hills. Most high-ranking state guests felt honored to be invited there.

Whenever we were invited, I enjoyed the privilege of being seated next to the Vice- Chancellor with various heads of states. In order not to lose my privileged seat by the host I read voraciously, and kept myself keenly informed and abreast of the latest and most interesting political affairs, both official and personal.

Later, the 'Watergate Scandal' was the hottest topic. Oluwasami was impressed that I could even relate details of the investigating committee hearings, led by Senator *Sam Ervin*.

While other expatriates were there on short-term contracts, we had become more like permanent residents, as we had stayed on for over a decade. We felt fortunate to be part of the educated elite from all over the world. Outside our gated academic community, a tragically poor, underdeveloped population still barely subsisted, except for the rich Lebanese businessmen.

Golden oil now proffered a generous allowance for education. Mujeeb acquired a new, well-equipped research lab and an impressive office.

Billions of dollars were being sucked out of the oil-rich Niger Delta during the oil boom of the 1970s. Nigeria joined OPEC and became the world's fourth largest oil-producing country. ***The success prompted a head-spinning 35 to 50 percent wage hike for the nation, retroactive to one year, and paid in one lump sum!*** The ecstatic nation went wild with indulgent shopping sprees. Those who formerly had no means of transportation rushed out to buy their first bicycle or motor bike. Those with a *Volkswagen* wasted no time in trading up for a *Cadillac* or a *Mercedes*. Cash was flowing in abundance.

The Art of Coping...

Despite all the wealth benefits, the expatriates had to go through a learning curve. When we would run out of cooking gas, a Nigerian friend would always bring me a spare cylinder. In fact, on each friendly visit, he would also teach me a little ***Yoruba***. When I managed to master a few words in their language, even the farm boy would reward me with extra fruits or eggs. On the odd occasion when the gas station ran out of gasoline, the manager made sure I had enough to keep driving. That's when our registrar Hugh Balmond dubbed me '*The Gasoline Queen*'. I wasn't sure if it was a compliment or a criticism, but it soon became my nickname on campus.

While many expatriates felt challenged and frustrated by some of the lesser hardships, for me life was beautiful. I found humor in the natives' response to me:

"*Aa, Aa, Madame, you're so fony.*" To my ear, it sounded like *phoney*. "*You're jost like oss blacks*" (just like us blacks) was a compliment they often paid me. And even though they called me *Oebo* (peeled orange), the fact that I was not very white earned me more marks, since the whites were generally perceived as the Colonialist rulers or the aggressors.

Many of the new arrivals we met were from the Ford Foundation, and the University of Wisconsin. I served on the housing committee and the welcome wagon. Since they were on temporary contracts, we developed the art of making *Instant Friendships.*

．．．．．

Babatunde, the Talking Drummer...

Once I led a group of thirty adventurous expatriates to Ajido village to experience the unique art of Talking Drum**...** it was delightful to watch the group of white women, wide-eyed and stunned. Babatunde Olatunji was known as the Father of African Drumming. Our guide informed us, "When the European expeditions came into the jungles to explore the local forests… they were surprised to find that the message of their coming and their intention was carried through the woods, a step or more in advance of their arrival."

We each had fun whispering different messages to the Nigerian drummer, who in turn relayed our messages by playing them on his talking drum. The locals on the opposite side interpreted these with astounding accuracy!

An African message can be transmitted at the speed of 100 miles an hour!

All those adventurous expatriates thanked me for this unique experience. "What a clever method of communication the locals had invented back then," some of them commented.

．．．．．

One special young lady I clicked with right away was Mezzie Wolgan.

Mezzie, a vibrant young Italian American lady married to Wilfred Wolgan, a Jewish American professor of Entomology. They were on a two-year contract linked with the Ford Foundation. Mezzie's first question to me was, "How come they call you the Gasoline Queen?"

We giggled and bonded over my rise to royalty. She was new to the region, and deeply curious about this strange and scary new world.

"To be honest I'm very fearful of the military presence in the country," she expressed. "Luckily things are calmer now." It fascinated her to learn about the military coup of 1966 we had successfully endured, before General Yakubu Gowon assumed power.

I became her guide, although in so many ways we were clearly the opposites. For example, she had brought an abundant supply of scented toilet rolls from America, while I was content with whatever was available locally.

I was easygoing and laid-back; she was uptight and meticulous. I knew how to throw a great party, but she knew which anti-malarial drugs were most effective. I've always believed that 'opposite' is what attracts people to each other. Mezzie became my good friend, my 'Surrogate older sister'.

Both of us joined the bridge club; together we soon attracted an enviable social circle of expatriate couples who held fun-filled potluck dinners and dance parties. Mezzie too learned the art of adjusting to a third world country.

Trouble in Our Bubble…

One fine morning, four of us expatriate wives had been playing bridge on the pool patio of the elite staff club. As I dropped my trump card on the table, Mezzie unexpectedly rushed in.

"Ladies, I hope you're ready for a shock because I have news for you."

"Oh no, here comes the bearer of bad news," my partner Helen whispered. I was ignoring Mezzie because we had just won the Rubber; but she was not deterred.

"**A major oil refinery has broken down!**" she warned, I remained engrossed in the game. "The two of clubs can sometimes beat the ace of spades, ladies," I said joyfully.

Mezzie went on, "Don't you find it ironic that this is the fourth largest oil-producing country in the world and now we'll have to line up for hours to get a couple of gallons of gas?"

This startling news was in stark contrast to the good news of the oil boom just a short while back. Mezzie went on. "I don't know about you, girls, but I'm starting to work on my contingency plan. What if another civil war breaks out, and we need to rush off to Lagos or escape overnight toward the border? We'll need gas in our cars to get away, won't we?"

The game and Mezzie continued unabated. "Well, you can ignore it if you want to, but I'm going to ask my gardener, Abedimi, to dig me a deep pit so I can store barrels of gasoline, just in case." With that she made a hurried exit.

Darlene suddenly stood to attention and asked in a quavering voice,

"Did Mezzie really just say that she's going to dig a pit in her backyard to bury gasoline?"

A silence washed over the group after Mezzie's warning. The playing cards were swiftly gathered up, as the bickering began. Other expatriate wives, who were sunbathing around the pool, quickly wrapped themselves in towels, joining in the gossip.

"Did you know that she keeps her bags packed and ready to go at all times?"

"She's being ridiculously paranoid, don't you think?"

"I can't believe she's going to ruin her gorgeous landscaping with an ugly gasoline pit."

One of the women asked, "Do you think there's going to be *real danger* here?"

The tension was growing as the women continued to give voice to their fears. There they were, a bunch of highly-strung, frustrated Americans, and there I was, the cool, calm Pakistani. "Why aren't you a nervous wreck like the rest of us?"

I responded, "Look, I come from what you call 'a third world country.' For decades, we have lived through shortages and threats of war. So, maybe we've developed resilience to this kind of pressure."

That afternoon, we decided to wait for the *future* to show what it had in store for us.

One day Mezzie asked, "Zohra, I was wondering if your neighbor has any barrels buried in her backyard?" Dr. Akande Kogbe was my Nigerian neighbor and friend.

"I doubt if she would be that organized," I said, wondering why Mezzie was so curious, but later realized it was because Akande's baby was suffering from a disease called *Osteogenesis Imperfecta*. As the mother of a sick child, she needed to always be prepared for an emergency.

We patiently tolerated the first few days of gasoline shortages, but after several weeks of constant line-ups, tempers were rising higher than the steam off our automobile hoods. Once we ran out of gasoline completely, and started lining up for hours at gas stations, our irritable underside erupted. It was torturous having to wait for two to four hours in the muggy heat, just to get two gallons of gasoline.

......

The Gasoline Queen

One morning, I got the news that a tanker was to arrive at 7:00 a.m. at the Shell station just outside of the university campus. I thought I would be the first to arrive, but word had leaked, and there was already a long line waiting when I pulled in. I greeted the gas station manager Adele Abimbola, with a few words in Yoruba, my usual currency to ensure courteous and prompt service, but he wasn't buying it that morning. On any other day, an extra gallon would have been added to my fill-up, for free.

I summoned my most casual tone. "How are you, Adele? *On sise takuntakun* (you are working hard). I heard the good news that you received a large tanker this morning?"

"Yes, Madame, but you have to line up like the rest," he bluntly insisted.

"Can't you fill me up now?" I asked with high hopes.

"Just get behind into line," How could he be so abrupt?

"You will surely run out by the time my turn comes," I pouted.

"Please, my friend, go to the line." *Friend* was a term loosely used by the Nigerians.

With no seeming choice, I joined the mile-long line-up. At least two hundred cars were idling bumper-to-bumper. Moving inch by inch I knew I'd have to exercise patience, but by now I feared that there wasn't even enough gas left in my car to return home! The arduous delay had begun so early in the morning. It was almost noon when I realized I could still have hours to endure mindless waiting, and they could run out of gas by the time I make it to the pumps.

I drove the car out of the line and parked it on the opposite side of the road. For the second time that day, I tried to butter him up by complimenting him in Yoruba, "*Kú isé* (well done)." His shirt was drenched in sweat and the glistening beads on his silky black face reflected fear, rather than heat. I followed his eyes to the two army jeeps parked by the front of the pumps. The second one was occupied by a couple of no-nonsense-looking soldiers. I sauntered over to the jeep and peeked into the back seat and what did I find? Several large gas cans that appeared to be full while at the pumps additional containers were being filled.

What power does the POWER have? I thought when suddenly a fresh idea dawned.

"Ekaaro O dara lati ri o (Good morning, it's nice to see you). My name is Zohra," I announced to the important-looking soldier in the lead jeep. "My little nephew suffers from *Osteogenesis.*"

"From what?" he grumbled in English.

"It is a disease in which brittle bones can break easily at any time. What if we have to take the baby to the hospital in an emergency, but I don't have enough gasoline to get home?"

Seeing little reaction, I dared to go on.

"The thing is ... you people are lucky, and maybe you have all the authority too. I'd really appreciate your power if you could get me some gas."

It was a General that stiffened his neck and stepped out of his jeep.

He looked down at me and barked, "I don't see your car in line."

"It's over there, the white Opel Rekord parked across the road. It's the only car that's not in the line-up." Now I was beginning to feel more than a little nervous lying to a General. In a military regime there were no casual rules about punishment.

"Bring it here, right now," he demanded. The way he roared and planted his feet on the ground, I fearfully hoped that he was just grandstanding for the audience.

I pulled my car alongside the General's jeep.

The soldier filled my tank then asked if I wanted additional supplies.

"Yes, please," I sputtered in disbelief.

I wanted one for Akande in case her baby did need to make an emergency run to the hospital ... and an extra ... just in case. Now all I had to do was, wait.

As I looked around I was shocked to see an angry mob, some with stones in their hands, and it seemed they were slowly heading toward my car. I secured my handbag under my arm, and looked toward the woods behind the gas station, paranoid that if I rushed into that thick dark forest, I would never find my way out.

One of the soldiers climbed out of the jeep and fired a shot into the air. The mob retreated. I jumped into my car and locked the doors. My head was spinning. Up until that moment, I had been taking so much for granted in this unusual land. But that day, I experienced raw terror, for the first time.

The Jeep escorted me from the gas station to the university campus and as I approached the entrance, they drove away. No sooner had I passed through the gates to the university, than Hugh Balmond, the university registrar, the man who had initially endowed me with the embarrassing title Gasoline Queen, signalled me to stop. He was a friend of sorts, with whom I had a love-hate relationship. "Take a U-turn, right now," he ordered.

My initial instinct was to defy him. "Why? I'm heading home."

"Well, I'll tell you why—I'm bloody hot and tired and have no desire to argue with you. This damn country and its shortages are getting on my nerves. There is no running water in our kitchen today and even the cooking gas has run out. My gas tank has been dry for days, and I'll bet that your bloody tank is full." He was so right.

"I need a ride, so just turn around Gasoline Queen."

His obvious frustration and my guilt surrounding my good fortune made me feel compassion for the man. On that day, even the Registrar could not enjoy the privilege that was afforded the military … and by extension, me!

"Yes, sir, I can drop you wherever you want to go." And I did.

At home our maid, Charity, had drawn my bath perfectly. My mauve hand-painted evening gown was ironed and spread on the bed, and matching shoes were set out for me. "Madam, the Sanfords have sent your orchid corsage. I've put it in the fridge for you."

While I leisurely soaked to get the morning's tension out of my system, I mulled over the details of the US Watergate scandal and the Committee hearings. I was geared up and ready for a stimulating evening of politics and history at the Vice Chancellor's villa.

That evening, Mujeeb and I were slightly late for the cocktail hour. Upon arrival, the vice chancellor Professor Oluwasami introduced me to his honored guest for the evening.

"I want you to meet this fascinating lady. You must talk her into inviting you to her home. Not only will you enjoy a splendid Pakistani curry meal, but as you dine, I promise you the white flowers at the dinner table will turn red!"

The gentleman glanced at me with a smile and tried to interject, but the host gave him no opportunity. "We used to call her 'the youngest bride on the campus' but then we found a new name for her: *The Gasoline Queen!* No matter how little gas there is in Nigerian pumps, there's always gasoline for Zohra."

I nervously shook the extended hand of the now smiling military General, who had loaded up my car with gasoline that very morning. I was relieved to discover that he was a gentleman who didn't betray a secret.

We said goodbye to our hosts around 1:00 a.m. The campus road was pitch-dark, and there wasn't a single vehicle on the road other than ours. We had not driven very far before I noticed smoke rising from under the hood of our car. In a panic, we pulled over and jumped out. Within five minutes, our automobile was ablaze. We stood there dumbfounded and helpless, holding on tightly to each other.

With a tank full of gasoline and two extra full cans in my trunk, we were terrified as to when the explosion would occur. Suddenly a set of headlights appeared. It was my husband's associate, Dr. Kirkpatrick, on his way home from the party. He professed to be equipped to put out the fire. I turned away and covered my eyes, but as luck would have it, Professor Wangboje, who was also on his way back from the party, pulled over to offer his assistance.

"Since Wangboje lives close to us, you can go and I'll join you as soon as the fire is under control." I put up no resistance.

Wangbode assured me, "I'm pretty low on gas, but we'll have enough to make it home."

When he pulled into my driveway, I noticed the lights were still on in front of Dr. Kogbe's house. "Wow, it looks like my neighbors are still up at two in the morning. That's a first," I muttered.

As I stepped out of the car, Dr. Kogbe came rushing out of the house in panic!

"I'm so relieved to see you, Zohra. It's my baby, he's very sick and I have to get him to the hospital but … my tank is dry." She broke down.

I never felt so helpless in my life, Professor Wangboje looked at me. He had brought us home on the last fumes of gas. In my burning automobile was the can of gasoline that I had earmarked for just such a traumatic occasion, but …?

Suddenly I knew what to do.

I rushed to call our cook Pious to bring Mezzie at once. He sped off in a flurry, gaining speed with every reach of his long, athletic limbs. In record time, he returned in the passenger seat of Mezzie's Range Rover.

True love and admiration is what I felt for my friend, as she helped me get Dr. Kogbe and her ailing baby into her car and off to the hospital. Thank God for Mezzie's visionary nature and her contingency plans that the bridge club ladies had so ridiculed.

For all intents and purposes, she was the true *Gasoline Queen*!

Now her 'foresight' mysteriously enlightened my 'hindsight'. There was so much I had to learn from life, and from her.

……

The Magical Mount Cameroun...

Mujeeb's quest to find rare mushrooms not only took us all over West Africa but also to an ex-French colony, Cameroun, a mountainous country situated east of Nigeria. The famous Mount Cameroun (13,350 feet above the sea level) is one of the highest mountains on the Equator!

At those high altitudes and the rugged terrain, two-way traffic was not permitted. Our driver knew ahead of time, which day we could travel in what direction. It was a scary but a fascinating experience. We reached the capital city Buea, situated at the foothills of the famous mountain. We were utterly captivated by the misty aura hovering over the hotel we stayed in. The dinner menu at the hotel made us feel as though we were back in Paris. In anticipation of the next morning, we retired early.

Rucksacks on our backs, wearing knee-high boots, we were armed with machetes and Mujeeb led the way. Discovering rare mushrooms not found in tropical Nigeria fascinated my Professor. It took us all day to climb until we could see the lava tracks and small craters. Venturing through the clouds, we got soaked, but once we made it above the clouds, the view below was incredibly beautiful and surreal.

"Zooby, I feel like we are in cloud *ten*!" I was jubilant beyond words.

However, on our way back, as Mujeeb bent down to pick a mushroom, his glasses fell off, rolling all the way down the valley. This meant he could not see anything anymore! What a dangerous escapade, as I held his hand … treading slowly down the slope, *one wrong move by either of us would have sent us tumbling down the valley, almost 5000 ft!* I reflected that, 'Sometimes descending can be more challenging than ascending—true to life as well' We finally reached to safety. A bubble bath in the luxury French hotel was a well deserved treat.

For identification and research purpose, we later took those rare fungi to Kew Mycological Gardens in London England (One of the world's largest botanical gardens).

……

The Fury of Fauna and Flora

The ongoing travelling facility we were able to explore Nigeria from West to East, South to North. While most of our adventures were pleasurable, two bizarre incidents occurred back to back were quite traumatic.

To my husband's delight, I had become quite adept at identifying wild fungi in the jungles of Nigeria. I considered myself to be his able research assistant. A professor teased Mujeeb, "Your wife can now spot an *Amanita Bulgaria* or a *Boletus* even before you've taken your glasses out." My knowledge was limited, but I loved our excursions into the jungles to uncover new forms of fungi.

While he snapped pictures, I sketched the beauty all around us for my husband, as his sketch artist. I felt honored to contribute to his upcoming book on tropical macro fungi. We looked forward to the weekends, when we would travel in a Land Rover. Every mile added a new and unusual image to my catalogue of memories.

One particular day, as we drove along, happily singing an Urdu tune, the Jeep abruptly stopped. Mujeeb and I lurched forward as the driver backed up without explanation...then he sped forward once again, halting abruptly...and then back again! He repeated this several times. Mujeeb's anger was rising, as was my lunch. Finally he called out, "Ojo, what in the hell are you doing? Are you trying to make us car sick?"

The dark-skinned driver turned to us looking quite ashen, and attempted to explain himself. But with his very strong Yoruba accent and fear causing a quaver in his voice, it was difficult to understand what he was trying to tell us. He peered through his windshield, turned back to us, and in an attempt at English, he asked us to get out of the car with him.

The sun was bright, the roads were fairly empty and we were ready to take a short break. Ojo led us toward the front of the car. It is hard to describe the panic circulating through my brain, as I looked at the source of Ojo's strange behavior. *There before us lay a wild lizard, the size of a crocodile!* It was quite dead, but still seemed to have the ability to intimidate and nauseate me. The horror show intensified as we watched Ojo grab the creature by its tail, drag it toward the rear of the SUV, and heave it into the back. Spending an entire day with my back to what I knew to be a four-foot long man-eating creature, it made the journey as uncomfortable as racing through a minefield on roller skates.

I asked Ojo, "Why in the world are you bringing this dead beast along?"

He looked at me as if I was a complete mystery, before he replied in the best English, we had ever heard from him. "Madame, I work hard to kill the meat. My wife she clean and barbeque it. Our neighbor will have party. So you ask why?"

Shocked, I had no words to reply. We continued on our way without singing or even humming. I had a creepy feeling that a pleasant melody might heal the horrid creature, and it would rise from the back to devour us all.

It seemed that every time we got in the car with Ojo, we were destined for a new, unusual, sometimes baffling, and even ***ghastly*** experience.

......

To get from Ibadan to Enugu, we travelled along cow paths and country roads.

It was a beautiful Sunday morning, as we were heading toward the city, we passed a procession of dozens and dozens of men, women, and children, who were happily marching along and chanting in their mother tongue. They were led by a tiny, dark-skinned, white-haired woman clad in a chocolate brown, loose-fitting look-alike jumpsuit. To see the contrast of the brightly tie-dyed costumes against a background of the lush green tropical rain forest was a delightful spectacle. The children were skipping, the women were dancing, and the men were sprinting along carrying primitive musical instruments.

We headed to our jungle destination and found, on that morning, some of the more exotic fungi that we had been hoping to collect. It was a glorious day. With our research bonanza safely tucked away, we headed back to our home.

As we passed the area where we had witnessed the procession earlier in the day, we noticed an unusual mound by the side of the road. I requested that Ojo pull over for a closer look. He turned toward me and asked, "Madame, you are sure?"

I brusquely replied, "Of course I'm sure, why wouldn't I be?"

He shook his head and stopped the car. "We're here, Madame."

I leaped out of the car and Mujeeb followed. Ojo stayed behind. I walked toward the dark mound and felt my knees give way as recognition set in.

This was not some sort of refuse that had been tossed to the side of the road. This was a human being, a female ... naked and ...quite dead.

Mujeeb and I were transfixed.

It was sad, puzzling, and tragic to think that this woman was left naked and all alone in the middle of nowhere. Had she been struck by a car, had someone stolen the clothing from this poor, dead woman?

I heard Ojo approaching. I was confused by the fact that he seemed more embarrassed than alarmed. I asked him, "How could this happen?"

He tried to explain how this woman likely ended up in this horrific situation … how different tribes have different customs, and in this particular tribe, they prefer to eliminate the elderly, rather than let them suffer old age.

Suddenly I recalled the image of the woman at the head of the grotesque parade. She had wool-like white hair; and what I had mistaken for a loose-fitting chocolate color jumpsuit was in fact her elephantine skin. I finally realized that the instruments the men were carrying were not for making music, but were most likely weapons they had used to beat the life from her.

Having lived through the experience of encountering another dead entity, I was certain that Ojo would be amenable to the idea of gathering up this unfortunate dead human and taking her with us, to give her a respectable burial. His response was not what I expected. The very idea was more repugnant to him than the death itself. I asked again and again in as many ways as I could, but he still resisted.

I feared that if I pressed too hard, he may abandon his duty and drive off, leaving us alone with the corpse in the middle of nowhere.

I hate that I acquiesced to my fear of intimidation, but there were so many strange and frightening things I had already experienced since my arrival, I couldn't take a chance.

Ojo spun around on his heels and returned to the vehicle, Mujeeb followed him.

I slipped my cotton shawl off my shoulders, and spread it over the dead woman.

I returned to the car and silently wept.

"Look at the variety of mushrooms we have been able to collect," Mujeeb tried to divert my attention away from the grief I was feeling.

Was it a primitive version of Euthanasia?!

In any case, there was no end to our fascinating adventures, here is another …

……

Bat Hunting and a Culinary Adventure

We were invited by the Palm Wine Drinkers Club on a hunting excursion, followed by dinner at Professor Halstead's home. The professor, a highly eccentric individual, was one of the executives of this unique club. He had a PhD in Zoology from Reading University in England, and was on a contract at Ife University in Nigeria. He wore shorts and shirts made from Nigerian tie-dye material, a huge Mexican hat, and rode a tricycle to work!

Amongst the chief guests for the banquet were the Prime Minister of Sierra Leone and Professor Halstead's girlfriend Jennie visiting from England, both were going to be initiated into the Drinkers Club that evening.

For this late afternoon hunt, he was accompanied by many Nigerian colleagues, students and of course an adventurous couple … my husband and I. In the middle of the thick tropical rain forest stood a dead tree, void of even the tiniest twig! Thousands of bats covered each and every branch, concealing the tree entirely. Several Nigerian hunters aimed and simultaneous gunshots rang out. But at the sound of these gunshots, thousands of frightened bats took to the sky. The hunt was on, and now the prey was identified, and in our sights.

We watched in amazement as the hunters dropped these injured bats into the cardboard boxes, still moving their wings, I cringed away. Struggling for their last breath but eventually giving up on life. Strangely enough, within just a few minutes, the idiotic bats that were spared made their way back to the dead tree! We had no idea what attracted them back to danger? The repeated gunshots brought more prey into the boxes, until enough were collected.

The club members claimed that after drinking their brand of palm wine, one could have a clear vision as far as twenty miles! *A blurred idea indeed,* I thought. Slender young boys had mastered the technique of climbing these tropical trees just using a thick rope around their waistline and the tree trunk. In seconds they could reach the top, to place the calabash right under the sapping fruit. Fermented for a few days, this juice apparently turned into the magic potion that's intended to get everyone intoxicated, except for my tea-totaling husband and myself—it just wasn't the Muslim style. Luckily it was a garden party, so I managed to *accidentally* spill the wine in the grass, thus spared from that farsighted insight. By the end of the evening, we were the only two individuals who remained sober.

Hungry and curious to see what their chef had prepared for us, I made my way to the buffet table, but the very sight of spit-roasted *bat* quickly abated my appetite. It happened to be the main dish! Bat may be a Nigerian delicacy, but we would've preferred chicken. I was relieved to see a small quantity of familiar and edible Nigerian *Daudau and Moyein-moyein,* and *akara balls,* which had never tasted so good. A European friend who did try the roasted bats satisfied my curiosity by commenting, "It's like chewing on a rubber eraser."

Mujeeb loved to entertain us by playing in reverse the video of our bat hunting, so it looked like the tree trunk sucks up all the flying bats, like a vacuum cleaner!

......

Other Expeditions in West Africa...

Our common interest in travelling took us to exotic places along the coast of African countries west of Nigeria as well as Cameroun, Kenya, Egypt, and Ethiopia to the east of Nigeria.

Professor Kenneth Daman was on a two-year temporary appointment as the head of the Department. He and his wife Donelda, an elderly couple, had a 'special needs teenage daughter,' Libby. They took us under their wings, and we travelled to many places together.

Once on our way to see a few West African countries, our starting point was Lagos. They managed to secure free overnight stay at the Ford Foundation Guesthouse. But only one room was available. Mujeeb suggested we call our dear friend, Mr. Zahid (Pakistani ambassador to Nigeria). We often stayed at each others' homes but their residence was too far to travel. Ken joked, "Let me be your special *Ambassador* today." So six of us in adventurous mood, stayed in one room with just two beds!

Once we changed into our night clothes, Ken came around and sat down on my bedside. "I'm fascinated by your gold bangles." I felt uneasy as he started playing with them. "What's their significance?" he asked. I replied, "Western women wear a wedding ring to indicate they are taken, we wear gold bangles." Ken got the hint, got up and said, "I just wanted to tuck you in, like my daughter Libby."

On our way to Accra in Ghana we stopped at a gas station, and while our driver was refuelling, the Damans sited a gift shop across the street and Mujeeb accompanied them to the shop. Kashif and I waited in that muggy sweltering heat, but once our patience ran out, we too decided to join them. ***Just then, a disaster struck***!

"Hello, hello, can you hear me?" I opened my eyes only to find myself lying in the middle of the road and a bunch of concerned and curious local Africans bending over me.

"Are you okay? Can you get up?" Kashif sat on the road with his legs crossed, my head on his lap. He was crying, "Mommy, wake up, I love you." I was dumbfounded as to what had just happened?

While crossing the road, a vehicle in reverse gear hit me on my right side, but Kashif was holding my left hand, or *he* would have been injured too. Fortunately, I had no fractures. However, without even getting any information about the reckless driver, we simply continued our journey! That was Africa in the early seventies.

Upon arrival I lay in bed 'bruised but not broken,' insisting that everyone must go Sightseeing as planned. A bit of privacy felt good. Two days later, we drove further west to a small country, Togo, originally a German colony, overtaken by the French.

Stretching over 40 miles wide and having a 90 miles long coast line, the capital Lome is the largest city, and chief port of Togo—coffee and cocoa land, and an oil refinery.

We never knew that such vast stretches of exotic beaches at the Gulf of Guinea, with luxurious tourist resorts existed!

Early mornings, the Damans, Mujeeb, and I would routinely take a plunge in the ocean. Though I was now less inhibited about wearing a bathing suit, I avoided it in Ken's company. They remained intrigued.

After a plunge in the ocean, we'd wobble across those virgin beaches before plunging into immaculately maintained swimming pool, then rush to enjoy a lavish Continental breakfast. It was an oasis in no-man's land…a Mini Europe.

What a fascinating display of delectable German baked goods, such as *Elisenlebkuchen,* and *Schwarzwälder Kirschtorte*, not to mention the best French croissants and pastries, from the classic *Éclair* to *Tarte Tatin.* These exotic names were printed on little cards beside each basket of goodies. African waiters pronounced them in perfect French accent. They were amused with us giggling and struggling with our clumsy pronunciations.

"Did you know all these fresh delicacies are flown in *daily* from Germany and France?"

Our chalets by the ocean had a deceptive exterior look, like crude huts. The interiors with modern amenities were contrastingly sophisticated. But we decided to also experience the local scenario and stayed in the city for two days.

The Manager of our downtown hotel was Sule (pronounced Soo lay).

"What's the meaning of your name?" I asked.

"Adventurous," he said and educated us further. "By the way, don't miss our Togolese funeral tomorrow... these are extravagant celebrations. The ceremonies can take up to a month or more." We listened on. "The families often sell or even mortgage their land or homes to pay for the funeral of an elderly relative they loved."

Luckily we got to experience such a wildly extravagant funeral which we would have missed out on but for Mr. Sule.

We took his advice to visit the Sacred Heart Cathedral. Known in French as 'Cathédrale du Sacré-Cœur de Lomé (the mother of the Archdiocese of Lome). Built in 1901 by the German Colonial Empire, now an iconic building of the new capital of Togo—a testament to German occupation and colonial rule in West Africa. A plaque in the church had names and cities inscribed in German, of the German people who helped pay for the restoration of the original church. However, *none of the local* Togolese people were mentioned! Ken commented, "I'm not sure if I were German I'd be proud of my colonial history."

"Incidentally, Germany had colonies in six modern-day African countries: Burundi, Cameroun, Namibia, Rwanda, Tanzania, and Togo."

"Yes, Ms. Geography major." Mujeeb tickled me on my waist.

"History in this case," I replied, moving away from him.

'Officially in 1922, one third of the area came under British control, and two-thirds under the administration of France (modern-day Togo), including the capital Lomé—deeply influenced by the architectural programs of the successive colonial regimes.'

Still, more than forty years of French administration left its mark, although traditional Togolese culture had voodoo cults and rituals. It was interesting that throughout the country, many different forms of Christianity and Islam were practiced.

"You must try the local outdoor buffet dinner at our hotel" Sule persuaded us.

"Togolese style food is a combination of African, French and German influences."

The mile long spread had great aesthetic appeal. Our hunger evidenced how we each piled up our plates with a variety of foods, while Mr. Sule walked alongside us to demonstrate hospitality. He started naming various dishes like *Agouti*, *Fufu* made from yam, *Koklo meme*, *Kokonte*, and *Akume*. The names sounded quite exotic but . . .

As we took our first bites, our mouths were on fire! It reminded me of the 'killer curry' I once made. Wide-eyed we exchanged glances. Sule had drifted away to greet others.

"Sorry, Togolese *local* food doesn't cut it for me." Ken put his fork down.

"Me neither, every dish seems to have some form of fish added."

"But … did you see what was at the end of the buffet table?" His eyes sparkled.

"*Ken's-tucky fried chicken*," I joked. We all rushed to attack that one platter the locals hadn't even touched. Luckily Mr. Sule had drifted away.

……

By the time we returned to Nigeria my purple bruises had faded away, but the vivid memories of picture-perfect water and the beaches like the *'French Riviera in Africa'* lingered on. Mujeeb was back to his lectures and me … always standing by, awaiting new surprises.

....

THE MIRACLE FEET

---

10 A letter from my dad created suspense. "We have good news in our family. Let's see if you can guess." So I listed various possibilities: 'Perhaps he was being transferred to Istanbul, maybe Nigma was getting married' ... my list was long, but Mujeeb added a one liner P.S.

"Shadan is going to have a baby brother or sister."

I told him not to embarrass his in-laws.

"Darling, in India and Pakistan *good news* means another baby, their best entertainment."

Upon our arrival that year, my in-laws seemed disappointed, curious women were stealing glances at my flat belly! I lowered my gaze and declared, "I'm not, but my mom is expecting!"

"Your mother is trying to teach you a lesson," they teased me. Once they booked for me an appointment with a Gynecologist, I revealed the secret to his sister-in-law, Tahira.

"Mujeeb's first words to me were: *It'll be just you and I, and no third life.*" She was shocked to hear that the two brothers had collaborated to supply me with contraceptives.

Upon our return to Nigeria, I accelerated my power of persuasion.

"Zooby, for me to feel complete, we must have a *Third life* between us."

We struck a deal, but not without a condition. "Never ask for a second child, is it a deal?"

"Deal," I promised, not realizing the full implications.

A month later, Mujeeb confirmed the good news with mixed emotions. I wanted to jump with joy as I gently touched my belly. "Aren't you excited ... Daddy-to-be?" I asked, but he responded, "I am ... as long as our child does not interfere with our lifestyle."

"Interfere?" I said with a concerned tone. 'Once the baby arrives, he'd be fine' I thought.

After three long months, I shared my joy with the family, everyone was delighted.

Once the reality hit me, I became paranoid about losing my figure, my tiny waistline which elderly women envied. Surprisingly though, the bigger my belly grew, the happier I felt. Barely five feet, like a football bouncing around all over the campus, bursting with vitality as though I was the only one who had achieved this feat—so childish I was!

In Mujeeb's family and mine, the firstborn were always girls. My aunt next door had two sons, so during my mother's third pregnancy she routinely asked me and my sister Nigma to pray for a brother. We raised our little hands, "God, please give us a brother."

Our chubby little green-eyed brother Sikandar turned out to be the family's most entertaining little toddler. Wouldn't it be nice if I too have a son? I secretly wished.

What a thrilling experience when I first felt the fluttering in my womb! Feeling a life inside you magically evokes intense love emotions. We got a kick by placing an empty matchbox on my belly, delighting in how it jumped off. I wrote in my diary titling my thoughts, *"The Miracle Feet"* which subsequently evolved into a poem.

As the Social Chairperson of the International Women's Organization, I was to coordinate the Annual Dinner Dance. It clashed with my due date, but ... my resignation was rejected.

"If the baby comes on that day, one of us will take over."

The dance party was held at the staff club, by the kidney-shaped swimming pool surrounded by tall palm trees and illuminated bushes that created beautiful ambience. The popular *High Life* music played on, each number lasting 30-40 minutes. Mujeeb and I were the last to leave the floor. At 3:00 a.m., friends commented, "We'll get the news tomorrow for sure."

Film Society and Our Movie Nights...

Our close friend Dr. Ghazi Farooq from the UN Population Council was elected the President, and I was the Publicity Director. Together we were able to secure the premieres of movies in the country, iconic films such as **Jaws** and **The Exorcist**.

The Nigerians being superstitious, we arranged for an ambulance to be on standby. The Theatre was always packed with students and staff. We ended up calling the ambulance twice!

In any case, it was the weekly Movie Night—an event we never missed.

I tried to excuse myself but Mujeeb said, "See what I meant, the baby hasn't even arrived, yet our life is being interrupted." Begrudgingly, I caved in.

Everyone was surprised, "So you're still around, even after your endless '*Highlife*' performance?" As if the baby heard them—my first contractions started! We rushed straight from the auditorium to the only Hospital designated for expatriates (Eighth Day Adventure). I had full confidence in my experienced Gynecologist, but with my luck he got transferred back to the USA, replaced by a rookie, Dr.

Michael Shea. The two recent stillbirths experienced by the staff wives worried everyone.

Regardless, I was destined for a C-section. But I wanted to be awake for the first cry of my baby so I insisted, "Please don't put me to sleep."

Once the epidural took effect, a few doctors stood around my bed and prayed for the safety of the child. I became paranoid, "Is there any complication?"

"No, it's our routine prayer at this hospital."

Doctor Shea yelled out, "It's not a baby you have a monster in there!"

"Is it a girl or a boy?" I asked.

"Told you it's a monster," that irritated me. I instantly lost confidence and whispered to the nurse, "Please make sure he doesn't forget any instrument inside my belly."

In that most precious moment of my entire life...I was pain free!

A Caesarean section can be a blessing in disguise, I thought.

I later heard that outside the Operating Room, 'Professor Photographer' was caught standing upon a stool, recording the *novel event* on his camcorder through the glass panel above the door. In his nervousness he went to the wrong room, it was empty. I had yelled at him during my contractions when he tried to videotape me, but now I chuckled.

The soft-spoken nurse from Finland protested, "You have too many visitors from Ife University. I've placed 'No more visitors' sign but now they're trickling in through the back door."

Who didn't show up, my own lover boy!

Mujeeb finally showed up, declaring his innocence, "I was in such a shock after your surgery I consulted the Chief Medical Officer on campus, and he gave me a sleeping pill.

......

Holding a beautiful healthy baby in my arms, *feeling euphoric*, I entered our brand-new bungalow. The first thing I said, "Zooby, let's have one more child please."

"Breaking your promise already? Never mention this again," he silenced me.

Being on the Housing Committee I had access to the blueprints, so we had reserved a bungalow with the bedroom window facing a lush green hill. I also booked one for Ghazi and his wife Janet, our first Canadian friends from Dundas, Ontario. During their doctorate at Yale University in the US, they ended up in an interracial marriage.

The following Thursday, Mujeeb got ready, with keys in his hand he said, "Let's go."

"What, can't we miss this ritual for once?"

"We'll leave the baby in the car, windows slightly open. He sleeps through anyway."

"What? There is no way I would do that," I tried to be assertive but eventually caved in.

Hardly ten minutes passed by when I rushed outside the auditorium to check up on him. The parking lot was semi-dark but considered safe back in the '70s, as all the cars belonged to the staff. I came back inside then went out again, back to the auditorium and out again—driving my husband crazy! "Darling you are disturbing everyone else."

Eventually, I just drove off myself—motherly instinct!

"That's why I didn't want to have a child, he is only a week old, and our life is already disrupted." *Disrupted?* Was he at fault or was I? His words rang in my ears.

"You and I, no third life between us" In fact I was the one who broke that deal.

......

It sneaked in our Bedroom!

A week later, I woke up in the middle of the night to feed the baby, his basinet rested on one side of the bed. In the dim light I noticed my black ribbon that I usually tied to my hair was on the floor. I was about to pick it up when it slithered, I screamed with fear. *"There's a snake, Mujeeb, there's a snake!"* I grabbed the baby and rushed out of the room, slamming the door behind me.

Mujeeb managed to kill it. The next day we took it to our Zoologist friend *Lawrence Cahill*, who identified it as a three-foot cobra! We didn't rest in peace until we confirmed it had entered through the plumbing, not fully covered during the construction.

Miracles do happen—within a few days I noticed a drastic change in Mujeeb. I teased him, "Was it the snake scare that did it?" Now Fatherly instinct took birth for the **Third life** to become the most significant. Mujeeb would cuddle the baby and capture each and every precious moment on his camcorder. The so called 'Disruption' turned into a 'Celebration.'

......

The Naming Ceremony...

In Nigeria the naming ceremony is also important, like we celebrate *Aqeeqa* in Pakistan, when a lamb is sacrificed, dinner guests are invited in celebration, and meat is distributed to the poor. We had booked a hall and invited two hundred guests. Shopping for two lambs became entertainment itself. Since our monthly 'meat-eating-marathons' Ghazi had become a pro. He took us and Pious in his station wagon. It was funny how he walked amongst the bleating lambs, checking the inside of their ears to find ones that will have better flavor and no odor! The two we picked remained eerily silent, all the way back to the campus.

Men conducted the operation on the veranda of the servants' quarters. Some meat was distributed to the needy in downtown Ife and the rest was used to make *West African Curry* (a version introduced by the British). Our Austrian friend Johanna Moody took weeks to bake a fancy cake, large enough to feed the crowd. We had already named him Kashif (Pioneer) but the Nigerians named him **Oluwafemi** (God loves me).

We now anticipated another adventure—this time '**with**' the third life. Mujeeb was granted one academic year of sabbatical leave with pay as a Visiting Professor at Uppsala University in Sweden, inclusive of travel expenses and free accommodation.

....

SABBATICAL IN SWEDEN

11 Our dream trip was not without warnings and apprehensions.

My Danish friend Aida shared her bias: "The Swedes are as cold as the Scandinavian weather. Moreover, with the newborn baby, you'll need your family's help,"

"His 'grand' mother would be travelling with us," She was baffled.

"Yes, Dr. Spock. He is known as the 'Grandmother of one million American babies' I carry his book like a Bible. *Doctor Spock's Baby and Child Care*,"

"So now, an American doctor will mother a Nigerian-born Pakistani baby? Good luck." Why would I miss once-in-a-lifetime opportunity?

As the **SAS** Scandinavian Airplane began to descend, I followed Spock's instructions: 'While landing, make sure to give the baby a water bottle.'

"Look, look at Kashif, Zooby. I've never seen him sucking the bottle so rapidly."

As the jumbo landed, roared loud in reverse gear, the baby's speed doubled . . . tripled. "What a sucker," Mujeeb said. He sucked and we giggled ... Our anxiety was distracted as we landed in an unknown territory.

The nearest airport *Arlanda* was in Stockholm, we had to take a train to Uppsala.

Before we unbuckled, I said, "Darling did you know that the University of Uppsala was founded in 1477, the oldest university in Sweden and all of the Nordic countries?"

He replied with a smirk, "I saw you pick up the pamphlet while in transit,"

"It is among the best universities in Northern Europe, even at an international level,"

"That's why I chose to apply there, my dear."

We gathered our 'tripled gear' and lined up for customs.

......

In 1970 Sweden was far more advanced than England, in many aspects.

The University had pre-arranged our accommodation. As though Ali Baba said, "*Khul jaa sim sim*" (open Sesame) and the magic doors opened. A modern apartment, furnished with light Scandinavian furniture, was a novelty compared to the dark wood in Nigeria. Humans are so enchanted by novelty. We were supplied with cutlery, crockery, even salt-and-pepper shakers. The laundry rooms were high tech—place a washed bed sheet in a machine, press a button and it would come out at the other end, ironed and neatly folded, wow!

I cuddled the fluffy pillows, those Ikea bed sheets and cozy comforter, and spilled my excitement, "How about Sweden as our permanent home. It doesn't *have to be* Canada."

Our neighbors turned out to be a young couple from Canada and our friendship developed through a negative experience. One night Kashif cried with colic, until three in the morning. Adding to our anxiety, they started banging on their floor—our ceiling! Mujeeb was angry and suggested we should complain about their reaction.

"Darling, they don't have a child, and this situation can recur."

We decided to place an apology card at their door, explaining that *"We tried our best not to disturb you, but…"* We bonded in friendship with Linda and Ed, a tall Canadian couple in their thirties. Once they learned we were considering moving to Canada, they reacted.

"Why would you or anyone, abandon a luxurious life in the tropics, for a 'freezer'?"

Mujeeb worked with Professor Nils Fries, a slim, tall, refined gentleman in his mid-fifties. He was an embodiment of grace, knowledge, and humility. He later introduced us to other staff members and …our social life commenced.

Right from the beginning, we found the Swedes to be exceptionally warm and friendly.

Most of the professors invited us over for High Teas in their immaculate homes. We adapted to their customs, and carried an extra pair of shoes or slippers for indoor use. We were surprised and felt flattered when our hosts routinely made a formal speech.

"We are honored to welcome Dr. and Mrs. Zoberi, the first Pakistani couple ever to visit our home."

Beautiful trays presented with dozens of assorted teas to choose from, that could put the English to shame. Tea was followed by a sophisticated smorgasbord—a variety of open-faced sandwiches. Contrary to Aida's feedback, ours was entirely a different experience, maybe because we moved among an enlightened academic circle?

Mujeeb's research routine meant he disappeared for the entire day, leaving me alone for parenting. Exhausted by the evening, I needed a break so I enrolled in an evening class to learn Swedish. Noticing my aptitude for languages, they recommended me to take full-time classes.

"But … I can't leave my baby with a sitter for that long," I said though their idea excited me. "We will see if a special arrangement can be made."

How musical the Swedish language is, I had first noticed when I met Kerstine, Mukhtar's wife. News that the Government paid bonus to foreign students added more music to my ears. Six hours a day, five days a week plus income—it was an opportunity too good to be missed.

Learning Swedish…

The *Aa Bay Eff* (ABF) Language Institute went out of their way to accommodate my needs beyond any expectations. They not only vacated one of the classrooms for my baby, but also provided a crib and a tiny fridge to store his formula! The instructor kept the classroom door slightly ajar, so we could hear him if he woke up.

With such surreal treatment I felt honored and *humbled.* During lunch hours, an international group of students started taking turns to feed him the formula, and even burp baby Kashif. He became everybody's chubby little kitten to cuddle. In fact our baby's popularity extended well beyond the language institute—opposites attract: In Uppsala our 'made in Nigeria product' was a novelty. We were charmed by Swedish babies having blue eyes, blonde eyelashes, but I never imagined our child would be a rarity to fascinate the Swedes and the Norwegian tourists. They would stop by his stroller and whisper, *"Titta pa hans ogon!"* (Look at his eyes). In the department stores, total strangers bought and placed toy gifts in his stroller!

"Maybe they think we are from a third world country, could this be charity?"

"Darling, blue eyes and blonde eyebrows are not as visible as black. That's all."

"So he may even win a baby contest over here?"

......

The United Nation's Silver Jubilee…

A group of Uppsala University students from Pakistan (all singles) were excited to meet us—*A first-ever Pakistani family on the Campus!* Our apartment became their escape venue. They hadn't quite adapted to the Swedish meatballs. Instead, they craved home-cooked curries.

They approached me about the upcoming Silver Jubilee of the United Nations to be held in Uppsala. Over two dozen countries were participating, but there was no representation from Pakistan. Mujeeb was quick to volunteer my services.

"My wife will participate, maybe perform a dance," he said with confidence.

"So you really expect me … to dance on stage … for the United Nations Silver Jubilee?"

My only dance experience on stage was the *snake dance* I performed in Grade 9. At the time the possibility of the cessation of *East Pakistan* (now Bangladesh) from West Pakistan was looming. We previously had emotionally charged debates with those students. Now my patriotism awakened, I said, "What about a classical dance to represent East Pakistan?"

"Life is full of surprises," exclaimed a student. "And enterprises?" Fehmida pitched in.

"Where there is a will…

… there is a Dance," I said. Everyone took it as a YES.

The UN office in Stockholm arranged for my costume through the Pakistani Embassy—a Banarsi silk saree, peach colored with a golden border. They also provided me with a classical LP record.

In the peak of winter, fresh white garlands were supplied for my long braid. To allow practice time, they even compensated for the babysitter. It was unbelievable.

"The *Will* is not enough I must find a *Way* but how?"

'Sometimes desperation is the mother of invention.' Where to obtain a video of Bengali dance in Uppsala? As if my wish was their command, one of the students presented me one.

I began practicing Indo-Pakistani-Bengali Classical *Kathak* dance on *Tabla* and *Sitar*— rigorous lessons by a unique teacher: *Myself to...* my... self?

In front of a tall mirror, I practiced various moves and postures, improvising all the while to suit my personal capability, or lack of it. Watching video and emulating the professional dancer simultaneously, was a multitasking challenge. Mujeeb was my audience and if I went overtime Kashif also joined us. He would start jumping on his 'Skip hop, explore and more,' then giggle and drool, even try to emulate my *Kathak* moves.

In a way, it became our family's 'joint project.'

On the day of the event, Mujeeb was allowed backstage. It took us an hour to dress me up. The colorful mosaic of international participants watched the novelty in wonderment.

No sooner did I take the first two steps, I almost skated across the wooden floor and nearly tripped. The costume designer approached me with a pair of scissors. "Let me cut her feet." Laughter broke out in chorus. "How did you forget to remove your nylon stockings?" She just cut and removed the feet part of my stockings, when my name was called. Nervously I whispered a in Arabic, *"Bismillah Hir-Rehman Nir Rahim"* (I begin in the name of God).

Facing a captivated audience of hundreds, my head was spinning but the prayer seemed to work, like a placebo. I survived the longest seven minutes of my life. Relief came with the loud applause. Jubilant, I rushed backstage to find Mujeeb. Of course, he had joined the audience with his pet Canon.

"I know I goofed several times." I admitted.

"But how would the Swedish audience know that?"

"Don't... ever ... get ... me ...into trouble again, ok?"

The next day ABF students greeted me with congratulations, even brought me clippings from the Swedish newspapers. *"Look, your picture is in the Swedish newspaper headlines."*

"It must be the novel costume or the fresh white garland in a long black braid." I concluded.

......

An Indo-American couple we met, Nancy and Sagar Krupa, who became our Travelling Companions; together we visited a number of cities.

The second largest city in Sweden, **Göteborg** (G pronounced as 'Y'), in the **Haga** district felt as though we had entered the 19th century. Nancy said, "These wooden houses, candlelit cafés, and pubs with terraced courtyards, give it the Bohemian look that I love," I added, "I really liked **Malmö**, for its medieval architecture."

Time in Sweden turned out to be one of our best ever!

Travelling back via Copenhagen, **we were stranded there** for five days during one of the nastiest snowstorms in Europe. Most of the continent was covered with a fluffy white blanket.

....

THE BLUSHING HIBISCUS
(Back to our tropical oasis)

---

12 "From *pure white* to *deep green*, this is unbelievable, am I dreaming?" I stood stunned. The freshly sodden lawn we had left was now a plush carpet. The entire foliage had sprung up in such a short time, it was a miracle.

Our gardener **Obeymi** was overjoyed to see his efforts reap such a reaction from us. With his gleaming smile displaying his pure white teeth, he tried to give the credit to me.

"Madame, you are the one who chose all those plants," he said.

"But … I never expected you'll perform magic to grow them so huge, so fast!"

Mujeeb added, "It's because we have two rainy seasons."

To ensure that various bushes would bloom during different seasons, before we left we had drawn a sketch for Obeymi—a blueprint, of our dream garden.

The professors from the Agriculture Department of Wisconsin had created an amazing nursery on Ife campus. Privileged staff could select and pick any number of tropical plants at no charge. I remembered the bumpy ride in a tractor trailer when I went to pick those plants.

"I'm ready for a hot cup of tea." Mujeeb went in the house, I carried on, "I like your blue and yellow tie-dyed shirt. By the way Obeymi, you have a green thumb."

"No ma, what ma, green?" looking at his thumb he asked. I explained the meaning.

I had picked a rare species of the Blushing Hibiscus. Looking at a pure white bloom in full glory I asked, "Do you know how long it normally takes for these flowers to turn from white to pink or red?

"About ten days, Ma," he replied with the confidence of a professional horticulturist.

"But I can make it turn almost red in one hour." I kept secret a special trick I had learned—the white flower arrangement placed in the fridge, when brought to room temperature, can change color within an hour or two. My experiments had worked, leaving our guests intrigued. For now, I let Obeymi remain baffled.

......

"The tea tastes so good when made and served by *others.* It beats all the variety we found in Sweden."

Kashif's nanny, Charity, must be in her twenties. I noticed that the burgundy and navy printed dress I had gifted her was now too tight on her sexy, protruding behind. Her hair was braided into a pineapple pattern that I really liked. She gave Kashif a quick bath which surprisingly he didn't resist. But then he practically fell from her arms into my lap. Freed from being bundled up for months, I cuddled his chubby arms and legs. He giggled for a bit then suddenly went silent, looking flabbergasted. Maybe he was trying to figure out the stark contrast between the blonde Swedes and the dark Nigerians.

"It would take him a day or so to adjust."

Early morning I opened the bedroom shutters, eager to
view the rolling green hill, I was shocked. It was a mound
burned black, smoke was still rising. All that greenery

I so enjoyed had been engulfed by fire! "Don't worry, Madame, the man kills *'juju'* every Ya (year)."

"What! He does this every year … and you people let him?"

"Soon it will be green," he said with confidence but I inhaled a sigh of regret.

Yet another disappointment—our television was out of order. Pious had no answer.

Saying goodbye to Lucille Ball, Patty Duke, and the Waltons was okay, but not the classic Nigerian dramas that fascinated us, especially seeing a Nigerian playing the role of God!

"But things happen for a reason," Mujeeb repeated his pet phrase.

How we Found Common Ground!

Our television breakdown led us to a 'breakthrough.'

With hubby's help, our versatile gardener marked a badminton court in our backyard. The net, the rackets, shuttlecocks all necessary supplies swiftly made their way to our home.

Initially our audiences were just Charity, Pious, and Obeymi, but later a battalion of kids, toddlers to teenagers, started trickling in from nowhere?

"Did you invite these spectators, there's no privacy here."

"It's okay, darling … let them enjoy." That's what Ammi would've said.

I remembered back in Pindi we were famously the first family to own a television set. Before moving to comparatively affluent Lalazar, poor children in our neighborhood flocked around our house in the afternoons, anxious to peek in at the Magic Box.

Ammi opened the doors of her heart and home to welcome them. She offered everyone lemonade and snacks. When criticized, she would repeat her mantra in Persian:

"Dil Bedast aawar ke hajj-e-Akbar asth" (pleasing someone's heart is the greatest pilgrimage). "This is my father's legacy," she said with pride.

Now, in Nigeria while we played badminton, children of the domestic staff living in the servants' quarters entered our backyard through a small opening in the thick plant fence.

Too lazy to run, I remained glued to one spot, expecting Mujeeb to send the shuttlecock right back onto my racket. So I expressed my dislike over the least bit of footwork he challenged me to. One day he spoke up.

"Don't be so lazy. See how the grass has disappeared from where you stand still?"

"I don't want to play with you anymore!" Like an immature teenager, I dropped my racket and stomped out, even though deep down I knew the proof was in the muddy bald spot.

I felt offended at first, but later reflected upon what Abbaji often repeated, "How can you discover your *'Chupee Rustam'* (The hidden champion) unless your try your best." I relived the memories of him taking me to Ayyub National Hall in Pindi, where he played badminton tournaments. In our home there was a glass cabinet filled with trophies he won. I had the desire to follow his footsteps.

So I got back to the court, determined to 'apply myself.' Practicing the swift spin with my tiny wrist, the possibility of the little bird angularly cutting across the court thrilled me.

"No one can handle that without touching the net," Mujeeb complimented me.

"No more bald spot, what do you say to a *love game,* Zooby?"

"My *Blushing Hibiscus*, I prefer a different love game with you." he whispered with mischief and I replied, "This title is far more artistic than being called Gasoline Queen."

We eventually joined the University Staff Badminton Club, and played every afternoon at the gymnasium. Friends teased us, "Is your new passion badminton, or *Bedminton*?"

From then on, after serving us afternoon tea, Pious never failed the drill.

"Sa, Madame, your joggers and rackets are in the car." Charity timed herself for our welcome returns. "The bath is filled, Madame." I could indulge, soak, and just walk away.

Two and a half hours of our joint daily activity seemed to fill *a vacuum in my life I hadn't quite identified as yet!* Sports are great for both physical and mental well being.

No more nightmares!

Consequently, I got noticed on the courts by Dr. Oyewusi, the official coach, known as Nigeria's first Doctor of Physical Education. He surprised me with an invitation to join the State Championship Team. The tournaments were scheduled in three months. For lack of female representation, he was eager to train me personally—I was at the right place at the right time.

Playing with *all male* professors and an ambidextrous coach, I was challenged to achieve my full potential. Abbaji was super delighted to get the news of my new adventure.

"Keep up your footwork and practice those sneaky angular drop shots at the net which will give you an edge." Surprisingly I won the State Championship! Mujeeb took more pride in me than I. Bit by bit he was winning my heart.

However, my price tag for getting seriously involved in badminton was expensive. Originally enrolled to complete my Bachelor's in Languages, now I switched to Physical Education instead. Dr. Oyewusi declared, "I have a future for you." How circumstances led me to an exciting new field. I too started dreaming big.

Having developed common interests; bridge, badminton, and dancing—we had evolved as: **A happy couple in solid friendship**.

Mujeeb remained steadfast with teaching and research, publishing scientific papers in International Journals. I accompanied him to Mycological Forays, both local and international. I practiced a Stippling technique and drew sketches from live specimens of fungi we collected.

......

A Unique Art Project...

Each time we ran into each other, Dr. Wangboje would refresh his request,

"I must talk to you, let's set up a meeting soon. It's something important." Known as Nigeria's First Doctor of Fine Arts, he was married to an English lady Margaret (Maggie). She and I belonged to a group of expatriate moms, who met once a week to socialize, while our nannies accompanied us to watch over our toddlers. Maggie also reminded me about her hubby's request.

Finally, we met at their home, where in an instant I noticed a blend of cultures—paintings of English landscape, side by side was a palm-beach scene in Nigeria. A huge pair of elephant tusks rested in front of a look-alike fireplace—never needed in Nigeria. According to the latest fad, the couple wore identical embroidered, tie-dyed cotton T-shirts in bright yellow and royal blue colors.

Maggie placed my cup of tea on the side table, along with English scones, and Nigerian *akara balls*. Their toddler, with a pale brown complexion and afro hair, came running and hopped onto his mother's lap. "Say hello to Auntie Zohra." The toddler murmured, and gave a curious look to his parents. I too waited in suspense.

Wangboje cleared his throat, gathered charm in his voice, and asked, "The thing is ... that... eh ...? He was reluctant to go on. I'm sure you've never done this before but ... would you mind if I ask you to model for one of my portraits? I'll pay you for it,"

Modelling?! Did I hear him right? He explained with reluctance,

"Actually I have an exciting assignment from the Iranian Embassy in Lagos. They've asked me to paint a life-size portrait of Queen Farah."

I was silent, and he went on, "I didn't want to offend you or your husband but ... eh ... you look exactly like her."

"What, Queen Farah Diba, wife of the Shah of Iran, the Reza Shah Pehlavi?"

No one had ever compared my looks to hers, I was surprised and amused.

"Yes, yes, Maggie also agrees with me," Wangboje insisted.

"Are you serious, I've never heard this before?"

"The Embassy has provided me a photograph of the Queen, so I will use that, but if you could please give me a few sittings, it would make my job a lot easier. I'll pay you for your time."

"This comes as a real surprise, I don't know what to say," with a surge of excitement I changed my tone. "I kind of like the idea—modelling for the Queen, wow!"

After the green light from me he asked, "Will you ask the Docto (R silent), or should I? Do you think he might say no?"

"Oh no, don't worry, my hubby never says no to me."

"I know Dr. Zoberi is known to be the most open-minded South Asian husband."

"That he is, thanks," as though it was a compliment to me.

I was excited to embark upon my short-lived modelling career. But on my way out I clarified, "I've always admired your art, and I love Maggie, and adore your kid. So I'm happy to do this, but accepting payment is out of question." I knew Mujeeb wouldn't agree to that either.

Funny, when we shared this with our friends of South Asian origin, *none* of them thought I had any resemblance to Queen Farah, but my Nigerian and European friends thought Farah and I did look alike!

The following week, I sat upon a high stool, beside Farah Diba's large portrait, while in front of me was Africa's distinguished artist, playing with colors on a huge canvas. It was bizarre!

Wangboje later made a special offer to compensate for my time.

"I'd be happy to enrol you in my upcoming workshop, followed by a National Exhibition:

'Islamic Art from Africa, South of the Sahara'

Despite knowing that I wasn't an artist, he was adamant on returning the favor.

"Maggie tells me that you have hand-painted your baby's clothes and your living room curtains. You could at least join the 'amateur artists' workshop." I was thrilled.

During the weeklong workshop, the main items I experimented with were a clay sculpture, which most Africans perceived as my self-portrait. The other item was the silk screen printing. In line with their religious theme, I chose Arabic calligraphy, a prayer which translated as:

'Oh! Giver of Life
The Sustainer of Life
Bless us with your Mercy'

The professional calligraphers would likely cringe over its amateur quality. I wasn't pleased with my own choice of colors either—apple green and royal blue with a touch of red. Strangely enough, people loved it as it was unique. That my first-ever amateurish attempt got included in the main display section, was nothing but sheer luck. As for Farah Diba's portrait, I wonder if it's still displayed at the Iranian Embassy, or...?

Both Mujeeb and I took pride in each other's endeavors. His research interests had already converged with mine. "How our Scientist/Artist union has worked out," I proclaimed. Mr. Romantic used any excuse to wrap me in his arms followed by passionate kisses.

......

Publishing a Scientific Book

Fresh off the press, it was finally in our hands! ***Tropical Macro Fungi*** published by McMillan, London, and Heffner in New York and the author—my own Dr. Mujeeb H. Zoberi. I gently wiped my tears of joy while Mujeeb smiled from ear to ear.

I gently massaged the green and white glossy cover with a sketch of the mushroom known as ***Boletus*** we had handpicked during one of our excursions. The book was the result of years of persistent research by Mujeeb, attending dozens of International Mycological Forays in Europe and Africa where I accompanied him.

"I'm so proud of you, Zooby."

I noticed his quivering nostrils whenever he was excited or about to give me a surprise—he dedicated the book to me? He had included the illustrations I had sketched from live specimens of mushrooms we collected from the remote forests. Memories of the wild lizard Ojo once killed, and the old woman beaten to death, flashed through my mind, but I soon returned to celebration. Charity and Pious sensed our festive mood.

"Sa and Madame are so happy today, I made *pakoray* and *halwa*." Pious placed the tea tray, and Charity forwarded us the plates and napkins.

"Is this the book *Sa* (sir) has been working on?" Pious asked with a sincere smile.

"Yes, take a look. Sit down, Pious, my neck is hurting trying to look up," as though his already long legs were on stilts. He knelt down beside us instead.

Flipping the pages, I said, "See what it says, *Dedicated to my wife Zohra Zoberi*," it went above his head, but once I flipped open the page with the termite hill and the Queen Ant about the size of a man's thumb, resting on the palm of Obeymi, Pious became over excited.

"Charity, please call Obeymi quickly," he hollered, and sure enough Charity showed up smiling. I noticed she had changed her hairstyle from pineapple to? However, everyone's attention was on her majesty, the **Queen Ant.**

The termites had once built a castle like a mound with reddish clay, about eight feet tall and twice as wide, near the fence of our backyard. Mujeeb had brought out his camera not to miss the special moment. Families of all three servants had joined us to witness the action in our backyard.

"Remember, Obeymi, how you used a machete to break up that hill?"

The mound is a world filled with nonstop activity. "Can you believe that each termite has a specific job—there are *worker* termites and *soldier* termites," Mujeeb enlightened everyone.

Once I reminded they all recalled: The sun was shining bright that day, everyone had enjoyed the drama. Poor queen peacefully lay in her chamber, when Obeymi slashed the hill, thousands of termite ants crawled out first. "***Horry op Sa,*** it's going to melt, wife waiting."

"Don't tell me you are going to eat it."

Obeymi spilled excitement, "Of course Ma, it's not every day we get a chance."

In fact it was considered a delicacy. "How could you eat it? To me it looks like a lump of pus."

After the photo shoot he rushed back to the quarters, and the battalion slowly trickled away.

So now, Obeymi was enthralled with that picture of his palm, published in that book, displaying the queen!

While sipping tea we flipped the pages over and over, to relish the memories of where and when we had collected various fungi. Incidentally, *Termitomyces* are a variety of edible fungi that grow on, or near, the termite mounds.

Remarkably it is not the termites that cultivate the fungi, but the fungi that are cultivating the termites.

'Researchers have discovered fossilized 'Fungus Gardens' created by termites 25 million years ago. Scientists are not kidding— the gardens revealed that these ancient termites cultivated fungus by arranging them along a complex plan and feeding them pellets of plant material. The researchers conclude: This is the oldest physical evidence of agriculture on Earth.'

"By the way thanks for dedicating the book to me, let's celebrate."

"How we celebrate is *my* choice and you won't say no." My jubilant hubby replied.

"Did you know that the *Aquarius* have special love for the *Intelligent*?"

"Are you expressing love for me, or trying to change the subject?"

......

Stacks of books and atlases were spread across our coffee table for months, as we contemplated where our new homeland would be. But for now, I placed Mujeeb's book at the top as if it was a decoration piece. Then...we were in for another surprise:

I held the hand-delivered letter close to my heart and said, *"Omne trium perfectum."*

"Don't talk riddles, show me the letter." I read the invitation from Dr. Oyewusi.

All Nigeria Open National Badminton Championship Tournaments will be held in the capital city, Lagos. We are pleased to announce that you have been selected to represent the University of Ife Team.

Mujeeb spontaneously rose from his chair to render congratulations *his style.*

"Thanks for the encouragement, Zooby."

Preparations for the National Championship required rigorous rehearsals. Hubby didn't mind me disappearing for three to four weeks, for camping sessions with a bunch of wild University students. Charity was trained to take care of our toddler.

Friends teased me, "We'll keep an eye on your husband, but who will keep an eye on you?"

The rehearsals during our camping sessions were so intense that it seemed all we did was practice badminton with short breaks for meals and siesta.

My tireless coach Dr. Oyewusi seemed more determined than I. With his ambidextrous skills, I never knew which direction his shots would come from, so he groomed me for surprise shots.

After dinner, while most students took to partying, dancing and drinking, I decided to practice for another hour instead. A teetotaler like me *Aanuoluwapo* nicknamed *Oluwa* offered to help me practice my back-hand. Poor fellow even carried my joggers and the water bottle. "What's the meaning of your name, so hard to pronounce," I asked. "It means God's mercy is great."

......

Upon my return from a rigorous session Mujeeb shared the news, "Our Canadian immigration has been approved, we must get the papers stamped and here's our date of arrival." Unfortunately it happened to be the same date as the tournaments.

"But we must travel to Canada, or it's a lost opportunity."

It was a tough choice, but we compromised—Mujeeb would fly **alone** to Montreal, and I would go **alone** to Lagos to avail the opportunity of a lifetime.

The National Stadium in Lagos...

Hundreds of players from all over the country gathered in Lagos. We were accommodated in one of the campus dorms. Early mornings we were transported to the National Stadium, all in white uniforms with the green and yellow logo of our university.

A massive inaugural parade was held by various participating organizations. While marching, with great interest I realized that:

I was the only non-black in the entire stadium!

Fellow athletes considered me '*Oebo*' (white), and treated me with extra warmth. Their best compliment to me was "*You are jost like oss*" (just like us, blacks). Beneath that statement was a deeper implication as to how they perceived the real *Whites*. After all up until 1966 Nigeria had also been a British colony like the Indian sub-continent.

The National Tournaments created a festive mood in the city. Driving back and forth from the stadium, people on the streets stopped to cheer us. In our special bus, students played English songs—Simon Garfunkel's 'The Boxer' was the latest hit we sang along to.

"*Lai La la, Lala la*" was the line when we raised our voices to their highest pitch.

I was the only married woman, mingling with all the black singles, feeling eternal bliss!

With the media hype and great expectations, pressure was mounting by the minute. After the semi-finals, gearing up for the finals, students kept warning me:

"If you don't bring gold for us, you'd be DEAD MEAT."

Consequently, the evening before the final tournament, I developed severe stomach cramps. In panic I approached Dr. Oyewusi with my problem, he started laughing. I was so annoyed.

"These are called the Athletes Cramps, young lady. Just relax … have a good sleep." To pacify me he gave money to one of the students to buy me the 'most expensive sports shoes in town.' I noticed that in his khaki-color *Safari Suit*, he looked quite handsome. I realized how much I had changed from the day I first landed in Nigeria.

First thing in the morning, as promised, I was delighted to receive one of the best pair of sports shoes available in town. Purchased with such sincerity and good wishes, enough to melt my heart … but my cramps took time to subside.

The Championship Champaign

Among a huge crowd in the packed National Stadium, most athletes had family or friends to cheer them. As I glanced around the stadium I felt lonely—no family or friends, even Mujeeb was in Montreal getting that precious pink paper stamped that would change our lives altogether.

"You're lucky you get to play with Adele-Oya the prince." One of the players revealed.

"Prince, no one told me this before!" The game was about to begin, there was no time to clarify. Adele-Oya entered the National Stadium dangling upon his chest all the previous medals he ever won—quite intimidating. First, a bottle of coke was brought for him to moisten his shoes with, a few drops poured on the floor, near the post. Our opponent demanded beer instead, so he stomped the floor to moisten his shoes with Beer. The crowd cheering louder and louder, suspense and excitement gaining momentum, Adele wasn't going to give up that easily. He then asked for Champagne. I felt another stomach cramp.

"What … Champagne? Sorry Sir, not available."

Amidst yet louder applause and rowdy cheering by the fans, one athlete emerged to produce a bottle from his backpack. *Surely this drama was pre-planned*, I thought. But all I wanted was the game to be over with, before my nervous stomach got the better of me.

The game commenced with outright cruelty. The opponents' strategy was to target *me*. Like a dart board, I started receiving full-fledged shots right on to my chest, *bang, bang, bang*— one after the other. For a moment I thought I'd die when my partner and I had a short exchange to alter our tactics. The match went into overtime. It wasn't until the very end that we scored our last two points, to finally deserve our Gold Medal!

The women's game, Akande and I won easily. With two Gold Medals in the All-Nigeria National Open Championship, I became a source of pride for Ife University—Oyewusi's joy was beyond description. I posed for a photo standing beside one of the tallest men, this time without worrying about my height.

We were in the National spotlight; due to Adele (the prince) we received additional coverage. Students marched alongside us on the streets. So at least I could take some newspaper clippings for my family to see.

"Is Adele really a Prince?" I was curious.

"It's true he is from the Royal Family in Lagos. Oba so and so's son." (Oba means the King) but I didn't quite get the complicated names.

To me, being the only non-black in the entire stadium, and wholeheartedly accepted by the Nigerians as one of their own, felt like a bigger achievement than winning the two gold medals.

To this day, when I listen to The Boxer, Simon Garfunkel singing Lai La la, Lala la, my spirit starts dancing with joy—<u>An abstract gift I'll carry for life.</u>

......

Decision of a Lifetime...

During those twelve years, we visited our family annually, enjoyed paid vacations in various African, European, South Asian countries. We made a list, altogether thirty-six countries.

Dianne and Ed, the Canadian couple in Sweden, had wondered, "Why would anyone in their right mind abandon such a privileged lifestyle?" Well, there were many answers … valid and invalid.

Mujeeb ruled out ever returning to Pakistan. We studied the possibilities of the USA, Australia, Sweden, Canada, and England. Australia had better job opportunities; however, a few professors from Ife who had migrated there reported there was racism. We wanted to be 'Accepted, not just tolerated.'

Canada halfway across the world was circled in red. I picked up the globe, wound it, and placed it back on the table. "Look at the distance from our loved ones. Scary, isn't it?"

Well, we were young back then, so we didn't realize how the distance could become longer … and longer … and longer as you get older … and older.

The next steps: applications and medical examinations. With hundreds of people wanting to migrate to Canada, we were surprised when two young Canadians from the Immigration Office in Paris, flew to Lagos to interview only two other couples and us. They told us, "You'll need to set aside six months of income for living expenses, the longest period it would take for a PhD scientist to find a suitable job."

Back then, the Nigerian *Naira* was higher than the Canadian Dollar. We were accepted just like that. The substantial dollars we were to bring likely raised our qualifying score. In short we were declared physically, mentally, and financially healthy to try and become hyphenated Canadians.

Mujeeb qualified for a generous pension income with two options. I was skeptical and suggested he should cash out the lump sum but he settled for lifetime pension instead.

This significant chapter of our lives ended on a positive note.

....

On our Wedding Day

Our only date (two days before the wedding)

Two days later!
All round best student (won a gold medal)

Our nine cousins-
siblings I grew up with

My father (Masters
English Literature)
Hameed Zuberi

My own siblings
with our cousins

Mom and dad suddenly
gained a son-in-law!

Just arrived Nigeria (Ife
University Campus)

At a dinner party
downtown Ibadan

Thorn carvings (my first purchase
of Nigerian handicrafts)

Barged in my parents'
bedroom (just wrote a skit)

Our Gardner Obeymi is
holding the Queen Termite
It emerged from the Termite
Hill in our Backyard

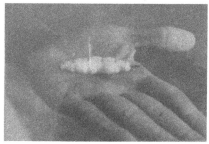

Scientific book: by Dr Zoberi,
illustrations: by Zohra Zoberi

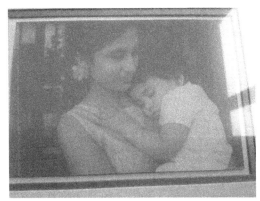

A proud mom

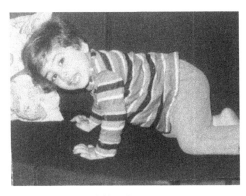

Our toddler became
popular in Sweden

Hyde Park London (on
our way to Uppsala)

PART TWO

Migration

(Quest for a Better Life)

En Route to Canada

13 During every discussion about Canada, images of red suitcases flashed through my mind! I had no idea why, but I felt compelled to purchase a lovely three-piece ruby-red set of Samsonite luggage before we began packing to leave.

On our way to visit family in London, we had planned to stop over in Vienna.

The excitement of our new beginning mounted by the day—to us it meant that our only son would not have to fly back and forth to England for schooling. He would get to live with us. That exciting reality in *his* mind was secondary to the fact that McDonald's hamburgers would be available round every corner. A private little delusion of mine was that Canada was a bilingual country, so people on the street would speak French and I would get to polish mine.

Excitement superseded any apprehension of possible adversities.

......

My Identity Theft!

For our stopover in Vienna, Mujeeb's brother, Dr. Mahmood who had qualified as a dermatologist in Austria, also joined us. Using cataract surgery to be performed by a Viennese surgeon was his excuse so he could meet us and also reconnect with his old colleagues. We stayed in the same hotel for a week and shared our latest news.

One day the two brothers decided to introduce me to a friend Dermatologist, Dr. Wagner. It reminded me of a similar name, so I said, "I knew of a Wenger in Nigeria." She got over-excited, "You mean Suzanne Wenger, have you met her? Do you know she married a Nigerian drummer and adopted Yoruba culture and religion?"

"Of course, in Nigeria she is known as 'Chief Susanne Wenger' or **Adunni Olorisha**- (Adunnii means adored and Olorisha is a deity) I continued, "We went there as tourists. In the middle of the forest, she has created huge sculptures in Osun Grove of Oshogbo village. That is the spiritual home of the **River Goddess Osun**, and she is the priestess who saved its shrines by dedicating decades of her life to this mission." They listened attentively so I went on:

"The day we met that *Deity*, she was busy sculpturing, dressed in a black bra and Nigerian wrap-around skirt. A white European woman in the jungles of Nigeria has created hundreds of Gods and Goddesses." Everyone listened with astonishment, however…

I had no idea a surprise was in the bag. As I continued the story, the Dermatologist got up to approach me with just "excuse me" then pricked a needle into the right side of my cheek and nose so I was frozen—emotionally as well. A harmless little black mole on the right side of my nose, very much a part of me, was removed from under my skin! The two collaborating brothers also got a mouthful for not giving me any advance notice.

"Oh, you wouldn't have agreed to it if we had discussed it with you," was the response to my grumbling.

Seeing tears in my eyes, they comforted me, "It could have possibly turned into cancer."

But this was my identity—that unique sign on my face that my mom and family considered as a beauty spot for which I was often complimented. Ammi opposed removing it from day one. I tried to persuade myself they had my best interest in mind but… *'What if I land in Canada and the Immigration Officer blocks my entry due to the missing sign mentioned on my passport?'*

Now in our less innocent world, would the explanation be accepted as easily?

We spent a few precious days in London with our best friends Sadiqa and Sal. He stayed up all night to tape classic old Urdu songs. Later, the news of his sudden demise at age forty-nine shocked us all and those tapes became ever more valuable.

We were also invited by Professor Kalmus, a highly revered retired Professor who had migrated to England from Eastern Europe. English food may have the reputation of being bland, but the rack of lamb they served with fragrant mint chutney, potatoes mashed to perfect consistency, and fresh green peas still crunchy, it was one of the tastiest dinners of my life. Though the *Hyderabadi Biryani* made with love by Sadiqa's mom will never be forgotten!

After that memorable dinner at his suburban residence, I posed my key question to the Professor, "As a well-travelled, enlightened individual, what would be your single piece of advice to a young couple migrating to a new country?"

"I'm confident you'll know how to handle the challenge," giving his vote of confidence he smiled and expanded, "Mingle with people of all ethnicities. Don't remain in a ghetto of one single community—adapt." I captured the essence of his advice.

......

The Land of Opportunities

What brings people to Canada? The assumption is that people leave their struggles behind to find a free and more comfortable life, but there are exceptions. Some of us pay a heavy price to achieve this freedom.

As I opened my red suitcases for inspection at immigration, a rush of memory overcame me. I smiled as I recalled the lovely lady Atiya and her red luggage that had so impressed me as a ten-year-old girl. I recalled that fleeting moment when I wished one day I'd also like to travel to Canada. 'Twelve years and 35 countries…rather a long detour' I mused. Here I was, red luggage and all, entering Canada just as she had; most likely with the same hopes, fears, and dreams she had experienced on her arrival.

I wondered if she had also found it uncomfortable to have to declare her most personal treasures. I laid the jewelry on the counter for inspection, and thought of my international collection of household items I had sold for next to nothing. The only remnant of our pampered past was the Royal Doulton *Carlyle* dinner set Mujeeb ordered when we stopped over at Harrods in London.

……

My Canadian cousins Rani and Riaz offered their place for a few weeks. Their hospitality was unsurpassed. Their apartment complex in Mississauga was cheekily referred to as the 'Taj Mahal' or sometimes more sarcastically as 'Paki Palace.'

An urgent search for suitable accommodations superseded our job hunt. 'Half-decent' was our minimum requirement.

3400 Riverspray Crescent, Applewood Hills—the address itself had a musical ring that implied a classy location. I imagined apple orchards and a flowing river nearby.

Once our credit rating from British and Swiss banks had been cleared, the apartment keys were handed to us. However, Mujeeb had not resigned as yet and chose to return to his full-time job in Nigeria, at least until a suitable position was available in Canada. It wasn't an easy decision, especially as it meant I would have to struggle on my own in a new country, with a six-year-old.

Our furniture, purchased from liquidation sales, was to be delivered later but for the time being cardboard boxes neatly covered with Nigerian tie-dyed fabric served as our table. A simple mattress on the floor would do fine, as long as my fancy stereo system was nearby to keep me company during my lonely evenings.

In the quiet moments, the wind made scary screeching sounds. I called a handyman to fix it. He told me, "The glass doors aren't sealed right so they need cocking." I was shocked to hear that word. First, I had been told, *"Here in Canada you must learn to sell yourself"* and now my *door needs cocking*? What in the world could that mean? I looked it up in the dictionary— "Oh, it is spelled caulking." I laughed at myself.

After my six-year-old was tucked into bed each night, DJ Glenn Darling, at the Burlington FM station, became my evening companion; and this lonely lady soon developed a taste for sappy English songs of the seventies—Barbara Streisand's '*Memories of the way we were.*' That announcer's voice remains in the black box of my memory.

......

Mujeeb's absence led my heart to green pastures where romantic letters bloomed. He was as miserable without me as I was without him. I had too much time to kill.

One day, I noticed an interesting ad on the bulletin board of a nearby grocery store. People could tear the telephone number off the sheet, take it home, and make the call? What a smart idea. Inspired by it, I too placed my ad on the Dominion Store bulletin board.

Newcomers, Women only!
Learn the English language in the comfort of a welcoming home
Socialize while you utilize your time
Charges are minimum and negotiable

Within a week I had lined up several elderly Portuguese, Italian, and Polish women to enroll with me. I set the price at only $8 per hour and no one even tried to bargain.

Repeated visits to the Manpower office were initially in vain until one day they referred me to the Shaw College in Toronto. A scholarship was being offered to a limited number of students. But first you had to pass an exam. In the early seventies in Toronto, being Indian or Pakistani was not ideal. Ironically, all brown people, East Africans, Sri Lankans, Guianese, and East Indians were labeled '*Pakis,*' an expression freshly imported from Great Britain.

It seemed to bother the Shaw interviewer that I had secured a higher score than most of those born in Canada. "Where on earth did you learn English?" he brusquely asked.

His tone was less than warm, but I replied respectfully, "In Pakistan and in Nigeria."

"You should consider yourself damn lucky that a great country like Canada has accepted you, don't you think?"

There was no further confusion about his tone, but now I had one of my own to share.

"Of course, I'm extremely lucky, but this country is also fortunate that great people choose to come and live here. Moreover, Canada needs immigrants."

I came out of his office jubilant as I qualified for a one-year scholarship at Shaw College in Business Administration and Accounting. Tuition paid, free books, and to top it all, $90 per week spending money! Once again, I had hit the jackpot. In Sweden, I had gotten paid just for learning Swedish language.

Our instructor at Shaw College was Professor Schuler, a chubby tall gentleman with curly dark hair and a glowing smooth white complexion. He had one of the kindest smiles, more suggestive of feminine warmth. In no time, he identified my weaknesses and my strengths.

I started out resisting the accounting class, but he offered to help me through it. After having learned that I played bridge in Nigeria, one day he invited me to join a staff lunch-hour bridge game. As a result my fellow students taunted me for *'kissing the teachers asses!'* Such crude expressions I initially found offensive, but each evening I came home and conditioned myself to accept all that was new to me, the good with the bad.

I hated accounting class, but this Schuler guy wouldn't let me walk away. He insisted, "The game of bridge that you play so well, is nothing but mathematical calculations."

I soon realized that in the dictionary of my perception, the phrase *'Ability to sell yourself'* initially had a negative connotation, but in reality it was one of the most essential qualifications required to succeed in North America. There were PhDs without jobs and people with Masters' degrees were driving cabs, while those with average intelligence and selling ability were enjoying great success. So I joined a three-month course in Personal Development.

At Shaw College, there was a young Pakistani Canadian in my class named *Yousaf*, the white girls raved over him as being 'Tall, dark, and handsome'. He dated a petite *Indian* girl Sumita. Both Soomi and Yousaf were engaged to 'Other' individuals from their respective countries, chosen by their parents. Poor cousin soon to be imported from Lahore likely had no idea what her fiancé was up to over here in Canada. Soomi's fiancé in India (*Hindu*) was also kept in the dark about her love affair with a Pakistani *Muslim*. "I have no interest in spending my life with a FOB," She said it means fresh off the boat, a newcomer. They expressed disappointment I didn't warm up to them.

My evenings were depressing. In stark contrast to my life in Nigeria, preoccupied with campus cocktail parties such as those I had enjoyed at Oluwasami's lodge, now a thing of the past. My neighbors in Mississauga were 'winter cold.' People in the building hardly even shared a smile while crossing each other in the corridor. On Ife campus, everyone knew us and cared. Now lost soul in a cosmopolitan city where even in a small, closed space of an elevator, people looked the other way.

Yousaf's mother Mrs. Khan invited me for dinner. They had a large family; it was house full. After a delicious Pakistani dinner, they drove me and Kashif to Gerrard Street. It was like I had found mini-Indo-Pakistan right here in Toronto. We could even buy *Meetha Paan* (leaf filled with beetle nuts and other delicacies).

"You people have opened up another world for me!" I acknowledged.

What a coincidence that once more in a new country, another Mrs. Khan had entered my life. She took me under her *dupatta,* so to speak. Still Rani and Nishat remained my nearest and dearest.

Learning about a different culture…

Professor Schuler advised me, "In addition to the Business Admin course, I urge you to learn typing. Someday you'd be thankful to me."

I didn't realize that my neighbor Ruth was observing my late-night *click, click, click*, practicing typing while Burlington FM radio was on. She once invited me for after-dinner coffee and dessert, when she and her husband squabbled throughout the evening. He told me, "Ruth is using you as a scapegoat." So I decided to avoid them. Thank God Mujeeb and I never quarreled.

During our Friday afternoon chat sessions, Mr. Schuler was once surprised when I expressed my positive outlook toward the institution of Marriage.

"Look who is talking—don't we know the kind of a messed-up marriage you have. Your husband is living in Nigeria while you're roughing it out in a new country, on your own!"

One Friday afternoon in our discussion group he posed this question:

"How are you adjusting to our Canadian culture which is new to you?"

I naively replied, "I watch *Mary Hartman Mary Hartman* every night to learn about Canadian culture." There was a murmur rumbling around my class before Schuler interrupted with a smirk, "That's not representative of Canadian culture, it's a soap opera with dark humor."

(*A late-night Monday-through-Friday soap opera which aired from 1976 to 1977)

He explained, "Norman Lear, the producer, wanted to do a show about a woman who had been affected by the media, her mind was shattered by magazines, radio—especially television."

One of the students joked, "It's a show about a 'sexually unfulfilled woman,' her husband is away, maybe she should watch it."

So, ironically it was the very show which was not suitable for me at that time. The class had a good laugh. Drowning in embarrassment, I proffered, "What I find interesting is how discreetly they warn that it's rated R:

'It's eleven o'clock do you know where your children are?'

"It's a sardonic take on modern life" they said. I looked up the meaning and was happy to add another word to my vocabulary, *sardonic.*

......

Those Magical Sound bites...

After a tiresome day I had said good night to Kashif and snuggled with a blanket on my couch with soft music. Suddenly I heard a familiar voice and rushed to increase the volume. "Oh my God, is it really *Ameen Sayani* from Radio Ceylon?" I hadn't heard that voice since 1963! A million memories surged invoking mixed emotions, I wanted to sing, dance and weep, simultaneously.

As mentioned earlier, 'Binaca Geet Mala' was my family's favorite radio program. I recorded the top three hits. I wonder if my family retained that diary or discarded it.

Broadcast since 1952 from Radio Ceylon (now Sri Lanka) with millions of listeners all over India, Pakistan, Bangladesh, and here I was listening to it re-broadcast in Toronto! DJ Glenn became secondary to 'Ameen Sayani Darling', who had the power to transport me into my buried past and excavate it, *one hit at a time!* It fascinates me how our brain stores memories. Regardless, Sayani was my past, DJ Glenn my present.

I met some immigrant couples who were always tossing around the idea of whether to go back or to stay in Canada. They referred to themselves as:

Dhobi ka kutta, Na ghar ka na ghaat ka

(Urdu Proverb--A person split between two things, and can't justify either).

But I was determined never to look back. *Tariq bin Ziyad* had burnt his boats once he landed in Spain, so did I when I landed in Canada!

Our First Snowfall…

One morning we were spellbound, as crystal flakes formed in space were gently floating down, creating magic. We had a panoramic view, from our floor-to-ceiling, wall-to-wall glass doors. Applewood Hills was slowly covered with a fluffy white blanket. Only a few weeks back all was green. Kashif wasted no time to change gear into his brand-new snow suit I had just bought. "Slow down, *beta*, what's the rush?"

"What if it starts melting?" he asked, as I helped him zip up his navy gear and boots, while he grabbed his scarf and a toque, he rushed out the door.

"Wait, wait, I'm coming. We are not about to miss a flight." I locked the door and rushed to press the elevator.

Soon we romped in the snow, rolling down the hill on the white fluff, giggling away hitting each other with snowballs. Children from other apartments started joining us. I too became a kid. At first Kashif was shy, but after some introductions we 'broke the ice with the snow,' running after each other squeezing with both hands to harden the balls, only to disintegrate upon slight touch.

Rosy cheeks, red nose, and sniffles, all part of the outdoor winter celebration, it was Kashif's first unforgettable experience.

"Mom, look at the trees, just like the postcards we collected in Nigeria,"

"Yes, our dream has now become a reality."

Over a dozen children energized with the season's first snowfall created a huge mound and Kashif remarked, "It feels like we've brought Idanre Hill to Mississauga, except that it's white." That reminded me of the annual *Ogun Festival* we attended in Nigeria. It was a spectacular traditional event held on top of the hill every October. While new in the country, we often found ourselves comparing it with Africa.

"Remember in Nigeria we were fed up with the same weather all year round, although the Canadians would love it." Kashif aimed a ball at me, I dodged.

Almost three hours flew by before I was able to persuade him to come inside. My hands and face frozen by the time we returned, panting and puffing.

"Let's have dinner, hot chocolate, and then the bedtime story. Today it would be about?"

"The snowfall?" he was swift. "But *my* first snowfall experience was very different."

I related the story of being stranded in Paris, on our way back to Nigeria. KLM could only take us via Amsterdam, there was snow. "We spent an entire day in Beatrice Park. Your father and I were so fascinated we played with snow like little children, just like you this afternoon."

"But I'm not little anymore." He yawned and I cuddled him good night, pulled the blanket over him and reflected:

Having a single child, a mother has to play the role of a friend and a sibling as well. But now, I had to also fill the gap of his absent father.

Once the salt was added to that dream-like white winter fluff, it turned into dismal brown muddy slush, a new reality for us. The sweet dream had shattered, and now we all seemed destined to freeze to death waiting for the right bus in bone-chilling muck.

......

Identity Crisis…

When you're new to the country to the ignoramus *you* may come across as ignorant. In Nigeria I never had to use public transport, here I had to rely on Mississauga Transit.

I was still struggling to get used to wearing clunky winter boots, so it was not easy racing from the train to the bus upstairs. One day I joined the line behind an elderly, somewhat chunky lady ahead of me, who was adorned with a mink coat and flashy diamond rings.

"Excuse me, please, but does this bus go to Mississauga?" I was still panting.

"They can find their way thousands of miles to Canada, but once they get here, they're suddenly lost," the snooty woman muttered, drawing everyone's attention to me. I felt embarrassed. We finally boarded the bus. The lineup was long, and because I was not up to speed yet, a seat was hard to find. Eventually I spotted one I could squeeze into, but the lady in mink spread her fur to occupy the space. She couldn't resist offering up another dig. "Now they're making our buses overcrowded too." My blood pressure rose to the max, as she continued her racist remarks.

A white Canadian gentleman got up and politely offered me his seat. The mink lady continued her verbal assault, looking at me all the while. I had become her dartboard and she was targeting me with every nasty verbal weapon at her disposal while everyone looked on. Some passengers offered me a look of compassion. I felt relieved when she got off.

I soon learned from others that Italian immigrants were the victims once, after that the Greeks and the Chinese took their turn. "Some people are feeling overwhelmed with the number of immigrants coming from the east. Sadly, this is just a bad year for Indians and Pakistanis."

That left me wondering again if we had done the right thing. We were so popular on Ife University campus but here I was experiencing an identity crisis. My status had suddenly shifted from 'Non-black to Non-white'! In Nigeria they called me *Oebo.* Here in Canada, I was visibly *Brown*; a fact made abundantly clear when my son came home from school one day. "Mom, the kids said if you came from Africa, why you don't wear skirts made of banana leaves?"

......

The Growing Stage...

This new life was a big adjustment for our son too, but we tried to handle it with reason and patience. Once he came home upset and bewildered. "Mom, why do the kids at school make faces at me and call me *Paki?* What does *Paki* mean?"

I was horrified, but I thought for a moment before answering, "My darling, you can proudly tell them P is for pure, A is for able, K is for knowledgeable, and I is for . . . ?" I needed a second to think.

"Intelligent," Kashif interjected with a broad smile. He understood my message. I was happy he was not going to let a bunch of ill-informed seven-year-olds diminish his spirit.

He returned from school earlier than I from Shaw College. So I decided to hire a sitter. One day she called me at the college. "Your son is crying, he has severe pain in his right leg."

I had to leave the last class and rush home. This happened every second day, and the pain became a persistent problem, sometimes the right leg, another time it was the left leg. Rheumatic fever was the possible diagnosis, and I was told the pain travels. However, one day by chance I happened to notice that he suddenly shifted his limp from one leg to the other!

"Is it this leg or that?" I had to question him.

I came to the sad realization along with some relief too, that the pain was only psychological.

After extensive talk he admitted his friend at school told him, "One day my dad left too, but he never came back. Maybe yours would do the same."

Kashif was afraid that one day even I might not return. From then on, I chose to skip the last class until my husband returned from Nigeria.

....

Together Again

14 We celebrated Mujeeb's return from Nigeria, but now he faced the harsh reality of job hunting with disappointment after disappointment. Finally, one day he broke some good news. "I got the job. But it's not in Toronto."

Mujeeb accepted a temporary position as a Visiting Professor in the Microbiology Department of the University of Regina. Energized, he drove all the way by himself in his pet Caprice Classic jam-packed with as much baggage as we could fit into it. The Prairies! I consoled myself with the word *temporary.* Once my exams were over, we had to join Mujeeb.

It was a great opportunity to experience fall colors at its best. Our train zooming along at the treetop level, Kashif and I sat inside the Great Dome, utterly mesmerized. Magic spell cast upon us by the falling leaves dancing their way down, we remained captivated! But as soon as we entered the prairies, my spirit began to sink.

One of my travelling companions advised, "Take a U-turn lady, after the kind of life you led, you won't be able to handle Regina—it's a dull city."

Our moderate apartment was nothing like the one we enjoyed in Uppsala, Sweden. In Regina most parking lots had electrical outlets as you need to heat up your car ahead of time. Sometimes temperatures drop as low as minus 55! I shivered with the thought.

"Cold or not, I couldn't have survived one more day without you, darling," Mujeeb said.

The next morning, he gave me a tour of downtown Regina. Parked near Simpson, Sears, and other 'sky scratchers', I spotted an S-shaped building and spontaneously said, "If I get a job in *this* area, in *that* S-shaped building, I may be able to survive."

"Wishful thinking" Hubby replied.

......

Entering the Work Force...

The Temporary Manpower Services found me a three-week assignment to work with the Task Force on Canadian Unity, a conference in Regina. Quebec independence was on everyone's mind. It was a great opportunity for me to meet the top politicians in the country.

After the three-week stint with Canadian Unity and as a result of a referral from Shaw College in Toronto, I was invited to an interview with the Director of Community Colleges.

A tall gentleman, in his early fifties, walked into the office to shake hands with me. I was nervous. As he glanced at my resume, I summoned up the courage to confess,

"In Toronto, my Placement Officer recommended that I should delete two items from my resume . . . but I, um, I haven't, um, done that,"

"And what might those be?" he asked.

"That my schooling was in Pakistan... and ... that I have three gold medals to my credit," as though I was pleading guilty for an offence.

"So why didn't you delete them?" His friendly curiosity was encouraging.

"Because these are the achievements I'm proud of," I replied and went on to explain, "The Placement Officer was concerned because people here in Saskatchewan are not as exposed to outsiders as they are in Toronto."

"Well, on that note, I'll say you're hired." With that he stood up and strode out of the room when I heard him say, "Those Eastern bastards think we're so ignorant here in the West."

I was thrilled with the temporary job offer as the Administrative Assistant to the Director of Community Colleges.

Much to my surprise, a senior officer from the Ministry of Education during an office tour gave me a warm welcome as '*The first Pakistani in that office*.' He directed one of the staff to replace my wobbly chair with a brand new one. Two days later, he even delegated me an important assignment in his own office. Those generous advantages made me a ripe victim for office gossip by much older women who probably sat on those chairs for too long.

......

The Credit Union...

I continued to look for other more permanent job opportunities. I applied and got called for an interview with George Clark, the General Manager of a Credit Union (Saskatchewan Power Corporation). I was taken aback with the bizarre coincidence—that office happened to be in the very building I had casually mentioned to Mujeeb on the first day!

Mr. Clark asked me, "Mrs. Zoberi, did you read our ad properly? Did you not see that I require a minimum eight years of banking experience?"

"But that is the *only* requirement I don't meet," I nervously explained.

"So then tell me, what requirements you *do* meet?"

"Presentable, professional, ambitious, willing to learn . . . and so on," I rambled on.

"I'll call you later," he said with a smile. It felt like his standard 'brush off.'

From then on, I called him every two weeks. "Mr. Clark, if any other opportunity comes up, please keep me in mind." But I didn't hear back from him.

Mujeeb advised me to give up but . . .

Three months later, on Christmas morning I received a call.

"George Clarke here, may I speak to Zohra." He had called to see if I was still interested. I found out that the perfect candidate they had hired suddenly left due to a problem with the staff. Instead of having to undergo the tedious process of advertising and interviewing all over again, George thought of calling the ever-persistent lady for a second interview.

"Mrs. Zoberi, my staff has never been exposed to people from your ethnic background. I, on the other hand, have lived in Vancouver, so it doesn't matter to me; but I'm somewhat concerned about . . ." he paused then reluctantly expressed, "As the only colored person amongst the entire staff, how would you deal with discrimination if it should happen?"

"I can only add color and spice to your Credit Union, Mr. Clark," I said with overconfidence.

"You're hired, young lady." Oh, how appealing was his smiling face with umpteen expression lines—the lines of wisdom giving me the vote of confidence.

"You just follow my instructions and if there's any trouble, come straight to me, okay?" His meaningful gaze invited intelligent interpretation. I just knew I had acquired a new Mentor.

First day on the job, George invited me into his office for an introductory meeting. He opened his drawer with a cheeky smile and pulled out a size 52 white cotton bra! I was shocked and embarrassed.

Back then, being a relatively traditional woman from an Eastern culture, I lowered my gaze and whispered to myself, *"La Hawla Wala Quwwat"*— Arabic, to ward off any evil.

I sat there dumbfounded as he explained how a woman had written a cheque on that bra.

"Should I honor it?" he asked with a cheeky smile. I remained silent then exited the room. But now, those memories amuse me to no end.

One of the duties assigned, however, was to 'spy' on the staff to find out what exactly was their problem, why were they ganging up on the staff member he had previously hired. *So that's why I was given this opportunity?!* At first the thought was depressing, however…

As for my job responsibilities, I knew I was 'raw material' trying my best. I couldn't have made it without George's tireless support. This wonderful teacher was my luck of the draw. Three months later, I couldn't believe my ears when he offered me the position as Secretary to the Board of Directors of the Saskatchewan Power Corporation.

"What about the terminology I'm not familiar with, how will I take minutes?"

"Look, you've taken Speed Writing course just jot down everything you hear. I'll help you transcribe it later." George seemed to know I'd meet his expectations. Thanks to him, my confidence leaped forward.

Mujeeb's niece Nasreen had sent an introductory letter from Karachi to her friend in Regina. Consequently, we were warmly welcomed by a small group of Pakistanis, a closely knit community. Our social life suddenly began to flourish attending private musical concerts, picnics, and other gatherings. We hit it off with fun-loving Wasima Kadri and Anwar Sultan.

Mujeeb wasn't yet entitled for a vacation, but I craved the warmth of my family. Entitled for three weeks' vacation only, I couldn't afford to lose a single day.

......

A Stranger in My Hometown!

To catch the earliest possible flight, I went to the airport straight from work dressed in chocolate color three-piece western business suit. I hurriedly tucked in my carry-on a wrinkle-free *shalwar qameez suit* to change before landing.

Regina to Toronto had added six more hours to what used to be an everlasting journey to my homeland. ***Time*** *does not fly when I'm flying,* I expressed my frustration looking at my watch once again.

The weather was turbulent before landing so I didn't get a chance to change. On the connecting flight to Islamabad, I noticed there were no women on the flight. Being the only female, I asked the gentleman seated next to me, "Is it designated as an all-male flight?"

"No, Madam, on early morning flights usually businessmen are the only travelers."

At dawn, my plane landed at Rawalpindi/Islamabad Airport. I could hear the ***Azaan*** (call for prayers) on the loudspeaker from an adjacent mosque, a familiar sound instantly connecting me to my hometown. As usual I rushed to peek through the door anticipating my family members holding bouquets, but for the first time there was no one there to receive me—and I had travelled halfway across the globe! Did they not receive my telex message?

In 1977 technology hadn't made its way into direct dialing from Regina, Saskatchewan, to Rawalpindi, Pakistan, let alone emailing.

In the late seventies, Islamabad and Pindi had not been as exposed to Western culture as Karachi. At the baggage collection belt, I felt completely out of place. Being the only female, hundreds of eyes were ogling me, dressed as I was in a western business suit. However, Senior Immigration Officers smartly dressed in white uniforms, politely warmed up to me right away, making me feel like royalty they had been waiting to receive. As usual a woman travelling alone instantly acquires *younger brothers* who start calling her **Baji** (older sister, turns into **Auntie** as you get older).

Mujeeb's brother Habib had requested me to complete an 'A Form' upon arrival to declare electronic equipment he ordered. "We will help you, Miss," said one officer. Once I opened my wallet, I never imagined the string of my credit cards would impress them so. Back then credit cards in Pakistan were so rare I heard a gentleman explain to the other, "These cards are worth thousands of dollars. She is a professional woman **yaar** (buddy), with these she can purchase anything, anytime, anywhere." I felt empowered like 'a woman of the world' a westernized female—*a stranger in my own town?*

Little did they know the curse of plastic money, I recalled a few victims of this North American contagious disease.

'A Form' completed, one officer offered, "Please have breakfast with us, Madam. We will arrange to drop you at your residence." But I opted for a *kaali peeli* taxi (yellow and black cab, initially English Morris, later the Japanese Hyundai). Once the old clunker rattled on, and my side of the window was impossible to close, cold wind piercing my face I couldn't help regretting my choice. For once I could have enjoyed a ride in a Mitsubishi Pajero.

On my way home, I realized that arriving here from Nigeria, Pakistan seemed relatively advanced, but coming from Canada it does feel like a third world country.

The surprise and delight on everyone's faces confirmed they hadn't received my telex message. I cuddled with my mom and dad right into the hand-stitched silk **Razai** (comforter), like a little girl who just woke up from a dream! Soon there was the aroma of fresh **parathas** being prepared in the kitchen by our maid Taaj Bibi. That surprise visit became most memorable.

Wide-eyed, they listened on. "In Saskatchewan temperatures drop as low as minus 55, Ammi! They sometimes announce that *Exposed human flesh can freeze in sixty seconds."* I related the story of my conquest as though I had conquered K2 (the highest peak of Himalaya mountain in Pakistan). They felt sorry for me. Gifts of glamorous party wear added another suitcase to my baggage. Weeks flew by it was time to return.

Family bid me farewell like I was on a mission to the moon.

Landing back to the Prairies felt as though we hit the Planet Earth with a thud—on a wrong location too! Fortunately, our newly acquired friends helped me cope with the 'alienation blues' they too were familiar with.

By the time Mujeeb's University contract ended in Regina, our minds were already made up to return to good old Mississauga. Time would tell if it was a hasty decision.

The departure was painful, the small group of friends had become like a closely knit family. When saying goodbye to George Clarke,

I became very emotional. He was a guiding angel who had done so much for me. His parting advice to me was,

"Make sure you do not end up in a Bank. It takes large organizations years to recognize unique talents—you could offer a lot more to a wise employer," but, do we always listen?

Regina was left behind and we were back to our good old Mississauga. This time we found a three-bedroom apartment in the same building—The Applewood Hills.

....

A DIFFERENT WORLD OF FINANCE

15 Against the advice of my mentor George Clarke, I ended up in a bank, hired as an MIT (Manager in Training). The first interview was on the 35th floor of the Wealth Management Bank (WMB) Tower in downtown Toronto. But a job opening came up near my home instead.

Mr. Jack Allcock, the Assistant Manager had barely watched me walk across the hall when he urged the interviewer, "Hire her, hire her." I later learned that he had a soft corner for any female between age 16 and 65 who wore a dress.

One day I was given a sack full of monthly statements to be stamped and mailed out to 1,500 clients. I felt offended and embarrassed by the idea of being reduced to mail clerk status. So the next time, I flatly refused. The manager stepped up to take the mail instead. His impressive gesture made me realize that in North America no work is beneath anyone, unlike in the third world countries where certain jobs are looked down upon. Coming from a privileged group in Nigeria, 'the Professor's wife' probably got into my head. Upon reflection, I realized Equality is in line with our teachings too, but we just don't practice it.

Three months later when my probationary period was over, I became more vocal "I was not hired as a Receptionist/Typist. How long do I have to wait for my MIT training?"

I overheard the Admin Officer Judy proclaim, "We don't invite immigrants to come and take management positions. We call them only to do odd jobs for us."

A Daring Step...

Judy took me by surprise. "Since you're unhappy with your working conditions here, the manager has decided to extend your probationary period to twelve months."

Twelve months! In a state of disbelief, I was quick to protest. "Incidentally, my three-month probation was over yesterday. I am now a confirmed employee."

Judy replied with delight, "Oh no, you're not confirmed yet, we have until 5:00 p.m. this afternoon."

I went home to study my contract line by line, and discovered that our Head Office had implemented a system where one could write to top management in complete confidence. The letter would be assigned a number so that the employee would remain anonymous. I quickly typed a letter to Head Office, sent it via inter-branch mail.

The next day our branch received a call informing that the most senior personnel manager was going to be visiting our branch the following morning. The fatal letter had been mailed and now it was too late for me, I became nervous. We had been depleting our savings, and the prospect of losing my job when my husband was out of work was terrifying.

Ms. Wendy Codrington, a senior most officer from the Head Office, Human Resource Department, showed up at 9:00 a.m. sharp. Everyone appeared to be nervous. Wendy had been misinformed by the staff that I had joined the company one day later than the commencement date on my contract. I was furious but able to provide time sheets that religiously logged my date and time of arrival. The staff Wendy interviewed also seemed to support the idea that Mr. Jack Allcock had rated my performance as substandard. My anger fueled me to speak up.

"Why can't you stop being a chicken for once Jack? If my performance is substandard, please be a man and say so."

He gasped for breath then became more confident. "In fact, I've always commended Zohra for her competence, so all this is news to me."

The silence that followed was loud and intimidating.

The Manager rose from his chair, shook my hand and declared, "Mrs. Zoberi, we've bull-shitted you for three months for which we apologize. Congratulations, you are now a confirmed employee of this Bank, and today we begin with a clean slate."

That was one of the most meaningful days of my life. Freedom and justice prevailed—becoming a Canadian was worth it. Jack later expressed his view, "Never pick up a fight with the ruthless North Americans." I was surprised that being an Englishman, he felt that way. In any case, Jack got transferred to another branch. As for me, even though justice had prevailed, my ambition was shattered when I was told:

"The only way you can get into a management position is by starting as a Teller and earning your way up." What! Take a drop in my grade and salary? **No.**

A promotional plan to gift $5.00 to staff for every Visa card they sold had been implemented. I sensed a gold mine and was prepared to dig in. Soon I not only ended up with most of the $5 bills, but also earned a title as 'The Visa Lady'. The Manager took me by surprise.

"Based on your record of highest visa sales in Ontario, we are happy to appoint you to manage our WMB Booth at the *CNE this summer to promote the new debit card."

"What . . . debit card?" I had to learn all about it to become one of the **Pioneers**.

(*CNE, Canadian National Exhibition held annually in downtown Toronto)

The branch manager Wim Faasen would often pass by my desk and whisper, "Just serve the counter, ignore the typewriter, I'll get someone else to help with typing."

Another turning point in my favor was when a new client had walked in to open an account. Noticing his Swedish accent, I became curious and was tempted to try my rusty Swedish: *"Pratar ni Svenska?"* (Do you speak Swedish?)

He was amazed. "I never imagined I'd walk into a Canadian bank to find a brown lady speak to me in Swedish."

"Jag har vaarit I Sverige nitton hundra shotty (I have been to Sweden in 1970)," I explained. This gentleman turned out to be the President of Astra Pharmaceutical! My spontaneous gesture resulted in the acquisition of a payroll account from one of the largest Swedish Pharmaceutical Firms—of course with the help of our branch manager. After all our Swedish language instructor in Uppsala had professed, "Once you learn a language it doesn't go away. Someday it may come in handy." Who would have imagined such a payoff?

Having discovered an easy ice breaker as a rapport builder, I decided to learn a few friendly phrases in several other languages spoken by our client base.

. . . . . .

Subsequently, I got invited to Head Office for an interview, but I was apprehensive I'd meet Ms. Sandra Wellington again who would repeat her mantra: *"Take a drop in salary, start as a Teller then work your way up."* That option was out of the question for me.

A handsome brown gentleman with crinkly hair briskly approached to offer a warm handshake. "Terry Campbell here, Ms. Wellington is under the weather, so I'll be interviewing you." My prayer answered, I almost danced my way behind him as he led me to his office.

After our discussion, he concluded, "Mrs. Zoberi, your sales results speak volumes. I can't believe how you've been batted around." He promoted me with a salary increase as an Appointed Officer of the Bank with official signing authority.

"Call from BCCI for Zee Zee." It was Sikandar calling to congratulate me. I was surprised. He said he saw ZZ00002 in the catalogue of the International Designated Bank Officials and assumed it would be me. I told him, "I've been promoted, waiting for a transfer. As soon as Mujeeb finds a job, we hope to sponsor one or two family members."

Since that was still a remote possibility, we desperately needed friends.

......

Creating a Library of Friends...

For new immigrants, alienation from next of kin creates a void. Many feel as though they have been uprooted and 'Trans planted.'

As Aristotle said, *"Man is by nature a social animal; an individual who is unsocial naturally and not accidentally is either beneath our notice or more than human."*

I had shortchanged myself on extensive reading; however, having known people of various backgrounds over the years, was like reading—some short stories, and a few novels. We had left my 'Library of Friends' behind in Nigeria. In Canada it was to be a fresh start.

For me race, color, or creed didn't matter, I just craved for the like-minded. In the Riverspray building I connected with my neighbors Sandy and an Australian couple Dave and Rudy. My cousin Rani and other relatives; Ayesha, Rehana and Ghizala Zuberi we just inherited.

I met a gentleman in our laundry room, he looked like an Arab, but his two kids looked Indian. Soft-spoken Hussain turned out to be a Hyderabadi Indian, his better half Tyaba jokingly called us 'Laundry room Friends' and introduced us to Prateebha and her group. Through literary events a bunch of writers were also added into our fold. We met Nazo Hasan, related to my cousin Dr. Farida. Mujeeb was excited that they were also into dancing. We were the only couple in that circle who didn't touch alcohol. Everyone was surprised how music intoxicated us.

Soon it developed into a sizeable 'collection' of friends. Each circle was drastically different, yet we seemed to fit in all. Our South Asians usually entertained at home. While men dressed western, the ladies loved to deck up in glamorous eastern outfits for fancy rotating dinner parties. It almost became overwhelming for me, but why?

Being an extrovert isn't always a good thing. While we were welcomed, I realized a bit late that in *some* gatherings I was invited for entertainment value?! I was expected to tell animated jokes, recite poetry, and be in the frontlines to cheer the poets or music performers. Even Kashif joked, "Mom the pressure is on." However, heart-to-heart connections were ***rare***.

......

Reunion with Manju...

One day I received a surprise call from an old friend from Nigeria. "Hi, this is Manju, remember your friend from Nigeria?"

"Oh my God you are such a globe-trotter, where are you calling from?"

"From Toronto airport, I'm about to check into a hotel."

"You better check in with me tomorrow."

The next day she arrived at our Applewood Hills apartment. Same old Manju in her hand printed, gossamer silk chiffon saree, decked up in jewelry and dark make-up. We caught up with each other's lives.

Much to rekindle, conversation about our worldwide travels transported us to Indonesia.

"I was fascinated to see the nude painting of President Sukarno's wife in your bedroom!"

"It was a secret transaction," she acknowledged. I also asked, "Is that life-size Tiger at the entrance of your home still there, it looked so real," "Of course it was *real* before Shiv hunted it in Bengal."

We had bonded through a Bridge Tournament. During our sleepovers on weekends to play bridge, we had no qualms about discussing the love/hate relationship between India and Pakistan. How intertwined our two cultures still are—even though the continent has split in two. Manju acknowledged, "I have more in common with you than the Indians on our Campus."

We spoke the same language she called *Hindi*. I made a candid remark, "Spoken *Hindi* my dear is the political name for *Urdu*, especially in Bollywood movies, right?" She readily agreed.

What was common between us was: 'Our **passion for people and the love of life.**'

Manju's chain of thoughts suddenly drifted:

"By the way, one of my Indonesian friend's sister *Chameli, lives here. Should we invite her over?" I replied, "Of course, if she is as passionate about life as you." I handed her the phone. Manju called her; I gave the directions.

Chameli arrived, breathtaking gorgeous. She looked like the film star *Sri Devi.* At first, I was taken aback to see a young face with premature grey hair but within minutes I found it stunning—a head turner.

"So your parents are from Pakistan, and you are an Indian, but my parents came from India and I am a Pakistani, strange isn't it?"

"Ya, but now we are both Canadians."

Her jovial self created such spark that we felt instant connection. Her eyes lit up when I quoted Rumi, "*Set your life on fire. Seek those who fan your flames.*"

Chameli and I decided to get together soon.

Manju left for the US to join her husband but promised to revisit before returning to Nigeria.

*Chameli (jasmine like white flower)

……

Like a Blood Sister in a Foreign Land!

Our meeting could not be better timed. Chameli and I were both in need of a 'close friend' even though for different reasons. I was relatively new in Canada, and she had recently been betrayed by some friends. Our international exposure in common, we therefore connected at many levels.

Chameli's husband Raees was passionate about music too. Mujeeb revealed a surprise:

"I believe I've already met your sister at our friend Ghazi's place in Switzerland."

Connecting the dots confirmed he was right. What a coincidence that one of Raees' sisters was married into our close friend Ghazi's family.

"For us, gypsies, this world is merely a village."

Me being older and a banker, Chameli looked up to me as my younger sister. Her adopted brother Mohsin and his wife Nasra were in her close circle. Together with two other couples we bonded in friendship without censorship. One only needs two or three sincere friends.

Every weekend we got together, watched classic Pakistani plays in Urdu such as *'TanhayyaN'* and *'Dhoop Kinaray'* followed by mutual discussions. We often enjoyed outdoor picnics, attended Raag Mala's live musical concerts at the University of Toronto.

Chameli once asked me, "What are you doing on November 11th?"

"Nothing special, Remembrance Day is also a bank holiday, so I'm off."

"Me too, working for the government. Let's go to Toronto and paint the town red."

"Yes . . . *Red and White,* forget about the green and orange."

"Or green and white," referring to our native flags.

"Would you believe I was fascinated with the 'Red' maple leaf since age ten," I shared.

"So, from now on, let's celebrate Remembrance Day also as our friendship anniversary."

From then on we religiously observed our friendship and spent the day downtown, window shopping, enjoying exotic meals in fancy restaurants in Yorkville and Distillery District. Despite close friendship we avoided one delicate subject— India/Pakistan relationship. Though we watched Deepa Mehta's movie 'Earth' together and were both deeply touched with what happened to our countries in the hands of politicians.

Over the years, I met her entire family visiting from USA and abroad, they lovingly embraced me as part of their family. Together Chameli and I coordinated larger musical events. She introduced me to Ghazala Zafar, who eventually introduced us to Fowzia Muzaffar, who became close. ***So we did manage to create a family abroad.***

After their tour in USA, Manju and Shiv invited us to join them for a long weekend at an exotic location in Sarnia by Lake Huron. "They are a group of Indian/Pakistani medical doctors who own luxury mansions. They are planning to spend a memorable weekend together." The offer was too tempting to refuse.

....

MIRACLE IN MISSISSAUGA

16 Driving back to Mississauga, Mujeeb and I were still raving over that luxury bash in Sarnia, our son fast asleep on the back seat on fluffed up bedding we had taken along.

"It was quite a treat . . . a 'Triple B Party' . . . Bridge, Badminton, and BBQ! Those medical professionals really know how to live."

We had been blissfully cut off from the world for the past three days. Mujeeb reached to turn on the radio. "Oh no," I pleaded, "Please don't turn it on 'cause I'll fall asleep."

I was tuckered out from three late nights in a row, and I didn't want to miss the last precious views of the countryside as we drove along.

"Weren't you amused that we the nondrinkers were at a gathering of mainly *meat-eating Hindus* and *wine drinking Muslims*?"

"It's true. What I enjoyed most was the whole-lamb roasting in the open fire pit by the lake. While you slept like a stone, we sat by the bonfire, chatting away until 3:00 a.m."

Immersed in conversation as we approached Mississauga, I noted something odd, "Mujeeb, there's not a single vehicle on the road."

"You're right. Not a soul walking on the streets either!"

Two police cars were blocking off the street. Emergency flares flickered across the roads.

Fear began to creep over us as we noticed more and more streets were blocked off.

"How could our bustling city turn into a ghost town in three days?" Mujeeb muttered.

Avoiding various roadblocks, we cautiously detoured to Applewood Three, our apartment building. As Mujeeb was about to insert the key into the underground parking meter, we heard someone holler, "Excuse me, Sir. Where do you think you're going?"

"To our apartment where else?" replied my baffled husband.

A policeman stepped out of his Peel Regional vehicle and approached us: "Sir, don't you know that there's been a train derailment in Mississauga? Poisonous gasses have leaked into the air and if a tanker bursts, you could be dead in minutes. Mississauga has been evacuated, so you need to get back in your car right now and drive at least five miles from here," he insisted.

Such a major disaster had hit our city and we didn't know anything about it? Being a BBC and CNN News junky, those must have been the only three days I was ever completely cut off from the world! With all those fun activities, none of us had wanted to turn on the TV or radio.

"May I at least go up and get our passports and some other essentials?" Mujeeb asked. "Go! You have two minutes," the officer warned.

Kashif and I waited in the car, scared stiff, while *Mr. Relaxed* on the seventh floor was slowly gathering what he determined were our essentials. Filled with anxiety, minutes seemed like hours, so I rang the buzzer to hurry him up. "Mujeeb, the cop is back, and he's about to give us a ticket for lack of cooperation."

I moved into the driver's seat to assure the police we were ready for takeoff. Mujeeb finally came down with a portfolio in one hand

and his favorite pillow in the other. That was his essential? He threw the pillow onto the passenger seat and jumped in.

I was in control of the steering wheel but had no idea where we were going. I mindlessly navigated along the 401. At the sight of the familiar *Martin Grove Road* sign, I took a quick exit and turned left.

"Where in hell are you going?" Mujeeb shouted. As I pulled into our friends' driveway, he now seemed pleased with my spontaneous decision.

"Fatima and Latique are sure to provide us with more details, before we check into a hotel," he concluded.

"What hotel!" Our relative Fatima asked as they rolled out their Pakistani carpets of hospitality while their little ones, Isa and Sadia, and our Kashif almost nine became excited over the possibility of a sleepover.

"Did you really think we'd let you leave now?" Fatima asked, as she served us tea and refreshments with her ever-generous smile.

I picked up a newspaper from the coffee table and read:

'On November 10, 1979, a train disaster occurred when a 106-car Canadian Pacific freight train derailed near the intersection of Mavis Road and Dundas Street in Mississauga, Ontario. The train was carrying chemicals and explosives including Styrene, Toluene, Propane, Caustic Soda, and Chlorine from Windsor, Ontario. As a result of the derailment, more than 200,000 people have been evacuated from Mississauga.'

The derailment caused a huge explosion, sending a fireball 5,000 ft into the air. It could be seen from 100 kilometer away. I also read, "As the flames were erupting, the train's brakeman, Larry Krupa, 27, at the instruction of the engineer, his father-in-law, managed to close an airbrake-angle spigot."

"What's a spigot?" Latique interjected with his wisdom: "Listen guys, the main thing is, this hero managed to save the undamaged cars and prevented a catastrophe."

"Someone always comes out the hero after a tragedy," Mujeeb added.

"Well, thank goodness, for that. His actions prevented those cars from catching fire. Had they exploded, imagine what could have happened to us all."

"In an instant, the city of Mississauga might have been wiped off from the earth!"

"But *we* would have survived at our *Triple B* weekend in Sarnia," Mujeeb tried to lighten the mood.

"Well, as you said, heroes emerge out of emergencies," Fatima repeated.

"There have been hundreds of stories of shelters being set up in schools, and friends and neighbors extending helping hands to each other. Officers even went back into homes to save people's pets!" Fatima updated us. "Let's not forget our Mayor Hazel McCallion, on a sprained ankle she hobbled from one location to another providing whatever support she could."

"I'm not surprised. She's incredible," I enthused. "Did you know I was still new in Canada when she was elected to be the Mayor of Mississauga, of all the famous personalities in the world I selected her as my role model?"

"Hurricane Hazel was a good choice. She inspires women every day," Fatima added.

The weeklong luxury of being so royally treated by the Qureshis brought us close to become like intimate family. Kashif had a great time with their kids Isa and Saadia.

For days Mississauga was deserted. The city partially reopened on the evening of November 16, the chlorine tank was emptied on November 19, but residents weren't allowed to return until the contamination had been cleared and the danger neutralized.

The Peel Police were applauded for smoothly handling the largest and most efficient evacuation in North American history. The Mississauga residents were proud to hear that Mr. Larry Krupa, the train's brakeman who had acted courageously, was recommended to the **Order of Canada** for his bravery. Would such a disaster be handled so efficiently in our countries?

We returned to our cozy apartment after several days. In the aftermath of it all, Mujeeb and I felt an overwhelming sense of gratification: "So we did make a good choice in becoming Canadians."

"Indeed."

....

Vertigo (1984)

17 Once I had invited Nasreen Irfan (our first Bridge partners) and other couples for a formal dinner. Creating ambience with soft music, candle lights, the fragrance of fresh flowers was important to me. I even used the Royal Dolton set sitting idle in a glass cabinet. Generous compliments abound.

"Working overtime, when do you get time to make these gourmet dishes?"

"You even use fabric serviettes?"

After dinner, we had our usual poetry recitals, joke telling, the evening was a blast with a sing-along segment at the end. I declined the offer to help clear up.

"Everyone deserves one evening of relaxation."

"My wife has the energy of two women," Mujeeb boasted in jovial manner.

It was well past two by the time I hand washed and towel dried all the dishes, wondering if it was worth using gold-plated dinnerware. Paper plates would've been just fine.

Browbeaten, I plunked myself in bed and fell asleep in seconds.

How life can change in an instant!

The next morning as I tried to get up from my bed, the entire room was rapidly rotating, I screamed with fear. As though the ceiling was swirling downward and the floor was shifting up. "Help… Help! I can't get up… Call the ambulance, please."

My heartbeat racing, I was perspiring, dizzy, and nauseated.

"Maybe I'm having a heart attack."

"Relax, darling, it must have something to do with your ears," Mujeeb comforted me. Dr. Borgeil made a home visit as an exception. He had a clinic in the strip plaza adjacent to our building. He diagnosed it as, "*Labyrinthitis* (inflammation of the labyrinth) is a virus that sometimes attacks the inner ear." As for the prognosis he advised, "There's no medication, just rest and it will eventually go away."

For two weeks, I felt as if I was on a ship engulfed in a storm, scary.

Wobbling my way around, I could hardly stand up without holding on to something. I was later referred to an ENT specialist Dr. Smith. He referred me to a downtown Hospital to rule out anything serious. On my way out, I was shocked as he touched me at the back and blurted, "A good F— might do you good." My head was spinning already, but reporting this outrageous harassment was still lesser of my immediate concerns.

Today with the **Me-Too** movement, he couldn't get away that easily.

After some grueling tests at St. Michael's—being tied to a swirling table, water injected in my ears that triggered scary dizzy spells, the final verdict was '*Benign Positional, Recurring, Left Head Hanging Vertigo.*' The word Benign was a relief but the thought of permanent damage to my inner ear was depressing. I was in it for life!

I spent a turbulent year. I felt sad having to bid farewell to the Badminton Club in Mississauga. I returned to work a bit too soon. Slightest wrong movement triggered debilitating dizzy spells.

One day, interviewing a couple for a Home Improvement Loan became an eye opener for me. The couple planned to change all the doors in their new bungalow to accommodate wheelchairs—for both spouses! Their disabilities were far more serious than mine.

I researched into inner ear functions, marveled at the minute particles that float in three tiny canals that help us balance. The specialist taught me how to cope. On the examination bed, he took me off guard and pushed me toward the wrong side to trigger vertigo. When I screamed for help, he said, *"Just turn to the opposite side as fast as you can."* I did, and the magic occurred as if I had put breaks on a vehicle running full speed!

He explained, "When one ear is not functional, the other takes over. Sometimes the part of the brain to which the inner ear is attached, also learns to assist!" That imbued me with confidence and offered me a subject for my diary as I learned a new lesson:

Vertigo Philosophy

How we appreciate the true value only when
an ability is taken away!
Nature's 'back-up' system I marvel at.
One ear out of function
the other takes over
How we learn to counter act

What if we apply this philosophy to
our negative thoughts floating

in the mysterious veins of our minds
causing emotional imbalance?

> *Nature's backup system, at our fingertips*
> *With brain power we may counteract*
> *Negative thoughts with the Positive*
> *avoid 'emotional vertigo' and achieve...*
>
> *Balance!*
>
> *.........zz*

I had to embrace my limitations—how far down or up I could move my neck. While serving clients at the bank, turning to my left triggered vertigo but if I turned to my right, gave me *relief!* However, that meant going in circles...so, a friendly client in our bank joked, "You are such an interesting lady even your illnesses are amusing." My colleagues chuckled.

Consequently I kept a supply of '*Conium 30*' a homeopathic medicine from Pakistan, far more effective than the *Serc* usually prescribed. A few vertigo victims were referred to me and I was dubbed as the *Vertigo Support person*.

....

Home Ownership in Canada

18 In Nigeria, as expatriates we could never own a property, so owning one in Canada was our dream. However, Ife University arbitrarily discontinued Mujeeb's pension. When I shared the dilemma with our Manager Mr. Stevens, he immediately called the bank's corporate lawyers—Strathy Archibald. One letter from them to the Nigerian University carried such power, that the outstanding installments were cleared without a problem! With the down payment, we booked a model home in the heart of Mississauga.

An 8 ½ x 17 inch application with multiple carbon copies seemed intimidating.

In that crazy branch no one had time to teach me what is TDSR (Total debt service ratio), and GDSR (Gross debt service ratio) So, I sought help from our Head Office.

After their Tele-training session, I completed my personal application and even added the Manager's recommendation myself:

'The client is fully responsible to meet all her commitments.'

Mr. Stevens smiled at *my* version of *his* comments. "Fully responsible, are you?"

"I just copied your remarks from one of the old client's files you had signed." He smiled and meticulously put his autograph on the exact spot.

Such a prim and proper, no-nonsense gentleman, always in an immaculate suit and tie, not a single salt-and-pepper hair was out of place ever. What a treat to see him lighten up.

That was the extent of my mortgage training when I got promoted as the Mortgage Officer in-charge of an offsite Mortgage Centre within the Meadowvale Mall in Mississauga. I was excited but nervous. The Loans Officer said, "It's just a larger loan."

We eventually became the proud owners of a 2,700 sq. ft. brand-new model home in the heart of Mississauga, a highly desirable location near a ravine.

"Human nature is so strange," I said. *Owning* that relatively smaller house with a sizeable debt was more gratifying than our larger luxurious furnished bungalows in Nigeria, cost free!

Our son ran up and down the circular stairway feeling euphoric, looking at the skylight and double ceiling, he asked, "Isn't this too big for us? We even have our own laundry room?"

"Yes. No more trips to underground Laundromat to wash our dirty linen in public."

The burden of borrowing hit us slowly—a huge loan amortized over 25 years!

"Most Canadians are used to this lifetime commitment," I said.

While clearing up my office desk before the move, I casually blurted, "Wouldn't that be something if Terry Campbell becomes the Manager of that branch?"

"He is. But I want to know how the hell did you two plan it?" Judy asked.

"Is he really the Manager there?" At first I was baffled.

"I bet you've known this all along." Overjoyed, I ignored Judy's sarcasm.

That afternoon I arrived home reciting Allama Iqbal's verse:

"Khudee ko kar buland itna ke har taqdeer se pehlay
Khuda banday se khud poochay bataa teri raza kya hai?"

(The gist: Build your confidence to such an extent even God's will is on your side)

What a bizarre coincidence that Terry Campbell really was transferred as the branch manager! He was the answer to my prayer once before, when he interviewed me at the head office. How my struggle was being rewarded, felt like Divine Intervention.

......

Becoming a Mortgage Officer...

We were excited about our reunion. Immaculately dressed, Terry Campbell was a handsome Executive of mixed race (black and white) wheat complexion and crinkly hair.

He welcomed me with a warm smile and jogged my memory. "I still remember how your face lit up when I said that instead of Ms. Wellington, I will interview you. By the way I haven't forgotten that bright blue dress," he recalled playfully.

"Oh!" I wasn't sure how to respond. Terry suddenly assumed a serious tone.

"See this?" he pointed out to his wrist and mine.

"This is a great country but remember you and I have the same pigment. We are being observed more closely. To deserve the same reward, we must do better than others." I respected him far too much to question his strange philosophy.

"Birds of the same pigment," I said, and he nodded.

"So let's stick together."

Once again, a flash of thought fluttered: In Nigeria I was considered **Oebo** (white like a peeled orange) but over here my status had changed as being *a visible minority—brown.*

As a rookie Mortgage Officer, suddenly in charge of a Mortgage Centre especially during the peak housing market of the '80s, I had to sink or swim. More flexible, overtime hours ensued and ... I got married to the Bank.

As though my husband and I were now heading in two opposite directions—ascending and descending. Terry got to know of my personal circumstances—a jobless PhD at home, so he empathized with me. Hearing me laugh heartily, he often commented with curiosity,

"There must be a method to your **madness**, lady."

"There is ...but I have never been a *Teller*." He enjoyed the pun.

Mr. Campbell knew that in the past I was pressurized to become a Bank Teller first. It was he who helped me climb the ladder without having to step down first. Working with him, my motivation accelerated. My role as a senior lending officer came with unexpected perks.

'Serenity One' A Yacht Cruise...

On a bright sunny day, early morning I zoomed along the scenic Lakeshore Boulevard to join a kickoff party to introduce a yacht for which I had approved the loan. Paul Anderson and Alan Archie welcomed and introduced me to their wives, Sandra and Johanna. "Ah so they did name it **Serenity One** as I suggested. "Why add one?" they had asked, and I replied, "Leaves the possibilities for a larger boat in future."

I couldn't believe they let me steer the yacht out of the Humber River dock/Harbor. Making me nervous they screamed in panic, "You are too much to the left. Oh no! Now you're too much to the right. Take it easy, Zeezee!"

My fear of water was inbred—as my mom often related to me the story of her brother, murdered prior to the India-Pakistan Partition. His college peers plotted to drown him in the river, and sadly he was later found deceased—still wearing his glasses and boots! However on that particular day, my excitement overpowered my fear of water, so I dared, though I was nervously clinging on to my life jacket.

"Hold it, steer straight ahead or you'll take us all to hell," Paul was now getting angry. I swallowed my agitation. With a false sense of accomplishment, I proclaimed, "Watch it, you guys, it's ***our*** boat, once the bank loan is paid off, you may scream all you want."

Paul apologized, and we lightened up.

Soon I felt a masculine hand helping me steer, so we finally came out of the narrow passage unscathed, and approached the vast open Lake. I took a sigh of relief.

Deep blue Lake Ontario always fascinated me, the white sail boats smoothly floating over the gentle ripples, so serene. An inner desire surged like the waves. *If only my parents witnessed me steering a yacht, even my siblings would be so excited.*

Both wives stayed down in the cabin preparing sandwiches. Men were busy discussing the engine horsepower and other details I had no clue about. Out of respect for me they restrained from binge drinking, ensured ginger ale was available. This is where I developed the taste for Phil Collins they played. I related the details to Mujeeb, even played the song '*In the Air tonight*' but it didn't interest him the least bit. What happened to the good old days, when I called him the Brown Englishman? But now, he was more interested in Urdu music.

I had the overwhelming desire to be Shadan—'live each day to its fullest, maybe this was the *Method to my Madness* Terry Campbell was curious about?

Working overtime hours, at times I had no energy to drive back. Our friends Neema and Zia lived nearby and always extended a warm welcome. "Is your tea kettle connected to the doorbell?" I asked. Within minutes a hot cup of tea with sumptuous refreshments tantalized my taste buds. Neema's cheerful company instantly energized me, I sometimes joked: "You are my Tylenol tablet." We formed a strong loving bond with her whole family. As well, their three little girls Hira, Ayesha, and Sabeen got attached to Kashif and me. I finally took Neema into confidence to share Mujeeb's job dilemma.

....

THE ROLE REVERSAL

19 I started viewing Mujeeb's ongoing research at the University of Toronto without pay as his hobby, but he felt he was working harder than me. As the tension between us mounted, I worried about its impact upon our son. However, both of us were fully aware that our stress was due to our Role Reversal we least expected to face in Canada.

There were times we would be arguing while driving when a hand would sneak from behind to hold mine. That silent support spoke volumes. None of my family members knew that in this land of opportunities, being 'over-qualified' limited his chances.

Knowing our mutual dilemma we always forgave each other. Anger often transformed into apologies. At times we resorted to humor. Once in the middle of an argument, Mujeeb blurted, *"You should've married a Mullah, he would've given you eight children and you'd be changing diapers forever."* I humorously retorted,

"Oh, then I'd have a whole team on my side." We both burst out laughing.

While Mujeeb regretted the decision of coming to Canada, I maintained my 'Tariq Bin Ziyad' philosophy. Many alternatives I suggested were ignored. His determination to stay in the academic environment blocked other possibilities but, deep down I admired his passion as he was still publishing research papers. He attended international scientific conferences on behalf of the University of Toronto and was content with nominal honorariums.

I sometimes met cab drivers with PhD or MSc degrees. Once we shared our stories, my countrymen refused to let me pay the full fare. When the anguish weighed heavy, I wanted to be heard, maybe write an article for the newspaper about the fate of PhDs in this country. *Where's the Speakers Corner, like the one in London?*

Sooner or later there was bound to be a breakthrough.

A Golden Opportunity...

"Darling here's an opportunity of a lifetime... and ... it is ... right in my field." Excitement spilling from Mujeeb's voice, I assumed it must be to do with Termites. I had recently typed a scientific paper for him— his research focus had shifted from *Termitomyces* mushrooms that grew on termite hills, into actual Termites.

He read the newspaper ad from the Federal Government:

"Independent Scientists are invited to submit their bids for a $6-million-dollar research project," he continued reading the details.

A torch lit up in my heart, racing with joy.

"Deir aayed, durrust aayed."

(An opportunity ... better late than never)

"What's the deadline date?" I asked.

"No worries, I've already done the related research. I have two months to put it together.

Snuggling with him on the couch I joked, "If you get this grant, you will literally become a *Six Million Dollar Man,* referring to his favorite TV show with that title (An American science fiction about a former astronaut).

"Would you prefer to be called Steve Austin, Lee Major, or ... better still *Lo Mujeeb?*"

"As long as I can name you 'The Bionic Woman',"

"But just yesterday you called me *Bhayanak Woman I said lightly (*Scary).

"So, Jamie Sommers, let's celebrate with *garma garam chai and pakoray*" (hot cup of tea and snack). We cuddled with each other at the prospect of such a lucrative project.

Termites are often thought to infest only tropical or temperate areas. Very few were aware that termites thrive in most parts of southern Canada, especially along the coasts. They are commonly found in large cities like Toronto or Ottawa. The most common type to infest Canadian homes is the subterranean termite (in the East, *Reticulitermes flavipes*, in the West, *Reticulitermes Hesperus*).

"I had such difficulty typing those scientific names." I said.

Mujeeb spent hours working on his research proposal, but now and then I'd enter his Study to remind him, "This isn't Nigeria, darling, over here quality of presentation is of utmost importance."

"Just because you have a job and I don't, you think you've become smarter than me?" This new version of my otherwise exceptionally polite hubby was hard to tolerate.

"Promise that you will quit your job as soon as I secure this contract."

I sometimes pointed to the sticker I had bought: *'A woman's place is in the home, as long as she goes there directly after work.'* In Nigeria, I was his utter source of his joy, where I celebrated my twelve-year-long honeymoon. Evolving as an Independent Canadian professional woman was inevitable. But ... was it too much for him to handle?

I reiterated: "If I were you, I'd hire someone just to polish up the proposal." Invariably, he got upset so I promised never to interfere again.

Only two days prior to the submission deadline he approached me, softly, "Shady, could you ask your secretary to type my manuscript?"

"What?" I got up from my chair, frantic, "I can't ask her to do my personal work in business time." But I noticed he called me *Shady* after a long time.

Our receptionist Marilyn agreed to type the fifty-page proposal after work, at a cost of $75. I kept it a secret as saving money was why he didn't hire help.

The following evening I proudly presented the finished report to him. We celebrated by a candlelight dinner. The next evening, Mujeeb declared, "Your secretary cannot spell scientific terminology, plus I have to make some major changes."

"So now, am I supposed to interfere?" I could literally taste my own bitterness.

Eventually, I decided to call up Fatima Qureshi and Latique who had their own computer business 'Logitek'. Once again, they opened their hearts to us. I remembered how we had enjoyed their hospitality during the Mississauga Evacuation in 1979.

I had just returned from work I gobbled up a sandwich before driving to their place. All night long, from eight in the evening to seven in the morning, four of us were consumed in a tiresome marathon. The unprofessional draft was transformed into a professional-looking Scientific Proposal. "I don't know how to thank you." We left Fatima and Latique yawning.

I barely had time for breakfast before I headed to my branch — wearing the same business suit!

That afternoon at 12:20 p.m., Marilyn handed me the receiver. Mujeeb's voice sinking like he was dying, "I've missed the deadline, I'm finished." I remained dumbfounded ... he broke the silence, "I was only fifteen minutes late but my submission has been rejected."

I plunked myself onto my chair holding my head with both hands, swiveled backward to gasp for breath. I then turned around with, "*I have nothing to say.*"

What was I to say or do? I put the phone down and headed for the restrooms.

The delay occurred for two reasons: that he had gone back to Latiq's place to change the title page again. Why, why, why? He still had the time, but there was a major collision on the highway causing further delay. I wanted to scream but I just banged the table.

After a whole decade he gets this golden opportunity and...? It wasn't really his fault, just Fate!

Clearly my partner was dealing with depression. If I didn't support him who would?

A close friend suggested, "Perhaps he needs counseling?" My attempts had failed.

"You have lost the opportunity to become a six-million-dollar man, but I still have to play the role of **Bionic Woman**." I learned to find comedy in our tragedy.

However, certain people walked into my life, contributed not only to the advancement of my career, but also blossomed into rewarding friendships. One such anecdote I'd like to share:

......

The Mystery of Malisa

Blessed with a figure like Sophia Loren, how could she go unnoticed? Her silky red hair that fell well below her shoulders bounced as she walked. Her light European complexion and lovely facial features didn't represent any typical origin, so she could pass as French, Spanish, Italian, or from just about anywhere in the Middle East.

Once she had settled herself in the chair across from my desk and the introductions were completed, I asked: "How much are you depositing in your account?"

"Five hundred," she whispered.

"And how much would you like to withdraw?"

"Five hundred," she replied again softly.

"You are depositing five hundred, but also withdrawing five hundred?"

"I'm depositing five hundred thousand dollars, withdrawing only five hundred dollars."

She handed me a draft—five hundred thousand dollars.

I gasped as I glanced at the information sheet which confirmed that she was only twenty-four years old! By the time I finished filling out her transfers of funds from other banks, the total amount came to almost two million dollars. This was definitely a God-sent gift for me as we were in the middle of an aggressive campaign for bringing in *new money* to our bank branch. Her name, Malisa Khan, raised my curiosity: "Miss Khan, may I ask where you are from?"

"Niagara Falls." She replied. "Niagara Falls? I ... I mean ..." She sensed my hesitation.

"Oh, you mean originally. I'm a *Parsee* from Iranian background, married to a *Pathan* from the Frontier (Frontier or NWFP is the North Western area bordering Afghanistan).

They had just moved to Toronto from Niagara Falls where they had sold a hotel they owned, which explained the hefty deposit that so delighted me.

Once the transactions were completed, we chatted for a bit. I mentioned that across the street from our new home was a four-bedroom luxury house that overlooked a ravine . . . and it was for sale. The next day, she and her husband Rehmat Khan came, and made an on-the-spot purchase fully paid. They were probably the only mortgage-free couple in that affluent locale.

Soon we were on the list of their favorite guests. Rehmat and Malisa loved to BBQ, and we enjoyed socializing with them and their friends. Malisa was a brilliant young woman, educated in a convent school in *Goa*. Rehmat worked at a butcher's shop in Mississauga; they were a very unusual match from the Indo-Pakistani cultural perspective, since being a butcher is considered to be a menial job often looked down upon. I found them interesting and mysterious.

In the entranceway of their new home, a huge marble pedestal supported an impressive, original bronze sculpture by a well-known French artist; and yet they cooked food in dented and stained pots, and served it in the crudest manner I had ever witnessed.

Once Mujeeb and I accepted their invitation to join them at a downtown night club called *The Heaven*. That evening on the dance floor, it seemed as if most of the young guys were finding themselves 'in heaven' while dancing with their girlfriends, but ogling Malisa wistfully as she sashayed on by.

"Some of these guys are sure to end up with sprained necks tonight," I whispered to Mujeeb. Malisa was fashionably dressed in a one-piece, turquoise silk jumpsuit with a halter top and plunging neckline that exposed her well-endowed bosom. As she gyrated erotically to Chubby Checker's *The Twist*, it was evident that beneath the flimsy silk, she wore no undergarments. "I think *The Twist* was instantly chosen by the DJ who spotted her."

In contrast to her exotic appearance, her husband was dressed ever so sloppily.

I had once asked Malisa, "Your husband seems kind of conservative, doesn't he object to the way you dress?" She replied,

"Please don't *ever* bring it up in front of him. This is the only area where I get to exercise complete freedom."

A few months later, Rehmat travelled out of the country for a three-month business trip. It was during this time that she and I became closer. She was a lonely neighbor in need of company. I often visited her and we watched sappy movies, shed tears, and shared stories of our childhoods that bonded us.

After a few months, she made the trip abroad and brought back some semiprecious jewelry to sell. I didn't fancy anything much except for a pair of black jade earrings set in pewter. But as I expressed my interest, she held them against her heart. "Sorry, my dear, but these aren't for sale they have deep sentimental value for me." Malisa didn't seem eager to share the details of the sentiment, so I didn't press the issue.

One day we were invited for a dinner gathering at her place. I was almost finished dressing when I received a call from Malisa who was sounding stranger than usual.

"Please don't come for dinner this evening. Rehmat is upset over how close my friendship with you has become, and that's something he cannot tolerate. I can't talk right now. I must go. Bye." I put down the receiver in disbelief.

Days and months passed when we hardly saw the couple, even outside of their house. I wondered how Malisa could be so cold, and how Rehmat could be so controlling.

After several weeks, much to my surprise and relief, Malisa showed up at the bank, profusely apologizing. "You are not the first close friendship my husband *made me* end."

"Made you?" is all I could utter. By then I was angry with both: Rehmat for being so controlling of such an intelligent woman and Malisa for being so submissive.

After that encounter, she mysteriously disappeared again for several months!

One Saturday morning, Malisa caught me by surprise when she dropped in unannounced at my home. She was dressed in a black leather miniskirt, fishnet stockings, and a plunging neckline that displayed her ample bosom. Even Sophia Loren might have felt a twinge of envy.

"I just wanted to tell you we've sold the house and we are leaving the country for good. Rehmat left yesterday. I'm following with the children tonight."

She said it as casually as if she had just mentioned, "I'm picking up the dry cleaning."

I was once again dumbfounded by this bizarre woman. I still invited her in. She had barely crossed the threshold. "I can't stay, Zohra. I've only come to say goodbye."

I was struggling with what to say, all I could utter was "Oh really?"

I turned to see Mujeeb. He took a rather a long look at her. Then in a flash she was gone.

In a jumble of nerves and confusion, I began to chatter away and asked Mujeeb, "Did you see how she was dressed? Who dresses like that for a long flight with two small children? Don't you think she kind of looked like a …hooker?"

"She's just very modern that's all. I didn't see anything wrong with it," he insisted.

"Okay, next time I fly across the globe I'll dress like that, darling. Then I'll see if you find anything wrong with it." He smiled and lovingly forwarded his hand to hold mine.

"Ah! My dear Shady, if you would dress like that for me tonight, I'd love it."

I wasn't in the mood for a joke. The reality was that this time Malisa had left for good.

As I stepped up to secure the lock, I noticed a small paper bag perched on the hall table by the front door. As I opened the package, I said, "Oh my God, these are the black jade earrings I had swooned over. But Malisa had said she could *never* part with them because they carried such *sentimental value* for her!" I took a deep sigh.

Clouds of emotion blurred my eyes. Mujeeb offered me the tissue box and a warm hug.

......

Getting to know people closely was adding to my *Library of Friends*. As I said, some relationships were short stories, others were novels. I considered Malisa to be a mystery novel." Moreover, the bank rewarded me for the sizeable investment she brought.

The new owners of Malisa's house were a lovely Hungarian couple. Next-door neighbors were a Portuguese family. By now I was woven into the fabric of the celebrated Canadian multicultural mosaic. The *duality* of living in two drastically different cultures was a reality I wanted to embrace and relish.

Yet the need to be with blood relatives sometimes struck like **hunger pangs**. Annual stopovers in Dubai and Abu Dhabi to meet Sikandar and family had now become routine.

The United Arab Emirates

20 Our initial trips to UAE were not hassle free. But by now my brother Sikandar, a gold medalist from the State Bank of Pakistan, was a senior executive in BCCI Bank in Abu Dhabi. At Dubai airport he had arranged VIP Gold service for us. In the arrivals lounge, petite Filipino girls in yellow-and-red uniforms held up signs with our names inscribed upon them. They also assisted us in breezing through various landing formalities. Fatigue vanished at the sight of dear Durdana and Sikandar's gleaming smiles.

Over the years we witnessed Abu Dhabi, one of the seven states of the United Arab Emirates, miraculously transform from a dessert into a perpetually blooming garden. Sikandar enlightened us',

"The Sheikh of Abu Dhabi has spent millions, even the topsoil has been transported by air from Europe." *Where there's a will, there are Dirhams to be spent.*

During the one-hour drive to Abu Dhabi, I was informed that apart from lunch and dinner invitations, I'm booked to give an interview at Radio Abu Dhabi."

"Interview, why? I'm here for quality time with you." My excuses didn't work, so I consented.

Lunches and Dinner parties were followed by jokes and or music. A most memorable gathering was at their closest friend Rukhsana Humayun's place. Sikandar and I worked ourselves into an enthused frenzy reliving the old memories of our favourite songs. Everyone thoroughly enjoyed our performance and commented, "We have never seen such a loving bond between a brother and sister."

On the day of the interview, on our way to the radio station, I felt nervous. In fact, the credit goes to the two polished hosts, Waheed and Lubna, who put me in a relaxed and upbeat mood right away. However, I still asked them, "Who are your main audience?"

"It's the South Asian community living in the Middle East, contemplating migration to Canada. They are curious if it's worth leaving the tax-free *Dirhams* they earn in the UAE. Canada has the reputation of being a progressive and peace-loving country." I took delight in it, as if I had something to do with it. I enjoyed relating my spicy stories about adjusting to Canadian culture.

"But, *Shadan*, I mean Zohra: our audiences are also waiting for a song from you."

"Oh no, I'm not a singer, please don't pull this trick on me."

"Just sing Geeta Dutt's song *Sundar Sapna.*" That's when I realized they had been tipped off by Sikandar. Behold! Such is the power of persuasion that ... there I was…on Radio Abu Dhabi, singing away as if I really could? However, with their sophisticated accompanying sound system, I didn't sound half bad.

That evening we visited a well-manicured Cornish park enjoying the sea breeze, peachy-pink sky as the sunset reflected upon the ripples of warm water of the Persian Gulf. Sikandar suddenly got up, opened all four doors of his parked car, and turned on the radio full blast. My interview was being broadcast! "Oh no, even I can tell where I went off tune." In any case, nobody expected a professional performance. At the end they gifted me the tape recording of it.

Despite our hectic schedule, we managed shopping sprees in those glittering, seductive lanes of the traditional *Souks* (Arabic for marketplaces) situated in narrow streets, abuzz with local salesmen, hawking items ranging from the most exquisite Persian rugs and exotic perfumes to just about anything our minds could conjure up. One souk bedazzled me with gold jewelry of many different designs. South Asian women flocking there, gold being their traditional weakness!

Seven colors of sand, encased in glass, fascinated me; Sikandar gifted it to me. These represented the various shades of sand, perhaps reflecting the differing personalities of the seven states, comprising the United Arab Emirates today. The locals would describe the Emirates though united, as seven offshoots of a tree, or rather seven sons from the same father. It made me think of my father, one of seven siblings, how different they all are. Sharjah, the less affluent more religious brother, Abu Dhabi, the established successful one, Dubai being the flamboyant, relatively wild one, the family is perpetually attempting to tame! Tilting my gift sideways was fascinating, how the multi-colored sand was forming the dunes of different shapes each time.

Memories of seven days, preserved in seven colors of sand!

......

Reaching Karachi...

At the airport, we were greeted by a battalion of family from both sides. Mujeeb's brothers competed as to whose place we would go to first. My sister Nigma always conceded, volunteering to take second place. Visiting them all was hectic yet extremely pleasurable.

My three sisters-in-law, being older than my mom, my natural inclinations were to become friends with their children, two of whom were even older than me. Upon arrival, I'd learn they had preplanned *Rathjagas* (all nighters). Sabeeha was a Chemistry teacher, Fawzia a Clinical Psychologist, Fareeda a lawyer and Naila a medical doctor. In such qualified company, we never ran out of topics. Fareeda shared mind-blowing legal cases she encountered. From Fawzia, I learned about the most concerning psychological issues prevalent in Pakistan.

Eager to share their intimate stories and also listen to the 'richly animated versions' of my own experiences, they gravitated toward me. That often triggered additional adrenalin! I blended in mightily well. Once I asked them, "What is your most enjoyable activity?"

"The highlight of our year is ... the week you stay over." Of course I felt elated.

Nigma was often "shortchanged," but never complained. She would go out of her way to make fancy dishes, get new *shalwaar kameez* stitched from fabrics gifted to me by many. I called her Mother Teresa for her giving nature. My nephews and nieces insisted upon Nigma and I to sing our favorite song from our teenage days. With fascination, they listened as we synchronized our identical voices: *"Nain so nain naheeN milao,"* (don't gaze at me directly) our song was captured in Mujeeb's camcorder.

We also stayed with my third sibling Rubeena when *Mazhar* was on wheelchair. She remained his tireless care provider. Yet their hospitality was unsurpassed. One day Chinese, the next day Italian cuisine, then exotic Pakistani dishes, I'd say, "The way you are spoiling me, I'd have a hard time adjusting back in Canada." I dedicated to her my poem *"Twin Emotions."*

Tanveer was like my older sister; sleepover at her place was mandatory. As a Radiologist she pioneered Ultrasound in Karachi, while her husband Dr. Khalid and I shared a common passion for poetry. Born in Burma he authored his memoir "Where the Irrawaddy flows".

They always arranged a potluck dinner with all my sibling/cousins from Rawalpindi. Reminiscing about our childhood, we lost track of time, wondering when the last years of our fleeting youth had rushed by, especially when steeped in discussion with Nasir, Khalid, Yasmeen, Nazo, and Paro. Having grown up together like siblings, we had a blast. Nasir made hilarious jokes about the funny nicknames used in our poor neighborhood, and the blatant four-letter words they uttered, strictly prohibited in our own homes! How they lined up as we emerged from our house: a parade of stunned, gawking spectators, eager for a spectacle, emerging from their abodes as if on command, whenever we went out dressed formally.

That narrow brick alley back then could be likened to a community catwalk.

The only way we could reciprocate dozens of dinners, was by inviting the whole clan together. Just like a wedding, outdoor tents, chairs with fancy covers, fresh flowers and a full-service barbeque was set up at a day's notice. Such enriching experiences, condensed into a few memorable weeks!

Let's Go Shopping in Karachi...

Most Pakistani women have an obsession for clothes, mine seems relatively moderate. Our men were content with casual menswear or a suit, whereas women made annual trips back home to import the trendy Eastern party wear to grace frequent gatherings in Canada*. Repeating an outfit previously worn was like a societal taboo; hence, a wardrobe of a wide variety was *Vanity's Necessity.*

At a Canadian conversion rate, everything sold in Pak Rupees seemed unbelievably inexpensive. Sometimes I'd burst with excitement, "Oh my God that's so cheap!" My shopping chaperones hushed me. "Don't be so loud, they'll figure out that you are from abroad."

Salespersons (always males) extended us warm welcomes. Switching on their brightest lights to bedazzle the customers and showcase unlimited oceans of flowing fabrics, ready-made *shalwaar kameez, sarees, lehengas, and chooridar pyjamas.* They would immediately order tea or cold drinks for us, as their revered customers—a great sales technique, and one which we fell for every time! A vivid memory of these trips is one of shoe shopping with my niece Afsheen, a soft spoken pretty girl ever-ready to spread love.

Rainfall of Shoes (Karachi)

Amidst the noise of rattling taxis beeping horns, motor rickshaws, I wasn't sure if we would find a parking spot at Tariq Road. Posh cars parked on the angle, each guarded by its chauffeur. Carefree, ultra-mod women emerged, weaving their way between obstacles, both moving and stationary, they headed to the stores. The majority of them having no head coverings, or just a stole casually draped across their shoulders. (Now many wear head scarves).

"*Baji* (older sister) I have hair clips, buttons, kamarband, children's toys from China, French crockery, English cutlery—anything and everything."

Amongst that shoulder-to-shoulder swarming sea of humanity, so unlike Canada, I felt overwhelmed. We went through a veranda like lane, behind which were a row of fancy shoe shops. We entered **Modila**, one of many such stores on Tariq Road (in contrast with fancy Malls).

"Why such a mad rush, is there a special sale on?" I asked.

"No, it's always like this," Afsheen replied.

Several young salesmen moved forward, eager to serve and sell to the throngs of potential women and girl customers. They selected from window displays, and men started calling out orders at the speed of lightening:

"Number 2459 brown *aur* 4350 black *mei dedey yaar* Size 7"! They spoke Urdu swiftly but interestingly, only the numbers and colors were detailed in English!

Dozens of white cardboard boxes started falling from the ceiling one after the other. I looked up and it was as if they emerged through an opening in an attic. My eyes following the nonstop movement, I was fascinated by the salesmen's skills in catching the boxes as they rained down, inexplicably into the hands of the correct salesperson each time.

"First time I'm witnessing a 'Rainfall of Shoes'" I said as I stared, hypnotized.

A scrawny teenage salesman, with thick black hair, wearing shirt and pants also hollered with the speed of lightening, "Number 346, 7 in red, 45 black, 320 brown and multi"— this time all was uttered in English!

"Oh my God ... shoes everywhere!" Some big spenders bought eight or even ten pairs?

"Who says this is a poor country?" I exclaimed.

"The rich are too rich, and the poor are too poor, that sums up our story," Afsheen said.

I heard someone holler in Urdu mixed with English, "*Jaldi ker yaar* ... 2232 size 6 black *mei deydey or* fawn color *bhee chalega.*" A captivated salesman ordered for a pretty young lady whose get-up spelled 'rich.'

While serving her he was all smiles, taking his sweet time, especially when tying the straps around her perfectly shaped ankles, pedicure with shiny maroon nail polish. She signaled him to put aside a tower of boxes.

"Please decide quickly or they'll attend to another customer." Afsheen acted as my tour guide, cajoling me to move things along and pick out my favorite designs. Under pressure, I pointed to a few shoes, but remained thoroughly distracted, questioning,

"How many sandals and shoes does a woman really need?"

"One to match every outfit…and she'd like a new outfit for each occasion!"

"And these ladies of leisure have **never** earned a living? I feel sorry for their husbands."

"Well, our husbands get their end of the bargain."

"What do you mean?"

"We *pamper* our men, so once they return from work, they don't have to lift a finger."

She went on, "Not like poor Mujeeb uncle, we heard he even washes dishes sometimes?"

"Yes, but I'm a working woman and don't have servants like you all do."

"But this is how we keep the poor employed." What she said now made sense to me.

By the time we left, I had acquired a half dozen pairs of shoes, but justifying my guilt nevertheless: "It's a whole year's supply and I would've paid three times as much in Canada."

*Here in Canada: Over the years enterprising businessmen and women have opened boutiques filled with Indian and Pakistani traditional clothes, eliminating the need to travel just to replenish one's wardrobe.

……

Arriving Rawalpindi…

My parents and Shahid had been patiently waiting for my arrival.

On the way from the airport, I noticed my home town had suffered neglect. Shops and fancy movie theaters appeared rundown, but the twin city of Islamabad was being well groomed. An American tourist described it well: *"Islamabad is ten minutes away from Pack-is-taan."*

What a pleasant surprise to discover that my parents and Shahid had moved to a newer, more modern locale. Our new Lalazar home was very different from the one I was raised in. However, Ammi lamented, "In richer neighborhoods people are cold, not sincere like the ones we left behind." Abbaji was happy his Rose garden was in full bloom and he also found a companion next door, a retired Colonel from the army.

I woke up to find myself surrounded by my nephews and nieces, little curious cats how they gravitated to me. My youngest sister Arifa Salman and her kids had sleep over. Between them and Huma Shahid's children it was full house. There was much to share, so we usually stayed up late.

One morning, at dawn I was drawn to the kitchen by a loud clinking of dishes. I tiptoed in through the back entrance and found my father elbow deep in dish water.

"Abbaji, what are you doing? With all the women in this house, you're relegated to dishwasher?" I asked with a playful chuckle. When he turned and gave me one of his mischievous smiles; I knew to duck as a spray of water flew from his fingertips.

"You missed! Abbaji, you'd fit in perfectly in my country Canada where husbands help with the household duties." He said with a pretense of disdain, "My country? So . . . even when you're in your own home, this is not *your* country anymore?"

"Oh, you know very well what I mean. I have two feet, Abbaji, I can have one foot in Pakistan and one in Canada, and my body can be a bridge, spanning both continents. It's not a problem for me." As we were beginning this impromptu political debate, I heard voices rising in the next room. I signaled for my father to shush while I crept closer to the dining room.

Ammi and Huma my sister-in-law were panicking, but the more I listened the more amused I became. In Pakistan, Tuesday is a meatless day (introduced in Benazir Bhutto's era in the 1990's). The problem was that the cook called to say he was taking his wife to the hospital and apologized for not having stocked their freezer with meat for the week.

But *meat-free day* was not the contentious issue. The fact that a sophisticated lady of the house, Huma, would dare enter the butcher shop herself was anathema to my mother's cultural sensibilities. Huma had no qualms herself and even I was eager to tag along.

The gradual change in me awakened the desire to know my people at a grass root level. I had this tendency even before I got married. Now that I was becoming a Canadian, feeling like a foreigner, there was a greater urge to interact and learn about our marginalized majority. So I liked the idea of visiting the local butcher shop as a native Pakistani.

The Bucher Drama

En route to the butcher shop, we stopped to say hello to folks we met along the way. I admit that I was beginning to feel more and more conspicuous on each visit to Pakistan; but I was sure that my identity as a foreigner was attributed to my ever-present camera.

It was an opportunity for us to enjoy morning walk and catch up on family gossip. As we passed a variety of shops along the way, I paused to read the signs and snap more pictures. I was amused that the shopkeepers probably felt they were upgrading their images by describing their services in English. The writing was in Urdu script, but the words were in English:

Tajjammul's Beauty Salon; Zulfiqar Tailor Master; Mustafa's Fine Fabrics and finally...**Fakhruddin Butt the Butcher.** It was evident that the British had left a lasting impression on Pakistan whether we liked it or not.

Something compelled me to bring my camera to my eye as we entered the butcher shop.

Before we crossed the threshold, the racket created by the bevy of chickens that called this space home would surely have identified it as the butcher shop, without the fancy signage.

To my left was a poultry condominium; five floors of chicken cages, fully occupied. To my right was a contented-looking goat that I hoped was a pet rather than dinner, since around its neck it wore a lovely gold-colored bell that hung from a pink satin ribbon. But the most picture-perfect image was displayed directly in front of me. There, poised yoga fashion in the middle of a two-foot high and ten-foot-long counter, was seated the king of butchers.

"*Ander ayyeh Baji* (come in sister)," the young muscular, raven-haired, Sylvester Stallone of butchers shouted.

"Thank you, sir," I replied. "You have a most interesting shop here . . . Um . . . Are you Fakhruddin Butt?" I controlled my chuckle. His face melted into a gleaming white Chiclets smile. "*No, Baji*. That would be my grandfather. My name is Shafique."

"Well, it's a pleasure to meet you, Shafique." I wanted this to be a most agreeable experience, once in a lifetime.

Huma placed her order. "Lamb chops for *pulao*, goat meat for *curry*, and skinless chicken pieces for *Qorma*." The butcher nodded his head, and I pulled my sister-in-law out of the way, so I could snap a photo before his smile diminished. The image of him seated like a king on his throne was one I had to capture. It was a strange paradox that such a handsome man in the Bollywood-esque manner would spend his days sculpting and carving works of art from raw meat.

He was as precise and deliberate in his preparation of the meat for carving, as a heart surgeon in 'pre-op'. His instruments were well maintained and lined up beside him in finite order from the teeniest to machete-sized, sparkling clean and razor sharp.

I stood in wonderment as the butcher carefully chose a carving knife, situated the handle between the toes of his right foot in a perpendicular position with the blade facing me and the back pressed against his apron. He then took a large fillet of lamb and proceeded to pull the meat toward him, thus separating it into two perfectly equal-sized pieces. He repeated the action over and over, cutting the meat into smaller and smaller pieces.

He then moved on to the chicken. I stayed behind the lens, not prepared to miss a shot. He began to chop the skinless bird into multiple parts when suddenly blood began to gush forth. I knew the chicken hadn't shed a drop because *halal meat* is drained of all blood and washed; so, I concluded it was the butcher's blood that was spurting all over.

I was already feeling light-headed, although my sick feeling was probably influenced more by my overwhelming sense of guilt—that it might have been the clicking of my camera which distracted him. I could replace a carving knife ...but fingers? "I am so sorry, should we take you to a doctor?"

He puffed his chest up to its full capacity, flashed another broad smile, and winked.

"*Baji*, I have my own first aid kit, it's free and it's the most natural treatment there is. You'll see." With that, he picked up the skinned goat leg (which had been destined to be bubbling in our curry pot later) and he deftly removed the fatty white membrane that encased it.

He sucked the blood from his wound (one finger only) and quickly bandaged it with the paper-thin goat skin. "The doctor would've charged me twenty rupees for nothing."

He then commenced to finish butchering the meat for us. By then our appetite for goat meat had abated. "Shafique, we'll just take the lamb for today, if you don't mind. Our cook will return for the rest of the order tomorrow."

When we walked in with only one packet of lamb, *Ammi* asked, "Where is the rest of the order?" Huma jumped in to explain, "The butcher was so busy we brought enough for tonight."

Abbaji entered in his jovial mood and announced, "Shadan, your mother and I wanted to do something special for you before you return to Canada, so we thought we would all go out to a fancy restaurant for a special meal tonight."

"Oh great! So where are we going?" I must admit, I was really looking forward to going out for an authentic first-class, Pakistani dinner of mutton *qorma, biryani,* and *seekh kebab.*

He looked over at my mother who was bursting with excitement and said, "How about a Restaurant with America's finest hamburgers?" I made a face.

I said, "I've experienced the Chinese cuisine around the world and it is at its best in Pakistan." They settled for my choice. "Chinese waiters speaking fluent Urdu seems to add to the flavor."

Ammi just stayed for late-night talent shows then retired. But we stayed up to play our father's favorite songs just for the pleasure of his radiant smiles.

"*Ulfat ki nayee manzil ko chalaa*" (Let's fall in love again—a classic)

Decades later, a renowned vocalist and a dear friend Azalea Ray took me by an astounding surprise! In the middle of a fusion concert at harbor front, to capacity audience, she cast her magic spell and rendered this song as a 'tribute' to my father! What a gesture, my emotional surge was bound to invoke tears of joy.

On our way back to Canada, if unable to spare a few days in London, we converged at Heathrow Airport. My best friend Sadiqa and my cousins Khalid and Rana joined us for tea and refreshments. Amidst the noisy hustle and bustle of one of the busiest airports in the world, we exchanged fun-filled memories of our childhood—at the top of our voices.

....

BACK TO THE FAST LANE

21 It was like waking up from a sweet dream, wishing that it had continued. After a vacation when you don't have to lift a finger, it's so hard to get back to the routine of a full-time job and household chores. However, realizing that over here the water flows with full force, no routine power cuts either, once again life's amenities in Canada seemed a bigger blessing.

What lengths we women of the East must go through to adjust ourselves to our new environment and to help our better halves (or *bitter halves*) adapt as well. They had accepted their wives' double shift lifestyle as it brought second income. But the idea of their wives attending work-related social events wasn't always welcomed. Here's my experience from a Christmas party.

Strip Loins

Despite all the convincing and pampering of my hubby, I was still feeling guilty about leaving the poor fellow home alone while I went out for a swanky dinner with my colleagues. I usually declined their invitations, but that night was an exception. It was my office Christmas party. He wasn't too happy to be left alone so he called out from the family room, "Immigration to Canada isn't cost free," I replied, "Everything has a price, darling."

I marinated the strips of sirloin with vinegar, black pepper, and garlic because he liked his steak spicy. I also added a large dash of sincerity and a heap of affection.

Despite running late, I took no shortcuts. He liked sautéed mushrooms and sweet peppers, so I sautéed. He was partial to having his gravy on the side, so on the side it was to be. And he preferred that the table be pre-set, so I followed the drill: plate, cutlery, napkin, and drinking glass . . . and I even floated a rose in a vase to adorn the table.

"Bye, darling, I'll try not to be too late."

"Yeah, bye," he muttered.

As I drove off in my compact Chevrolet, I felt a wonderful sense of freedom. I could point my car in any direction I chose to go. I was the last to arrive at the fancy restaurant my colleagues had reserved for this Christmas gathering. They had wasted no time in overindulging on expensive booze while I, on the other hand, was content to sip pure ginger ale.

By the time the meals were served, I was the only one excited to see my delectable fish filet arrive. Everyone else was sloshed, the conversation had grossly deteriorated, and the talk had turned to Peter—the young extraordinarily handsome and sexy part-time teller in my branch. He was a teller by day and, I was shocked to discover, a male stripper by night.

Darlene panted, "I've been dying to see his hot naked body."

My colleagues opted to forfeit dinner and drive to Peter's Bar to see him strip.

In a staff of seventeen, where the women were in the majority, there was only one 'No' vote. Their decision was to get blind-drunk and embarrass their colleague at his questionable workplace. I decided to go home early and surprise Mujeeb.

A reel of reflections began rolling in my mind, focusing upon this strange world of ours where some women choose to cover themselves from head to toe, while others choose to expose it all. In any case, many of my female colleagues were scantily dressed.

I was taught to 'follow the middle path.' So in Canada I tolerated those who drank or told dirty jokes, I accepted LGBTQ, and I tried to keep an open mind on many other elements of Western culture strange to me. But when it came to strippers, my colleagues were well aware that no one could talk me into participating in that *flash of flesh* adventure.

A few Indo-Pakistani girls I met had been lured into watching male strippers, and while a couple of them were thrilled by the sight, others were a little traumatized over the experience. And now, my colleagues were anxious to launch me into that seedy world. I found drinking and drooling over a naked colleague, plain vulgar. I heard them whisper, "There's no way you'll get her to come with us." "Of course, we will." "Wanna bet?" "We've got her cornered tonight."

The caravan of vehicles was ready to proceed. "Go ahead, you guys, I'll follow," I coolly suggested. "Oh no, Miss Smarty-pants, you aren't following US, we're following YOU!"

They seemed to take delight in their plan to entrap me, with a few cars ahead of me, and the rest to trail behind me. Realizing there was no way out, I tried rationalizing it somehow.

We kept driving along the unlit and unfamiliar roads. I had no idea where we were going, but I sensed it was north. I regretted ever attending this Christmas dinner. It would have been so nice to stay home, have a candlelight dinner with my husband, and share that delectable, juicy sirloin. But now, I was at the mercy of a group of drunkards.

The cars ahead of me went through an amber traffic light but it turned red, so I had to stop. I could see just past the intersection that the other cars had pulled over to wait. Their taillights and signals were flickering red . . . danger!

Suddenly I spotted a road sign: Hurontario Street, with an arrow pointing to the right. *'Oh my God, Hurontario runs close to my home'* I thought. As the light switched to green, I accelerated, and took a right turn. I entered the house singing. "Hi, darling, I'm baaack."

I knew Mujeeb would be excited to see me back early.

"But ... eh ... but ..." He seemed at a momentary loss for words.

"But what" I queried.

"The steak," he murmured as he pointed to the kitchen.

"What about the steak?" I asked. He mumbled, "There is only one."

"Oh, don't worry, darling, go ahead and enjoy it. I'm full up with fish, and believe me *strip loins* hold absolutely no appeal for me tonight."

Later on, Mujeeb admitted that he had plans to watch an adult movie he would never get to see if I was home. So it turned out that while I avoided partaking in some questionable 'strip loins' myself, I happily prevented my hubby from enjoying a double dose of his own.

. . . . . .

The following year I got transferred to a branch in the west end of Toronto. The new environment brought new experiences. I often worked overtime and was usually the last person to leave the depressing parking lot. Here's an anecdote about the immigrant fraternity, how we identify with, and feel compassion, for each other.

The Immigrant Connection

The dark underground parking lot of the rundown building remained dead silent between the hours of nine to five, except of course, for the odd vehicle racing out, creating a thunderous noise. How boring was the job of that parking attendant, snoozing inside the suffocating, prisonlike cubicle all day long. If he didn't wake up by himself, a driver would lean on his horn, pay him the money, and then hurriedly accelerate away, on the fast track toward his or her fast life.

After five, the place became alive again when the fatigued employees from that office building hurriedly raced out, one after the other, to merge into the outside traffic. No one had the time to say two words to the parking attendant. I felt sorry for the poor guy.

One afternoon, I observed that the driver in front of me showed his middle finger to the attendant then tore out of the darkness into the street. At times like these, I recalled my mom's lesson: '*Dil badsat aavar ki hajj-e-akbar-ast*' (Pleasing people's hearts is the greatest pilgrimage).

I felt the urge to say a few comforting words to the victim in his prison.

"How was your day?" I asked as I approached his booth.

The attendant looked up, surprised that someone was talking to him. "Okay, I suppose." His voice was sullen.

"Just okay," I asked sympathetically.

"Time seems to be at a standstill in here."

"Don't you keep something to read or play music to keep you amused?"

"I can listen to music only so much. The fact is that this job isn't what I came to Canada for." He started to share his story with me, it perked up my curiosity.

Since there was no car behind me, we chatted a little more. As it turned out, Fernando Oliveiro, a slightly built gentleman in his forties, was a successful lawyer back in the Philippines with a well-established practice of his own. Here in Canada his degree was about as useful as trash. I comforted him by saying that he wasn't alone in his struggle as an immigrant. I learned that Fernando was married with three little children, and that his wife Josie was a qualified accountant presently at home out of necessity. Back home, her family could have been providing care for her children while she went to work.

From that day on, it became a daily routine that unless there was a car behind me, I would stop at the booth and chat with him for a few minutes. Careless as I was, sometimes my monthly parking pass would expire; other times, I simply forgot to put it in the bag while changing purses.

One afternoon I was frantically looking for my pass as I was next in line. I took out $2.00 cash instead. To my surprise Fernando just opened the gate with a polite smile and signaled me to go. It was a gracious favor once, but just as our two-minute chats had now become an expectation his automatic gesture to open the gate as I approached also became a routine. Fernando said, "I know you have the pass; I don't need to see it."

As for our chats though, there were times when even I couldn't spare those two minutes of my precious time. One day, I hurriedly accelerated out of the parking lot and merged into the traffic. I felt guilty leaving his wondering face behind, as if his disappointed eyes were still following me. Ammi's mantra entrenched within my inner conscience, I spontaneously decided to go back, even though taking a U-turn was somewhat risky; I almost hit an oncoming car.

"I'm sorry to have rushed off like that, Fernando," I said.

"All morning I was waiting to share my good news with you, Sora (Zohra)." In his sparkling eyes I could see how happy he was to see me back.

"So tell me, what's the good news you were so eager to share?"

He delightfully shared, "I've passed my night course, and I'm getting a job as a paralegal in a law firm."

"Congratulations, Fernando! You deserve it. I'm happy for you, but I'll miss you very much." He assured me, "I'll miss you too. After I settle down, I'll come to see how you're doing." I was truly excited for Fernando. However junior a position, at least he would be working in his own field.

The next afternoon, after work as I got in the car and switched on the ignition, I suddenly remembered: Fernando is no longer there. In a hurry, I scrounged through my purse—no parking pass! I searched my coat pockets in vain. The new parking attendant would make me go back for cash, and so he should. I finally managed to collect $1.90, not quite the required two dollars. I figured I'd owe him a dime and beg his mercy.

Before I made it to the barrier, I saw a frail young Asian male hanging more than halfway out of the attendant's booth. One more inch and he would have somersaulted onto the pavement, or onto my hood. As I approached, he eagerly asked, "Are you, Sora?"

"Yes, I am." How did he know my name? I was surprised.

He immediately pulled himself back into the booth with a sense of 'mission accomplished.' Bright-eyed and with a wide smile, he swiftly opened the exit ramp for me. Obviously, he had been tipped.

He too was a young Filipino who had apparently taken over not only the job of parking attendant but also the unique responsibility of his predecessor—to take care of me! I insisted he accept the $1.90

and I would pay him the missing dime later; but he determinedly said, "Ms. Sora, I was told never to check your pass or take any money from you, ever." On my way out I drove home in a somber mood, wondering about the inside story of this young man's struggle. Was he yet another educated, overlooked immigrant?

The overall atmosphere in that Toronto branch was different than Mississauga. Client base was very different so new and unique experiences were added to the journal of my life.

......

Therapeutic Banking...

Stressed-out couples with over-extended credits, on the verge of marital breakdowns also approached us for help. I approved second mortgages to clear their debts and cut up the credit cards. But it was easy to slip from credit counseling into personal and emotional counseling—somehow they were interconnected. Subsequently, sometimes our clients extended me lunch invitations.

Even my female colleagues shared their personal stories of broken hearts from recent romances or break-ups. It gave me a glimpse into the western women's struggles to find a life partner. On Friday nights, they went for ladies' nights out, for a few drinks and to get their fatigue and frustrations out. But I'd rush home to get ready, usually for dinner gatherings and enter the Orient. Farewell English language, welcome Urdu/Hindi instead. *My colleagues' social lives were drastically different from mine.* They made jokes:

"Your life is one big party you come to work only to take a break."

How do women in western culture find their soul mates? I became intensely curious about their relationship dilemmas. Consequently, I accepted the odd invitation, but one turned out to be a Psychic party. All of them were single, how the mysterious-looking Psychic

Woman attempted to resolve their relationship issues, and instantly transformed their moods! Eastern women didn't have to search for soul mates (others helped them) but they had their own peculiar problems. I concluded that the grass isn't all that green on either side!

My intense curiosity and probing was perhaps leading me to something ... but what?

Incidentally, banks and the bankers are not popular, so whenever customers saw me in the mall wearing the WMB badge, they commented, "Please take it off, because it doesn't suit your personality." One client referred other customers to me and introduced me by saying, "She is a banker with a heart, and that's why we call her a *Therapeutic Banker.*" Some of them requested to meet me after work, and I felt compassion when they poured their hearts out to me. A Polish Dentist on my portfolio, making over half a million, stormed into my office one day--in tears! "My husband has swindled me, destroyed my marriage, my finances, and . . . and . . . betrayed my trust forever." A seemingly independent strong woman was crying like a child. I counseled her over lunches.

"So while you were busy pulling your patient's teeth, he was pulling dirty tricks on you." I wrote her story and many others in my journals. It never occurred to me that someday these real life stories may emerge in my literary endeavors.

Once I got engrossed in trying to resolve other people's issues, mine seemed much easier to deal with. As a teenager it had been my dream to become a psychiatrist. As though my *latent* desire was now coming to fruition in a strange way. I became a self-appointed Amateur Therapist. *Counseling added an interesting dimension to my banking life.*

A precondition for portfolio managers was to take a Chartered Financial Planning accreditation. Like my Mutual Funds Course, it was also sponsored by the Bank.

In the sales industry, the more you achieve, the more is expected of you.

My portfolio comprised of 250 upscale clients. Once I studied the demographics of the Bloor and Dufferin area, I realized it was a gold mine—most clients lacking language proficiency were from European countries: Portuguese, Polish, Italian, and Greek. Not every banker would have the patience to explain to them concepts such as *dollar cost averaging.*

English being my second language, I had more patience to better understand them. Especially since I provided them financial services in the comfort of their own offices, my clients loved to be *spoon-fed.* Once again, luck had brought me to the right place at the right time.

Surprise of a Lifetime

After a one-week vacation in Flint Michigan with my niece Dr. Lubna, I felt re-energized. A telephone message from my branch surprised me.

"Will you be coming to work tomorrow?" as if they were not expecting me.

When I entered, I noticed our branch had a face-lift, appropriate signage displayed, pamphlets filled in every slot of the kiosk. The Vice President arrived; camera crew was present.

"We are here to celebrate your branch's outstanding success." After providing us with national sales statistics he said, "However, one staff member has outperformed everyone across Canada. So ... here is the key to ..." he put his hand in his pocket. Everyone waited in suspense, as the cameras were pointed toward him while I stood beside him. "Here is the key to a ....," he paused again then announced: "A GM sports car for... Zohra Zoberi, winner of The Top National Sales Award as number one in all of Canada." I was dumbfounded first then started stuttering. "What, me ... a sports car?"

I looked around at our staff in disbelief. "How did you all keep this such a secret?"

"We wanted it to be a complete surprise." My eyes blinked faster than the hummingbird flutters its wings. Everyone started hugging and congratulating me. I was then escorted to a nearby Dealership, like a dream it was surreal. Without a second thought I chose red color.

Then I was taken for a trial run in my red convertible around Lakeshore Road, Parkdale area. My colleague Mary Lourenco and I celebrated over a lunch. "Salesmanship seems to be in your blood, isn't it?" I then shared my father's stellar success in sales...out of desperation.

"Abbaji was once persuaded to resign from his twenty-five years of service with the Government, cashed out his pension funds and invested in business. Naively he put hundred percent trust in the two salesmen he hired, who swindled him off his entire investment within two months! Having a family of six children, he resorted to insurance sales at EFU (Eastern Federal Union), soon to become the number one salesperson in the entire Rawalpindi Division. His motivation had its roots in 'desperation,' but what about mine?"

"Well, you seem to enjoy it," Mary replied.

I took great pride and delight in becoming truly my father's daughter.

With those memory surges, I was bound to feel the urge to cross the oceans once again. Mujeeb wasn't in the mood so I travelled alone.

....

A Confidante in the Air

22 On board a British Airways in an all-night flight from Toronto to London, I found myself surrounded by fatigued moms with screaming babies. Fortunately, at my request the staff upgraded me to business class. I slid in next to an exceptionally large gentleman who appeared to be quite flustered. The poor guy could have utilized an extra seat during this eight-hour journey but ... I wondered if this happened for a reason?

I introduced myself, he responded, and the conversation began. I soon shared the fact that I couldn't sleep on a plane. "Likewise," he replied. I noticed he was holding something in a tight fist, but I didn't ask, although I was curious. I did discover that my new seatmate Paul Anderson was a Therapist and a Family Counselor who lived in Brantford, one of Toronto's suburbs ... and was ironically now heading to London to deal with his own family crisis. His eighteen-year-old daughter Amanda had just suffered a nervous breakdown and was in a hospital. He was apprehensive and had been imagining the worst. To console him, I shared my innermost secret that my mother had experienced a major breakdown and I had to deal with it, at age twelve.

After relating in detail the story of his ugly divorce and its emotional impact on their daughter, he became curious to learn about my situation. I willingly shared the traumatic experience I had been withholding for so many years.

"My beautiful mother was always the life of a party with her songs, poetry, funny jokes, and impersonations but… there came a time when she started singing louder, laughing harder, and crying irrationally. She started dyeing old outfits for *__Basant Season__ and got so obsessed with it, even my school uniforms were not spared despite my protests. It was clearly her abnormal behavior."

"What is Basant season?" Paul was curious so I replied, "Basant is spring season when Pakistanis celebrate Kite Flying Festival with great pomp and show,"

"Sorry I got side-tracked. So what did your family do about her condition?" Paul asked.

"Well, no one said anything, at least not in front of us children, but her angry bouts and manic moods began to last longer and longer, as did her endless poetry recitals."

"What happened then?" Paul was encouraging me to speak.

"Then one day she suddenly disappeared from the house!"

"How tragic, I am so sorry."

"There was no police report, no 911 call," strangely I carried on sharing what I had held back for so long! "In a panic people rushed out to look for her. I didn't know what to do, how to react, who to turn to as my heart pinched with grief and fear. After a few hours, thank God *Ammi* was found at my cousin Salma's place, about a mile away.

"It was late at night, and we had already been tucked into our *lihaafs* (comforters) when my uncle came to speak to my father. Hearing him utter the words 'nervous breakdown,' I was petrified. I plugged my ears, gravitating between wanting to, and not wanting to hear. At first I pretended I was asleep then I started sobbing under the comforter."

"Did you ever come to understand the root of her problem?"

"They said her initial depression resulted from the trauma of the India-Pakistan Partition in 1947, but this complete breakdown happened twelve years later, after the birth of my sibling. They diagnosed it as 'post-partum depression,' I think."

How bizarre is it that you meet a total stranger and end up sharing intimate secrets you've been holding back for years! My mom's past illness had been such a 'hush, hush' mystery all those years. After I got married, I had tried to share the heartache with my husband, but he too avoided the subject completely. Now it felt as though someone released the seal on a pressure cooker. **A God-sent-by-air Therapist!** One who was also in need of comforting … and who wanted to hear more, "Go on."

"My mother was the youngest and most beautiful pampered daughter of a brilliant and rich father—a Magistrate who was awarded a title by the ruling British Government as: *'Nawaab Khan Bahaadur Mohd Saleh Khan.'* Nawaab means Lord. Before the partition, he had experienced a sudden stroke which paralyzed him from the neck down, but his brilliant memory remained intact for the remaining decade of his life.

"When his daughters and their husbands had to flee for 'Freedom' leaving everything behind, sadly that included my young uncle and my grandmother. During this mass exodus from both sides, trains were looted, homes were burned, and shops were raided. Girls were kidnapped and raped. Women's breasts were cut off, thrown into bags, and discarded! Apparently, there were almost one million casualties during this historical tragedy. The result was a divided India and a free country called Pakistan!"

"Do you think the price in human suffering was worth it?"

"Ask my mother. Birth of her first child—me—followed by the trauma of alienation from her parents must have been too much to handle. She was after all just a teenager, around the same age as your daughter."

"Prior to the Partition, she had lost her brother, a victim of a premeditated murder. He had been pushed into the river with his boots and specs still on,"

Whether it was a result of those traumatic experiences or just post-partum depression, her illness was a taboo subject. I had no idea how long her first bout of depression had lasted before she completely recovered. For me it was a first experience and a very painful one."

"So did they get her back from her cousin's place?"

"She came back, but her songs got louder by the day. She would stay awake all night long, reciting poems from '*Shahnama-e-islam*' (Religious poems by Hafeez Jalindhree). My siblings didn't say anything, they just looked terrified."

As difficult as it was, for the first time I had openly spoken about the suppressed taboo subject. "Go on," Paul encouraged me to speak. After all he was a professional counselor.

I'm sure he never could have imagined he'd end up counseling a stranger 30.000 feet in the air! As he listened, I paused to gain composure, and asked him what he was holding in his fist so tightly.

He opened it, smiled, and said, "A tranquilizer I was about to take just before you sat down next to me. I'm a bit of a nervous flyer." I offered him a bottle of water.

"So why don't you take it?" I asked. "I don't need it now. *I have you.*"

That's when I decided to also share my fear of flying, which surprised him and I had to explain. "It was after my dad's cousin lost his life in a plane crash."

"I'm sorry to hear that." Paul said after a brief pause, "Go on with your story. How old were you at the time your mother got sick?"

"Twelve. Anyway, no one could persuade my mother to go to the Hospital. CMH Military Hospital was the best facility available to my father through his work. So, I had to use all kinds of tactics and come up with a new excuse each time we had to take her for ECT (Electroconvulsive Therapy). My father and I held hands for support, but never uttered a single word about it to each other or anyone else."

Paul asked, "Did she recover?"

"Yes, but full recovery took almost a year. I took time off from school but then eventually life became normal and *Ammi's revived smiles brought the daylight back into our lives again.* From then on, my father treated her like the delicate petal of a flower. It was during this time that *Abbaji* and I built an ever-stronger bond. No one knew that even as a child, I detested the fact that my mom's family blamed him for bringing traumas in her life. The Partition was not his fault."

The plane was descending, we were asked to fasten our seatbelts but Paul continued to listen, and I rushed to finish the rest of the story.

But all of a sudden, we felt the turbulence caused by London's thick clouds.

As the wheels touched down and the roaring engines went into reverse, it was time for me to set my emotions in reverse. Finally, Ammi's case was dealt with!

In the immigration line at Heathrow, I got to see his full height at 6'4"! He was more than a foot taller than me. As we inched forward, he gave me his business card and added, "Promise me when we get back to Toronto, you'll stay in touch."

I pulled Paul Anderson's card out of my purse several times but I never called him.

However, I ended up writing my story *'Humraaz'* (*one who is privy to your secret) in Urdu and decided to use it as a therapeutic approach for my siblings and Abbaji.

One night in Rawalpindi, they all sat around as I read that story. Emotions were powerful, tears plentiful but one of my sisters thanked me later by saying,

"From now on, it'll be easier for us to talk about what had long been bottled up."

Luckily, Ammi has been back to being her jovial self, and she seems to have even accepted the isolation from her brother. As usual my visit came to an end a little too soon.

On my departure, Abbaji's favorite phrase was, "I almost wish you hadn't come."

My standard goodbye was, "You have no idea how I long for my family to visit *me* for a change."

....

IS BLOOD THICKER THAN WATER?

23 "Hello, I'm Mateen, you don't know me I'm your uncle from India, but I am calling from New York and I would like to visit Toronto and meet you. Would you be interested?"

"What a surprise...Mateen *Mamu* (uncle)! Of course I'm interested to meet you."

Throughout my childhood I heard his name fondly mentioned hundreds of times by my mother and her sisters, but to me, Mateen was just a mystery –an imaginary figure. Now, after all these years, I would get to meet this 'celebrity' of whom everyone spoke so highly.

The truth is that I secretly resented him. I mean if he was so good, why didn't he ever write to his sister in Pakistan (my mom), who always shed tears for him?

On the way to pick him up at Buffalo airport, I couldn't keep my thoughts from rushing back in time. I was only five in 1952 when my mother took her three children to meet her parents in India. Apart from the wild monkeys hovering on the rooftop of my grandmother's grand villa 'Kothi Dilkusha' sometimes also called **Chaman** (garden), I didn't remember much else. The only monkeys we saw in Pakistan were the tamed ones that the *Bandar waalas* (monkey owner) occasionally brought around to entertain the children in our neighborhood. But I wondered why in India those annoying little primates were left loose, to hop freely across roads, ride undisturbed on top of buses, and pester pedestrians.

As I drove toward Buffalo, New York, I began to wonder how I'd receive my long-lost uncle. How would we react to each other? Why he was suddenly interested in meeting me? We finally arrived in Buffalo, but at the wrong terminal. I was about to give up when I spotted a tall, regal, well-dressed gentleman standing before me. With one hug, everything instantly changed and it felt like love transfusion—*Blood is thicker than venom too.*

"Do you know that of all my nephews and nieces, you are the only one I have actually been able to visit?" I replied, "Well, do you know that in over the thirty years of my married life, you're the first blood relative who has ever visited me here in Canada?"

When we reached my home, I raced to the phone to call my mother in Rawalpindi, Pakistan. "*Ammi,* I have a surprise for you. I'm going to put you on the phone with someone I know you'll love to speak to." I handed the receiver to Uncle Mateen. Of course, there were no words, only silent tears on both sides. After several minutes of sobbing and sighing, they managed to exchange a few words before they put down the phone with a promise to call again in a few hours. The two siblings hadn't met for decades. The victims of the India-Pakistan Partition; but now they finally heard each others' voices, *after fifty years!* I held a second receiver and got to enjoy the excitement in their voices.

After dinner that evening, I asked Uncle Mateen if he was into music.

"When I have a headache, I don't take an aspirin. I listen to a good *ghazal* instead" was his reply. So, like me, he too had found refuge in old melodies. My spirits danced as I headed for my stereo to select something special for him. With an air of confidence he said,

"But you're from modern times. I listen to the old stuff."

What he didn't expect to find in Canada was a South Asian woman whose prize possession was a revered collection of old Urdu/Hindi songs, the same ones my parents always listened to. I proudly challenged, "*Kanan Devi, Kamla Jharya,* or the legendary *K.L. Sehgal,* you name the singer and I'll play their songs for you." He was completely taken by surprise.

"My favorite song by *Kanan* is—" I finished the sentence for him: "*Dolay hriday kee nayya*

Pug dharat darat hai khewayya"

(The Gist: This restless heart of mine is like a rocking boat, even the oarsman is apprehensive of)

We hummed together, both of us in tune. We each had suffered alienation. In my case, I had to **leave** everyone behind whereas he was **left** behind by everyone.

It would have been wonderful to spend his entire visit conjuring up music from the soul at full volume, but the sound was soon turned down as the pressing urge to share our life stories took precedence. He told me all about his first marriage, the turmoil of his divorce, and then his second marriage. I caught him up on all the family history he had missed. I shared with him my myriad of travel adventures, including my airborne counseling session with a total stranger at an altitude of 30,000 feet. He shared a few tears, so did I. "Now *you* have become my 'Confidante.'"

We laughed, we cried, and we reminisced; but he couldn't get over the fact that I was now a married lady. "Woman of the world, I still remember the time you came to India as a little girl, all dressed up in a pink frock with two ponytails."

The visit continued uninterrupted until three in the morning, when we spontaneously called the airport to cancel his morning flight. We stretched his twenty-four-hour stopover to forty-eight. We talked right through breakfast and lunch. Eventually, however, we had to say goodbye, but not without his firm promise to return as soon as he was able to.

An emotional letter of a few lines from him touched me deeply:

> *"Dear Shadan: I thoroughly enjoyed your asides but underneath that jovial girl, I found a very serious woman."* —Mateen

Of all my relatives, how could he make this assessment in such a short time?

......

Soon He Revisited...

Within a year of that emotional visit, Uncle Mateen returned to Toronto as promised.

This time he stayed for several weeks. I learned a lot about my uncle and his position on the 1947 breakup of our two countries. He had succeeded for years in hiding behind a brittle veneer; but inside, he suffered the same fear, loss, and confusion as did all those affected. Uncle belonged to the Congress Party and was vehemently opposed to the India-Pakistan Partition. Among the many issues he was left to deal with, there was his father who suffered a stroke and was confined to a wheelchair. Uncle said, "My four sisters with their husbands, all my friends everyone simply disappeared."

My circle of friends—Hindus, Christians, Muslims, Sikhs, and other mainstream Canadians warmly received this *Indian* uncle of a *Pakistani* niece and were quickly drawn to his charisma, reputation, and intelligence. But sadly, even an educated man like Mateen had a hazy opinion of Pakistanis that needed to be enlightened.

The president of the Association of Pakistani Professionals and Academics in Toronto, the retired Pakistani Army Colonel Anwar organized a seminar about:

The Nuclear Disarmament between India and Pakistan

Uncle Mateen, who had represented India at the United Nations meetings in the past, was invited as the guest speaker. He concluded his address by stating, "What a unique experience for me to address an all-Pakistani group of individuals in Canada, something I never expected. You people only played with *Phuljharees* (firecrackers) tonight, while I was expecting gunshots." The audience applauded vigorously, and I was filled with pride.

As his stay came to an end, I promised Uncle Mateen that I'd visit him in India at the first opportunity. We made such a heart-to-heart connection I made video tapes of our conversation in which one by one I **'role-played'** each of his sisters, pretending to be *them*, conversing on their behalf in their accents. He also directly addressed my father to acknowledge:

"Hameed Bhai I'm so grateful to you for taking such good care of my sister. Shadan told me what a devoted husband you have been." I listened on... posing as 'Hameed Zuberi'.

In my next visit I played those videos. I was delighted to see how excited they all were to listen to Mamu (uncle) addressing them as though in person! My father made repeated requests to replay *his* portion.

Before Mateen Mamu left, I asked him, "What are your impressions about North Americans?" He paused to think for a few minutes, then smiled and said, "Money minded and sex obsessed."

At that note I shared with him the story of recent *Karate Attacks* introduced by our bank. He was surprised, amused and …?

……

The changing Corporate Culture…

The Steinberg brothers (both Psychiatrists) were much better salesmen than my father or I put together. They made millions by selling their psychologically driven sales program to our Bank, including the *Karate Attacks* they introduced. A colleague defined it as a 'Corporate Cultural Revolution.'

Soon the entire frontline staff from all branches was mandated to take a weeklong sales seminar at an exclusive location in Queen City to learn how to 'cross sell' and 'up-sell' by way of '**If then**' and '**What if**' clues—new jargons were introduced.

However, employees with track records of sales success were slotted in the same category as novices, which was unacceptable to my mind. After winning sales awards year after year, would it not be redundant for me to learn the ABCs of selling?

Appropriately named, those Karate Attacks were intimidating. In the new environment your Area Manager could make a surprise call and ask,

"How much new money do you have in your pipeline for this week, next week, next month and over the three months?" You had to have that information at your fingertips or . . . ?

Those who spoke the new jargon such as '**If then**' clues in front of their managers were favored.

In the meantime, Mujeeb's situation was status quo. I knew of immigrant couples in similar situations, in most cases the wives had left their spouses and moved on. I too was influenced to think along that line but Mujeeb's failure was not his fault… or *was it*?

Kashif once asked me, "Would you rather be in Abu's shoes?" That got me thinking.

Mujeeb was a self-made man who financed his own education, travelled abroad, and completed MSc and PhD while supporting himself. He had published dozens of scientific papers in reputable journals and was still volunteering his time.

How could we … let his passion go to waste?

He had given me a luxury life, taken me to the Wonders of the World. Each time I recalled his loving romantic gestures, my heart melted. Those precious moments are stored in the hard drive of my mind:

I once sat on the steps singing, *"You don't bring me flowers anymore."* Mujeeb was off running some errands. When I came out of the shower, what did I see? On each of the thirteen steps on our circular staircase, there sat small planters with Gerberas resembling sunflowers, in vibrant rainbow of colors: sunny yellow, bright pink, orange, and ruby red—smiling at me in full bloom. Love emotions overwhelmed he repeated, "You are the only woman in my life I have truly loved, who also ***lived*** to love me."

Being sensitive to my hectic schedule at work, he sometimes tried to make dinner. One afternoon he came to pick me up from work. On our way back he asked me, "What are we having for dinner?" His quivering nostrils were a giveaway. I even noted turmeric stains on his white shirt, but I feigned ignorance. "Don't worry darling, I'll just whip up an omelet."

Umh! The smell of that *Aloo gosht* (meat and potato curry) he made was so delectable. Only the previous evening, I had suggested he should consider teaching Urdu once a week (at TL Kennedy School nearby). He had flared up because he took it as an insult.

I concluded that this delicious ready meal was a form of apology, so my heart melted again.

"Zooby, for a South Asian man from your generation, you've come a long way."

"What do you mean 'your' generation?" I swiftly changed the sensitive subject.

Aloo gosht was too delicious to let the usual concerns interfere with my tantalized taste buds. He served it with sizzling hot *Naan*. One affirmation we had agreed upon was:

'Never go to bed angry with each other, even if it means just a kiss on the forehead.'

My thoughts took me back when I first read his diary. How he felt at age five when he witnessed his mothers' burial. 'Why did they take a five-year-old to the cemetery and no one explained anything?' Loss of his father at age sixteen added to his challenge.

After reading that diary was when I vowed my lifelong commitment:

'No matter what, I will always be by his side.'

However, my chain of thoughts always had a dead end: The First Letter—why did he not mail it? What did he hold back and why?

......

The Last Drop...

At WMB I still wanted to meet and exceed my ever-increasing targets. If I didn't, I'd get a call: "What's your success story this month?"

'Successive success sucks you in!' I coined the phrase from my own experience. A colleague of mine Sandra once warned me, "They will squeeze you till the last drop." She physically demonstrated it.

"See this lemon, there's nothing left but ..." she squeezed it harder. When nothing came out, she chucked the lemon and I chuckled.

Miraculously, my 'Internal Flame' remained intact. I readily accepted invitations to serve as Emcee in various concerts, private or public. To introduce the legendary vocalist of the sub-continent Mehndi Hasan was a great honor that delighted me to no end. In those private musicals everyone still considered me to be the life of the party. Friends said, "Somehow, you seem to inspire the artists."

Our social calendar was filled with fun events. My colleagues teased me: "You come to work to take a break." But working overtime year after year caught up to me. I started experiencing panic attacks on the road. Driving to Montreal once, approaching the city during the peak traffic hour, I became paranoid that one of the cars will hit me from behind so I had to take an emergency exit.

Eventually I started having nightmares about work, there was a recurring one:

'I've misplaced a valued client's mortgage file. On the closing date his lawyers are screaming at me. At the same time there's a call, 'What's in your pipeline for new money this month?'

I'd suddenly wake up and rush to the washroom with IBS (irritable bowel syndrome).

Despite family resistance I decided to consult a psychiatrist at a nearby clinic. Dr. Johnson prescribed an antidepressant which was like a swear word in my home—strong opposition began. "Look at yourself— being creative, working hard, looking spiffy, who says you're depressed? Don't even touch that addictive stuff."

One day, I nearly tripped over the edge...in forty-eight hours I did not wink for a second! Mujeeb stayed up to comfort me and I begged him, "Read to me, please read something ... anything." So he did, but I could no longer concentrate. "No, don't read." I got up pacing up and down.

A flash of temporary sanity whispered the irony: 'The person trying to comfort you may also be contributing to your insomnia.' I shuddered with the idea that **His** being depressed is depressing **me?** Yet he sleeps like a log.' The thought even invoked a smile!

Rainbow Epiphany and the Magic Pill...

The next morning, home alone, feeling suffocated I rushed outside for fresh air, and to water our flower-beds. Lately I had taken up gardening and ironically, for once our lawn was greener than our neighbor's—a refreshing thought. The *Impatience flowers* that I planted were bursting with vitality, even though mine was depleting.

While watering the lawn, suddenly I saw a rainbow through the sprinkler. With the movement of my hand, switching from one spray option to another, I could control the pressure of the water. I noticed that from a certain angle, the rainbow would disappear. I turned around and there it was again! So I started experimenting –only to discover that once I had my back to the sun, the rainbow reappeared. That epiphany dawned on me like a 'Message from Divine.'

With that sprinkler I could expand the rainbow, shrink it, and ... it was all in my hands! I mumbled to myself:

'I must take control of my life in my own hands.'

With a sudden surge of energy, I rushed inside the house, grabbed my car keys, and off I drove to the nearest pharmacy to fill the prescription tucked away in my purse for months.

Playing cautious, I settled for half a dose only. For the first few days I felt a strange sensation in my head wondering if hubby was right. But I gave myself two weeks to decide.

Soon, I started sleeping better. I could *digest* my food as well as the challenges on hand.

To get off that Magic Pill as soon as possible, I read about mind body healing—meditation versus medication.

'A holiday would do you good.' I readily took that advice.

We didn't want to lose a single day of the four-week vacation I was entitled to. Often I went straight from work to the airport.

......

Reaching my Comfort Zone...

Being enclosed inside a capsule can be so liberating!

After the take-off, I reclined to recollect the previous day:

The night before departure I worked late to cross my T's and dot my I's placing sticky notes: whose credit line had to be increased, whose investments were to be reinvested. I heard a tap on my window around 11:00 p.m. Dr. Zogala our Polish client was passing by. He touched his belly and signaled to ask if I had eaten dinner. I pointed to the plastic container on my desk. The dinner was delivered compliments of Mr. Mercouris, the owner of the Greek restaurant across the street. I felt privileged to have such a loving rapport with my clients. They were worth going the extra mile. *After all, being married to the bank isn't that bad,* I thought. *Or was it?*

As usual halfway through the journey I switched from English music to Urdu, gearing myself up to embrace the cultural contrast. Once the plane lands in your homeland, there is a sudden surge of mixed emotions, in reverse gear the engine roars: *You are now in a different world!* I always needed time, so I let everyone else exit first.

I disembarked as a traditional Pakistani woman. Family was like a magnet, I rushed toward them, to wave through the glass, before claiming my baggage. Over there, knowing someone with clout helps.

Mujeeb's nephew Saleem an Aeronautical Engineer at the airport, always assisted us with smooth checkouts.

With too many next of kin initially I felt overwhelmed. Everyone spoke Urdu (English words only inserted when convenient). Their clothing, the language, the air to breathe, the attitudes—everything felt DIFFERENT! With a promise to revisit my in-laws soon, the next morning I went straight to my sister Nigma's place.

Upon a king size bed, freshly made by someone else, jet-lagged, I lay with my eyes closed, holding one hand with Nigma, the other with Rubeena. The outpouring of affection was intoxicating; I closed my eyes. Their children had joined us, someone was gently massaging my feet, but which of my nieces was doing so? I called out names. "Is it Afsheen, Maheen, Sameen, or Ayesha?" I extended my limbs they took turns, lovingly running fingers on my arms… someone lifted my foot and kissed it.

It didn't take them long to figure out something was not right.

"Why don't you share what's bothering you?" But I responded with the bare minimum.

"Just move back, Mujeeb Bhai can get a decent job here. Moreover, we'll all be around you." Their comforting words had immense healing power.

A Bridal Shower…

Everyone catered to my whims, and I was treated like royalty.

One afternoon my cousin Tanveeer took me to a book launch. On our way she suddenly asked the driver to stop at a boutique.

"How did you know I wanted to go to Zaman Zar?" She said, "I have my resources."

In that bedazzling display, my eyes landed upon a fuchsia georgette silk, three-piece shalwar suit, hand embroidered in aqua and mustard. I held it against me in front of a mirror, the look on my face was enough. It was too expensive but before I could say anything Tanveer paid for it and said, "Let's go or we'll be late for the book launch."

"But I'm leaving for Pindi in two days, there's no time to get it stitched."

"We'll see about that." I felt embarrassed at her generosity.

Already feeling indebted to my siblings and in-laws, how am I ever going to return all their favors? However, that suit piece and my sample outfit instantly sent to Tanveer's Tailor Master, was stitched to perfection … in one day!

That afternoon, Nigma skipped her siesta and returned with shopping bags.

"Oh, wow, you got me fuchsia sandals to match my new outfit, thanks."

"Look, here's a matching purse, and these are gifts for Kashif and Mujeeb."

Then Rubeena also arrived with a gift bag, "Earrings and bangles to go with your outfit."

"Who gave your all the details? It's exact match with the embroidery!" I got beaming smiles in response. Everyone took such delight in pampering me, I was deeply touched.

"How about modeling for us?" my cousin Shanno requested and my little nieces already lined up as spectators. Like a teenager I rushed in and decked up.

"This feels like a bridal shower in Canada."

As I was having fun with modeling, even their maid emerged from the kitchen. I had a flashback when in 1963, Shehnaz Khan brought her toddler and dressed me up as a bride in Nigeria. Now, everyone was clapping when a long-distance call interrupted the fashion show.

Shahid from Rawalpindi called to confirm my arrival and requested, "Just keep a party outfit in your carry on, okay?"

"Party outfit, why?"

"There's a *__Qawwali__ musical evening with dinner at the Marriott Hotel in Islamabad, remember our cousin Tabassum, she has extended a warm invitation to you."

"But I'm coming for my parents and you all, not to meet a million other relatives,"

"You'll meet everyone and won't have to make individual visits."

"By the way, I happen to be modeling a hot-pink outfit in front of a sizeable of audience. It's the bridal shower I never had, I've been gifted all accessories too."

"So you didn't leave anything for us?"

"All I need is to be with you all, I'm sure Ammi can hardly wait." We said goodbye.

......

At the Rawalpindi /Islamabad airport, after hugs and kisses, I noticed Shahid's facial expressions change as if he was up to something. He took out a small paper bag from his pocket.

"What? I don't believe this—hot-pink nail polish, who told you to get that?" He smiled. Overspill of such TLC for me was enough to trigger an emotional surge.

"Since when have you become so sensitive?"

"I'm touched because these small gestures have such big meanings."

I barely rested for two hours then decked up in my fuchsia gear for the evening. During the intermission I had brief exchanges with dozens of cousins from our Zuberi clan.

Incidentally, that **Qawwali** gathering of two hundred at Marriott Hotel turned out to be a Wedding Party in disguise—to circumvent government restrictions imposed on lavish weddings!

(*Qawwali is a form of Sufi Islamic devotional singing, notably popular in India and Pakistan.)

Apart from relishing in my parents' affectionate outbursts, I spent the rest of my fun time with Shahid and Arifa's families. Their four children Umair, Saad, Abdullah, and Zainab happily growing up together made me think that, '*My own son is deprived of growing up with his cousins*'. During his few visits Kashif had become everyone's favorite. After those visits he commented,

"I don't understand how you could have left such a loving family behind!"

In any case, for me it had been a close call—I was just glad I made it there while I was still SANE. A great sense of gratitude prevailed for I really got *pampered to life*.

Moreover, upon my return I had a landmark event to look forward to.

....

Trip to Montreal Mont Royale

Visiting Pakistan,
connecting w cousins

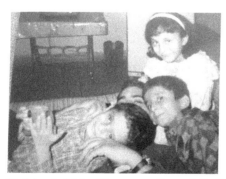

Rubina's kids (Sameen, Saeed & Shaheer) also gravitated toward
Kashif

Kashif w Ayesha & Sabeen
(Neema's children)

My brother Shahid and
sister Arifa's children

(L to R) Umair, Zainab,
Abdullah and Saad

I'm Jet lagged, but the kids can
hardly wait for gifts from Canada!

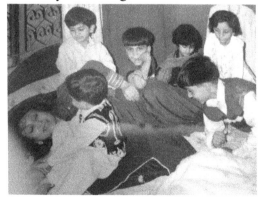

Admiring my dad's garden, but he said "You are my favourite rose!"

Shahid's wife Huma enters early morning: *"What are your favourite dishes?"*

Kashif bonding with uncle Shahid

Enough of spearheading
investment campaigns

Instant escapes to be with
the family

Their daughters Saman
and Madeeha

Stop over in Abu Dhabi,
pampered by Sikandar &
Durdana

PART THREE

Depth of Struggle and…
Height of Success

GRADUATION

24 I arranged a pre-graduation party in which I invited a few of his Ophthalmology classmates: Tony, Adam, Paul, and Pierre. Tony was the only one I had met previously.

Over a simple curry meal, Kashif's friends connected with me, cracking jokes as though we had known each other forever.

"Did you know that Kashif once had hair longer than mine, and it was bleached and permed?" At their incessant urging I finally brought out his photo album.

"Are you okay with this talk?" I asked Kashif who seemed completely at ease around his buddies.

"Ms. Zoberi, we like your son a lot, but we can never be *like* him," Pierre mused. "I mean, he's so disciplined, he stays away from night clubs, and now he even avoids girls. That's mission impossible for us."

"If I want the girl I'll marry to be a certain way, I must preserve myself to be like that," Kashif clarified, "But it's not that easy," he added with a smirk.

"Let me share another mission of his you may all want to follow," I said.

"One day I came across a piece of paper in his room, upon which he had scribbled twenty values he wanted to live by. One of which read: *'Examine each patient as if he or she is my immediate family member.'* I cried tears of joy."

"Sure," I heard one of his friends remark in approval.

But soon enough they went back to making fun of his long hair again, flipping the pages of the album over and over, laughing heartily. Kashif for the first time shared how they ganged up to set booby traps when he returned late from the library. "Booby traps, why?" I asked. "We didn't want him to study so hard."

The Ceremony...

After a few days, Mujeeb and I drove from Toronto to Waterloo to see our son graduate as a Doctor of Optometry. We headed toward the Convocation Hall, thrilled to watch him receive his degree. There he stood all decked out in his grand robe and cap. "Remember your Grade 8 graduation when I got upset to see you in T-shirt and jeans?" As I whispered and patted his shoulder, he smiled back.

His classmates introduced us to their parents. We seemed to be receiving more felicitations and congratulations than the other parents, so I was curious. It became clear when a parent commented, "Too bad you couldn't be here for last night's Gold Medal ceremony."

"What Gold Medal?" I was surprised.

"Oh wow, you didn't know that your son took home the prize as the top student?"

I couldn't believe he'd keep such a secret from us.

"Kashif, why didn't you tell us?" I protested.

"I didn't want you to have to drive here two days in a row, Mom."

I gave him the warmest hug of my life.

"Mom, please don't broadcast it 'cause it sounds like bragging."

"Yeah, well, like it or not, I intend to share it with my parents, and siblings, and friends, and shout it from the rooftops to anyone else who will listen. I am nothing, if not the proudest mother on earth!"

All my hopes and aspirations were geared to our one and only son's future. I secretly thought that his outstanding success compensated for my hubby's career sacrifice.

Both of them finally found their niche, wanting to make a change. I found myself having to take a tough decision.

......

Farewell Financial World…

After being married to the bank for twenty years, closing that chapter was more like a divorce. I had thoroughly enjoyed the *honeymoon period,* the first sixteen years, but the changing corporate culture lately did not suit my personality.

One day I was called into my boss' office.

"Do you realize that this week there is a million-dollar dent in your portfolio?"

"I do." Caught off guard, I realized it was likely a *karate attack.*

"How did that happen?"

"Mrs. Smith is a hundred-year-old lady in my portfolio. I've visited her at the Evergreen Retirement Home across the street. A young couple invited the lonely woman for Christmas and the New Year and treated her royally." I paused when Mr. Esposito pulled his chair forward waiting further explanation.

"She wrote a half a million-dollar cheque in their name to buy a house and furniture."

"What else?"

"$400,000 was withdrawn by a Mr. Wong and his brother who recently emigrated from China. They jointly purchased a million-dollar home and paid cash," I replied with confidence.

"What did *you* do about that?" Offended with such lack of faith I still explained.

"I congratulated my Chinese client and requested to introduce his brother to me, reminded them that I'm there for all their future banking needs."

Like an intimidating question mark, he sat on his executive chair with the high back, certificates of his achievements gracing the wall. Power emanating out simply by the way he swiveled his chair around, he then faced me again. "What about Mrs. Smith?"

"I requested her beneficiaries' contact number, Dianne and Earl Walker. I called to congratulate them and offered my services for any future needs."

I awaited his reaction. "Well, you could have in fact *increased* your portfolio."

"How so?" I held back my anger.

"You could have invested half of the Chinese assets into mutual funds and given them a mortgage. Same applies to the young couple who could have partly invested in Mutual Funds, instead of spending all their cash."

I faked a smile. "Do you call us 'Relationship Managers' really?"

Mr. Esposito wasn't expecting this answer so he picked up a pen to make a note. My thoughts travelled back twenty years when I was new in the bank. A senior rep from our Marketing Department had come to observe my stellar success in sales. I summoned the courage:

"At this point I would like to say goodbye to the Bank." My throat felt dry as I spoke.

Taken by surprise, his tone softened. "Hope you are not planning to resign, are you?"

"Yes sir, I am. No longer on the bank's side, let's say I'm more for my clients – *A Relationship Manager*. In fact, it would be in the bank's interest to let me go."

Mr. Esposito pushed his chair back, with a markedly altered tone, he acknowledged, "You know how much the Bank values your work. I hope you understand it's my job to stay on top of the situation."

"I understand, you have to do your job, but I must do mine."

I was surprised to receive emails from my colleagues *not only to say goodbye* but also to express their envy: "Wish I could quit; you must have another job offer?"

There was no job prospect lined up, only apprehensions. Kashif had started optometry practice but clearly stated, "Never work with your own family member." However, it was a relief to have qualified for a golden handshake of one year's salary, plus moderate pension.

I had kept journals of real-life stories of my clients and colleagues, and the valuable lessons learned from my mentors like Wim Faasen and Marilyn Muir.

......

My New Career, an Eye Opener...

I began an aggressive job search. But one day Kashif took me by surprise:

"Ammi, before you start applying elsewhere why don't you work at my clinic, try it for three months."

Excited with the unexpected offer, I spontaneously blurted, "Who could have predicted that one day my passion could become my profession?"

My thoughts had drifted to a decades' old memory:

"You would be amused to know in my first letter to your father I asked him to change his old-fashioned glasses to something modern."

"Really, that's funny." He smiled but cautioned me, "Let's not jump to conclusions Mom, it's only on a trial basis."

"You could've saved me from gut-wrenching debate about resigning from the bank."

......

Having played various roles, mother, sister, best friend, and now I was becoming his colleague. Subordinate? Oh no!

From day one, I stipulated that no one would refer to me as his mother, he too would call me Zohra and I'd call him Dr. Zoberi, like everyone else. Only when patients came out of his office praising how thorough he was, or when older women raved over his looks, I couldn't resist the temptation to claim my 'ownership.'

Before learning about any optical illusions or training in the dispensary, I had to temporarily work as his Receptionist.

My friends remarked, "From a limelight job as the Manager of Upscale Portfolios, don't you feel you've downgraded yourself?"

"The heaviness of being successful has been replaced by the lightness of being a beginner again." I personalized Steve Job's quotation, as though it was meant for me. But I felt sorry that our Indo-Pakistanis still had their old-fashioned mentality.

'Customer Service' in the bank versus 'Patient Care' at the clinic! Banks and the bankers were generally not liked. On the contrary, patients were respectful of doctors. Regardless, concerns about peoples' nose pads and temples were not nearly as demanding, as worrying about their ROI (return on investments).

As for promoting the clinic, twenty years of banking experience now paid dividends, although I had to learn medical jargon. I figured out that the key to expansion was via referrals but—building rapport with physicians was less important than knowing their secretaries.

The real challenge was to alter the fixed mind-sets of the elderly patients.

"Why should I see just an Optometrist, I have had an Ophthalmologist for decades?"

"He is not *just* an Optometrist he is a gold medalist, a GP of the eyes, so now you are under the care of both." I recalled Kashif's list of values:

'Examine each patient as if he or she is my immediate family member'. With that philosophy he easily won the patients' confidence and together we became a good TEAM. Before three months had passed, he said, "Don't ever leave this job," "So my probationary period is over?" I recalled when the Bank had made a blunder regarding my probationary period. When I had to take a daring step before justice prevailed!

Now I had the luxury of on-the-job training by a pro, all about single vision, bifocals, and progressives. I didn't know I'd enjoy fashion consulting so much. Just by choosing the right pair of glasses, one could make square faces look less square, long faces not as long. We could make the bags or dark circles under the eyes less noticeable—by choosing appropriate frames, wow! I relished the experience whenever the first pair I suggested turned out to be the right one.

Friends jogged my memory:

"Didn't you say if you ever left the bank, you'll open a match-making business?"

"I am match-making—glasses to faces." They were amused.

In fact, I had long pondered upon the idea of opening a unique dating club "Match Making fusion style" especially after that singles' Psychic Party of my colleagues. I had successfully match-made some of my *Mangia-cake* colleagues (Italian slang for white Canadians).

Now I got my business cards, assigning me Dispensary Manager, so once again I looked forward to going to work—with an added zest that it was our own son's private practice.

······

Kashif soon moved his clinic to a bigger location. A white patient once asked, "Is this clinic run exclusively by brown people or what?"

"Yes, one way or the other they must be brown," I joked.

Dale Brown was our white receptionist, so it became a joke she didn't mind. However, a pretty blonde lady Debbie as the Dispensary Assistant expressed, "Over here I feel reverse discrimination. People prefer to deal with you. Maybe they don't like me because I'm white?"

"No, not at all Debbie, just add *'passion to profession'* and you'll see the magic."

"Sorry, I can't be you," she said, bemoaning her regretful status in life.

"But you are far more efficient in processing the orders than I'll ever be."

"It is all about understanding the client's psychology, affordability, and peculiar tastes of different population segments." I took joy in remembering what brand, and even which code numbers most of our Sri Lankan patients would buy, and similarly had my finger on the trends and styles preferred by the Italians.

A Patient named Merridy once travelled from out of town to see us. "I've recently retired, and at my age I want something conservative to complement my face," But I surprised her with a funky samples to try on. "Oh no that's not me I have a dull personality."

"That's all the more reason for you to make the switch. Here, try this one, it'll uplift you, and your soul," I humored. She spent hours debating. After much dilly dallying, she finally did decide on a trendy model I had recommended, but not without my solemn promise that, "If you don't like it after one week, I'll exchange it with that dull-looking one."

I vividly remember the glow on her face once she came to pick it up. A friend later accompanied her and said, "I'm here to see if you can alter my image with one of your *fashionista* suggestions." Life outside the bank was proving to be so much fun.

Connecting with people of all ages and ethnic backgrounds was my passion. Now I penned journals of the *patients' interesting stories.* Some people bought glasses as if they're buying a pencil, while others fussed as though they were purchasing a million-dollar mansion. I discovered that many men were just as vain as women, taking selfies to invite second opinions.

Sales Reps, wanting to promote their designer brands, gifted me with Versace and Dolce & Gabbana frames I may never have otherwise bothered to purchase.

Mentored by the Optometrists, I eventually became 'hands-on as the Dispensary Manager' so I was able to also train other staff. A young Optometry student *Sameer* had to complete three months training as part of his Optometry Internship. He was a sharp and eager learner, even though he was half my age, we connected well and became good friends.

"Why is it that I can't think of you like an auntie?" he asked.

"By the way, I dislike the word *auntie,* so let's stop being so old-fashioned."

I couldn't tell him 'Auntie is visiting' was our code for the dreaded monthly periods, it reminded me of stomach cramps.

Once *my pupil* Sameer became adept and confident in measuring the *pupils* and learned all about progressive lenses and bifocals, he made me an offer I couldn't resist,

"Zohra ji, I'd like you to take a day off, relax and I will man the ship for you."

I felt sad when Sameer broke the news of moving to USA to complete his doctorate.

"Does that mean I'll never see you again?"

"Never say Never," he said and I wondered *would he ever be back in my life again?*

......

Kashif had received an honorary award from CNIB (Canadian National Institute for the Blind). He expanded the clinic to include Low Vision Rehabilitation, complex devices were needed to help those with serious vision challenges. Consequently, he became everyone's go-to person, teaching them about Assistive Devices and grueling paperwork for funding requirements.

"Ask Dr. Zoberi … ask Dr. Zoberi" was the phrase echoing, that pleased my ears all day long. The lineups were increasing by the day, and I felt proud.

"You are one lucky mother," patients paid compliments for raising my son well.

Working at the clinic was an eye-opener as most clients requested lenses with 'the best panoramic vision.' That evolved into my personal philosophy that:

We must also develop the best *'Panoramic Perception of our World.'*

I never once regretted leaving the bank. There was life and a thriving, bustling world outside of the bank.

We now had leisurely time to connect with the like-minded. Chance encounters sometimes bring us precious gifts that life has to offer, provided we are open to receiving them.

......

Zamir—A Classic Addition to my Library…

At a literary gathering, we met a classy couple who *had it all*. Zamir Ahmad a scholar, retired from the United Nations as Auditor General, had settled in Mississauga. Iram, with her gentle loving presence, complemented their partnership culminating in a sublimely *perfect couple*, whose artistically decorated bungalow became our cozy corner in the city. Zamir was a walking encyclopedia of poetry both in Urdu and English who masterfully translated poems by Nobel Laureates such as Wislawa Szymborska, T. S. Eliot, Pablo Neruda, Joseph Brodsky, and many more. Two of his collections were published.

We developed such emotional connection—outside of my family I'd say Iram loved me the most. I wrote a poem dedicated to her *"Aroma of Iram"* (heaven).

......

Having common interests in poetry, art, movies, and classical music, we attended numerous events together. After a gathering at York Library in Toronto, Zamir offered to translate the two poems I had recited. At first I thought he was joking, but I later had first-hand experience of how he delved into the minds of the authors to capture the essence and the mood, to convert into more poetic Urdu. *"Valentine Dance"* and *"True Colours"* he translated for me were so appreciated. I said, "There's only one problem with your translation." He looked surprised so I explained.

"Your translation is superior to my original." I received an affectionate slap on my cheek.

We also developed friendships with their children, each uniquely brilliant. A terrible tragedy struck when Iram had a sudden and fatal heart attack. It felt as though she sneaked out through the backdoor, to the hereafter. Zamir attempted to lighten up and added, "More in the style of an errant and wild escaping teenager!"

At the cemetery I overheard her grandchildren conversing— Aemin (eight) and Rischard (fourteen). While gazing at the clouds one said, "See, the sky is weeping for Nano." Observing small opening in the clouds above, the other replied, "But the heavens are smiling at her."

After her loss, Zamir endured prolonged illness. During the ensuing decade, Mujeeb and I visited him regularly. Our conversation was sprinkled with his recitals, most appropriate and apt to suit each and every situation.

My friend Reva once accompanied me to meet Zamir. She was entranced by an Urdu-speaking Pakistani's delivery of Shakespeare –verbatim.

To watch an art movie with Zamir was a unique experience, passionately he relished subtleties some others may miss out. Some classics included French *Ille Postile*, Bengali *Charu Lata*, and a Swedish film *The Seventh Seal.*

Even during his prolonged illness, he used the iPad with his aching warped fingers to share musical masterpieces. Passion intact, he still managed to introduce us to rare classical performances!

Zamir had a live-in support worker, yet the dedication and personal attention his son Fawzie provided was exemplary. I was touched whenever I saw them interacting with each other. Fawzie too is extremely witty and has an eye for art, décor, and literature, maybe inherited from his parents. We met his daughter Tazeen and her husband Naseem Rehman, witty as ever!

It was Zamir whose advice I took seriously: "Big pleasures are few and far between, like weddings, birthdays, graduation etc. but small pleasures you can enjoy a hundred a day."

Such a Classic Novel has to be revered and frequently referenced.

…………………………

A Visionary's Foresight
(Vision and Literacy International)

---

25 Before Kashif qualified as a Doctor of Optometry, a three-month internship in a third world country was mandatory. Pakistan was his first choice (Al-Shifa Eye Hospital in Rawalpindi was one of the most reputable). Marginalized communities, especially children, had little access to general eye care. This sad revelation to a young doctor raised in Canada became his moment of awakening! There was an endemic of vitamin A deficiency and *Trachoma* (bacterial infection of the eye). Early detection of these diseases in schools as well as health education concerning their prevention and treatment was inadequate.

Almost 50% of Pakistan's population happened to be children. WHO classified it as a country with severe subclinical, vitamin deficiency!

Study showed that 32–43 % of children under 5, were deficient serum vitamin levels.

This harsh reality impacted him to the core. He decided to embark upon a meaningful project, but the reaction from family and friends was skeptical.

"Establishing a charity clinic in Pakistan, while living in Canada, is a tall order."

That did not deter the *determined*. However, issues to deal with were: Who would monitor the project locally, and where would the funding come from?

An Unexpected Benefactor…

Mujeeb owned a house in Karachi, rented out to a Mr. Farooq, a cricket player with business acumen. His 'discounted rent' was our spending money during our annual visits.

For years, family insisted that Mujeeb should sell it, but he refused and now he suddenly decided to do so. Farooq purchased it for half the market price, quadrupled its value overnight—by constructing a four-story, nine-bedroom mansion.

Mujeeb pledged a portion from the house sale as two years down payment to rent a bungalow in Rawalpindi. His noble gesture was a welcome surprise. With my younger brother Shahid's help this residential house was converted into a clinic. After overcoming the red tape, Kashif succeeded in establishing a free eye clinic in my hometown Rawalpindi. Our family was thrilled to see the large billboard on the front wall:

Vision and Literary International
Free Eye Care for Children 1-16 years of age

An ophthalmologist was hired at a charitable rate. My entire family happily performed sundry chores, writing, printing, and folding up the pamphlets. My father complimented him,

"Kashif, we're proud to see how you've mobilized all your cousins too." Abbaji also had a charitable heart, and Mujeeb's father was a philanthropist as well.

To manage the clinic locally, a trustworthy person was needed. Shahid was already volunteering. He now had to decide if he should manage the clinic or remain a banker? He took a big risk for a higher cause and lesser monetary compensation!

Excitement built up when a few children who came for checkups also enrolled in a school named 'Nishan-e-Haider Academy.' Everyone was surprised when and how Kashif made all those connections.

After receiving the remaining funds from his house sale in Karachi, Mujeeb became the proud owner of an upgraded semidetached bungalow in a new subdivision in Mississauga, Mavis, and Britannia. "This cute little house would be perfect for our retirement niche," he said.

Since it generated income, Mujeeb now felt justified in pursuing his research passion. What a difference in his demeanor, he regained his self-esteem and the happy man I married was back—peace returned!

Our family of three formed
a stronger bond with a common cause.

Meeting the Beneficiaries in Person...

We now needed to monitor the new project abroad. Regular visits by Kashif or us to meet VLI children provided us with further insights:

An intelligent twelve-year-old, Faizan had been enrolled in the school program. He became our enthusiastic 'Self-appointed Tour Guide.' The villagers informed in advance, geared up to welcome us. Little girls wore western dresses, likely purchased from *Lunda Bazaar* (where clothes donated from rich countries are sold for a pittance). To impress us, mothers permitted their teenage daughters to even wear lipstick. The mantle pieces were decorated with hand-embroidered runners, just for us. Some even used old newspapers with edges trimmed to intricate designs.

I was deeply touched to see a tiny fridge proudly displayed in the middle of their living room as their prized possession. Pasted on it were red roses clipped from a glossy magazine. Shahid educated me later, "One of their family members working in Dubai must have sent the fridge as a gift." How they expressed their gratitude to VLI for providing their children a chance to study! We felt gut-wrenching compassion.

During one visit to the clinic, we met *Reshma,* a mother of six daughters. Consequently, the poor woman suffered merciless and sustained verbal abuse from her in-laws. Finally, her seventh child turned out to be a male, appropriately named *Kamal* (Perfection). What a trauma when they found out he was almost blind in both eyes!

But the day we met fourteen-year-old Kamal, he was all smiles as the surgery of one eye funded by VLI had been successful. With obvious delight Shahid shared the news with us,

"The whole village had a party to celebrate his vision in one eye."

Wearing brand-new, crisp, white shalwar kameez (traditional attire), he arrived to book an appointment for his second eye surgery by himself—as if he had conquered the world. His mother Reshma raised her hands beseechingly upward to the heavens and vehemently prayed for Kashif. "May Allah bless your son and your family," wiping tears of joy away with her wrinkled-up dupatta. That touching sight is etched in my memory and tugged at my heartstrings.

One afternoon, we finally visited Nishan-e-Haider school. A two-story, four-bedroom house with a veranda on three sides of the courtyard, now converted into a school. Boys and girls in blue-and-white uniforms assembled in the courtyard to sing the Pakistani National Anthem for us. It invoked nostalgic memories of my youth when two other girls in my school and I led the singing of our anthem *'Pak Sarzameen Shaad Baad'*

(Long Live the Land of the Pure).

I began to sing along spontaneously; although deep down, a sad reality hit me hard.

The children were surprised and excited that I knew every word. Their teachers looking down from the veranda of the second floor seemed equally joyous. A Grade 5 humble-looking, undersized student named *Ajmal* wore the thickest glasses I had ever seen on any child of his age (his prescription was -12!). After receiving free eye care, he had been admitted to this school and had won a position in the Board Exams. The announcement was loudly applauded. The children presented us with a bouquet of flowers, and then re-assembled in several rows to sing for us a famous poem by our National Poet Allama Iqbal:

"Lub pe aati hai dua bun ke tamanna meri
Zindagi shamma ki surath ho khudaya meri"

(God bless me with quest for knowledge. May my life become a guiding light)

Thousands of children in schools across the nation have been singing this prayer every single day, yet to be answered. Ironically, ours remains a country with one of the lowest literacy rates.

"Ho mera kaam gharibon ki Himayat karna
Dard mandon se zaifon se Mohabbat karna"

(May my mission be to favor the poor and also love the elderly)

Touched by this irony, I felt the urgency of Kashif's mission. Many philanthropists in Pakistan serve this noble cause, but the harsh reality remains that the affluent couples have two or three children, while the poor would produce eight or ten! So it's a 'one step forward, two steps back' scenario.

Kashif expressed his sentiment, "You guys enjoyed a good life in Pakistan, then sacrificed and left your loved ones behind to give me a better life in Canada. Now it's our turn to give back to the deprived." His passion resulted in many annual fundraising events. To add pizzazz and panache to our fund raisers, I would often find myself organizing musical concerts. One such event from my journal I finalized as a stand-alone story.

......

Oceans Apart, Close to Our Hearts

It was a musical concert to raise funds for Vision and Literacy International, at Meadowvale Theatre in Mississauga. Our caption for the flyer read:

Young and the Restless, Hand in Hand with the Golden Oldies

For the first generation of South Asian immigrants, it was a challenge to attract youth to their events. With this in mind, I met with a father-and-son team of professional artists—David Dean Sr. and David Dean Jr., who hailed originally from the subcontinent. They were singing to nostalgia inducing old, toe-tapping, contemporary Bollywood and *Lollywood hits – (this refer to the Lahore and Bombay film industries).

The father expressed his delight, reminiscing, "Eleven years ago, this was the location where our son David Junior had his singing debut at age seven!"

"So now, he's going to resurface as an eighteen-year-old heart throb for our female teen audience," I responded. It was a sold-out show.

Four hundred guests lined up in front of Meadowvale Theatre in Mississauga 'ahead of time'—almost a miraculous feat for our Indo-Pakistani community!

As an extra precaution, I had booked a spare room just in case anyone missed the fine print on our flyer, which politely but firmly specified that 'Children under ten not permitted.' The theater management had inadvertently left the room dark, so one of our eager volunteers rushed forward to turn on the lights. As luck would have it, she mistakenly pressed the wrong button, and … the fire alarms went off!

"Vacate the premises. Vacate the premises!" A panic-stricken theater manager made the urgent announcement, as he fought his way around the congested hallway, swarming with now bemused guests.

Knowing it was her own mistake our volunteer simultaneously ran across the hallway and hollered, **"False Alarm…no need to vacate."**

Chaos and confusion followed, which as one can imagine, felt barely short of a stampede! Shortly thereafter, the streets around the theater were blaring with the sirens of fire brigade trucks, ambulances, and police cars, as their emergency lights flashed and illuminated the streets surrounding us in red, white, and blue.

Being the main organizer of this venture, I stood dumbfounded. Everyone could sense the anger in the Manager's voice as he shouted out, "Mistake or no mistake, no one is allowed entry until the entire premises has been checked out." The poor audience had to wait outside the theater for one whole hour.

"So much for her persistent reminders about punctuality," I heard them whisper.

"It's all because you dressed in flaming red hot, looking like a fireball!" one friend joked aloud. Laughter rose from the crowd.

One of our more astute board members suggested, "How about serving the *Shawarma* now, which we had ordered for later? Just shorten the intermission."

"Brilliant idea," I replied. The catering company was happy to make early delivery.

What a memorable picnic it turned out to be—nature was on our side, as it was a beautiful sunny afternoon in May. The hour flew by, before we were finally welcomed back inside the theater premises. As the show started one hour late, our request to extend the end time by one hour met with instant approval.

David Junior sang a selection of the latest hit songs, his father interspersing these with warmly familiar older numbers, each of the father-son duo outperforming the other.

The mood of our audience uplifted, during the intermission I heard nothing but praise, "Such a wonderful show, a rare gathering of older and younger folks together—what an amazing novel concept!"

"The delay was really a blessing in disguise. The outdoor picnic was a bonus."

Feeling ecstatic that the show was unexpectedly a hit, notwithstanding our decidedly shaky start, I announced the second half, commenting that "Adversity sometimes turns into advantage." A murmur of consent was audible from amongst the audience.

The Deans had introduced me to a talented community of Pakistani Christians for this memorable day. One of the organizers happened to be a patient of Kashif, which naturally infused added enthusiasm into the event.

A solo dance performance by Cheryl, a beautiful Pakistani teenager, was to be the highlight and climax of that evening. Amidst thundering applause, the young girl dressed exotically, poised in a squatting position. Her back facing the audience created suspense and anticipation, before she would turn around to finally perform and enthrall the crowd. The music commenced, but as she turned to face her audience amidst applause and whistles, with a sound of sudden blast it became pitch dark — a power failure!

"Oh no!" a loud murmur erupted from the audience.

Candles and torch lights were provided. In that semi-lit room, I came up onto the stage, confused. All I could say was: "What were the chances of two emergencies in one night?"   "Don't wear that fire-red color again!" Everyone laughed. It must be the same culprit who had joked earlier, but the feeling of relief washing over me was palpable. *So the audience is still in good mood.* I asked, "Are you guys prepared to wait?"

"YES!" was the overwhelming response, loud and clear. "But how long can you wait?"

"Indefinitely, especially for that dance!" replied someone.

Power outages in Mississauga were rare. Five minutes of darkness had ensued, after which the Manager of the theater, *without our consent*, rushed up onto the stage and announced:

"The show is over due to the power failure."

No sooner than the disappointed crowd of 400 began to disperse, blazing lights came back on! That instantly triggered anger. Skeptics suspected it could be intentional. Maybe the staff didn't want to stay the extended hour and work overtime? Eager for his **Debut II,** David Dean Jr. had his masterpieces still to be rendered. So this event meant a lot to all the artists involved. They even wondered if the theater lights were turned off intentionally.

Consequently, I bore the brunt of interrogations as to why I let the theater manager get away with cancelling the show, without my approval. "Have patience. Since I was in charge, let me handle it." I placated those affected, as I promised to follow up.

At my request, I was invited to meet the office manager of the theater. A well-groomed, blond gentleman rose from his chair to shake hands, and signaled me to take a seat.

I spoke, as he listened, but did not utter a single word. I went on with my story, the purpose of the event, how the poor children with eye problems were being helped through this charity. He listened on, said nothing, just gesturing me to continue speaking.

I wondered about his odd silence and emphasizing the importance of my concerns, as well as the depth of our dissatisfaction, I explained, "To satisfy our disappointed artists and audience, all I want is confirmation that there actually *was* a power failure that night in Mississauga."

He brought out a document to prove it, including details and timing of the power failure, the areas affected, when the lights were restored. However, the gentleman still did not speak!

Relieved to receive the proof I could show to skeptics, it was only when he jotted down something on paper that I finally realized that this gentleman had <u>speech impairment</u>!' Only written communication was possible. Instant thoughts that triggered in my mind were:

What would be his fate in a third world country? How fortunate he is to be in Canada, a country that has given him the fair, equitable and equal opportunities to attain a managerial position today despite his challenges.

Now it was time to settle the bill. I had already paid half the amount as a deposit.

On the piece of paper he provided, I wrote, "The two mishaps in one evening were unfortunate."

He wrote: "I agree but it was your volunteer's mistake to turn on the wrong switch."

I wrote back: "The Theater Manager should have ensured the room lights were already on," He nodded in agreement. I wrote, "But he cancelled the show without consulting me."

"Agreed, he should have spoken to you first," he wrote.

By then I was beginning to enjoy our written conversation:

"We owe you $1,200 balance, but I have a request,"

"Go on …" his facial expression spoke, *what a hard bargain you drive lady!*

"Technically I am obliged to pay you that amount but …" His curious gaze was intense.

"If you give me 50 percent discount, we could get two more children's eye surgeries funded by VLI—your decision." I put the pencil down.

The Manager pondered for a few minutes, leaving me in suspense …then wrote down,

"You don't have to pay *anything.* Use the whole amount for charity." I was ecstatic beyond words. We exchanged glances of mutual gratitude.

Just as I left his office, it started raining cats and dogs. Holding an umbrella above me, and in a truly gentlemanly manner, he covered me until I reached my car. Joy and sorrow mingled, it was raining in my heart too. So many people would benefit from the grandeur of his philanthropic gesture.

One eye surgery of a poor child and the recovery of a single child's eyesight can impact their entire family, in fact even a whole generation. The memory of Reshma and her son flickered and was ignited in my mind. Oceans apart, but close to our hearts –two more families would receive life-transforming benefits through the gesture of a fellow Canadian and to this day I am proud of him.

Each time my eye catches the infamous or even notorious 'fiery-red' outfit I wore that day I have vivid recollections of this entire episode. It now belongs to my granddaughter Marzia.

That episode further boosted our will to give back to the local community in Canada. Together with **Kehkashan Ladies Club**—especially with the help of friends like Ashy Habib, Farhat Abid, and Mansoora Ghani, we coordinated large-scale concerts for the Indonesian Tsunami, and donated funds for cancer research to the Free Care Hospital in Mississauga.

A dear friend, Javed Mughal, also donated his time and talent to the VLI cause. The most memorable fund raiser was held at the Huron Park Recreation Centre, when he mesmerized a capacity audience with various genres of music including *Sitar* and *flute*.

The Love Boats...

Kashif later found innovative ways of raising funds for VLI. With the help of like-minded young professionals, he coordinated annual boat cruises at Lake Ontario. Those seemed to serve dual purpose—eligible singles were able to mingle, even meet their ideals.

Funny how everything was tying in with the theme of arranged marriages!

Mujeeb and I, as Board Members, invited a few of our friends.

The parents of single girls felt comforted by our presence. There was no booze, just wild music. Mujeeb and I danced crazy; they said, "We want to be like you when we are your age."

Memory of one Gala Cruise, attended by 150 guests, at Mariposa (perhaps?) is etched in my mind. It was a perfect summer evening; the kickoff was a bedazzling dance performance on the upper deck by a group of twenty decked up boys and girls. They replicated a dance from a latest Bollywood romance 'Kaho na Pyaar Hai' (Just admit it's love). Our Love Boat cruised along; music reverberated on the ripples of Lake Ontario.

"Pyar ki kashti mey hein
Lehron ki masti me hein"

(The gist: In our love boat, we are intoxicated as the rippling waves)

Five hours of sheer fun ended at sunset, with a stunning view of Toronto's skyline, the city lights reflecting upon the sparkling waves as we inched our way ashore.

*Kehkashan name is changed to Kiran Ladies Club, under the enthusiastic leadership of Nuzhat Khalid.

....

Financial Freedom

26 It was the day I thought I'd never get to see. I gloated over the slip confirming our last mortgage payment. As well my golden handshake (one year salary) was deposited in WMB stocks. We celebrated my 'Freedom Fifty' at the Black Angus Steak House in Islington.

Still, the biggest source of gratification for me was to witness Kashif continuing to honor his resolution of treating every patient as his family member.

We had raised him to pick and choose values from the East and West to achieve the 'best of both worlds'. The next step was obvious—the topic of his marriage was often discussed. A gold medalist doctor, an only son of an established family, he was perceived as a good catch. Being a Canadian citizen had enhanced his value for girls in Pakistan.

"Are you looking for an Urdu-speaking girl?" they asked and I naively replied,

"Of course, both English and Urdu speaking." It upset me to discover that our people still differentiated between *Urdu speaking* and *Punjabi speaking* families.

"What kind of a girl would you look for him?"

"It's up to him. Our job was to raise him to the best of our ability." I went against the traditional thinking Eastern mothers.

I had heard through the grapevine that Kashif said "the main reason I want to marry a Pakistani girl is because she would understand the traditions better. A girl who believes that close relationship with her husband's parents is important—just as he would also respect *her* parents."

It so happened that a couple we hardly knew invited us to their daughter's sixteenth birthday. It was a grand event in a banquet hall, almost seven hundred guests. Kashif was reluctant to come along, but we persuaded him. Barely half an hour had passed when he whispered to me, "There's a family here that I think we should approach to see if it might be a good fit."

He later had a chance encounter with the girl at a student function. Things progressed; once he made up his mind to pursue this relationship further, he requested us to facilitate a family meeting through a common friend. Their first visit at our place lasted until 2:00 a.m.

Subsequently we got together every weekend. I later found out why Kashif had become *overexcited:* It was the thought of acquiring a brother and a fourteen-year-old sister!

I had once asked him, "Other boys your age are driving around, but you never asked us to buy you a car," From the back seat of the car I heard him mumble, "What's a car when you deprived me from the most important thing in life?"

Startled, I turned around and asked what he meant. "Oh nothing, it's okay."

As a family of only three, we were happy to be welcomed by their larger clan.

Though their family background and social circles were very different, we were charmed by their extraordinary hospitality. We spent months dining together, going to picnics. Some friends, especially Ghizala Zuberi often teased us, *"It's a family romance."*

......

The artistically choreographed **Henna** *or* **Mehndi** ceremony was a combined event.

Kashif wrote a dance/drama—a woman reliving her romance on her fiftieth wedding anniversary. The story was interwoven with dance songs from **Bollywood** and **Lollywood** (Lahore Film Industry) including old classics.

As I recited parts of the story, the groom and his friends performed dances. The bride's sister and her friends prepared their dances, some of which I choreographed. *Wijdan Nizami*, the Master of photography covered the events.

The last item was a competition between the two groups:

The boys had rented **Ali Baba** costumes. The performance was at its peak, when our lead Ali Baba's black satin baggy pyjamas started slipping off! I rushed to his aid with a safety pin but was turned away. Kashif continued performing, jumping, swirling, holding his pants up with both hands, the entire hall was roaring with laughter. A lady even fell off her chair!

Once I got a glimpse of his white shalwar and *kamar band* peeking through while he jumped up and down, I felt relieved. "Was it preplanned?" the guests wondered.

Kashif being a philanthropist, indifferent to luxuries, never before did he care for material things or display of glamor, but now...?

He even arranged for a ***white horse and carriage*** that would take us to the wedding hall.

To our delight, my brother Sikandar had arrived. All four of us in the carriage leading the way, inching along behind us in a procession were fifty pedestrians in glittering *sarees* and *lehngas*. Accompanying us were ten black cars driven by his friends dressed in tux, slowly moving along.

My Montreal cousin Nilofer strolling along waved, "Hello, Queen Mother."

I mischievously stood up and waved majestically, posing like a real queen.

"Look at the King and the handsome Prince," Rani complimented Mujeeb and Kashif.

"And here is Sikandar our Alexander the Great." I joyfully patted his shoulder.

(Alexander the Great in Urdu is known as Sikandar-e-Azam).

Valeema… (Dinner Reception hosted by the Groom) evolved into a 'literary fusion' event.

One of the top Urdu Scholar from the subcontinent Dr. Gopichand Narang was in town.

He even spoke prose in poetry, after him a celebrity poet Ashfaq recited his love poem in Urdu.

In my poem *"The Miracle Feet"* originally written for Kashif, I added another verse.

'The miracle feet have now multiplied into four.'

I related that Kashif had learned to walk in Mecca, between *Safa* and *Marwa.* After the ritual of seven rounds, he wouldn't stop. His diapers filled with *Zamzam* (a holy spring) water, giggling away he ran back and forth, me running after him. To witness that hilarious scene a crowd had gathered to enjoy the spectacle. Kashif's colleague Dr. Nicolicci became curious…so I had to explain the full context to her later.

I had splurged by inviting a professional Odissi Classical Dancer, *Elora Patnaik.* She took our breath away with her version of classic songs I chose, leaving our guests stunned especially when she danced to depict a flickering flame about to be put out. I did add a Punjabi love thriller '*Longawacha*' when everyone sang along, almost started dancing while seated.

*Safa and Marwa are the two Holy Hills situated in Mecca. The story of the sacred Hills belongs to Bibi Hajra (Hagar) and Prophet Ismail (A.S). As a ritual to commemorate Hagar's devotion for her son, Pilgrims run back and forth between Safa and Marwa. (A version of this story is in the Bible too)

......

The Inter-cultural Dilemmas...

Fancy weddings are not as important as Marriage Planning, but not all immigrants are at the same level when it comes to *adapting* to a different cultural environment.

Kashif had spelled out his views *before* committing to his marriage:

"Although the best part of our culture is that the eldest or the only son lives with his parents, but my 'wife-to-be' would get to choose one of the three options:

"We either live in the same house, two homes side by side, or at least in the same neighborhood." However, being a forward thinker, I clarified my <u>firm conviction</u>:

"Joint-family living system, considering this culture, isn't the best option."

On the other hand, her traditional family strongly believed in the joint-family system. Incidentally, many of us in our culture remain obsessed with 'what will they think' syndrome.

Consequently, our basement, previously utilized for musical concerts and poetry recitals, with traditional Eastern décor including *Divaan,* and *Gao-takyas*, was transformed into a modern luxury apartment for the newlyweds. A brand-new kitchen, remained untouched, and three months later his bride declared, *"I always want us to live together."* We celebrated her decision and opened the doors of our hearts, home, and *hearth* to her family. In place of just three, our dining table often had eight of us seated around! Friends noticed the drastic changes to our lifestyle. But we were happy to have acquired a Ready-Made Family.

Kashif's clinic was thriving with an ever-increasing clientele. So was the Optometric Dispensary that I managed. Our lifestyle could now be perceived as being 'Ideal'.

It was time to make good on my promise to Uncle that one day I will visit him in India.

....

A Visit to Taj Mahal

27 I marveled at how easy it was for this Canadian to land in India! My heart was throbbing with excitement as the Immigration Officer stamped my passport, explaining that his seal was all I would need at the time of my departure.

Uncle Mateen sensed my excitement, and took the longer route to show me the historical buildings along the way.

When he pointed out the grand old villa of our Qaid-E-Azam, Mohammad Ali Jinah (the Founder of Pakistan), I felt a sudden burst of patriotism and gratitude that the Canadian Government allowed us to retain dual nationality. I also felt a sense of pride visiting New Delhi, the Centre for Learning and Culture in the subcontinent. It was renowned as a majestic capital city during the rule of the Muslim Mughal Empires that governed India from 1576 to 1857, as well as two hundred years' long rule of the British Raj.

Though it was the power of 'blood-ties' and a desire to explore my roots that enticed me to travel to India, there were other compelling reasons to be there. En route from the airport, we passed the Holy Family Hospital where Ammi had given birth to me, a Pakistani from Rawalpindi born in New Delhi. Ammi had once taken us back to India again when I was five, but this visit felt like my first.

We got caught in a traffic jam caused by a cow that was simply meandering across the road! In India, the cow is sacred. Everything stops out of respect for the cow.

We finally reached the campus of *Jawahar Lal Nehru University* where Uncle Mateen resided with his wife *Nasreen* Auntie and their son *Irfan*. To them I was yet a stranger. *Banarsi Apa* was a petite, elderly lady of seemingly timid disposition, who was happy to assume her duty as my temporary caretaker. At night, she spread her bed on the floor beside me and told me how my *Naani* (maternal grandmother) looked after seven ailing and ageing servants who had taken care of my grandfather and the family for decades.

She said, "Your Grandma lived to be ninety-five. On the day of her demise, she prepared her own bed, where she peacefully departed!"

Surprisingly, Banarsi could even relate minute details of my wedding in Pakistan, as though she had attended the event. "Your grandmother loved you very much and talked about your sudden departure abroad, wondered if you were happy in your marriage." I was touched.

Uncle's son, my slim fourteen-year-old cousin Irfan, was into classical music at such a young age and was learning to play *Tabla* (traditional drum). It was amazing how Irfan and I developed an instant blood bond that allowed us the freedom to tease each other constantly. Irfan being a single son, like my Kashif, Uncle Mateen had dreams for him. I assured him, "Something tells me *Irfan would grow up to be an extra ordinary individual, you'll see."

Parveen Auntie was a simple, soft-spoken refined lady who blessed me with tender care. She put up with her husband's second bedroom without fuss. Uncle Mateen shared one with her and the second one with his beloved books piled up on half his bed; he slept on the other half.

My lifelong dream to visit the *Taj Mahal* on a moonlit night with live *sitar* accompaniment serenading my senses did not materialize, but I got to see several historical buildings in New Delhi before heading to the Taj Mahal.

Passing through the poverty-stricken city of Agra was depressing; but once you encounter the grandeur of the Taj, it is sensory overload. The impact of such an extreme contrast is hard to describe; you just stand in absolute awe and wonder as you witness visual and timeless proof of the Mughal Emperor *Shah Jehan's* selfless, eternal love for his beloved queen *Mumtaz Mahal*.

It had taken them twenty-two years to build one of the Seven Wonders of the World, all in white marble. While I couldn't help but admire this historical masterpiece, I continued to feel disturbed by the downtrodden poor I had seen along the way that affected me to my very core.

A sad song that played in my memory didn't help my mood either.

"Aik Shahansha ne banwa ke haseen Taj Mahal
Hum gharibon ke muhabbat ka uraaya hai mazaaq"

(An Emperor has made a mockery of us poor, by building a palace as a symbol of his love.)

I had lived away from South Asia for so long maybe I behaved like other western tourists. One of the cameramen made such a sales pitch we hired him. He asked me to stand on a bench to pose so he could produce a photographic masterpiece.

"Wear your goggles, Madam, wear your goggles," he insisted.

"Raise your arm, Madam, higher, even higher. And now point your finger down please." He seemed amused with my incompetence, but he continued to instruct me, even resorted to fixing my *dupatta* (stole) as I became the object of attention for almost a hundred or so seemingly poor women and children who seemed to find my goggles fascinating, making me feel like a celebrity. "A Lollywood Star" I heard uncle whisper. (*Film industry in Lahore)

It was a free-admission day for the poor. They were lined up against a wall waiting their turn to enter. The photographer produced an amazing photo in which I appear to be a giant figure touching the top of the Taj Mahal tomb with my fingertip. "Yes, now I can see that the Taj Mahal did belong to us, Uncle!" He smiled at my cheekiness and gently slapped my face.

I realized that he had preplanned the photo session. I mean, who goes sightseeing in an outfit like mine? He had requested me to wear my brand-new, snow-white *shalwaar kameez,* hand embroidered with black silk thread—his special gift.

In the evenings, we shared our love for music. Apart from Pandit Jasraaj's classical rendition in Hindi, we listened to Urdu ghazals by Begum Akhtar or enjoyed *Shehnai* from Bismillah Khan, *Sitar* by Vilayat Khan, and *Sarodh* by Amjad Khan—the legendary Muslim artists from the subcontinent who were now … just Indians?

I began to feel as though we were robbed of our culture. How was it possible for me to separate myself from our rich heritage, which was now claimed to be only 'Indian culture?' Pakistanis could no longer claim the all-time greatest Urdu poet **Mirza Ghalib** even though Pakistan's official language is Urdu?

Mateen Uncle, Irfan, and I had friendly cross-border squabbles as to who owns or disowns who. Uncle was a patriotic Indian, and I a patriotic Pakistani. Art and culture transcend politics, we concluded that:

Accents don't matter, as long as we speak the same language of love and respect.
Lines drawn on maps are superficial.

One evening, Uncle took me to a cultural show in New Delhi. It was to mark the eightieth birthday of a legendary Muslim poet Ali Sardar Jaafri. I had the privilege of meeting Jaafri Sahib in a private gathering during his tour to Toronto.

The New Delhi event began with Sardar Jaafri's recital of his own classic Urdu poem *"Mera Safar"* (my journey). The English translation was followed by an artistic performance representing all three faiths and cultures. The *Hindu* artists performed a classical dance; the *Muslim* artists sang and played a variety of instruments, while paintings by a *Sikh* Artist Sarbjit Singh, were projected on the back wall, depicting the sunrise and sunset.

Adorable little girls all outfitted in pink and green *Pishwaz* joined in the dance of the budding plants, symbols of 'continuity of life and hope' that captivated the audience . . . and me.

I was suddenly jolted away from the lure of the sweet fantasy being presented on stage and compelled to rise and join the standing ovation.

"Did you see the interfaith display of art and culture at its best, complete harmony? This is what our India is all about," Uncle Mateen proclaimed with pride.

"Yes, but only on the stage. Had it been the case, why would we be divided? And what about all the communal riots you've had?" I questioned emphatically. He offered up another light slap on my cheek, an indication that he agreed with me.

Several years later in connection with the ugly Gujarat riots of March 2002, Uncle finally admitted, "This definitely is a stain on the soul of our country."

Apart from his cultural and historical collection, Uncle also possessed India's largest personal library on Nuclear Physics. In later years, he was instrumental in drafting the Indo-Pak Nuclear Treaty.

Many years later while I was living in Canada, he came to Pakistan on an official trip. That was when he became the Zuberis' celebrity. He was surprised to note how well educated and refined were his Pakistani nephews and nieces.

*Decades later, my cousin Irfan Zuberi became the Chairperson of the National Archives Section at International Association of Sound and Audiovisual Archives. Though not actively in contact, I secretly celebrat his many success stories.

Soon after my return from India I had a strange dream:

There were three passports shown to me by a scary giant of a man. The three were Indian, Pakistani, and Canadian. He ordered me to choose one and cast the others into a blazing fire pit.

It was a strange request, but it was a dream, so …

First, I tossed the Indian Passport with less remorse, since my parents had made that decision before I was born. I held the other two passports in my hand until the terrifying giant again ordered me to choose. Fearful I reluctantly cast my Pakistani passport into the fire but . . . in the same instant, I reached back into the flames to try and retrieve it.

Suddenly the ringing of my alarm clock awakened me. My first waking thought was "Thank God, for the privilege of dual citizenship."

I felt happy I was now clearly a Patriotic Canadian of Indo-Pakistani origin.

•••

Bridging the Gap Post-9/11

28 When the clock struck 9:15 that day, it was like a massive earthquake—with one big jolt, a major fault occurred. How our world had changed! One of the many emotional outpours as a prose poem was therapeutic for me:

Twin Towers

Awestruck, I slouched into my couch
Horrified, in disbelief I watched
panic-stricken executives running for survival
raging police cars, speeding ambulances
The ominous cloud that choked all of humanity
>   *Oh God! Let this not be by the people of my faith*
>   *which taught me love and peace*

Night after night I stayed awake
My fingers nervously flipping channels
if only I had the power to change
the channel of violence escalated

>   *"God, Allah, Khuda, Yahweh or Bhagwan*
>   *are you not one and the same?"*
>   *Can you hear me lament in the middle of the night?*
>   *I cried for the American mother*
>   *whose son vanished in the towering inferno*

I felt the pain for the Afghan women
I also wept for the young minds purchased
in exchange for a few morsels
                  In vain were my laments

Destruction and counter-destruction
the 'New World Order'
Repercussions of yet another war lingered . . .
        Images across the ocean of innocent children
        dodging weapons from up above!

Lost for answers,
I travelled back in time to reflect
upon the day I said goodbye to my loved ones
Just one suitcase, a few jewels of a newlywed
fistful of strong values from the east
Prized possessions I had brought along
In the new homeland I had chosen
I sadly recalled my initial days
I spent lonely Christmas holidays
envying the family gatherings of my colleagues
Unable to attend my brother's wedding
or my father's surgery but . . .

        Adept to adopt and adapt
        I remained adamant,
        continued to weigh the tradeoffs
        soon I blended in, and felt proud

Three decades of learning,

passing on to my offspring
moral values from the two cultures
best of both worlds, East and West
a fine process of combining, retaining,
rejecting, and upholding
            that balancing act I so enjoyed

Shared stories of Prophets Moses, Jesus and Mohammed,
visited Sikh Gurduaras
attended Jewish and Buddhist ceremonies
celebrated Hindu Divali festivals
learned to sing Christmas carols
with such abundant joy

On that morning my dream of
a unified peaceful coexistence . . .
                        Shattered!
What about millions of peace-loving people I speak for?
what about My Twin Towers of Values
that took decades to build?
On that ominous day when the clock turned 9:15
it wasn't only precious lives lost
            A faith was hijacked, humanity swindled
            a small brown chip
            in the multicultural mosaic,
            how could they separate me from it?

Confined to living room whispers
our apprehensions and fears concealed
*Who defines **We** and **They...** and why?*

Aren't we all human beings?
In the interest of humanity,
*we must safeguard ourselves—**Together***
... ...zz

Our otherwise vibrant community where poetry and music flourished entered a somber phase and mood. The 9/11 discussions even led to memories of the Japanese concentration camps. But Muslim apprehensions and fears remained concealed from the mainstream Canadians.

"Would our faith be shaken up or strengthened?" Some were in denial while others expressed anger, "An act of desperation by a handful. There are so many mind-boggling conspiracy theories out there we'd never know the truth."

A young relative Sahar Zuberi, chartered accountant by profession, showed up at our clinic wearing a baseball cap backward. I asked, "Didn't you recently start wearing a scarf?"

"My friends are experiencing racial slurs, I'm afraid of the backlash."

A patient brought her eight-year-old son for an eye exam. I overheard the Receptionist: "Eye exam doesn't hurt."

"Oh no, he is crying about why we named him *Osama*, because children at his school have started calling him a Terrorist." Children!

My non-Muslim friends said, "But the silence is condoning." So, speaking from the 'Media's blind spot' I strived to relay messages on behalf of our peace-loving majority who were not vocal. Here's one of the various poems are wrote:

Fear of the Unknown
With one big jolt a major fault occurred
our world got split in two!

Gravity pulls me
to the half I may not connect with
the other half, reluctant to rescue
Clinging to the cliff
I'm dangling in the air
How deep is this crevasse?
How steep would be the fall?

I gathered people of diverse backgrounds in our home where ideas began to materialize. We established a nonprofit organization 'Bridging the Gap' with a mission of *'**Enlightenment through Entertainment.**'*

My husband never fasted in Ramadan, but Kashif and I woke up for *Sehri* (pre-dawn breakfast). I expressed, "Somehow I feel a heightened sense of purity this time,"

"Me too, in light of the negative news maybe we've become more aware of our own innocence." I shared, "I respect people of all faiths. Faith is a very personal matter."

Kashif said, "Here's an article by Martin Bright, Sunday, September 1, 2002."

'Sales of the Muslim holy book, the Koran, have gone through the roof. Penguin, the publishers of the best-known English-language translation of the Koran, registered a 15-fold increase in the three months following 11 September and sales have held up well since.'

Some people felt their faith was shaken, I had to question mine.

Naturally, I first reflected upon my own upbringing, the characteristics of my peace-loving parents and grandparents as *believers*, what high moral values they upheld:

All they taught us was charity and purity, never cruelty!

My religious uncle reminded us:

"We pray to 'Rabbul-Aalameen'— Creator of the **Universes**, more than one Universe (in line with science). We pray for the descendants of Prophet Abraham (Christians, Muslims, and the Jews). At the end we look to the East then turn to the West to bless all *Humanity*, signifying inclusivity."

I tried to lighten up, "As a daughter of a Humanist father and Religious uncle, maybe I'm a cross breed?"

Religious rituals were secondary to me. I made a point of watching programs about various other religions too, only to find they **all share a common message of peace**. But none is free of any wrongdoing either. I can understand why some people are almost 'allergic' to the word Religion; sadly, many wars and crimes have been committed under the name of faith. Safe landings are taken for granted...only air crashes make the headlines. Similarly, 'Faith-motivated good deeds' don't make the headlines. Regardless, Religion has been hijacked by politics.

On a lighter, humorous note I said: "Being a banker, I think all good things provided to us are like a Credit Card. You may use it to your advantage or abuse it to complete destruction."

My friends asked me: "Is it true that Muslims believe that besides the three Prophets, there have been 124,000 other messengers sent to humanity?" "Yes." I said and added, "wouldn't those include the scientists, philosophers, and such eminent personalities as Epictetus; Plato; Socrates; Marcus Aurelius; Buddah; and Krishna?'

One verse I reflected upon proclaims that:

'God is nearer than your jugular vein.'

The need to awaken my essential self prompted me to also read spiritual books. Helminski's book 'Living Presence' became my source of finding the *Essence.*

Concepts such as 'polishing the mirror of your heart' and, how to tame your Ego so it becomes your 'Servant, not Master' appealed to me much.

'Moderate Muslim' became a new expression whereas I was taught that being moderate was a necessary part of our faith, *or any faith for that matter.*

<u>How would any peace-loving person like to be stereotyped as a terrorist?</u> Being a good human being is what matters most—in that sense I'm a Humanist like my father.

One of the most unfortunate outcomes of 9/11 was the Iraq War. I believe if an opinion poll was taken, most Americans may have voted against it. Even the British Prime Minister (Tony Blair) was overwhelmed with emotions while admitting that it was a gross mistake.

*Anyone who wants to learn more, I refer them to listen to Christian Scholars Gary Wills 'What the Quran Meant' as well as Matt Davies 'Understanding Islam.'

....

LAS VEGAS
(*Prelude to Change*)

---

29 One evening after dinner, Kashif handed a package to us with a smirk on his face.

"What, two airline tickets to Las Vegas and Cancun, wow!" Attached was the itinerary, hotel bookings were taken care of! "It's a prelude to a significant change," he left us in suspense.

In that Gambling Capital of the World, I must be the only person who spent ten days without touching a single slot machine. Mujeeb made one attempt and was thrilled to win one dollar. "Let's go" as if he had won a fortune. There was more to Las Vegas than gambling.

We first stayed at the Caesar's Palace. Walking around in the hustle and bustle of festive Forums, we arrived just in time at the main fountain when a free audio-animatronics show was about to start. The static statues gradually sunk down and disappeared. Instead, the historic figures automatically popped up and started talking to each other, fascinated tourists swarming around. This monument was built to mark the Battle for Atlantis. We had witnessed the *Talking Drums* in Nigeria, but I could never imagine that these hefty cement statues could even hold dialogue with each other!

But nothing could beat the experience at the Venetian Hotel. Over six hundred square feet of luxury room with en suite, which we were fortunate to savor the sheer opulence for two nights. I still remember the plush white towel gowns and fluffy slippers, not to mention other luxury complementary gifts.

Out in the mall's second floor, it was as though we had entered a dream world and found ourselves back in the Italian City of Venice, especially enjoying the gondola rides as we were serenaded with live Italian music.

"This can't be the second floor," Mujeeb was in awe, looking out across the water canals.

"Darling, the blue sky you see above is the ceiling. Look carefully it's just painted with fluffy white clouds," I explained but he remained adamant until we reached an elevator.

"Well, we've witnessed the stunning beauty of Venice in Italy, and now this luxurious replica, but I can't forget the *Venice of Africa. What a world of stark contrasts we live in!

'Makoko village is an informal waterfront settlement off of the capital city Lagos often referred to as the 'Venice of Africa.' It is also the world's largest floating slum, where thousands live cheek by jowl in stilt houses nestled deep in murky black waters.'

......

Soon we reached the *Icon in Action.* Those breathtaking Dancing Fountains of Bellagio, with accompanying symphony, were destined to invoke romance. Mujeeb gave me a tight hug, "This honeymoon is at Kashif courtesy." What a spectacular show of thoughtfully interwoven water, music, and light to mesmerize us tourists! Each performance was so unique that we couldn't help but fall in love with this aquatic wonder. "What an enchanting composition of opera, classical, Broadway and pop tunes." We delighted in that pure invitation to romance, as our senses exploded with awe. As we strolled to return, Mujeeb suddenly gained pace. "I can tell why you are so eager to reach the hotel."

The shows we enjoyed the most were *Cirque du Soleil* and *Titanic*. "How can they create such visual effects that the surging waves appear so real?" I was in awe.

We toured around the city visiting replicas of the Eiffel Tower as well as the Egyptian Pyramids. One of the landmarks is the pyramid shaped hotel **Luxor**, three-fourth the size of the great pyramid in Giza Egypt! There, at one of the largest atriums in the world, I picked up a brochure:

'The Hotel is named after the ancient Egyptian city Luxor. It is 365 feet tall and has 4,400 guest rooms. Guests are greeted by a 140-feet obelisk and a 110-feet reproduction of the Great Sphinx of Giza.'

Mujeeb interjected, "How captivated you are with the *Replicas,* but darling I've taken you to all these locations in real life, remember?"

"I remember but it's fascinating to see them all in one place, thanks to our son." I read on: *'The Luxor Sky Beam has 42.3 billion candle power spotlights that shine from the top of the pyramid nightly.'*

My thoughts wandered off to places in the world where basic electricity is considered an unattainable luxury, "I'm awestruck by the display of 'Ingenuity and Insensitivity' side by side!"

......

Once we returned to Canada, we learned that our generous son had also treated his in-laws with a fully paid ten-day trip to the Bahamas, including hotel and car rental! His sister and brother-in-law were treated with a trip to the Disney world. Mujeeb asked in a sarcastic tone,

"Has our son won a lottery or something?"

I replied, "He likes to spend on others."

"But they have two other children of their own. I don't think Kashif should put his in-laws on equal ground as us," Mujeeb said with considerable disdain.

The following evening, we received a dozen long-stemmed roses as a surprise. The couple asked us, "Would you rather win a million-dollar home or become grandparents?" Choice was easy—immersed in sheer joy we *all* celebrated the evening ***together.***

A Star Is Born!

A miracle unfolded before my eyes, how a supple body opened up like a lotus flower in blossom, I watched in awe! Since I drove them to the hospital, I was extended a last-minute invitation to join my daughter-in-law, her mom, and Kashif in the room.

Childbirth, especially of your own grandchild's, changes your world view. Mother-child bonding taking place before my eyes invoked memories of my own.

Holding little Elina in my arms feeling euphoric, I could forget the world's sorrows. Her lips like rose buds, long eyelashes, soft chubby cheeks, as I felt her gentle breaths close to my heart, I reflected: '*How we take things for granted. Somewhere in this world a grandmother is holding her beloved child too. Not as fortunate as I for she may be seeking shelter from bombs, protection from disease, or escape from poverty.*'

"What about *Azaan*?" (The Call to Prayer is traditionally whispered into a newborn child's ears). Mujeeb was glad to perform tha ritual. Azaan at birth has *no prayer* in response. However, the prayer at a funeral has *no Azaan.* This supposedly symbolizes our brief worldly existence, as short as the time lapse between Azaan at birth, and the Funeral Prayers at demise. In Urdu, the best word for death is considered ***Intiqal*** (transformation).

Choosing a meaningful name is important in our culture. The meaning of Elina is different in various languages, countries, and cultures. The Greek and Finnish meanings are the same: torch, *bright light*; but Indian meaning is *smart.* Elina or Elenais is a star amongst the cluster of Gemini. Gemini happens to be Kashif's sign and Zohra means *morning light* or the *planet Venus.* It was a mere coincidence that the three of us were named after stars.

I secretly wished that I am able to play a positive role in her life, like both my grandmothers did in mine. I whispered, "Elina, you've given more meaning to my life."

An Intercultural Impasse…

With the arrival of the baby, more space became a requirement. We expected the new parents to move out. Instead, they insisted we move to a bigger house *together.* I personally opposed the idea and tried to convince my daughter-in-law.

"Please don't choose old tradition for the sake of your parents, your husband, or the community. Just listen to the voice of your heart." I reiterated, "If you regret this decision later on, I will be devastated."

To leave our cherished home where we had created fond memories was difficult.

However, both our families were on the same page. Mine was **a single No vote!**

My discretion succumbed to *indiscretion*—we sold our paid-off home, plus the investment property, just like that. As for their share, long lives the world of creative financing in North America, even Kashif was swept away.

Always opposed to borrowing, his previously firm conviction rang in my ears at night: "Moderate living within means, and the excess income for charity and the rainy day," was now a forgotten fantasy. What happened to our son?!

……

Since the construction was delayed, Mujeeb and I spent three weeks of luxury in a motel. Fluffy white bedsheets and fresh towels supplied daily, I could live like that forever. But a trip to Montreal to meet our cousins Nilofer and Minhaj was overdue. In 1963, after my wedding reception, they had invited close family over for a BBQ dinner in their exquisite rose garden. That's when the two families had bonded. Now we travelled back four decades and relived our past, "Look at the beauties of our bygone era, how we have aged!"

The following day we toured the city, visited Point-du-Moulin (a park) and other sites.

……

The Train Journey
(An Awakening)

In that cold October afternoon in 2003, returning from Montreal to Toronto by Via Rail, our train sped across land and time. Passengers clung tightly to their invisible cloaks of privacy, each engrossed in a book, snoozing away their fatigue, or gazing out the windows. All ages, all races, heading in the same direction and not casting a single glance at one another.

A sudden bump shocked everyone as a barrage of stones and debris were hurtled against the train. Was it an earthquake, or were we under attack? Panic-stricken passengers grabbed on to anything they could. The train slowly tipped almost onto its side, then straightened up and came to a stop with one harsh ominous jolt.

Scared to death, each of us spontaneously began reciting our own prayers. Verses from the Torah, the Bible, and the Quran were all magically merging. The sighs of relief that we were all alive were our commonality, so we quickly found ourselves consoling each other.

The longest twenty minutes of our lives elapsed before a uniformed black man with a heavy Jamaican accent entered our coach. "Our train has collided with a huge tractor trailer! The engineer is alive but unfortunately the truck driver is in critical condition. Please do not panic. Stay inside. Help will arrive soon."

Stuck in the middle of nowhere, in cold darkness waiting for help to arrive, we had no acceptable alternative but to talk to each other.

Coincidentally amongst so few of us, there was such a diverse group of people from various faiths. In our group were a handsome young Palestinian Muslim, a graduate from Queen's University; a well-travelled Orthodox Christian girl from Mount Royale; and a refined Jewish woman from Toronto who was a voice of calm and order in the chaos. Together, we cleared away debris, cleaned our fellow passengers' cuts and soothed some children's fears with songs and stories. I even recited a poem to an elderly lady. To the amusement of some onlookers, she placed her hand on my head and cast a loving glance. I couldn't help recall my grandma.

A group of us discussed religion; politics; poetry; poverty; modern-day achievements; and the lethal injustices mankind inflicts on itself, often under the name of religion. How had we all connected so deeply in such a short time? Perhaps since everyone felt equally vulnerable during our life-threatening experience, *it awakened us to realize how similar we all were*.

After more than five hours, help finally arrived … in a fashion. There were ambulances for the critically injured among us; but for the rest of us, we had to trek two kilometers along a narrow, uneven dirt road, peppered with stones and broken glass, to reach the waiting buses. Those who were injured and needed assistance were aided by their fellow passengers.

We all made it TOGETHER!

......

Within weeks of our move to our much-anticipated new mansion, we were told that,

"Moving together was a huge mistake!"

Near derailment of a train we had just survived, but this jolt, out of the blue, had the potential to derail much more.

In my diary I've written the details, but here I'd prefer to express an 'objective' view: We were not the only ones impacted by this intercultural dilemma. Often the immigrant parents import their set of values, which do not make sense to their children growing up in Canada. Sometimes parents put undue pressure, especially on their daughters.

That one moment of indiscretion, when **I** did not act on **my** pragmatic sixth sense, changed the course of our lives. But now 'wisdom of the heart' was summoned.

We were presented a calendar with a solution: "On Red weekends you leave the house and we'll invite whoever we want. On Blue weekends we will leave, you may invite your friends, until you find another place." We agreed; <u>selfless love can be a recipe for disaster</u>.

Before their next trip to Hawaii, the couple offered, "While we are away, feel free to throw a housewarming party." We availed the opportunity, and had a fully catered lavish dinner party, entertainment included. Everyone had a blast.

Were it not for our beautiful chirping bird Elina, coming to our bedroom first thing in the mornings, I would want to erase those two years of my life.

I'd often cuddle her and ask, "What's the best thing that ever happened to me?"

"*Me*," she would joyfully reply, with her beautiful bright eyes and breathtaking smile. We cuddled, she giggled, as she wobbled along taking baby steps. Mujeeb and I sat at opposite ends to prevent her from falling, and one day she walked. We were enthralled!

But, our friends no longer felt comfortable visiting us as they did in our previous home.

•••••••••••••••••••••••••••••••••••••••

Farewell Joint Family

30 During an evening walk, a sign 'Open House' in our neighborhood invited our curiosity. I was enamored by that fully furnished, upgraded bungalow for sale, inclusive of custom drapes and other accessories. But the price was out of our budget, plus Mujeeb's heart was still in Mississauga. The following evening, Kashif returned from work and declared,

"I've booked a perfect house for you guys,"

"Don't tell me it's the model home on the next street." He confirmed it. Mujeeb couldn't hold back, "Your mother was drooling over that house last night,"

"But you know well we can't afford it," I added.

"Ammi, Abu, it's just a down payment. We have uprooted you at this age. We should try and mend our mistake." I secretly thought of the irony, people dream of freedom fifty-five but I had achieved it at fifty. Assuming a huge mortgage at retirement age meant I'd have to work more hours. However, an ideal house on a unique street leading to a heritage area felt like a reward we deserved.

How community thrives on gossip, "*You just moved, what went wrong?*"

"Nothing, I wanted to be the first mother-in-law to move out," I said lightly.

This silenced others, but Chameli commented, "Your house-*warning* party said it all."

One week before the closing, our new model home was struck with lightening!

All the electrical wiring had to be reinstalled so there was indefinite delay in closing. Sikandar was already upset why we had to move out from our new house. When he got this news, he booked me a return flight, I readily availed it. Mujeeb didn't stop me.

......

Three days later I was in another hemisphere, it was magic.

Now that Sikandar had moved from the UAE to Karachi, instead of Mujeeb's family, I stayed with mine. Up until now Shahid and Huma looked after our parents in Pindi, now in Karachi, Durdana Sikandar had taken over.

On our way home, it was a sea of humans—in a city of almost twenty million, population explosion visible and also *audible*! To cope with Karachi's crazy traffic, most of them hired drivers. The number of cars and noisy motor rickshaws had increased. A speeding motorbike whizzed by—a man with his wife, plus two children clinging onto their mother, a scary sight.

Jet-lagged, I squeezed myself in the middle of my parents and fell asleep like a baby.

Early morning, I took immense delight in seeing Sikandar looking dapper in his business suit and crisp white shirt. His face glowing with gratitude as he touched his designer tie I had brought for him, one of many I gifted to him over the years. "It looks so nice on you,"

"My colleagues at Faisal Bank ask me where I get these unique ties from,"

"Paris airport, London airport, the designer shops in Toronto, you name it," I boasted. "After all you are now the Operations Manager for thirty-six branches across the country,"

"Well, what I need to know is: *How could... an award winning banker... hand over her money power into the hands of others?"* I replied, "Dear brother Sikandar, my only choice was to **Rebel** but I opted not to." He sensed my mood and said, "Okay, we won't talk about it again. You are here to relax before a fresh start." As usual he entered our parents' room to greet them, I watched Ammi kiss his hand as usual.

After Shaista gave oil massage to Durdana's hair, she asked if I was interested too.

As she poured coconut oil on my scalp she commented,

"So dry *Baji,* who oils your hair?"

"Nobody, I do everything myself. But I have no time to oil my hair," I said with my eyes closed. Inhaling the mild aroma of coconut oil I relished the experience but was amused at the irony: That a housemaid in Pakistan was feeling sorry for an independent professional woman living in Canada. Her life was so simple.

Durdana then booked my appointment with Meher's Beauty Parlor for a manicure, pedicure, the whole works! Soon I started to unwind.

Green tea was served in the lounge as a midmorning routine. Gourmet lunches included specialty dishes I craved for. I entered the kitchen like a *foreigner.* Their maids giggled as I cracked jokes with them, I opened the lid of a huge pot, smelling the mouth-watering **Qorma** (gourmet version of meat curry) I asked: "Is there a large gathering tonight?"

"Not really."

"But this food seems enough for fifty people," I said and Durdana replied,

"It is not just us, there's our cook Zubaida, Shaista, Ammi's care providers Safia, plus the two drivers who also have families." *So this is their self-developed social welfare system,* I concluded. Well-off families not only enjoy the luxury of servants, but also support marginalized families.

It's interesting to live in two cultures simultaneously, but one habitually starts comparing and noticing even the subtle differences.

Any visitors, family or friends, would make a point to first chat with my parents. I noticed that whenever Ammi or Abbaji intended to get up, someone swiftly reached out to help them put on their slippers. *Respect for the elderly* is such an integral part of our culture.

Concerned about me, all my siblings embarked upon a mission to go the extra mile to pamper me. Sikandar took me to the Karachi School of Arts to watch a play *'Run for your Wife.'* How masterfully they delivered dialogues in typical English accents, the entire cast was Pakistanis from Islamabad! One could hardly tell they were not British. In that packed theater, the audience cracking up throughout the performance.

He also took us to the Defence Golf Club, where after a lavish meal I was in for yet another treat. We took a stroll by the seaside where I saw hundreds of lawn chairs, and an outdoor stage, under a decorative canopy with *Tabla* and *Harmonium* (traditional instruments).

"Live music by the seashore, really?" I spilled my excitement.

The crowd built up gradually. We sat in the front row relishing the sea breeze caressing us, the sound of waves tantalizing our finer sensibilities. Soon, the vocalist and a *Tabla* player arrived and bowed as we applauded. Sikandar and Durdana requested songs of my choice, and the artists smiled and willingly obliged us. With those favorite lyrics, we tightened our grips and moist eyed, we exchanged glances of affection.

My grown-up nephews and nieces also treated me to dinners in fancy restaurants. Over the years, I had built a special bond with them. My sisters complained why they were not invited. "Well, the youngsters just want my company for a change." I could easily step into their age group. They felt less inhibited to express their more modern views about life.

My baggage packed, a small suitcase was added to accommodate all the gifts. Usually my appetite abated as I dreaded the long enduring journey. However the smell of *Nihari* from the kitchen told me everyone would be joining us for dinner.

As usual, the night before my departure, we had music by candlelight at the

'Grand Central Station' (Sikandar's house) Youngsters selected and taped special songs bearing my taste in mind. I preserved that memory in an emotional poem titled "*In Tune*."

The next morning, on our way to the airport, even their driver played an old song:

"Chal urh ja rey panchi
Ke ab yeh desh hua baiganaa"

(Little bird, fly away from this estranged land)

"For God's sake, please switch it off. This isn't the time for such depressing songs." I felt sorry for **Khalil Sahib** the poor fellow had strived to score marks for his timely choice. To lighten up, I said, "Our family's passion for poetry has also rubbed off on your domestic staff."

In the loud silence of that somber moment, I marveled: For religious people he plays the Quran recitals, for my nieces the latest Lollywood tunes, and poetic Bollywood hits for Sikandar.

I thought of sharing our Canadian icon Anne Murray's "*Somebody is always saying goodbye.*" However, continued silence only raised the volume of my self-awareness—I was soon to be distanced from them all. Thankfully, I had something to look forward to.

......

Our New Beginning

Even though my flight back was tiresome, I was emotionally energized. Mujeeb greeted me with a passionate welcome. The best outcome of moving out was that we became closer to each other than we had been for some time. I had fun going to various kitchen places looking for spice bottles, a tea kettle, everyday crockery, and cutlery, like the newlyweds.

"Zooby, let's just pretend we are on our honeymoon."

"Ah ha, you're calling me Zooby again," he seemed elated. A memory of 1963 flashed by; so I hummed the first English song I had learned during our honeymoon.

"*Zooby Zooby Zoo means that I love you.*"

While emptying the waste basket in his study, an old folded paper fell out. I opened it, dated April 10, 1963, I called out with excitement, "Zooby wait, I think I found the letter you held back!" But Mujeeb was already at the door, "Darling I've been waiting for you, the Mall will close in an hour." I rushed out. But when I looked for it the next morning, it went missing again." I suspected Mujeeb but he said with a smirk, "If you kept it you'll find it, just like your car keys."

......

Before my trip I had attended a few meetings of the *'Kehkashan Ladies Club' which was established by South Asian women from the Middle East. Most of them wore hijab and just wanted to let their hair down in all-female gatherings. Now nominated to serve as their President, I didn't feel I was suited for the position, so I declined. However, due to the internal politics they chose me as an outsider who would be impartial. I resisted, they persisted, I succumbed:

'Maybe there's a calling for me?'

Being new in Canada, they faced unique social issues. One we identified was 'confusion about arranged marriages.' Cultural conflicts between the first and second generations needed to be addressed. Consequently, I wrote a customized script titled 'Arranged Love' to be staged at one of their monthly events.

As if the stage was set for me!

What a surprise ... those talented women usually in hijab now emerged from their shells of inhibitions to perform on stage, surprisingly even wearing tank tops or dresses with spaghetti straps. Being an all-female club, to play the male roles, their daughters had to dress as boys.

To watch my own written words being spoken on stage was a thrilling experience—not to mention the positive response from the highly engaged audience. Having touched a raw nerve a heated debate was triggered. This prompted me to bring awareness to a wider audience.

Mothers started calling me about their personal concerns, many *daughters* not allowed to date perceived arranged marriages outdated. Easy to get along with youngsters, I utilized every social opportunity to probe into their concerns. They expressed, "Zohra Auntie, at least you are interested to learn about our problems our loving parents don't seem to fully understand."

"Please don't call me Auntie, it creates a barrier and also reminds me of cramps. It was our code word for monthly cycle." They settled for Zeezee or Zohra ji. Subsequently, candid dialogues with them became my ongoing Research Project.

An outspoken member *Zeba* and I hit it off. South Asian mothers often sought **gori chitti** girls (fair-complexioned girls) for their sons! Zeba and her girls had perfectly tan complexions to the envy of most white women. "But that too is sometimes a hurdle," Zeba confided in me. I was disgruntled, so together we formed an alliance:

"Since you are familiar with both generations' points of views, maybe you could 'bridge the gap' between them." She really hit the nail on the head.

The open mic discussion after the skit triggered such heated debate it prompted me to write a story titled '*Window Shopping...for Lasting Love'* which I also translated in Urdu. I aimed to stage a play at our next annual fund raiser of Vision and Literacy International.

Carried away with my obsession, without knowing *if's and buts*, I booked the RBC Theatre at Mississauga's Living Arts Centre. "Aren't you going ahead of yourself?" Mujeeb asked. I said with audacious confidence, "Zooby, we still have eight months to find our way."

Two Chance Meetings...

One day, out of the blue I received a call: "I'm Samina a new immigrant. I was referred to you, that you hold large-scale events. I'd like to join your art projects."

We met in my office. She needed an introduction to the community, and I needed a creative diversion. Samina turned out to be an award-winning artist from PTV (Pakistan Television) and was interested in producing plays. With overflowing enthusiasm I shared,

"I already have a story to be converted into a play."

I noticed Samina's face with flawless skin, glowing with excitement. With such instant click between the two of us, it was like a lucky blind date. We decided to collaborate.

Within a few days, Samina converted my script for a stage production but …

The reality hit me later that I had blindly plunged into a huge financial commitment, the RBC Theatre! A desperate need for funding propelled me to approach our Optometric Clinic suppliers of frames and contact lenses. They readily accepted my proposals to advertise their products via community outreach—it was a win/win.

Our lonely *house* soon became a *home* for accomplished artists. I believe in the Chinese philosophy of *yin and yang*—everything is in balance. Marriage between Kehkashan and VLI now served a dual purpose: To raise *Awareness* as well as *Funds* in line with our mission of: *'Enlightenment through Entertainment'*

Samina had a theater group with Tariq Hameed, Azaad Daanish, and Zehra Naqvi, those artists volunteered their talents. I also invited Kashif's in-laws to participate; they were excited.

Within six months we were knee-deep into a live production of my play. Samina's new Urdu title was *'Pasand Apnee Apnee' (Of one's own liking).

Our unfinished basement became the Rehearsal Hall. Mujeeb was thrilled to play the dual role as our friendly host and an ever-ready videographer.

The Second unexpected Encounter…

It was after the tragic bombing of July 7, 2005, in London, UK.

At a monthly brunch meeting of the Writers and Editors Network, the topic of 7/7 was discussed—suicide attacks on the public transport system in London that killed many innocent civilians. Once I noted a comment or two with a hint of 'stereotyping' it triggered emotions. Being the only Muslim in that gathering, I was prompted to speak.

"We should guard against stereotyping *all* Muslims because of the unspeakable acts *of a few.*" I went on: "According to our faith, taking one innocent life is like killing humanity."

Instead of my love poem, I decided to recite my poem *"Juzdaan"* I had written after 9/11.

At the end of my recital, a woman approached me. "I'm so sorry for your pain. Believe me I understand how you feel. Being a Jew I know how it feels to be ostracized just for being who we are." I was touched by her compassion.

"You are so kind … but I am sorry I didn't get your name?"

"I am Reva." Encountering each other in circumstances of chaos and fear, we offered compassion to one another, with open hearts and no thoughts of creed or the burden of historical conflict. What started as a bad day was the beginning of a valuable friendship.

That Takes Ovaries…

What a pleasant surprise that Reva once ran a theater in Toronto and directed many plays! "Had I known that, I would've invited you to a play recently staged in Toronto—how my story 'The Gasoline Queen' from Nigeria entered the Distillery District in Toronto." Another WEN member Karen Allison was listening in. They were both intrigued and curious, so I shared:

"The original play titled *'That Takes Ovaries'* was written by a Jewish American producer, Rivka Solomon. Later on, Sally Jones of Rasik Arts Theatre reproduced it in Toronto." I carried on, "Since the play was about gutsy stories of brazen women around the world, Sally included two stories from Canada, one of which was mine from Nigeria."

"Oh, that's sounds so intriguing, what did you do?"

"Nothing really, Sally happened to know about my experience of the Nigerian military coup when dozens of soldiers pointed their guns toward me and I burst out laughing. She included that humorous episode as well as the excerpt from my Gasoline Queen story."

"Wow! But who would've thought that decades later a bizarre story from Africa would make it into a theater in Toronto?" Noting their interest level I was tempted to share more.

"By the way, a young Indian girl played my role. It was staged for three days, followed by open mic." Reva said, "Let me know of similar events, I'd definitely be interested."

"As a matter of fact, we are about to stage our first play, but it happens to be in Urdu."

Our first Socio-drama
(And, the Kashmir Earthquake)

Excitement mounted as it was to be a sold out show but...*'Life happens when you are making other plans.'* A few days prior to the production, a massive earthquake with a magnitude of 7.6 hit our homeland. It occurred on October 8th of 2005, in the Pakistan administered areas of Kashmir. Centered near the District of Muzaffarabad, also the Indian administered Jammu and Kashmir. The tremors impacted the regions in Afghanistan, Tajikistan, and Chinese Xinjiang. The remote and rugged mountains were shaken and crushed the entire population; children's schools were flattened. Almost 75,000 people lost their lives!

I called an emergency meeting in which Bridging the Gap and VLI decided to donate 50% of the funds raised to the earthquake victims. To raise awareness about the tragedy we decided to add half an hour segment prior to the Play. Emotionally impacted, many people rallied around us. Two renowned vocalists *Munni* and *Afzal Subhani* volunteered to render the opening song. *Shela Minhas* was one of the supporters of VLI as well as BTG. Her teenage son *Saad Minhas* readily took up the challenge to be our Emcee. We also put together a skit.

The event commenced with an emotional rendition of my new poem titled *"Under the Rubble."* Dressed in Kashmiri outfits, my friend Maleeha's children and Elina, acted as the injured children. A friend Meena Santdasani and I choreographed a 'Dance of Hope.'

"Mein ne tujh se chand sitarey kub mangay
Roshan dil baidar nazar de yallah"
(God, I'm not asking you for the moon and stars
Only pleading to raise awareness and the loving hearts)

During Santdasani's stellar performance, our little Elina under three, oblivious of the audience's presence, sat on the stage innocently shredding a business card of one of our major sponsors! She looked up and realized she was supposed to follow the other children's actions, quickly raising her hands in prayer for the earthquake victims.

Elina's acting debut with such adorable innocence invited loud applause, a timely distraction that set the stage for the main event—the play in Urdu *"Pasand Apni, Apni."*

I was ecstatic to see the capacity audiences, celebrating with us our first venture of this nature. The crowd had laughter outbursts, especially at *Tariq Hameed's* comedic role.

Reva, Karen, and Mickey attended the play to provide us moral support, even though they didn't know the language. I knew Reva would notice glitches in directions, so I admitted, "It was an amateur production." But their response was extremely encouraging:

"We were utterly fascinated to see how engaged your audiences were," "We Pakistanis have such a fetish for plays that over there even the wedding dates are fixed to avoid clashes with popular serial drama episodes airing on TV."

The next morning our landline continued to ring all day long, congratulating us.

"Thank you for bringing my story to stage" expressed several eligible girls.

Evidently, we had hit the right notes.

While the older generation enjoyed the crisp Urdu dialogues and humor, the younger crowd was pleased that this controversial issue was brought to light. "What about an English version so we may understand better?" My aspiration for a wider outreach was energized.

The After-shocks…

After the production, I was glued to our TV. I called my family in Pakistan to check if anyone I knew was affected? Sadly, it happened to be Moonis and his wife! They lived in the only building in Islamabad that collapsed during the earthquake. Unfortunately, they could barely identify his finger with a ring. To deal with that shock I invoked old memories which morphed into a poem, here are a few verses:

The Eternal Child

Like a precious pearl inside its shell
submerged in the mysterious depths
of an ocean unknown—the subconscious
Mind and heart in deep romantic combine.

. . . .

"Unexpectedly emerges from the ocean
the eternal child that never grows old
Through intricate memory lanes
it comes to rescue

> *Tensions ease, inner being smiles*
> *How wisdom flirts with simplicity*
> *as if an innocent child is helping the old man*
> *cross the bridge once again*
>
> > *Mature love remains... intact."*
> >
> > > ......ZZ

Nonetheless, that tragedy tarnished the image of the Eternal Child—*the pearl in its shell.* It was replaced with images of horror under the rubble. In due time, we accept it all.

In any case, repeated requests to take the arranged marriage issue to a wider audience occupied my mind. For the purpose of staging our play in English, Zeba vowed full support.

....

'Window Shopping …
for Lasting Love'

———————

31 At the Annual Banquet of Kehkashan Ladies Club, Zeba entered the hall like a Celebrity in our Community, wearing her apple-green and royal-blue saree; she attracted everyone's attention. "That's what you wore on stage for Zohra's play at RBC Theatre, right?" I felt happy that her acting debut at our play was so appreciated.

A few days later, I returned from work when Mujeeb broke the alarming news:

"Zeba passed away in a car accident." In disbelief I felt my head spinning.

She was simply walking on a footpath when a teenager without a license, driving her parent's car, inadvertently pressed the accelerator instead of brakes—it crushed her body. For weeks, Mississauga residents placed bouquets on that pavement; her townhouse was packed with mourning families and loyal clients from the hair salon she owned.

With her tireless commitment, followed by her sad and sudden demise, Zeba became an added source of inspiration for me to carry on the project.

……

For the English version, I reverted to my original title.

My old dream of state-of-the-art Hammerson Hall (1300 capacity) resurfaced. In my frenzy I went ahead and booked it, naively assuming that our Board members would help raise funds but? Only *I* seemed to be married to the project, Zeba had left me.

Help came from an unexpected source.

Apart from sponsorships from our Optometry suppliers, **Fatima Qureshi** came on board. With the growing number of South Asian weddings in the community, it was the perfect opportunity to showcase her custom-designed exotic wedding wear collection.

Engaging the Community at Grassroots Level…

For the lead role I invited *Filza* from our previous play, all the way from Calgary, at my personal expense. She arrived with two giant suitcases and a bundle of surprises—she had no place to stay! Now we needed a mother for her.

Part of Bridging the Gap's 'mandate' was to promote talent and engage individuals from all walks of life. This was challenging, yet the most interesting task which I thoroughly enjoyed. I called *Reena Grover* whom I met at a private musical. Enchanted by her melodious voice and stage presence, I thought 'she may be ideal for the role of our heroine's mother'. Bold and beautiful Reena Grover came for audition but asked me,

"Zohra ji, I've never acted before, what makes you think I can play this role?"

"It's my gut feeling because you are confident, have stage presence, plus you can sing so well. Let's just read the script first." Her initial attempt was flat, after that I read it with a *zing*, which she picked up fast. Her melodious live songs were bound to add flavor to the play. To add glamor as well, I persuaded a gorgeous and glamorous lady, *Amina Haqqani,* to play our heroine's mother-in-law.

The Multicultural Perspectives...

"Wouldn't it be best to have direct feedback from different ethnic groups?" I asked.

Fatima presented a practical solution, "Bring them over for lunch at my place. After the meeting, everyone may select their outfits for the wedding scene."

The authors from WEN agreed to play five-minute roles—Mickey Turnbull; Bev Laugheed; Anne Ptaznick; Jack Livesley and Stacey Balakofsky. I only needed a Palestinian. So, I approached *Gada* from my dentist's office who succumbed to my *Power of Persuasion*.

Everyone was excited to see Fatima Qureshi's exquisite place which was once 'The Hammond House' –Mississauga's heritage home built in 1866 by Captain Thomas Hammond. Lunch was served in their roundtable conference room. I later jotted down candid opinions and authentic dialogues of people from ten different nationalities. It was highly educational for me too. One of the most interesting comments was passionately expressed:

"Back in 1667, over in France, the clergy pushed parents to send their young daughters across the Atlantic to marry up... or so they were told. Basically, they were shipped here to service the pioneers— soldiers who were fighting the Iroquois. So I know it's not just the East Indians and Pakistanis who arrange marriages."

Various races and ages tried on *sarees, shalwars, churidars, and lehngas,* which immensely delighted our hostess. Fatima's showroom buzzed with chuckles and wisecracks. ***Girls will always be girls—*** after the catwalks, everyone picked up their outfits and danced their way out. How easily we all bonded, they said,

"A great afternoon like never before, now we await our five minutes of fame."

By then our Hallstone basement was finished with *East meets West* theme; we became one big multicultural family. Mujeeb and his camera remained fully charged.

Being a Rookie Producer, I ended up hiring a director who needed help. Reva turned out to be our 'Friend in Need' and helped us direct our multicultural scene. I received on-the-job training so I could direct individual rehearsals during the week.

I enjoyed Filza's wild sense of humor—together we had a lot of late-night laughs. She connected me to a renowned music group *Awaaz*. We were lucky to use their iconic songs.

......

Only two days prior to the production, Filza broke her sad news:

"My boyfriend has broken up with me, so my Calgary apartment is no longer available. I need accommodation in Toronto. Unless you pay me the first and last month's rent I cannot perform in your play." I felt the earth shifting from under my feet. Over a thousand tickets had been sold and the show was to take place in two days! Our board members suggested,

"Get someone to read the script on stage." But that option was not acceptable to me.

They say that Retirement Savings Plans (RSP's) are meant for the rainy day—for me it was a *Tornado Day*. I rushed to cash $2,500.

When she signed the loan agreement, I had doubts if she would ever pay me back.

During a TV interview in Buffalo, USA, they asked me if they could record our upcoming production and also air it on their channel. Obviously there was appetite to probe this issue.

On the morning of the event, we received a surprise mail delivery at our door:

'Certificate of Recognition from the Government of Ontario'

It was to congratulate us (Bridging the Gap) for the upcoming production, wishing us success. Only in Canada!

To introduce the play, facing a crowd of twelve hundred, I forgot about my nine months pregnancy and contractions. *'Less money in my RSP, longevity has no guarantee.'*

Filza's acting was superb. But she was asked to leave right after the production.

Junaid Waheed's lifelong dream was fulfilled; he zestfully played the father. Being on the Board of Directors (a Chartered Accountant), he took charge of all the financial matters.

A young actor *Fuad Ahmad* stole the show even though it was his acting debut. (Since then he has become a professional actor performing in films, television, and theaters across Canada). *Rafia Khokhar* was another gem of a talent I discovered who acted in both our plays.

Bridging the Gap received the 'Best Emerging Performing Arts Award' from the Mississauga Arts Council, plus $1,000 cash. But they say, 'Awards have a hidden agenda—we expect more of the same'. So how about the next play?

"I know there's interest, but I need a breather."

Post-production comments were worth noting:

"You guys are just like us!" What?

Some people asked, "Is it true that your Prophet's first wife Khadija was fifteen years older than him?" "Is it true that she proposed to him?" Other comments we received such as:

"More of you should share such information."

However, no longer willing to compromise our Club 23 parties, it was time for me to enter the 'Theatre of Innocence' to play the fairy-tale stories for a change.

......

Home Theater–Club 23 Dramas

Two of my granddaughters and I have birthdays on the twenty-third of different months, so we named our group Club 23. The Youngest Daania missed my birthday by two days, so in recompense we let her join, justifying her membership status as "She rushed to celebrate the first black President of USA."

"Ya right!" was her response once she learned to speak.

Together we either created artwork or dancercised.

On each visit I was assigned a different role.

"Ma, today you have to be Princess Adriana."

"Oh, but first you should tell me what Adriana is like so I may play her role."

For our *pretend* games we constructed a Club House, cost free! With the dining-room chairs facing outward we created a room in the centre and used my fancy stole for the ceiling. The exterior was my innovations, but the girls decorated the interiors and requested me,

"Ma, please come inside."

The invitation was tempting so I'd squeeze in, feeling like a giant for a change.

Inside that Club House, we utilized foot-rest stools as the dining tables, decorative serviettes made lovely tablecloths. At times, Elina even prepared a menu *a la carte*.

"Ma, let's name it Radial Restaurant (named after our previous house).

"Smart idea, but don't turn me into a waitress,"

"We will," they teased me back. The girls loved to serve **real tea** in the miniature bone china tea sets I bought from Chinese stores.

During our cooking sessions, they learned to make *kebab* and *puris* (deep fried flat round bread). Excitement surged when they were sufficiently skilled to create puris; when filled with steam the puris would puff up into a ball as they were dunked in hot oil. Their Filipino nanny Ms. Josie sometimes accompanied them in their culinary endeavors. Those video clips continue to excite us all to this day. Inspired by them, I wrote several poems. Here's one for when they first learned to speak.

Simple Words
New words she just learned
my granddaughter only two
"Because and Of course"
Uttered in appropriate context too

> *'Because' and 'Of course'*
> *Ostensibly simple*
> *yet their complication to an adult, ample*
> *Many words she'll continue to learn*
> *The older she grows*
> *the more difficult they may become*

*It's taken **me** decades to conclude:*
My 'of courses; should never be
reflections of submission;

Of confidence and determination
And my 'Becauses' won't be excuses,
only justifiable justifications

> *Lessons for her I'll save for future*
> *For now just relish the spontaneity*
> *with which she keeps repeating*
> > *Those simple words*
> > > *… …zz*

Once the children's innovative spirits were nurtured and aroused, they loved listening to their father's childhood stories such as,'

Baby Kashif Missing from a Hotel....

They sat around me captivated, as I related:

"When I travelled to Pakistan my favorite transit spot was Nairobi, Kenya, it is in East Africa. I took your dad on a real safari you know...

Flying from Lagos to Nairobi once, I met a couple we knew from our embassy in Lagos. We stayed in my favorite hotel, New Stanley. The couple convinced me to come down and have dinner with them at my favorite Tree Top Restaurant. Somehow I was persuaded to put your daddy to bed before I came down."

"How old was Daddy?" they asked and I went on,

"Only two and half years old, but he slept like a log. During the dinner, I felt restless and kept checking up on him many times. I had told the couple that he sleeps through the night."

Attentive and wide-eyed, the girls listened on waiting in suspense for the climax, so I continued, "Well, past midnight we said goodbye to each other, promised to meet at breakfast before taking the bus to Safari Park together. But after dinner, when I reached my room, I got a shock," One of the girls dramatically jumped up and said, "and Daddy was missing!"

"Yes, and I nearly lost my mind, you know. I ran up and down, crying for help, but later found him in the back office of the hotel lobby. He was sitting on a highchair, relaxed as ever."

"But how did baby Daddy come down from the fifteenth floor?"

"Well, they told me that a waiter was passing by and heard him crying."

"How did he open the door?" I told them that the hotel employees are given master keys.

Once a traumatic experience, was now being utilized in the *Art of storytelling* they so enjoyed. I only had one son, but now these three sweet girls had become the joy of my life.

Creating Club 23 Diaries became our ritual. When I visited them, they asked, "We hope you didn't forget to bring your computer, Ma." They would sit by my side and dictate, while I'd capture their thoughts on my net-book. For each new episode they chose a different color.

I thought '*By the time they grow up, handwriting may be a thing of the past.*' So I preserved their artwork and handwritten stories as well.

Urdu songs I taught them, sounded more adorable in their Canadian accents. But they made fun of me when I sang English nursery rhymes. "You are so out of tune, Ma."

We had a fancy diary titled '*Life's Lessons*'— values we should live by. At times I'd give them a surprise quiz, "What happens when you face adversity?"

"Turn it into an advantage!" Each of the girls was eager to be the first to respond.

During our sleepovers, their inquiring minds craved for more real-life stories. Once they fell asleep in my arms, I'd stay awake to enjoy their soft, melodious breathing. Those memories will always be my music.

Nonetheless, an underlying fear that haunted me for some reason was, that one day they may not even be allowed to see me. I shunned the thought as my silly apprehension.

……………………………………..

The Ageing Parents

32 A seed had already been planted in my head for a follow-up socio-drama.

I was committed to BTG's mission but not at the cost of family time. My parents had been longing for my next visit. "When are you coming?" rang in my ears. *What if I never get to see them again ...* made me decide to go, despite the exorbitant travelling expenses!

At the airport, we were excited to see a battalion of relatives armed with smiles and hugs. But once I reached home and witnessed my parents' declining health, my heart sunk. When you *live* with them, you accept gradual changes more easily.

In a ten-hour distant time-zone, I couldn't fall asleep. Everyone in deep slumber, I sneaked out of bed to express my concerns for them through outpourings on paper.

"I'm currently experiencing two opposites. My growing granddaughters residing in Canada, the ageing parents in Pakistan, I stand in the middle, my feet astride two continents—oceans apart in time and space." Those thoughts morphed into a poem about lifespan:

A Relay Game
To my right is playful joy
she has learned to stand on her own

To my left, a reluctant cane
His legs faltering, so is the will power

On my right
I hear her giggle and wiggle
singing nursery rhymes
but on my left:
sighs of aching and ageing
dwindling vitality
harsh reality
> *Playful innocence unaware*
> *of the inevitable!*

Wisdom of the years
whispers in my ears
"Bygone achievements and awards, now insignificant"
the 'adrenalin' of pursuit—depleted
endurance is fatigued.
> *While she is eager to learn*
> *he is at a stage to unlearn!*
> *Dreams and aspirations in one hand*
> *acceptance of the inevitable in the other*

Much of substance I possess
I've received from my left
To relay it to my right—
while I prepare myself for...? My poem continues...

One comforting thought was that our parents were being pampered by my siblings. They were surrounded by children, grandchildren, and full-time in-home care providers. Yet I felt guilty that I had never played a role in their care.

We now kindled old memories: "Remember those spring mornings, basking in the winter sun of Rawalpindi, in your rose garden at the Lalazar home?"

"Yes, sixteen different varieties I had planted there!"

"Do you remember your trip to Canada?" he called the maid to bring the album of his trip we made. To amuse him we had added catchy titles and captions.

"Do you remember the Annual Mosaic Festival in Mississauga, the Belly Dancer, in the Saudi Arabian stall?" He shied away from that memory, Ammi looking on indifferently. Flipping through the pages he said, "I told you, you'll get me into trouble with your mother."

He quickly turned that page –him standing beside the Hawaiian Hulas. I winked and he switched the channel and started quoting Mirza Ghalib's poetry. He requested Ammi to recite a love poem she had written for him titled "*Meray Hameed*" (My Hameed).

As she recited it verbatim, I could see love oozing from his marble green eyes.

One day while he was getting ready for a bath, I seized the opportunity, "*I* want to give you a bath." Everyone readily rejected the idea. "Why would you? There are so many men ready and willing." But I persisted, so he agreed but also assured me, "I do wear shorts you know."

Shocked to see him reduced to skin and bones, my sobs, merging with the sound of the shower, still I teased him, "Abbaji, you once looked like Sean Connery, but now…"

"Didn't anyone tell you I just got liposuction?" he joked.

"But now you look like *Goray* Gandhi Ji." (Fair skinned*)

"I'm honored," he said then turned around to relive the tragedy.

"Sadly, he was assassinated by an advocate of Hindu Nationalism."

"Please change the subject," Ammi swiftly interjected.

Once the maid helped him dress, he called me in and whispered a generous compliment,

"Many men have given me a bath, but you are the best."

"Feminine touch," Ammi said with confidence.

Goodbyes are never easy: The day before my departure, I barged in their bedroom and found them holding hands as usual. I gently unlocked them, and sandwiched myself cozily in between both of them. My early morning routine always kindled their spirits.

"Imagine I was just born,"

"Time has flown by!" Holding my hands, their grips somehow felt tighter.

I resisted the temptation to ask him about his *secret* artwork—the figurine collection. I had vivid memories: Only when their *close* friends visited, that the cabinet was ever unlocked. How they giggled, making me curious. Once they were away, I found the key and sneaked in to open that cabinet. I was shocked. The exotic postures he created from Plaster of Paris, replica figurines of the ***Ajanta Elora Caves*** in India. I refrained, lest he felt embarrassed. My humanist father now prayed fervently; 'Old age does that.'

On that last morning, when I lay between them, his *silence* spoke louder. Ammi was still asleep when Abbaji gently placed my right hand upon his chest, then on his eyes and kissed it. Placed it back on his chest, then eyes, and kissed it again, repeating the drill several times.

"Please *say* something Abbaji."

He said, "Sometimes you don't need to *say* anything."

Could this be our final goodbye? I shuddered at the thought.

I apologized for my rare presence in their lives. But he reassured me, "We appreciate the annual trips, costly and tedious journeys you endured. You've paid your dues *Beti* (daughter)."

How we eventually become the *parents* of our parents! I had a pep talk with him.

"All your life you have inspired us as an exemplary strong-willed and positive individual." He listened and I said, "Sometimes you look sad, not your usual self, why?"

His continued silence prompted an idea. "Saleem, please bring Abbaji's favorite cap."

His care provider rushed to bring a round white cap with golden embroidery. On the inside with a black marker, I inscribed,

'Abbaji's cap of positive thinking' Childlike, he obediently listened.

"Whenever you're depressed, just repeat these words, put on this cap and think of me. I guarantee you'll start smiling." It invoked a spirited smile.

On the day of my departure, after all the hugs and goodbyes, I was at the exit door when Abbaji summoned me back, "Shadan, just wait for another minute," I took a step back … waited in suspense … as he called Saleem.

"Please bring that white cap." Saleem ran back and handed it to my father. He first read the caption I had written 'Abbaji's cap of positive thinking,' put it on, tilted his head sideways, and with a languid smile he asked, "Are you happy now?"

"Very happy," I replied. That he said goodbye in *English*, my Canadian language, meant more than just a goodbye. *Would I ever see him again?* The door closed behind me.

Fortunately I had planned a stop over to see my baby sister Arifa.

……

Islamabad—a Memorable Week...

Entering the highway leading to the city was a classic stunning view of the foothills of the Himalayas, as though affectionately embracing the white Faisal Mosque. How the slim and tall minarets caressed those magnanimous mountains, always captivated me!

Since Shahid had also moved to Karachi, Arifa was the only sibling left there. What a memorable time I spent with her.

Salman being an architect had built their luxurious villa in Anchorage (a suburb). The weather was perfect and I'll never forget our breakfasts on their patio. Home-made guava jam and *malai* (fresh cream) served on crisp toast. Chirping birds joined our memorable reunion, echoing our songs of affection. Of all six siblings, Arifa and I have the most in common. I'm the eldest, she is the youngest; so I improvised a short poem *"The Book Ends,"* she loved it.

During a morning walk, we decided to visit a nearby village of many unfortunate 'have- not's' and what did we find? A bed without a mattress, a house without doors, yet the old man's smile of contentment we adored! We even joined them to bake *Roti* on *Tandoor* (clay oven). We had touched their hearts, their hospitality was unsurpassed.

In contrast, the 'affluent' had invited us to the Annual Prize Distribution Day of a Montessori school named **'*Brainiacs'*.** Little boys and girls held sports competitions. They demonstrated karate skills, danced on stilts to the delight of their parents and grandparents, followed by the adults' Tug of War, women against men. Amidst the clapping, I suddenly heard my name being called! I got invited as a 'Special Guest from Canada', to distribute the prizes. Caught by surprise, in my extempore speech, I said great things about life in Canada, but also expressed, "Over there we hardly hear the positive side of Pakistani life. So I feel as though I've landed in the *Media's Blind Spot*." Adding to their amusement, I jokingly remarked, "Over there we get the news about our maniacs, not about our Brainiacs."

Time flew by and I had to endure another LONG journey back.

......

On that return flight, I met one or two acquaintances. They also expressed that they feel guilty for abandoning their ageing parents. We finally landed back in Toronto.

Apart from my full-time job, our next play was to be a welcome distraction. Our community had approached us (Bridging the Gap) and expressed that,

"The divorce rates are rising, and the South Asians are catching up with the West."

"If love wins the debate, what causes people to fall out of love?" they questioned.

In my opinion, *Happily Ever After* had become an old myth. The divorce rate at 45 percent tells us that lasting love is hard to achieve and the new reality is:

"Questionably ever After" so that could even be the title of our play.

We wanted this production to be even more inclusive—the issue of rising divorces affects all communities. We commenced research in order to put together real-life stories of Mississauga and Toronto. However, a project of this magnitude required funding. The pessimists warned me: "Funding for a theater production is impossible." *Negative Incentive* is a term I had coined which my boss at the bank, Terry Campbell liked. So now I felt ever more determined to apply.

Life happens … so does Death…

I received the saddest news of my life –my father passed away! Motivation plummeted. I informed everyone, "Our project is on hold until further notice." Abbaji's words echoed:

"When happiness is shared, it multiplies but when grief is shared it gets divided."

In such moments, you want to be with your family but …? But we humans always improvise.

I took out my father's masterpiece photo captured by Mujeeb— reclined on his bed, watching the India-Pakistan cricket match on TV, with a bright smile he is clapping over a *Sixer*. Living true to his words: "Live each moment to its fullest."

Initially I thought of planting a tree in my dad's name in one of the many parks in Mississauga but eventually decided, 'why not plant one in our own backyard.' It was peak season, so most landscapers flatly refused me. However, I was in for a surprise.

One of my interesting Encounters…

While shopping for patio furniture at a Canadian Tire store, seeing my overloaded trolley, a gentleman asked, "May I help you?"

My abrupt "No thanks" seemed to offend him. Later in the lineup, he stood behind me and said, "Why is it so that all the pretty women refuse my offers?" It was a bad hair day for me, and with sloppy looks, I thought *this man sure needs an eye checkup.* But this time I accepted his polite gesture.

While loading my trunk he handed me his business card. I gave him mine. 'Dispensary Manager', he replied. "How do you know I need an eye checkup?"

"It's because of your compliment I didn't deserve." I probably shouldn't speak to strangers like that, but sometimes I can't help being spontaneous.

I glanced at his card: Dominic Costa—a Landscaper. Wow!

"Do I ever need a landscaper, in fact I'm looking for one for this weekend," I said.

Mothers' Day weekend coming up, it was my golden opportunity to convince Mujeeb; he no longer had the energy level for gardening as he did before.

"But this weekend is my wife's birthday," Dominic explained.

"In that case, I'll try and find someone else. My father just passed away and I wanted to plant some trees in his name." Dominic said goodbye.

Just as I turned the ignition, in the rearview mirror I saw him galloping towards me.

"It's okay. I'll carry my jeans along. After the church service, before I go home I'll visit you." I felt so blessed. Pleasant surprises greet me now and then. Just then I noticed his salt-and-pepper hair and his facial features had a strong resemblance to Richard Gere.

The next day, someone rang the doorbell. "It's Richard Gere for you," Mujeeb joked.

Each member of our family including the little baby Daania placed various plants after Dominic professionally dug up the ground and poured black soil. We recited *Sura Fateha* used to bless the deceased. Dominic joined us and also recited a Christian prayer.

Holding a fistful of soil in my hand, the sight invoked an image of my father being buried—that's when I broke down, a somber moment for us all.

Dominic later accompanied me to Sheridan Nursery to purchase tall evergreens and other bushes using his professional discount.

He planted the evergreen spruces in a row in our backyard, one in the name of each sibling. A special one was earmarked for my mom. A tall solitary pine in front of the house stood firm—to mark my father's demise or ***Intiqaal*** (transformation). With Dominic's green thumb the row of evergreens flourished, and invited many compliments.

That summer, we the Club 23 also planted a great variety of flowers. Abbaji's portrait remained surrounded by colors of nature, in his company we enjoyed breakfast in the patio. I shared with the kids, "Your great-grandfather used to take me on motorbike rides, also took me to movies like your dad does," they listened with fascination.

The voice of wisdom and reason finally beckoned me, "Enough with the mourning. It's time to put away the portrait," I complied.

......

A Dream Closure!

One night, after tossing and turning for hours, I got up to pray and meditate, and eventually fell asleep. What a picturesque dream I saw:

To the ends of the horizon, I saw deep blue ocean waves surging to land upon the sandy beach then gently retreating. Clear blue sky, fluffy white clouds floating with breeze, perfect temperature, it was heavenly!

Strangely I wore a white georgette saree, a royal-blue corsage, on a beach? Mujeeb was ready with his camera, I requested,

"Why don't I stand against the ocean, so everything is 'blue and white' this could well be the most amazing photo you have ever taken?"

As I posed for the picture, a wave landed near my feet. I felt as though someone gently touched the edge of my saree—was it my imagination?

Again, I posed but before Mujeeb clicked, I felt a gentle touch again, as though someone was drawing my attention. I looked back ... a wave surged and gently laid my father's body upon the shore. I screamed with excitement:

"Oh my God, Abbaji has travelled all the way to Canada just to say goodbye!"

Instead of the traditional outfit, he was wearing a Western formal suit and tie, arms folded, smile scattered on his face as though telling me,

"I remember telling you if something happens to me, you need not bother coming, that's why I've come to bid farewell."

Feeling the ecstasy, absorbing the moment I stood, when suddenly another wave landed then gently swept him away, and he submerged back into the ocean.

I stood still, gazing at the deep blue ocean and contemplated, 'Water is the source of life' I slowly inhaled serenity and the purity of that moment...

Music of the soul merged with the sound of surging waves.

When I shared my artistic dream with Kashif, he asked me, "Do you remember what you wore at uncle Shahid's wedding?"

"Oh yes, I wore the same white saree, and Abbaji did wear the same gray western formal suit, how strange!" Many women had objected to my white saree, instead of the colorful lehnga Ammi bought for me. Only Abbaji had backed me that day by saying,

"Suno sub ki, karo apney munn ki" (Listen to everyone, but follow your own instincts).

One day I'd like to learn more about DREAMS, such a fascinating subject.

That vivid dream had immense healing power. Moreover, the thought of dedicating the play to my father perked me up. I'll no longer mourn his demise; I'll celebrate his life instead.

…………………………………..

'QUESTIONABLY EVER AFTER'

33 The letter of approval from Ontario Trillium Foundation excited me beyond words. However, our grant was approved with a stipulation—that I could pay everyone else, except myself, unless I step down as the President of BTG. A project so dear to me, I opted to volunteer my services to embark upon a new journey, without the fear of flying. I sent out an email,

"Our Divorce project is to be resumed, hoping all of you are still on board."

For a more inclusive project, I had drafted the following storyline:

> *'A Pakistani <u>Muslim</u> Psychiatrist, whose qualifications were not recognized in Canada, becomes a Marriage Therapist and opens a clinic 'Creative Marriage Counseling.' He is in an ideal marriage but his assistant, a <u>Jewish Canadian,</u> single woman, who is dead against marriage, plays as the devil's advocate. She quotes Emma Goldman, "I'll never walk down the aisle to make false promises." Couples from various cultural and religious backgrounds bring relationship issues to the clinic.'*

We hired students from the Universities of Toronto and McGill, who conducted surveys and wrote research-based articles. Most of us were surprised that the 'official definition of marriage in Canada' does not have the word *Love* in it! Most of our Committee members felt the play title depicts exactly what the project is all about. Reva agreed to be our Dramaturge again.

Thanks to our board member Amira Masud; while she couldn't devote time to the project herself, she became a great source of valuable referrals.

Our basement now became the **Board Room** where several organizations converged.

The Executive Directors of Intercultural Neighborhood Centers of Mississauga and Brampton joined hands with us. They willingly facilitated focus groups with their Case Workers who were familiar with unique issues of different ethnic communities. We also invited a Psychotherapist Dr. Sohail to our focus group and Roohina Gilani, Counselor from Victim Services of Peel who provided statistics relating to domestic abuse. Many marital issues ranging from money problems to infidelity or boredom were addressed.

For one of those full day focus groups, Brian Hull accompanied me as a member of our Advisory Panel. I joke with Brian that since his last name *Hull* means 'solution' in Urdu, I may call upon him anytime for advice. He tells me, "You have *chutzpah*" (Hebrew for incredible guts).

The leading figures from Canada Pakistan Business Council, Samir Dossal, Andy Merchant and group, also came forward with their support.

Such cooperation from all directions I least expected. Our comprehensive brochure was a Resource Book diligently compiled and printed by *Jamil Qureshi.* A renowned visual artist *Sabiha Imran* offered to design the Cover Page. Once again our WEN authors rallied around me. This time *Anna Stitski* a tall and gorgeous lady from WEN also joined us. Wearing mini leather skirt she played a comedic role of a woman addicted to serial marriages. My friend *Nain Amyn-Lalji* graciously offered her talent as an experienced Costume Designer. I was simply LUCKY.

The Theme Song—thanks to *Porchia Waheed* we got permission to use the latest release by a Celebrity Vocalist of Indo-Pakistan, Adnan Sami Khan:

"Pal dau Pal pyaar ka
Aao ji lein zara"
(Similar theme as: *Cherish the Love we have*)

Community Casting— a Fun Challenge...

Our grassroots approach involved everyday folks from different ethnic backgrounds to participate. Once again, I seized every single opportunity.

Once at a wedding I sat next to a tall, outgoing Italian lady in her forties. Within a few minutes chat with her, my inner voice detected: *She would be perfect for the role of a feisty Italian in my script*. Once I explained the project to her, she said, "I'm excited but also amused that you think I can play a feisty Italian." We laughed while she was lured by my passionate pitch: "You get paid for five minutes of fame on stage, at a state-of-the-art facility."

Discovering a ***wealth of talent*** within reach (in Mississauga) was a rewarding experience.

The Astronaut Families...

Based on our research, I had added a scene about the 'Astronaut Families', highlighting how one spouse shuttles back and forth to and from their country of origin. But I was unable to find a Chinese female in late thirties or early forties.

One day, while inviting the President of Kehkashan *Nuzhat Khalid* for support, I dialed with one-digit error, only to hear a Chinese voice at the other end. My antennae raised, I left her a message: "Please call me about an important community project you may be interested in." Luckily she responded.

When *Cindy* walked in for the audition, wearing a bright red business suit, I felt a spark of excitement. In her late thirties, a senior executive in a production company –just the character I had envisioned! Taken aback, she said, "This is exactly my story, but how do you know about the *Astronaut Families and their issues?" I explained to her that we had interviewed Community Case Workers.

The dilemma of her husband shuttling between Beijing and Toronto for a few years was exactly what I had depicted. "Even the ages of my two children match your script, how strange."

First time she read the script, I was tempted to change my mind but I didn't give up:

"Now *I* will read it to you, with *feelings*. Please listen carefully the words I emphasize upon" …as though I was a pro myself. I also reassured her, "Our Director will train you."

She signed the contract and wiggled her way out, looking chic. It reminded me of my shapely bright red business suit and my 'once upon a time' slim waistline. I sighed but I smiled.

That night at two in the morning, I checked my emails. One from a stranger that read:

"Dismiss Cindy from your project immediately. I will not let my wife participate."

Blunt enough to keep me awake. The next morning Cindy sent her apology.

"See what I go through. I WILL play the role, no matter what."

*Incidentally the 'Astronaut concept' also impacted the immigrants from other communities.

......

The second interesting episode occurred at 'The Host' restaurant in Mississauga, at a formal reception arranged by a friend *Ghazala Shah*. As I saw a woman enter the hall, I joyfully blurted, "Oh my God I've finally found my mother-in-law."

My amused friends made fun, "Our women usually look out for *daughters-in-law*."

"But I've been looking for a gutsy lady to play mother-in-law, who is well versed in both Urdu and English." I briefly spoke to her and we booked an appointment.

The next day *Rakhshi Zahoor*, a sophisticated Pakistani woman in her late forties came for audition. She expressed her reservations to me about being overweight, but was amused when I responded, "Don't say overweight, you are pleasantly plump and … playing as a domineering mother-in-law, it would only add weight to your role." Rakshi cast a charming smile and passed her audition with flying colors. "But what makes you think I can act?" I replied in Persian:

"Qadar-e-gauhar-shah danad ya badanad jauhree"

(The true value of a precious pearl can only be appreciated by a jeweler or a King),

I suddenly realized that I had inadvertently paid a compliment to myself!

With the help of our director Derek Thompson, Rakshi's acting debut was outstanding. She found her niche and later said, *"You have given a purpose to my life".* I felt humbled and gratified. <u>Those who volunteered their time are now happy to be acknowledged in my book.</u>

Our *Second Generation* South Asians (Indians and Pakistanis) find much in common, some refer to it as Bollywood Culture. But amongst the first generation, the Hindu Muslim marriages are not easily acceptable. I approached Shahzeb Humayun, a handsome young Pakistani (Humayun's son a chubby little toddler I first saw in UAE). He and Namrita had fun putting up a silly fight on stage, having to deal with their 'joint family dilemmas'. This resonated well with our young audience.

The Intercultural Hiccups...

Knowing how competent Derek was, one day I took time off to be with the kids. When I returned, I was surprised how the *Directions* had gone in the wrong direction. In one scene, the wife of an interracial couple wanted to break the news of her pregnancy: "*Are you ready for a surprise?*" Her husband Adeel replies, "*Ever ready is my middle name.*" Derek interpreted it as ever ready to make love. When I saw Adeel climb over Tracy, I interjected, "This is a family drama, and their spouses will be amongst the audience." Derek lost his temper and shouted,

"What kind of a stupid culture is this?" I explained to him that even in real life we do not kiss in public.

Once again it was a full house (1,200+). Our Publicist Mary Ellen had put out Press Releases in various newspapers. The Mississauga Arts Council also helped promote the event.

At the end of the play, we handed out laminated copies of our **'Magic Formula for Healthy Relationships'**. It was posted on YouTube and also published in *Canadian Asian News*. The editor Latafat Siddiqui provided us full coverage of various events. The videos of both plays were shown during the 2009 Multi-cultural Festival at the International Centre in Mississauga.

I did get in trouble for showing a inter-racial marriage being successful!

An 'In-home Interview' by Omni TV…

They asked me if we were a perfect couple. "No, we fight every five minutes, but also forgive every five minutes."

"Could you put up a fight?" they requested, so I asked Mujeeb, "Remember those good old days, when we squabbled a lot, can we replay it on camera?" He agreed. After our petty squabble about fingerprints on the microwave, the Omni interviewer asked if we could also demonstrate how we 'make up' so I played a CD, and my ever-ready hubby and I danced.

That hilarious extempore clip was aired more frequently than the serious interview. Consequently, during some South Asian weddings that summer, a few eyes followed me with smiles as I passed by. "*You fight really well. Our husbands are asking if we can learn to 'make up' like you do.*"

*Unfortunately Rakshi Zahoor, our Director Derek, and Ursula have since passed away.

……

Marty's Annual Gala 2009 …

The event was like the Mini Oscars. The red-carpet Awards ceremony at Stage West was held by the Mississauga Arts Council (2008). Distinguished guests, accomplished artists, and the media were present. The Mayor of Mississauga, Hazel McCallion, literally danced her way to the stage. She zestfully promoted and appreciated the arts. I wished our lead actors had accompanied me but they said, "The tickets are too costly; competition is tough, and it's not as though we have a chance of winning." As I was missing their presence I heard the announcement:

'The Best Performing Arts Group is … Bridging the Gap Productions!'

Totally unprepared, in utter disbelief, I was escorted up to the stage. Lost for words, at first I stuttered, trying to gain composure. After thanking the Arts Council, a thought flashed 'that our men are often stereotyped as being controlling.' So I added a tribute to my father:

"*There are Pakistani men who adore their wives and some are ideal husbands too.*" The enlightened audience rendered the loudest applause of the evening.

That moment was also a stark reminder—**that 'I' without 'We' is nothing**. Even though I was there to receive the award, our win was all about '**Us**'. Reflecting upon how many people had participated in that project, I recalled a verse from renowned Urdu poet Majrooh:

"Mein Akaila Hee Chala tha janib-e-manzil magar
Loge saath atay gaiye aur karavan banta gaya"

(I embarked upon this journey alone, others kept joining in, and it became a huge Procession)

Good luck greeted me right after the ceremony. A charming lady introduced herself, "Hello. I'm Cheryl Xavier, a publisher from 'In Our Words Inc.' We would love to publish your two award-winning plays."

"By all means..." I was thrilled with the offer.

All other material was ready. I rushed to submit the book cover photo as well.

……

Cop Scare...

It's a great feeling when you first see your work in print. I remembered how excited we were when Mujeeb's book about tropical mushrooms was published.

On a stormy night, with a box full of books in the back seat, I turned into a gas station when out of the blue a police car followed me. Oh no, why is my life always a *Natak?* (drama) A uniformed young female emerged and walked toward me. She bluntly asked,

"Were you planning to kill yourself, or someone else?"

My heart skipped a beat but I dared ask, "What did I do?"

"It's the way you took a sudden turn...without any signal."

As she was about to issue me a ticket, I humbly admitted my guilt. "Sorry, it is my fault, but I have good explanation."

"What's that?" her voice was intimidating.

"I just picked up my books from my publisher. Please let me celebrate, I'm just overly excited."

"Is that an excuse to kill someone? Anyhow...what's the book all about?"

"It's all about ***love***," I said dramatically, reaching out for the box.

"Let's first see your license and the insurance slip," As a cold shiver travelled down my spine, I worked up the courage for one last stunt:

"Officer, I'm *really* sorry, please let me off just this one time, and I'll gift you the book."

"What? Show me the book," her tone softened.

Flipping through a few pages of the book, she read, *"Window Shopping... for lasting love,"* then smiled at me. "Catchy title but ... is there such a thing as lasting love?"

Probably in her thirties, she too was looking for it.

"Umm … this could be an interesting read. I have an off day tomorrow and the forecast predicts a snowstorm. Give me the book, but remember … don't … ever … take a turn without signal, okay?"

I swiftly signed the book as though I was a polished author, and cautiously steered my way home, feeling doubly festive and smiling to myself at my good fortune.

......

The Robinson Bray House…,

What could be a better place for a book launch than the artsy historical Robinson Bray House, one of the oldest buildings in Streetsville (1867). The popular Tea Room built in 1989 was known for freshly baked scones and Irish Soda Bread. Over a cup of Jasmine Delight and English scones, we finalized the launch plans. Brian Hull as a moderator instantly captivated the audience. A charming young lady, Seema Wain's daughter *Iman* enhanced the occasion by her rendition of a heart touching solo on guitar.

Perfect weather and the historical location attracted an overflow of 'walk-in' guests!

......

It was a mere coincidence that on that very day, I received a congratulatory message from Professor Rodica Albu of the 'Alexandru Ioan Cuza' University of Iasi, Romania. In her message she informed me that: On Canada-Romania Friendship Day, when Romanians celebrated ninety years of diplomatic relations with Canada (starting in 1919), her English students translated and recite my poem *"Time Theft."* Such encouragement from scholars like her and Zamir boosted my morale. I conceived a new dream, my own poetry collection, maybe one day?

Rodica was once our welcome guest at the Writers and Editors' brunch meeting. After my recital, she said, "Although I'm here to study established Canadian authors, why not cover emerging authors as well." This charismatic, down-to-earth scholar interviewed me over lunch, gifted me a beautifully hand-painted ceramic plate, and said, "I purchased this art piece with the intention I'd present it to the most 'spiritual person' I meet in Canada." Only two days prior, a close friend had commented, "Spirituality and you don't go together"—a point to ponder!

I cherished that navy-blue ceramic plate with white continuous circles, reflecting upon its meaning:

'A circle represents eternity. There is such a vast canvas for circles to show up in life, and depending on where you are in your cycle of growth a circle can mean something different.'

I hoped that this symbolic gift would bring luck and growth for me.

....

OUR BILINGUAL LITERARY SETTING
(Excerpts from my Diary)

---

34 Living in two cultures meant we had exposure to both Urdu and English literature. In fact Mississauga and Toronto have become the Hub of Urdu Literature in North America.

Numerous literary groups organized dozens of events. *Ashfaq Hussain* of Urdu International (winner of the highest literary award) held large-scale *Mushaira* (Urdu poetry recitation event) three to four hundred guests gathered usually in Marriott Hotels. For decades, we the South Asian immigrants benefited as Ashfaq invited renowned scholars and authors from India and Pakistan. His life partner *Narjis Zaidi* with her contagious smile, hosted private events at their Castlemore mansion, where we got to meet many celebrities. I was honored when he once invited me for an interview at ATN (Asian Television Network).

Mujeeb and I were warmly welcomed in both English and Urdu events. One week I'd be reciting an English poem at WEN (Writers and Editors Network) monthly brunch, another week at an Urdu literary event. The following month could be a gathering by the Writers Forum at York Library, and yet another event held by Courtney Park authors, followed by an event by *Dr. Khalid Sohail*'s literary organization 'Family of the Hearts' (a Thinkers Forum). At times it was overwhelming to keep up with such a hectic schedule!

Munir Pervaiz, a Scholar/Social Activist and a poet, conducted numerous literary events on behalf of The Writers Forum at York

Library in Toronto. He once invited me as the feature author to showcase my small contributions: prose, poetry, and plays in both languages.

Once a memorable Urdu Mushaira was held by an Organization named Effort in Mississauga (350 guests). Conducted by Munir Pervaiz (an outside-the-box thinker), he commenced the event with the recital of my English poem *"The Deserving Hands"* a tribute to women I had written for a Mother's Day event. Occasionally, I was even accommodated to experiment by reciting Urdu poem mixed with English. "It adds a unique flavor," they said.

Dr. Sohail was making a documentary titled *Mixed Messages* about interracial marriages. Our interests converged as I was supporting the controversial marriage of my relative Shazia, who was marrying someone from Barbados. I was asked to choreograph a Hena Ceremony with Shazia and Henderson which was videotaped in my home. Henderson Leacock was by all accounts a wonderful young man we all love. When it comes to racism, my own husband advised me not to attend that wedding. I told him he doesn't have to come, but I will go. Funnily, before I got dressed he had his suit and tie ready. He danced all evening and told me, "I'm proud of you for taking a stand." Incidentally that documentary *Mixed Messages* was aired at CBC.

A gentleman *Athar Razvi* once handed me his business card. I was intrigued that even his address 'Hidden Valley' was translated into Urdu—such passion for his native tongue even though he was married to a German lady named Rita. He had established the ***Ghalib Academy**.

(Mirza Ghalib was known to be the greatest Urdu poet of the subcontinent)

Attending an annual *Mehfil* (formal gathering) in his basement felt as though we had travelled back in history, to New Delhi. Like the Mughal Emperors in their palaces, he invited numerous poets. The surrounding walls were adorned with portraits of renowned authors of India and Pakistan. With the floor seating and the lighting, he recreated a truly historical ambience. He said, "*My Mushaira is incomplete without you and Mujeeb.*" German-speaking Rita felt like a stranger in her own home, so I broke the ice by relating our extensive travels in Germany.

After Mr. Razvi's demise, a poet friend Nasreen Syed stepped in to take charge of Ghalib Academy. Soft-spoken and down-to-earth, Nasreen staged large-scale Mushaeras in Mississauga, as well as her own book launches. She kindly translated a few of my English poems into Urdu.

......

Over the years, I coordinated the Annual International Peace Poetry events in partnership with the Women's Federation for World Peace. Some interesting anecdotes I recall with relish.

One event 'Connecting Hearts, Crossing Boundaries' was held at Rogers Theatre in which we invited established and emerging authors, traditional poets, as well as spoken word artists. The Executive Director of Mississauga Arts Council, *Mike Douglas*, was one of our special guests. As well, I received a surprise call from the Indian Consulate. A very humble Counsel General *Mr. Akilesh Misra* who also wrote Urdu/Hindi poetry was interested in gracing the occasion.

It happened to be the tenth anniversary of Bridging the Gap, so our cake-cutting ceremony turned out to be a true example of inclusivity. People of various colors, faiths, and age groups joined hands. Interestingly, *Asma Warsi*, the only lady wearing *Hijab*, rendered the most hilarious poem. Our guests provided feedback that they were pleasantly surprised!

I had invited Athar's daughter *Neila Razvi* who had become my colleague at WMB. It was to be her poetic debut. Just as she commenced, there was a sudden loud blast and the theater became pitch dark! It reminded me of the previous fiasco at Meadowvale Theatre. But our house full of very spirited audience wasted no time, amidst the whistles and cheers, dozens of cell phones suddenly lit up… kudos to Steve Jobs. Neila continued the recital of her poem **"Distant Daughter of the East"** while Meena Chopra kindly cast light upon her.

What could have resulted in a disastrous end turned out to be a memorable moment!

I mischievously complimented Neila, "Your presentation was a blast."

At my request Sahar Raza composed on guitar my poem *"Fear of the Unknown"* written post-9/11. Two of my favorite poet/composers *Max Layton* and *James Quinn* enhanced our event with their stellar performances on guitar.

Hindi Writers Guild once invited me as a feature author at the Brampton Civic Centre. An author named *Bhumneshwari* and I bonded in meaningful friendship. A lawyer by profession, here in Canada she was content as a homemaker and a poet. During the private gatherings at her place and our one-on-one encounters, I was deeply inspired by her 'Traditional Wisdom.'

Whenever I shared those joyous stories, someone retorted, *"Jungle mey more nacha, kis ney dekha?"* (Who sees a peacock dancing in the forest) It implied that 'what's the joy in life, living thousands of miles away from one's immediate family?' But my assertive response was,

"In Canada we have created a new world of our own where we flourish in both cultures." As Kashif says, we live in Mississauga, our favorite city of the best country in the world.

Mujeeb concluded, "If there is a lifestyle you may call 'Utopia,' this is it."

Consequently, 'Creativity' had room to flourish, another opportunity presented itself.

......

'From a Widow's Closet' (play #4)

An award-winning playwright Jasmine Sawant of Sawitri Theatre requested me to write and direct a play about women's issues, to be staged at the 2009 Annual Multicultural Mosaic festival. I wrote an educational script comparing the widows' status within the South Asian society … cultural baggage they bring along and what are the changes in their outlooks after coming to Canada? In line with Bridging the Gap's theme of inclusivity, four different faiths were represented: Hindu, Muslim, Christian, and Jewish.

The premise was: A Hindu widow, a social worker introduces Pakistani Muslim widow (Rakshi) to a Jewish widower who resides in their building. Our widow also meets a handsome younger Pakistani. *Azfar Tahir*, a real estate mogul and a friend, joyfully played that role. The modern Pakistani woman recites Iqbal and Ghalib in Urdu, as well as Keats and Shelly, verbatim! Both men fall in love with her, but once she decides to get married, the audiences are left to guess as to whom she ends up with?

"I've decided to marry the one who will love and respect me the most."

Breaking cultural barriers through our theme invited a standing ovation.

Something very strange happened. After I introduced the play and the performance commenced, we noticed Mujeeb comfortably seated on the wing videotaping the play. During the performance he decided to cross the stage and fell down! The prompter lady *Shobha*, hidden behind the couch ready to feed the lines, rushed out to rescue him. It became a hilariously *slapstick scene* when Mujeeb tried to get up wearing his *short* shorts! Luckily, he wasn't injured.

The next day, I received a few calls. "Your play was excellent, but the Oscar goes to Dr. Mujeeb Zoberi." Someone had recorded the fiasco; we all found it funny.

"Submit it to America's funniest videos," they suggested.

The play *'From a Widows Closet'* was later published in an anthology in the USA.

......

'Prison in Paradise' (Play #5)

Perhaps because we were producing socio-dramas, a few South Asian women dealing with marital issues but reluctant to seek therapy approached me. Inspired by their experience of infidelity, I wrote another play *'Prison in Paradise.'* Mujeeb insisted that I should stage it on a large scale, but Reva suggested 'Stage Reading' instead which we held at the Masonic Lodge in Streetsville. One morning, I woke up with the following caption:

'Is cheating in marriage as common as speeding on the highway? Only those who get caught must pay the fine?'

The cheated women loved it. Surprisingly, even my learned friend Jamil innocently expressed, "But this phenomenon does not exist in our community." Oh really?

Meena Santdosani with her bubbly personality loved playing the suspected cheater. Amongst our multicultural audiences were the 'cheaters and the cheated.' The follow-up open mic highlighted the psychological impact upon families; it triggered such heated debate that we went into overtime. A male guest urged to make his last comment, *"Every woman should be like Hillary Clinton."* The female audiences booed in unison.

The play was later published in an anthology in the USA.

How one thing leads to another!

......

Literally Gala at the Embassy
(Washington, D.C., 2011)

Authors from various countries were invited. I felt privileged to represent Canada, as the invitation from our Embassy in Washington came as a surprise:

Tracing the Tradition, Embracing the Emergent

(Celebrating the launch of Pakistani Creative Writers in English)

Mujeeb's vehement opposition surprised me, "Don't even respond to this fake invitation. There are all sorts of scams to trap women into sexual harassment." So unlike him!

"Darling, the Gala event is at the Embassy," I read the invitation to him.

'Ambassador of the Islamic Republic of Pakistan, Husain Haqqani, cordially invites you to a cultural evening and dinner—featuring a book reading by Eminent Pakistani Writers of English Literature, short dramatic enactments of their works, panel discussion, and a musical performance.'

"Fake, fake, this is how they trap you. You know what the Ambassadors are like."

Now that statement really baffled me! He was always supportive, so I explained to him, "Remember the play you wanted me to stage, it's published in an anthology in the USA, and I'm invited to the launch." He panicked about me travelling alone. To pacify him, I invited Chameli to come along, who persuaded me to take the Mega Coach.

"In the nine hours road trip we can catch up with all the gossip." Hubby felt relieved.

The day before our departure she backed out, now it was *her* husband objecting. Once again, Mujeeb's paranoia kicked in. "You could be kidnapped, and I'll never find you."

"P\please don't treat me like a kid, I've done all my research," I remained adamant.

My friend and neighbor Fatima Jalil offered to drop me at the station. I packed after he went to bed but *"Life is what happens to you while you are making other plans"* (Balzer)

Before the sunrise on November 16ᵗʰˑ I woke up with a nasty sore throat and fever. Torn between yes and no, I texted Fatima that maybe I shouldn't go. She literally ordered me,

"**Get ready,** you are going, and I am dropping you at the station downtown."

My morale boosted, I rushed to gargle with salt water, also added Advil to my carry-on.

If it weren't for Chameli, I would've utilized air miles points and travelled by air but … this time things did happen for a very good reason. So let's find out!

……

371

During that lengthy journey, I had a long chat with a Jewish lady named Judie. She was surprised to read the invitation. "I would never have guessed you are from Pakistan." An expression we often hear and tolerate with stoic patience.

I replied, "You're not alone. Most people form a certain image about Pakistani women through the media but fail to realize many of us don't fit that image."

"By the same token, wearing a head covering, I didn't think you could be Jewish. So we both struggle against stereotyping."

Judie then asked what I would be presenting.

"We will be re-enacting a scene from my play *'Prison in Paradise'* about infidelity in marriage."

Apparently, a co-traveler who could be either Indian or a Pakistani was eavesdropping. He closed his book and became interested in our conversation. An average-looking soft-spoken fellow in his late forties, he introduced himself as Dilip Verma, an Indian Hindu name. He had a firm bias against Muslims, especially Pakistani women. My Bridging the Gap's mission automatically kicked in—I felt compelled to engage him in our discussion.

With each new piece of information he would learn about us, he reacted as though it was a revelation to him. He kept repeating, "But you are not a normal Pakistani woman, they should clone you," all the while shaking his head sideways, quite adorable!

"What do you mean by *normal* Pakistani women? We come in all sizes, shapes, colors and … mind spaces," I said jokingly.

Once I shared the caption line, Verma was flabbergasted. He repeated, "They should clone you," followed by one or two offensive statements, but I exercised restraint.

"Do you realize the dangers of stereotyping us all as terrorists? We are *185 million strong even if one million, or let's say two million amongst us have become terrorists, what about 183 million wanting peace? Why label us all?"

Verma repeated his 'clone' mantra.

I replied, "Millions of women are like me, or better versions who reside in the *'Media's blind spot.'* You just haven't met them."

Verma later said, "Nothing is common between Pakistanis and Indians."

"Listen, I have many Indian friends, Sikhs, Hindus, Parsis, and Muslims, never met anyone who is so opinionated." He remained skeptical, so I asked him,

"Hypothetically, if you are travelling with an international group from all over the world, would you have more in common with a Frenchman, British, Mexican, Chinese, Japanese, Italian, American, or…

He said, "Okay, okay, I agree we do have much in common but…

"We should clone you," I mimicked him. We all lightened up and laughed.

He then asked, "If it's true that Pakistani women would be reading in public, I'd love to witness it." I sent urgent text to Mr. Salman Sharif at the Embassy if we could invite him.

The reply was disappointing: "Formal gathering, house full."

Salman Sharif received me at the station and dropped me at the hotel where an accomplished author Shadab Zeest and I had planned to join each other.

Having endured a nine-hour journey, I was browbeaten. We ordered Chinese dinner after which I became sick. At midnight, the hotel called an ambulance and I ended up in the ER of a Washington, D.C. hospital! Perhaps it was the combination of Advil and MSG in Chinese food?

After waiting for hours in a room filled with sneezing and coughing patients, I lost patience. My heartbeat had normalized, so I secretly escaped and hailed a taxi. The taxi driver was a young Pakistani with his peculiar story—an MSc with no job prospects in his field. He stopped at a convenience store to look for salt and Tylenol for me, not available.

The next day, I lay in bed feeling disappointed. Out of the blue I received a call. "Verma here, I'm so excited your Embassy has extended me an invitation, so I'll see you this evening."

"Oh, but I'm down with high fever." I coughed to clear my throat but Verma Ji instantly assumed a younger brother role! (Just like our Pakistani tradition)

"Zohra *Didi* (sister), please come over for a hot lunch and rest, we'll pick you up."

"Thank you, but I can't even get out of bed. It's likely I'm allergic to Advil. If only I had Tylenol and salt to gargle with, I might have recovered by now but …" Verma's voice dropped.

An hour later, the front reception called again, "A couple is here to see you."

Lo and behold, Verma Ji showed up, with his traditional-looking sweet wife, wearing a saree and red *Bindi* (a dot on her forehead).

The couple brought me freshly cooked *Parathas*, sizzling vegetarian dishes in an old style *Nashtay daan* (Tiffin carrier), Tylenol tablets, white salt as well as *Kala Namak* (black salt), fruit yoghurt for dessert, and Gatorade—an energizing drink I had never tasted before. "No matter what, we want you to get well for this evening's Gala."

After all those remedies, I was so fit that no one could tell I had spent the night in ER of Georgetown Hospital. Verma Ji arrived at the Embassy, immaculately dressed and ready for what he called, "A life-changing experience." Dr. Fawzia Afzal Khan, Professor of English literature from Mont Claire University and I were seated at the Ambassador's table. I couldn't ask Verma to join us, so I whispered to one of the Embassy staff, "I've partly converted him in favor of Pakistanis. The rest is up to you." Ambassador Haqqani came to the podium calm and collected as ever, delivered an impressive speech paying tribute to all the Guest Authors, emphasizing the importance of creative writing, and how authors can influence the thinking of our masses. I wish!

We rehearsed only once, but Dr. Fawzia is such an accomplished and multitalented lady, we successfully reenacted a feisty scene from my play *'Prison in Paradise'* when the cheater and the cheated finally confront each other. My eyes were automatically reaching out to observe Verma Ji's reactions, and I noted how he was casting smiles our way...in amazement! On his way out, he said, "Thank you for inviting me. This has been an eye opener for me, so let's stay in touch." That he did via emails for a while. Once my diary was shared, the editor of 'Solidarity International Magazine' from Islamabad, Mr. Khurram Siddiqui, requested if he could publish it? "Of course," I consented.

Life provided ample opportunities. I felt both thankful and euphoric in equal measure.

As for Mujeeb, he was exceptionally happy I returned from Washington safe and sound!

Rationalizing his recent behavior, I suddenly thought of the odd remarks he had made about the ambassador. Why he was so paranoid about my Washington trip and what did he mean by *'You know how the Ambassadors are?'* that excavated an old memory:

The Ambassador in Nigeria...

It amazes me how even one associated word can sometimes resurface an entire episode filed away in our mind's archives—I unlocked it...

Once I was flying back from Pakistan with Kashif, only three. Mujeeb was returning from Europe and we were to meet in Lebanon to fly from Beirut to Lagos together. Hubby didn't show up, but I still boarded the flight to Lagos. After I checked in a nearby hotel, I called our close friend Mr. Zahid, the Pakistani ambassador to Nigeria. We usually stayed at their place. As I related earlier, they sometimes drove down to Ife Campus as an escape from the overload of Embassy events. So now Mr. Zahid sounded almost offended.

"Why would you check into a hotel when Mujeeb would assume you'll come here?"

"Vicinity to the airport, as I'm sure Mujeeb would be eager to reach home."

"I'm sending the driver to pick you up," he said in a matter of course manner.

In his black Mercedes, the flag covered for non-official trip, I reached their residence in Victoria Island, a posh area of Lagos. Mr. Zahid welcomed me with his usual kiss on my forehead—an unusual custom for my family. *Where is everyone I wondered*, but I got a shock when he told me his family was away visiting Pakistan.

In the evening, we had a lavish dinner in his fancy dining room. His chef waited to pour iced water in special Pakistani hand-engraved silver glasses, then he served gourmet dessert before we retired into the living room. It was a huge room divided in several conversation areas. I always admired the tasteful décor which reflected masterpiece artwork from various far Eastern countries, Indonesia, Singapore etc. I glanced around the room, a treat to my aesthetic sensibility.

Mr. Zahid was a charismatic individual, slim and tall, maybe in his late forties, dressed immaculately and with intelligent speech he perfectly rendered. He explained about some of the artifacts which fascinated me. "This hand-carved antique rocking chair is one from the Dutch colonial era (eighteenth and nineteenth century). This stuff was very popular with the expats." He went on, "And this carving is fragrant sandalwood from Nusa Tenggara."

There was a seating section with displays of Pakistani décor. Zahid explained, "This painting depicts our ancient Indus Valley Civilizations in **Mohenjo Daro** and **Harappa**." I commented, "I suppose through this you enlighten your guests that Pakistan has such amazing ancient history." Observing other details in the painting, I exclaimed, "I wonder what calamity wiped out such an advanced civilization 5,000 years ago!"

"Would you like to go dancing?" He took me off guard and my answer was a flat No, so he changed the subject. After updating me with the latest political events, he asked if I had experienced the Marine Drive along the seashore. "I've heard a lot about it." He immediately summoned his driver to bring the car out. I became super excited, Kashif was already asleep and their maid was to watch over him. Mr. Zahid whispered in Urdu that it was time for his chauffeur to be off duty… then took the keys from him. 'Oh!' is all I said with a bit of surprise.

Somewhat nervous at first, soon I became entranced by the magic. How could I not capture that moment, the full moon shining upon the ocean's raging wild ripples shimmering as if an artist was playing with his brush dipped in silver paint! Perfect temperature, windows open I relished the lukewarm breeze caressing my face, feeling privileged that our respected Ambassador has taken the time to show me much talked about Marina. *Do I have a story for Mujeeb* I thought as he sometimes teased me as: "Your Ideal."

Once Zahid parked the car we headed toward the ocean, I struggled to walk, wobbling on the rippling sand. Suddenly he stopped and held my hands and made a long winded, what sounded like a romantic speech. Cold shivers travelled through my spine I was dumbfounded.

"Maybe it's time for both of us to change the course of our lives" were his last words.

As he tried to embrace me, I swiftly pulled back with anger and blurted, "You did not tell me, and I had no idea that we were coming here *alone*."

He swiftly receded to apologize then admitted that even his family has known that his feelings for me were more than admiration.

We drove back in ominous silence, looking out the window, he was aware I was seething.

I felt as if my dream was shattered. My ideal was 'but an ordinary man trying to take advantage of the situation. How could **I** be so naïve?!

At night, I locked my bedroom door, but at dawn I heard a gentle knock. After a few attempts he softly whispered, "Shadan, I know you are awake, I just want to let you know my plan." Plan … what plan? I was scared. Around nine when Kashif was starving, I opened the door, tiptoed carefully, and found an envelope in front of the doorstep, addressed to me.

"I profusely apologize for last night but I want you to know that I was sincere."

His note also stated, *"I'm going for official trip to Cameroun. I've instructed our chef Tayo to plan meals of your choice. Please consider this as your own home, stay until Mujeeb arrives."*

I felt numb!

I recalled that Abbaji once asked me, "What have you done to Mr. Zahid? He made a point to visit me in Islamabad. He asked if you were happily married, he went on praising you!"

I explained that he was impressed just because at an Embassy event, I got a thrill out of a three-way communication with the Chinese ambassador's wife who didn't speak English, so we used an interpreter. But his introvert wife was absolutely disinterested.

When I shared it with Shehnaz Khan, she advised me, "Forgive him but don't share it with your husband." Months passed by when Mujeeb decided to invite them over. As usual, he insisted we give them our master-bedroom, simply for the view of a hill from our window they admired. During their two-day visit, uneasy at first but soon I felt as if all was forgotten.

One day, when I was getting ready for a cocktail party, I found a small gift box in my jewelry drawer. Inside it was an exclusive hand-carved ivory necklace—from the tiniest to the largest pearl right in the middle. There was a message slip in a small envelope.

"Thank you for forgiving me. Please accept my small token of appreciation."

I did forgive him, especially after reflecting on my dad's comments. I learned to cherish that necklace but finally decided to explain to Mujeeb where it came from. Sharing everything with him was usual for me until an elderly American friend Helen Holton advised me,

"Never tell everything to anyone, especially to your spouse, or one day it will come back to haunt you."

So it did come to haunt me before my Washington trip. But I still **made** the trip and some *valuable connections too. We later learned that Mr. Zahid eventually divorced his wife and married an Egyptian Diplomat. Mujeeb said, "So he really was serious to break up our marriage!" Later on, the news of his sudden demise saddened both of us. I remember hubby's witty remark. "Had you accepted his proposal and married him, you would have been widowed at a young age,"

"*Ouff ...* how can you be jealous of a dead man. Spare the poor fellow."

Now I realized why my ivory necklace mysteriously went missing!

......

*I connected with a scholar Waseem Anwar, Professor of English & Dean of Humanities (Forman Christian College, Lahore). After attending an international conference in Vancouver, he visited Toronto. We invited him as our guest speaker to address the Writers and Editors Network where he spoke about the South Asian Literature. I felt humbled and honored to learn that in the conference he acknowledged my literary contribution as well. I have yet to make good my promise to visit the college in Lahore.

....

A visit to India and the Taj Mahal as promised

(Uncle gifted me this new outfit)

Mom kept his picture
under her pillow

With Aunt Nasreen,
Cousin Irfan and Uncle

Samina Tabassum directed my
Urdu Play "Pasand Apnee Apnee"

Reva Stern & family (2nd from
R)...partner in my literary projects

Fuad Ahmad's acting debut
'Window Shopping...for Lasting
Love' Now a popular Professional
Actor in films and Television

Our award winning play 'Questionably Ever After' (Adeel Ahmad and Tracey)

'Windows Shopping ... for lasting love' (In the Green Room) Amina Haqqani, Rafia Khokhar w Dance partners, Wajeeha Zuberi

(R to L) Junaid, Zehra, Adeel & Tracey In the front Live performance by Reena Grover and renowned vocalist Tariq Hameed

Kashif with his eldest
daughter Elina

The youngest Daania, at
her favourite picnic spot

Marzia also learned
to plant flowers

Daania and Marzia
up to mischief

Nasreen Syed (R) of
'Ghalib Academy'
Darakhshan Siddiqui, Zakia
Ghazal (L) & I
*(Founder of the Academy
late Athar Razvi)*

At Nasreen Syed's 'Dil Derya' poetry
book launch

Gala Launch of Rubina's
Short Stories collection

Author & Columnist Rubina
Faisal (3rd from R)

Konrad Brinks book launch 'Travellation'
With Kim and Marlene Leighton

Our Guest Professor Waseem
Anwar of Christian Foreman
College Lahore Addressed the
Writers and Editors Network about
South Asian Literature With Judie
Oron (R) Jasmine Jackman V.P,
myself and Maria Marchelletta,
President

Kim Cayer (author
of Kitty Casino)

Celebrating 'Literary Connections' Anthology
(Lindsay Albert & Susan Munro)

PART FOUR

Challenges, and . . .
Creative Escapes!

A Storm Was Brewing

35 One afternoon, Mujeeb didn't return from the University. From 3:00 p.m., I waited until 6:00 p.m. Eventually, I called the police. The cops were surprised I had no way of contacting my own husband, that he was neither willing to carry a cell phone nor would give me his office number. His reason, "No one picks up the phone, now everyone uses their cells."

The search began. A myriad of scary thoughts worried me, *What if he was alone in the office and had a heart attack?* It wasn't until 8:30 in the evening that the police called.

"We have located an elderly gentleman circling the parking lot at Erin Mills Town Centre. It's raining heavily, but we are heading there." Accompanied by three cops, he arrived, smiling as if nothing had happened. "Why didn't you stop at a gas station to use a payphone?"

"It wasn't necessary." He appeared cool, even amused by the episode. Only when Mujeeb saw the Town Centre landmark—a large globe, that he turned in the Mall. His license was suspended, conditional upon us consulting a specialist.

Mujeeb insisted, "Can't our son just change the prescription to help his own father?"

"No, he cannot or he'll lose his license," nothing registered. But I have no idea how he got his license reinstated. So one afternoon, the police called. "Your husband has had an accident at Steeles and Mavis area." I rushed out and a neighbor gave me a ride. Both the cars were totaled, but Mujeeb persisted, "I know the other driver did this on purpose because he wanted a new car." A thought flashed by, 'Is he losing his mind?'

Losing a license is like losing one's independence—it's traumatic.

......

The Iron Man

Hallstone Street where we lived on was designated as the *Gateway to the Heritage area of Churchvillle*—a village located in an exclusive portion of the Credit River Valley. Down the road was a scenic spot with a quaint little bridge that connected our new subdivision to the village. The stream flowing below was an offshoot of the Credit River. Tall weeping willows' branches bowed down as if to caress the stream. This view inspired the author in me. Members of our Club 23 also enjoyed that picnic spot by the water.

On the morning of May 9, 2013, we headed for our usual picnic. The kids asked me, "Can we take some bread to feed the ducks, Ma?" I could feel their excitement.

After a heavy rainfall the previous day, the stream was like a full-fledged flowing river. The kids were excited to watch a few people fishing. As they started feeding the ducks, I made a stern warning: "Please do not go close to the water."

"Relax, Ma, we'll be careful," It was hard to tame their excitement. "Let's forget about feeding the ducks today," so they agreed.

We sat on our Hyderabadi *Rallee* (multicolored hand-stitched, quilt). I spread out snacks and sandwiches. As we settled down, Mujeeb suddenly started running toward the river, full speed. "Stop, Mujeeb, where are you going, stop!" I ran after him and tried to grab his shirt from the back, but . . . there was no stopping him. Just like a

Diver takes a start *'On your mark, get set and GO,'* he somersaulted into the river, right before my eyes, I was helpless!

Had I grabbed him, I would have also plunged in with him.

Thank God, he surfaced. Blood was trickling down his face, children in panic hurtling helter-skelter near the lake, and there she was, our neighbor and savior Arooj! We had just exchanged greetings when I found her seated on a rock in somber mood, feeding the ducks.

Like an angel sent from heaven, Arooj reached out, held Mujeeb's hand, gently leading him until his foot finally rested firmly upon a solid rock. I rushed to call the paramedics, while trying to calm down the frightened children.

I had always admired Arooj as a talented artsy lady, but being in different social circles, we hardly saw each other. Strangely enough, only two weeks prior, we had run into one another, had a heart-to-heart conversation about the myriad of challenges in life we each were facing. We had promised to meet soon and provide moral support to each other. Who knew she would suddenly emerge as a mighty savior in a time of such dire need?

During those long six minutes until the paramedics arrived, I was able to calm the children, knowing that my hubby was in 'good hands.' He was all smiles, trying to pacify us while shivering in cold water. "Don't worry, I'm all right."

Kashif and the paramedics arrived simultaneously. We decided that Kashif would accompany his father to the hospital, and I'd stay with the children.

We ordered their favorite pizza and turned on a TV channel they liked, but not without some words of comfort first. I asked, "So, what was the positive outcome from this tragedy?"

Together we made a list, each of them took turns:

"Luckily, Abu wasn't injured seriously,"

"Our grandfather is so brave he was bleeding but still smiling,"

"The paramedics were quick and professional,"

"Arooj Auntie was there to help," I also added to their list, "And … for the first time, I found out how much you girls love your grandfather."

Only when they cracked up laughing at a funny scene on TV, I felt reassured they had in fact calmed down. But we anxiously awaited a call from the hospital.

Mujeeb had to get stitches in his skull and a few on his forehead— luckily there were no fractures. Though released the next day as having a non serious injury, I secretly worried if this trauma would exacerbate his dementia?

Our favorite spot became an *out of bounds* territory. The girls were too scared to ever return to that spot. I enticed them, "If you write a diary about the event, we will never go there."

Let's title the story *The Iron Man,* said one of them. "Okay. **The Iron Man** he is." Grandpa felt flattered and that diary was preserved in our journal titled *Life's Lessons.*

……

Cognitive impairment was now more evident. At the Urgent Care Hospital, Dr. Chandrakumar broke the sad news. "Your husband is diagnosed with Alzheimer-related dementia." Dumbfounded at first, the reality sunk in later.

How could all this happen to such a learned man?

But this disease does not discriminate. Early stages of Alzheimer dementia often go unnoticed. I started connecting the dots: His paranoia about my Washington trip—the negative comments about the ambassador!

At bedtime, I recalled other confusing episodes of his 'out of the norm' behavior.

I now envisioned a rough ride ahead; it was a call for 'Amor fati' (embrace fate bravely).

For immediate comfort I searched for interesting reads in my library.

The Magic of Morning Pages…

It must be faith or 'fate' that I stumbled upon what was referred to as '*The bedrock tool of a creative recovery*' a book about morning pages invited my curiosity so I read:

"Morning Pages are three pages of longhand, stream of consciousness writing done first thing in the morning. They are about anything and everything that crosses your mind—and they are for your eyes only. Morning Pages provoke, clarify, comfort, cajole, prioritize, and synchronize the day at hand."

Why did I abandon this practice . . . maybe because of our various stage productions? However, in 'The Artist's Way', Cameron gives her own example of when she faced challenges and needed to get her artist mojo back. I took immediate action and religiously followed the instructions: "*Do not over-think Morning Pages; just put anything on the page*," Though my keyboard skills coaxed me otherwise, but I agreed that, "*We get a truer connection to ourselves and our deeper thoughts when we put pen to paper.*"

My revived hobby became a ritual again. I poured out my anxieties 'uncensored.' Able to reach my inner self with a clear head, apart from the current situation, I analyzed other concealed apprehensions—whether my son's marriage was stable? Meant for my eyes only, this therapeutic drill provided space for creativity. I could even revive 'Bridging the Gap' activities I had planned.

My muse returned and poetry became a great escape. I quote one poem here:

Immigrant Woman

She likely had no say
in the decision to migrate
thousands of miles away
from her siblings, parents, and friends
Expected to tag along
walking two steps behind

But in this new climate
free from suffocation
Opportunities unlimited
she put her best foot forward
walking two steps ahead!

Migrating thousands of miles
did not deserve as much credit
as those four steps
she has taken on her own
                    ….zz

'TRUE COLOURS'
(From the Universe to the Inner Mind)

36 It seemed like yesterday when Mujeeb and I gave space to each other. But with his condition, to work independently at home was now impossible, therefore …

To finalize my poetry collection, I discovered a small French café in Erin Mills Town Centre, where I managed the new Optometric Dispensary. The moment I entered that quaint café, knowing my ritual the owner prepared a cup of chamomile tea and served it with a slice of banana bread. I sat comfortably down in a secluded corner to edit my poems for publication.

Later, my favorite poet Brandon Pitts and I met in the Second Cup in Streetsville, for the final edits. '***True Colours** –From the Universe to the Inner Mind*' an eclectic collection of pros poems was my humble attempt to paint the world's beauty as well as the ugly scars. A professional artist Salim Khan enhanced a few poems with his sketch work, at no charge! What a tough time it was for him…his partner Naheed was losing her battle with cancer. I'll never forget how she instructed him to prepare a lunch plate for me as I was rushing off to the Publisher. True Colours was published in 2012—I craved for a unique book launch, so I sweet-talked Mujeeb.

"I know you'll let me splurge just once," he agreed, in exchange for a romantic evening.

In the Montreal Room of the Living Arts Centre in Mississauga, some two hundred audiences applauded our nine-year-old granddaughter Elina's flawless recitation of the 'Acknowledgements' in my book. Club 23 girls wore deep-red matching dresses I had bought.

Memory of Elina's shy facial expressions kindled my heart especially when she read,

'This book is dedicated to my granddaughters Elina, Marzia, and Daania.'

Linda Thomas, the Executive Director of Mississauga Arts Council, Luiza Sadowski and Marilyn Garshowitz presented reviews, their articles were published in Canadian Asian News. One of the chief guests was my brilliant dentist Dr. Ante Bilic. Once my client at WMB I'm now his client/patient. He is into poetry and politics and has been supportive of my work. Ante teased me about my East-West combo. "You can't sit on two chairs at the same time," My response was, "I have two comfortable chairs so I may switch around depending upon the circumstances."

I felt honored when several authors recited my poems of *their* choice. My friend poet Ivy Reiss dressed in red bridal *lehnga* to recite *"Suhag Raath"* (The Wedding night). During the rehearsal the lady who lent her wedding gown, broke down into tears and confided in me:

"Your poem truly exactly depicts my personal experience." I was deeply touched.

The next poem *"In Tune"* was a dedication to my nephews and nieces. One of the songs they gifted me played in the background while an author Saskia van Tetering recited my poem.

I didn't realize how that scenario would come alive and trigger intense emotions. I wept through the entire recital, in public, and the videographer Najm Saheb had a field day focusing right onto my face. A friend comforted me, "There's nothing wrong in being true to your-self."

Here's that poem which created an unplanned **melodrama**.

In Tune

Their precise perception
of my taste for tunes
Abstract is this yearly gift of love
from my nephews and nieces
>*Upon my arrival they commence*
>*selecting special songs*
>*latest tunes I'd like best*
>*what lyrics would caress my finer senses?*

Prior to my departure a listening session
under the dim light I secretly observe
Delicate expressions on their serene faces
stealthily glancing at mine....
Wondering... confirming
if their selections were appropriate

>*Abstract love preserved in a compact disc*
>*I play over and over to relive the moments*
>*Though I reside thousands of miles away*
>*so accurate is their perception*
>*of my taste*
>>*Together or apart, we're always in tune.*
>>>......zz

The next recital by another artist instantly brought me back into a festive mood.

James Quinn, an accomplished poet/musician composed my two poems on guitar. Our guests compared him to Leonard Cohen. The audience truly appreciated the inclusive nature of that event—*Pakistani* Sitar Maestro Anwar Khurshid's delightful composition was accompanied with classical *Indian* dances by Jenevieve Bauleu, a *French* Canadian.

Dewdrops

Gently place the hand
of your caring nature on the shoulder
of my spiritual, sensuous being
  Like dewdrops upon a rose petal
   you will feel my fragrance enhance in response
    Life is too short.
      ......zz

A friend Braz Menezes, the author of the Matata Books, who had also attended the launch, surprised me with a welcome request,

"Your poem *"Editing Myself"* is exactly the theme of my second book, 'More Matata.' Would you be receptive if I use it as my Epilogue?"

"Of course, it would be a great honor for me," I replied. One line in my poem that resonated with them and many others was:

"Isn't life but a first draft?
We edit as we go along"

After reading his novel, I too was astonished how well my poem slotted into his story! I maybe an ordinary poet, but my simple prose poems have touched a few. Though I rarely meet a friend Anne Henderson she tells me, "Many real life situations often remind me of one of your poems." Zamir gave me full marks for the wide variety of subjects in my collection. Luckily, an organization 'Endless Possibilities' honored me with their 2013 'Woman of Courage Award' in the literary category. Their gala event was held in Woodbridge, Ontario.

The two poems composed on Sitar circled in my mind alongside innovative ideas:

'Why not combine traditional poetry recital with spoken word?'
Soon that unique concept materialized into a stage show.

The Internal Flame
Celebrating the 30th Anniversary of
Mississauga Arts Council, in 2012

Aptly named Celebration Square was the ideal venue I thought; having been invited to participate was an opportunity on a platter. I approached The Vibonics, an award-winning rap band, who were receptive but unsure of how my idea would work. "Just send me whatever you wish to present, and I'll incorporate it into my poems." Haunting me still were Khurshid and Genevieve's dance and sitar ensemble on my poetry. So I combined a few verses from my *"Dewdrops"* with another poem:

Canvas of the Heart
Step by step
How gradually you've descended
into the depths of my heart
reached its canvas
> *With gentle strokes you have enhanced*
> *the colours of my emotional landscape*
How easy it's become

to withstand adversity
Instantly I'm able to step
into my colourful world
......zz

Club 23—my granddaughters were tickled to watch their grandma rehearsing in our basement, a musical performance with young rappers. Four guys and two girls, under 21! How well their lyrics gelled with my verses! Thousands applauded when the Vibonics kept repeating,

"Lights out, party is over," but I kept insisting that party is not over,

"Keep your Internal Flame Eternal" (my message to the younger generation).

Repeating that mantra over and over during our rehearsals had a positive effect on me.

I remained determined to continue life as normal. There was always something to

Celebrate! Our performance was repeated at 2013 Marty's Annual Awards Gala.

....

A PARADIGM SHIFT
(*Financial Tsunami*)

37 One can work hard to reach the heights of success in life, but…one mistake can wipe out a thousand good deeds with a single stroke!

I thought I would cease to breathe as I received the head-spinning news.

"So would this be the last week I'd work at the Vision Centre?" I asked in disbelief, Kashif replied, "Yes. The clinic no longer belongs to me, I've sold it," his voice was sinking.

"Sold, what do you mean sold, when did that happen and why?"

I got no response, shock and anger simultaneously colliding against one another in my head.

"How could you do that without uttering a single word to me?" Still silence!

Observing his emotions, his face changing color and his tensed-up body posture, I felt a jitter and decided to refrain from questioning him further . . . only for the time being. For Kashif to take such a drastic step so suddenly there had to be some sort of crisis. I was sure he would share the details later. Reality struck me—that I too had lost my job as the Dispensary Manager, without any advance notice.

We both sat in deafening silence while I reflected:

What about Kashif's intellectual capital and dedicated patient care? It had taken him over a decade to develop one of the most flourishing Vision Centers in Mississauga? A Gold Medalist from Waterloo, recipient of an Honorary Award from the CNIB (Canadian National Institute for the Blind), he had mentored his associates every step of the way, especially in Low Vision Rehabilitation Services not offered in most other optometry clinics. Two of his associates had become his partners, more were being hired. My thoughts continued: I too had put my heart and soul in the Center, and played a significant role in the lucrative optometric dispensary I had managed now for thirteen years.

After establishing two other Optometry clinics and one Full Service Medical Clinic, he had embarked upon a much larger project— to establish several full-service medical clinics in partnership with three other Physicians. In that four-way partnership, his 25 percent comprised of investments from us, plus a bunch of his contacts and friends, of whom I wasn't aware.

I had questioned, *"Why invest in so many clinics simultaneously, why not one by one?"* "You don't realize, it gives us more buying power," was their response.

Kashif had hired his in-laws in various capacities. Father-in-law; sister and brother-in-law; his uncle and aunt in-law; and their sons— so there was manpower unlimited!

We were the 'non-interfering in-laws'…more so ever since we had moved out from our joint home. Even for the expansion plans, they did not seek my opinion, so I stepped back. Even as the Dispensary Manager, I was not consulted about the new Optometric Dispensaries.

Now, the deafening silence grew, as did the myriad thoughts ensuing in its wake:

I couldn't solve the mystery, but I wondered, "What about the *solid base* of the thousands of loyal patients, would one of his associates have acquired them all, won the lottery?" Compliments for Kashif by GPs, referring Ophthalmologists, and his patients rang in my ears.

Hit with such a serious blow, my elders would have concluded, 'Someone must have cast an evil eye upon him.' Junaid Waheed's wife Ashraf said, "*I feel guilty, perhaps I was the culprit?*" She clarified, "Once you were profusely admiring your daughter-in-law, but I said, '*Your Son is equal to ten, you should be proud of him.*' *It's not always the evil eye, you know.*"

Eventually, I learned more details. It was not just the Mississauga Vision Centre that was sold, that was only one component of the Total Collapse! The big project that involved multiple clinics had been expanded much too fast. Subsequently, our partner relatives and friends as well as us, lost our investments. But…as for my family of three, we additionally lost all our other assets, optometry clinics, our homes, and our entire life savings!

The most devastating news was when I found out that the list of his joint investors included three of my closest friends! They never whispered a word to me, **why…why…why?**

No one is ever prepared for such a sudden 'Paradigm Shift' in one's life. Having experienced hubby's job struggles, all my hopes and dreams were invested in my son who always made us proud. Reputed to be one of the most successful young men in our community, nothing is worse than losing one's solid reputation built over decades.

Kashif expressed regret for me. "Your friends can say all they want to me, but why are they involving you?" Subsequently, two of my closest friends abandoned me! At times of difficulty, I would have naturally turned to them.

A Willow that gifted me the Will…

As it is, day by day I was losing my partner to Alzheimer, and now my son was dealing with his crisis. His statement haunted me: "Falling to the ground from standing up is not as devastating as falling from high up the ladder of success into a ditch!"

Juggling simultaneously with multiple challenges, destiny had taken me to places I had never imagined I would end up.

How could my best friends believe it was *I* who master-minded the business venture? Our dear friend Zamir felt deep compassion for me and said, "In my entire life I've met only two people who got blamed instead of being rewarded, and you are one of them."

One morning before dawn instead of saying my prayers first, I felt the urge to head out toward the ravine. Avoiding our abandoned picnic spot to the left where Mujeeb had fallen, I turned right, only to find a uniquely mature willow tree. Its trunk surrounded by lush branches caressing the earth in a complete circle. To enter that secluded spot, I drew apart the branches as you would a curtain. Therein I released my calm for once, wailing out loud,

"God, what have I done wrong? Why are you putting me through such tests?"

"Are you all right?" A strange voice hollered, but I ignored it.

The gentleman came closer, opened the willow curtain, and peaked inside. "Is there anything I can do for you?" he probably assumed I was abused. "I want to help you," he persisted.

"Don't worry. I'll be alright," I replied.

It reminded me one of Rumi's quotations,

"When the world pushes you to your knees, you are in perfect position to pray."

Under that weeping willow felt like the best *Janamaaz* (prayer rug). Better than the various velvet rugs I had in my home, I thought.

What a place of refuge I had discovered! Blessed with the love of nature, some mornings I got enchanted by the music of chirping birds, witnessing peaceful dawn turning into the hustle bustle of the city. I returned home somewhat refreshed, ready to face the world. 'I have passed all other tests, maybe this is the last one I must clear.' No more wallowing under the willow.

At bedtime after meditation, I started repeating over and over Frederick Nietzsche's words: "What does not kill me makes me stronger."

......

Self-Evaluation and Reconciliation...

Part of the healing process is accepting one's own mistakes. When and where did I go wrong? Our First mistake was back in 2002, well before any business ventures were conceived. Moving out of our paid-off home in the heart of Mississauga, against *my* will is what had initially set my life on a different path. I should have single-handedly taken a firm stand.

What about our Second mistake? Despite the lawyers' warning, we moved out of the house where we had invested our life's savings. 'Reason is powerless in the expression of love.'

Viewing things from a 'subjective' point of view I could blame others. However, from an 'objective' point of view I realized that giving my financial reins into the hands of others was
My blunder!

I reconciled to such an extent that, at times I even hummed an Urdu song, as if the lyrics were written just for me:
> *"Sub kuch luta kay hosh mey aye toh kya kiya*
> *Din mey agar Chiragh Jalaye toh kya kiya"*

(What good is a lesson learned **after** you've lost everything?)

405

However, with my Vertigo Philosophy activated, I could see the positive outcomes. It's AFTER we moved out from our joint home, was when Bridging the Gap's mission of *'Enlightenment through Entertainment'* truly flourished, resulting in five socio-dramas in five years, two books of my own and numerous publications in various anthologies.

......

A Bookmark Friend...

One day I was engrossed in reading Dr. Lise Jeanelle's book, 'Conversation with the Heart'. That's when a handmade bookmark fell off, on which Chameli's phone number was inscribed! I had met the Therapist Dr. Jeanelle at our writer's club, she recommends,

"Learn how to find the perfection in the events of your life."

I sometimes followed her advice that we learn to interpret the Language of the Universe. Holding the bookmark in my hand, I interpreted it as a call to invoke forgiveness. A friendship that lasted for thirty-five years should be celebrated. So I wrote a poem about my friend titled, *"A Bookmark Friend."* Don't we sometimes put away even our favorite novels?

I resolved that:

On November 11, apart from honoring our Veterans, to my Poppy I'll also add the fragrance of Chameli flower.

I smiled at both of my 'Creative Closures'— hopefully permanent?

•••

MORE PRECIOUS THAN GOLD!

38 We were destined to lose our house, but in the meantime, I had to sell my gold jewelry, not a pleasant chore. I thought '*Shireen* would be fun company' so out of the blue I called her and asked if she would come along. I was managing the optometric dispensary in a new location, a full-service medical clinic. That's where I first met Shireen. We hit it off well as we discovered we had some things in common. She too had been married to a much older gentleman, at an even younger age than I. Whenever we had lunch in the mall, there was so much to talk about that we never ran out of topics. However, we had lost touch since I took retirement. Now she was surprised to get my invitation for a novel excursion.

"Sure, selling gold . . . that's one thing I've never done. Shall we combine it with lunch?" "That's the idea, let's take one car." So she picked me up.

Being able to invoke genuine laughter in someone is so flattering. Shireen laughs easily and wholeheartedly. Her beautiful eyes with 'Arab style makeup' exude positive energy. Able to switch from a serious topic to something lighthearted is her most admirable trait. She brought out the best in me, so lunch with her could be a source of stress release.

Now, on the way to the shops, I related my recent experience.

"I went to the Indo-Pakistani gold bazaar near the Airport Road and Derry. I should not have left Mujeeb at home." Shireen asked me what happened.

"The store owners were a husband wife team, each quoted me a different price. By the time the second partner weighed my gold, one bangle went missing!"

"Missing… how? And what's the lunch connection?"

"There I was worrying about money, but he was obsessed with food. Just when they were arguing that I had seven and not eight bangles, hubby kept calling me. "What's for lunch?"

"How frustrating, so let's make today a fun adventure,"

"Why do you think of all the people I chose *you* to come along?"

Together we drove around town, stopping at different jewelry stores, pricing various items—pendant sets, gold chains, necklets, rings, and earrings. Cracking jokes, mimicking the store owners, and their cheap haggling styles.

Near Dundas and Highway 10, we happened to see a sign.

'Halal KFC Lunch Special $1.99 only'

KFC has played quite a role in my life, I mused and said,

"Let's have the cheapest lunch ever. After all we are selling gold,"

"Moreover, it's halal," (kosher) I said as Shireen is very particular about that.

How much we enjoyed that unhealthy greasy lunch, which tasted better than a gourmet meal. Having to sell jewelry was a sorry state to be in, but seeing us in such a jolly mood, no one would guess what we had been up to. Upon parting Shireen offered,

"I can bring out some of my gold jewelry I hardly wear,"

"No way, but thanks for the generous offer." I said.

On my way home, I reflected a great deal about Shireen's personality. What a gorgeous, down-to-earth, fun-loving lady she is. But why did her Arab parents living in Canada, decide to marry her off at such a young age? I sometimes teased her, "By the Canadian Law, my dear you weren't even of legal age for marriage, so it was an illegitimate marriage."

She chuckled and said, "You have a point." At that time she was going through her own divorce.

……

Kashif had been separated for a while. The following year, he shared the news with me. "I'm going out with a lady you know quite well. I'm lucky to find just the right person for me."

"Is that the lady who works at Erin Mills?" His eyes cast a smile of delight.

Mujeeb and I later discussed, "In second marriages, people come with additional baggage," but Kashif responded, "No one has a bigger baggage than I do right now." Incidentally they each had three lovely daughters from their first marriages.

Subsequently, we started meeting her more regularly. Shireen's presence in our lives brought us a great deal of sweetness. Every time she visited, we all felt the fragrance of her loving presence. Mujeeb told her that the meaning of her name was **Sweet**. He pronounced it with his Urdu accent Shee-reen ('n' silent like in French).

"Thank God, Kashif has now found someone just like him," Mujeeb said.

"My only concern is that they are too alike,"

"So that's better than being like the opposing North and South Poles."

……

Once I jokingly asked her, "What did you find in my son that you fell for him?"

She spontaneously replied with a serious face, "The fact that he lost his investments, and he is always overworked," But observing my worried look, she started laughing like a teenager, then continued, "I was just kidding but … seriously speaking if you want to know the truth, I fell for his heart of gold. The best heart any woman could wish for," Shireen went on to share "Moreover, since I work there, I knew the doctors who took him for a ride. He trusted them blindly. I witnessed what happened to him. So I understand him the most."

It was comforting for me to know that at least *someone* understood his situation, maybe even better than I did?

She later shared that the day he discovered the ownership of the clinics had been lost to his doctor partners he sat in his car in the parking lot . . . and wept for two hours! Grief punched me in my gut. Constantly worrying about him since his separation, fearing alienation from his children, I secretly hoped *this would be the end of our agonizing days.*

Proceeds from the sale of gold couldn't last forever. We had no choice but to sell the house. In the meantime, my dear friend Fatima Jalil appeared as an angel. "No more selling gold, I'll help out until your house sale is finalized." I offered her to hold my remaining jewelry as security, but she didn't feel the need. **Now that's a true friend who trusts**.

....

OUR EXODUS!

39 As a family, we had once achieved our Canadian Dream, which was now on the verge of being shattered …or was it?

The morning of upheaval approached when my house was like a cardboard box, being dismantled. With the ominous sound of the truck outside, I knew it was the movers.

When they knocked at the door, I heard Mujeeb holler, "Tell them to go away."

"Please come inside so I may properly introduce you guys to him."

"What a day you picked, lady. Hope you'll offer us a cup of coffee," one of them asked, blowing steam into his hands. It was the coldest day of the year (*-22*!).

The three sturdy-looking young men turned out to be, Joshua, Muhammad, and Eric (a blonde Jewish fellow from Israel, a brown Palestinian Muslim, and a black Christian from Jamaica)! What an interesting partnership *Only in Canada* I thought and tried to invoke humor.

"So even the United Nations is bent on kicking me out of this house."

I poured tea instead of coffee— "That's all I can offer you guys."

"Let's get cracking," one started moving the boxes, another swiftly began to tape shut the loose ones, and started converting flat cardboard into boxes, at the speed of lightning.

From Mujeeb's office I could hear angry exchanges get louder and … LOUDER.

I called one of them to the side and whispered, "He is traumatized just agree with him, and all would be fine." They abided, and soon I heard them laugh like best friends. Thank God! I took a sigh of relief. Too friendly, too soon, was a surprise. I rewarded them with a nice lunch.

Sofas taped up, dining table bandaged, coffee table dismantled for separate packing … one by one … by one, I saw it all disappear. And now, like that empty living room, I too felt hollow inside. Through my family room window I took a peak in my backyard. My Seven Evergreens stood tall and majestic, six planted in the names of my siblings and one for my mom.

A solitary pine near the front entrance that represented my deceased father stood firm, as though reminding me: "Discover the positive aspect of every negative situation." Positive, really!

It was not easy to abandon our model home referred to as a Doll House, but thankfully I never got attached to bricks and walls. Odd as it may sound, but saying goodbye to those evergreens was more painful. Only two months ago, we had experienced the disastrous ice storm of 2013, and had been scared of losing those shriveled up trees. How excited the girls were when the trees bounced back. "Look, Ma, your siblings are standing up again!"

The buyers were a delightful young couple, I told them,

"We made history here, celebrated multiculturalism. This house welcomed dozens of artists, poets, singers, and people from multicultural communities."

Just then, I felt a piece of paper in my coat pocket which turned out to be a poem by an author friend Saskia. I had requested it at a writers meeting as the wording resonated with me.

Exodus

We did not want to depart but no longer have we any choice
We must leave this fate we have hollowed out of the
hard-stained, steely existence that passes here for industry,
for survival
Collect our possessions, our burdens together
Box up all of our celebrations, our heartaches
our memories—we must carry them away
...... Saskia van Tetering

But for this poem to appear at that moment was so bizarre!

I exhaled my stress out. The art of positive thinking is a honed skill, is it not? Thankfully by now the movers and Mujeeb had formed an *alliance*.

"Sweet guy, that Doctor, says he took you around the world, thirty-six countries, yes?"

When Joshua asked, "Could you put some music on?" I didn't waste a second as I recently found two forgotten old CDs which I set aside to kill the boredom of packing on the last day. Another strange coincidence, back-to-back, the very first classic song stirred emotions:

"Ek bungla banay niyara,
Rahey jis mey kunba saara hamaara"

(I crave for a unique bungalow where the whole family could live together)

In reality, our bungalow was being abandoned, and even our family was being dismantled … referencing our son's separation and lingering divorce.

Winston Churchill Boulevard (Feb 2015)

Our new address had royal connotations, but the approach to the townhouse was depressing—having to pass through the street with garages and everyone's trash cans on both sides. What a come down from our model home in a posh neighborhood!

It was past midnight by the time the huge truck reached our new abode, only to find out that our landlord abroad hadn't lived up to his promise. Snow had been piling up for weeks! Holding Mujeeb's hand, I strode slowly through semi frozen crunchy ice, up to our knees.

The front door had to be dismantled to push the designer furniture into that little townhouse. Suddenly everything seemed too bulky for the tiny rooms. From the 12 ft ceilings in a custom bungalow, low ceilings initially felt suffocating, but suddenly I thought I wasn't such a short woman after all. I looked for *any excuse* to cheer myself up.

The 'United Nations' of movers took advantage of my vulnerable situation, doubling their charges. Well past midnight, a little woman dealing with three aggressive men, plus a confused husband, ouff!

Mentally and physically fatigued, I came downstairs and plunked myself on the couch.

At dawn I had a unique experience which prompted me to jot down my outpour:

Choreographing my Breakthrough
Having lost everything, coping with
another night of insomnia
Sluggishly I descended
down the stairway
Step ... by step... by step

> *Financially 'fondled'*
> *Emotionally 'embezzled'*
> *Physically 'frazzled'*

A potent mixture—as though I could explode
Breakdown... or maybe.... disintegrate?

Lethargic, I plunked myself
upon the living room sofa,
barely conscious

    Suddenly I felt a presence—:
    Mysterious, majestic, mystical
    arms outstretched as though
    reaching out to rescue me
    A tall evergreen
    beside my living room window
        A rising symphony of epiphany!
        He too has weathered
        the harshest of all weathers
        Thunder, lightening, the ice storm of last winter
        I heard him whisper:
        "Why not choreograph your own breakthrough?"
                    …..zz (WIP)

With a great sense of relief, I put the pen down to finalize my draft poem later.

Recalling the events of the past month I had a refreshing thought about a magnanimous gesture by three amazing Vocalists –*Zaheer Habibi, Sadiq Azam* and *Rafat Alam*. Before the closing of our house sale, they coordinated a musical concert in my basement, at no charge. They each sang my favorite songs too! Sixty of our friends thoroughly enjoyed the evening. In my intro I said, "Instead of a housewarming, it's a *House-cooling* party to remember forever!"

With those pleasant thoughts I finally fell asleep.

Who knew that early morning I would rise to a pleasant surprise? I seemed to have received another Divine gift: From each window of this compact house peeked at me tall and majestic pines, the 'Evergreens' replacing the ones we left behind. I noticed the floor plan of this townhouse was a miniature replica of our Hallstone home. The sun rays were shining through with full glory. Even little Elina had recently reminded us:

"Ma, didn't you say a happy home is better than a luxury house?" *Even a child has grasped the concept... it's time to practice what I preach.*

Mujeeb went room to room looking for box # 79. He had secretly handed it to the movers with $2,000 cash enclosed, all his savings bonds, as well as my briefcase. Now I knew why those guys befriended Mujeeb. The police said it was their words against ours, no proof.

Two days later we watched a documentary on CBC showing an elderly couple who lost $9000 worth of goods. "It's not uncommon to exploit the elderly" they reported.

Tracing the Canada Savings Bonds could take up to nine months I was told.

......

Mujeeb developed a serious kidney problem and was admitted to Free Care Hospital. It turned out to be a blessing in disguise. Only because he tried to escape at midnight, a Geriatrician was called for a full assessment:

"His *'Neurocognitive Impairment'* is progressing fast." Dr. Waheed (a friend) explained, "The more intelligent a person is, the more they are able to camouflage this illness."

I was advised to ensure Power of Attorney is in place as soon as possible. What a head-spinning discovery about his Nigerian pension—he had not collected for 20 years! I had a job cut out for me. But for now I was happy he was released with a medical treatment plan.

Respite help for me was approved through Ontario Health Program, CCAC Community Care Access Centre. *Rajni Iqbal* came as a breath of fresh air, as she always arrived sporting a bright smile. Mujeeb took to her, especially when she made fresh **Chappatis* (flat bread) for us.

Curious friends asked, "How can you afford such a luxury in Canada?" It was a stroke of good luck. Overqualified for that job, we knew Rajni would soon find something in her field.

Our utmost priority for now was to engage the children in fun activities, while their parents were going through separation. Children often pay a hefty price, but it was up to us to minimize the impact. So in the basement of our compact townhouse, the girls played games with Kashif and dancercised with me to blaring music— Adnan Sami's upbeat tunes. Those bulky beanbags the children had 'prohibited' me from selling, provided such fun—I'd lift them up and plunk them onto it, invoking loud giggles. Such moments of joy we preserved on camera.

The upgraded house was forgotten and that rundown townhouse did become our '**Nayara Bangla.**' (a unique bungalow)

....

My Fatherly Brother

40 Sikandar and I communicated daily, we called ourselves Black Berry Partners.

He would repeat, "Remember, in the absence of the father, the brother takes over."

"Thanks for helping me get through this *Abbaji*," I would joyfully reply.

True to his words— Sikandar had taken over VLI's financial responsibilities until we recovered. Neither Kashif nor I could carry on with fundraising events.

But one day, he called, when my sixth sense produced an alert signal.

"Rather than you hearing from another source, I need to share something …" He paused as I grew increasingly fearful, he went on, "I've been diagnosed with cancer of the jaw." I felt my throat choking.

But how did **he** get cancer of the jaw? Never smoked or ate *Paan* (edible leaf with beetle nuts) Mujeeb's instant conclusion was, "Told you doctors want to make money."

Our family was shaken up. Sikandar had visited Canada twice at my request. Now I had to be with him. I also thought this would likely be Mujeeb's last chance to meet his family.

……

Ammi was super-excited that we both showed up. She always celebrated that Mujeeb was a year older than her. Once my father said, "I deserve an award for my hat trick because my three children are Gold Medalists." Ammi spontaneously blurted, "But I deserve an award for being the *only* mother-in-law younger than her son-in-law." Nonetheless, ever since I got married, Ammi and Mujeeb ganged up against me, teasing me endlessly. I just pretended I was offended.

They played *Antaakshri* or *Bait Baazi*, a game when one person recites a verse the other has to respond with another verse beginning from the last letter. They recited Urdu poetry verbatim, how their memories lit up, was astonishing, we felt overjoyed.

That distraction comforted Sikandar. At times when even morphine didn't work, I'd place my hand on his swollen jaw and start humming his favorite songs. Religious relatives recited verses from the Quran. One day when I was singing, a cousin arrived with a beard longer than any Sardarji in Brampton (Sikh).

I said, "All these *Saints* are praying for you and here I am the *sinner* in your life."

Sikandar smiled back. "It relieves my pain, keep singing,"

"Did you say keep **sinning**?" He struggled to invoke another smile and...I shuddered.

......

Could this be the last I'll see my Mother?

Ammi's mild cold soon developed into pneumonia, and she was admitted to Agha Khan Hospital. I was amazed by how many family members visited her—children, grandchildren, even siblings' children and grandchildren, only Kashif was missing. Ammi always kissed her guest's hands but now an oxygen mask was in the way; everyone kissed her forehead instead.

I spontaneously lifted her bedsheet and kissed both her feet, her face turning radiant. The next morning, as we got the news of her passing, while simultaneously Sikandar called out, "Abbaji, Abbaji!" as if asking our father to receive her. It was so strange because he had not yet been informed of her demise!

Like a foreigner, I observed how different the Pakistani lifestyle is. Within two hours, her body was brought to the house. Even the extended family was mobilized. The tents and chairs with starched white covers were set up outside the house to accommodate umpteen expected visitors. Their large family room (they call lounge) soon filled up. Sikandar gave instructions from his bedroom to ensure all the ladies had comfortable seating and refreshments.

As I noticed my sisters and nieces sneaking out, I ran after them, "Where are you going?" Her body was being taken to ***Edhi Centre** for her final bath. "So why am I being excluded?" they explained, "You live so far away, you may not be able to handle it."

"More reason for me to participate," I said and followed them.

After two professional women bathed her, each of us did the ritual of pouring water to purify her body. A million thoughts circled in my mind, questions cropped up. What is *Rooh* (soul), void of life how the body becomes like an *Empty Cage?* Ammi was a beautiful lady. As she lay there lifeless, a semblance of portraits from *The Louvre* art gallery in Paris flashed before me. I quickly shifted the thought to reflect about the mystery of life.

I had read that 'a Soul is made up of the spirit, tangible and intangible—something that represents **us**, our spiritual being, maybe?' Hindus believe in reincarnation; my atheist friends even deny that there's a soul. Muslims believe that *'A soul is created at birth and the time at which it would depart from the body is* *predetermined!'* Debating those confusing ideas in my head was perhaps my way of dealing with grief. I eventually concluded that,

*'The mystery of the **human soul** is unknown to humans.'*

But participating in Ammi's final bath gave me closure and conviction—that she will always reside in our memory (isn't that the Afterlife for her?). I'll try to embrace her pet phrase:

"Dil ba dasth aawar kay hajj-e-akbar asth" a legacy she left behind.

Her purified body, wrapped in a *Kafan* (shroud), and brought back to the house, everyone blessed her soul through prayers, and related their personal experiences of her immense love.

What a timely departure—as if she waited for my arrival and avoided the loss of her beloved son.

*Abdul Sattar Edhi was a Pakistani humanitarian, philanthropist and ascetic, who founded the Edhi Foundation, which runs the world's largest volunteer ambulance network, along with various homeless shelters, animal shelters, rehabilitation centres, and orphanages across Pakistan. (Wikipedia)

Nominated for a Nobel Prize, he was the recipient of numerous awards. This irreplaceable icon passed away peacefully in 2016 and was buried with full state honors.

......

Two days prior to our departure, Sikandar invited us into his bedroom—Shahid, me, and Abdullah (our nephew). Holding one hand with me he declared, "I've decided to stop chemo or any other treatment. Please explain to everyone that my days are numbered, so they are mentally prepared." Both Shahid and Abdullah were sniffling and sobbing. Sikandar meticulously stated his concerns and

I addressed them one by one. In his languid voice he whispered, "I feel better with your assurances." Surprised at my own strength, I wondered how I remained so calm?!

That afternoon, Sikandar was hallucinating under heavy medication. I could decipher him discussing a corporate financial transaction between Dubai and Australia –heartbreaking. On that somber night of my departure at 2:00 a.m., my heavy heart left him fast asleep.

It was a very dark night, the neighbours were asleep, silence was echoing loud.

Amongst all the hugs and emotional goodbyes, Ammi's maid suddenly recited,

"Abhee abhee toh ayi ho
Bahar bun kay chaee ho
Abhi na jao chor kar
Ke dil abhi bhara nahee"

(You just arrived like Spring Don't leave ... for our hearts aren't content as yet)

I touched my heart with an outburst,

"Oh my God, Shaista, that used to be Ammi's goodbye song to me."

"Of course, Baji, your mother taught us many songs." Somehow it eased the tension?

Observing my *calm* Saman complimented me, *"Sipah Sallar number 2"* (The lead soldier).

Being Sikandar's doctor/daughter when she played a proactive role at the hospital, I complimented her as 'Sipah Salaar' (The lead soldier).

As the plane took off, down below I saw Karachi city shrinking away, miniature houses and dinky cars, slowly diminishing. Knowing that I'll never see my beloved brother again, my outpouring of emotions merged with the Takeoff noise! As usual Mujeeb had fallen asleep on the runway. Eventually, I too dozed off and saw a sweet dream:

'Ammi was cuddling a toddler with green eyes and chubby cheeks.'

I then relished Sikandar's childhood memories.

Contrary to common perception I found that living abroad somehow made grieving *easier* and not tougher. I rarely saw them so I was able to imagine or pretend they are still around.

....

The United Nations Conference
(CSW59 2015)

---

41 Upon my return to Canada, an opportunity knocked for another healthy diversion: An invitation for CSW 59 United Nations Conference to mark the 2015 International Women's Day in New York. It was the Fifty-Ninth Session of the Commission about,

'The Status of Women—to achieve Gender Equality by 2030'

Our Support Worker Rajni offered to stay with Mujeeb and he was thrilled.

Lilly Tadin, President of the WFWP, Women's Federation for World Peace and *Eveline Stewart* represented their organization, but I attended on behalf of 'Bridging the Gap'.

Eveline willingly took charge to plan our trip together.

My connection with them commenced since 2011, introduced by Farzana Hassan, a scholar from our community. In challenging times, we gravitate to our comfort zones. Although WFWP's mandate was different from BTG (nonreligious), our common goal was promoting peace and interracial, interfaith harmony.

Together with the Universal Peace Federation they had honored me with the Ambassador of Peace award. I was invited as a Guest Speaker on numerous occasions, including a memorable International Conference on Multi-culturalism held in Ottawa. That's when I had discovered Eveline's jovial side, as we shared our hotel accommodation.

Now in March of 2015 in New York, thousands of brazen women from all over the world converged to gather in that hub to celebrate 'Women's Empowerment, Current Status and Future Progress.' Eveline had booked a room near the UN building, so we attended as many conferences and lectures as possible. One session I enjoyed most was named *'He...for She'* when the male CEOs who implemented gender equity in their corporations received awards.

One afternoon, at a gala lunch inside the UN building, the main topic was Child Brides as Victims. The passionate speaker was a young woman (I forget the name) who presented a motion: *'Marriages under the age of eighteen should be prohibited.'* Motion seconded, the crowd cheered as everyone raised their glasses to propose a toast; I spontaneously cracked a joke at my table: "But here's a happy victim."

My peers spoke in unison. "We know you've been a pampered wife—an exception."

Who would have thought that five women of different races and ages sharing one room could have so much fun? There were two beds only, so I got to share mine with a lovely young Japanese girl, Miho. During the seven hours journey and five days together, we became like family. After attending conferences, in the evenings we strolled along the streets of New York, made spontaneous choices of restaurants to dine in. Stayed up late nights and shared each other's cultural stories. "This is *Enlightenment through Entertainment* at its best," I rejoiced. Miho gave an enquiring look; Lilly explained about Bridging the Gap and its mission.

Miho confessed, "In five days I've learned more about the South Asians, especially Pakistani culture, than I would have by reading several books."

As for me, I never thought I'd meet white European women who also practice the culture of arranged marriages?! On the contrary, my socio-dramas attempted to influence the South Asian Canadians that arranged marriages in Canada aren't always the best option. But those happily married women enlightened me with the *how's* and *why's* of their *arranged* unions. Behind these successful women I discovered their 'He for… She' spouses —Lilly Tadin had the backing of her 'Super-smart *Stoyan*' and, Eveline enjoyed full support from the 'Dedicated *David Steward'*. I observed that their families truly practice what they preach:

'Living by the Logic of Love'

Mujeeb was happy I was back safe and sound but …?

Sipping tea one morning, looking out the window he noticed the exhaust outlets on the rooftops of other townhouses. "We are breathing dirty air from these exhausts. I'll die unless we move as soon as possible." Luck on his side, our landlord raised the rent, so I called my previous neighbor friend *Sophie Alam*, a go-getter realtor. The first home she showed us was in Streetsville ... music to my ears.

What an unusual multi split-level bungalow. Sunlight was illuminating the interior in all its glory, through ten windows upon one wall, from lower levels all the way up to the top floor.

"This is it. No need to see any other property." To see my hubby so excited was a relief. After a year at the previous townhouse, this bungalow was an upgrade. In contrast to the previous movers (thieves), the new ones 'Movers with a Heart' truly lived up to their name.

This artsy town, once home to Mayor Hazel McCallion, was known as a *'Village in the City'* with which I had a shared history that brought back an abundance of sweet memories. We had celebrated a Literary Festival at the 150th birthday of Streetsville, and recited poetry in the *Second Cup* and *Starbucks.* My first book launch held at Robinson Bray; stage readings of plays; open mic; even the Courtney Park authors' anthologies were launched in the Masonic Lodge, now within walking distance. What more could I want?

Whoever entered our bright home with an open concept plan spontaneously reacted,

"Wow! What a lovely and unusual house."

But…one thing was missing…our main source of joy.

During separations and divorces, children sometimes become hostages. We found temporary comfort in watching their videos of the happy times we'd had at the splash pad at Celebration Square or picnics in Jack Darling Park by Lake Ontario.

The Planet Sun has such a hold on the human spirit! Those glorious mornings invoked poetry.

What an interesting irony that during our economic meltdown, we got to live in a million-dollar bungalow! It was bound to raise suspicion. However, the hidden fact was that we inherited a severely neglected backyard (a jungle) and we also had to put up with serious plumbing issues. With our luck, *Paul*, our co-tenant downstairs happened to be a professional plumber. In exchange for my curry meals, he was ever ready to fix the taps or any leakages at no charge.

……

Oh…those $20 Bills!

In the meantime, Kashif remained adamant about re-establishing new medical clinics so he could return shares or ownerships to previous partner-investors. I just couldn't convince him that his

single-handed rescue effort may even lead to more losses, but he worked around the clock to rebuild.

How times had changed? Managing with limited income and 'unnecessary' legal expenses, we now shared one car. I drove him from one end of the city to another. He wanted to drive but I wouldn't let him. "You are too exhausted, I prefer you take a nap." He dozed off, I felt relieved.

At times he reluctantly asked, "Do you have $5 on you?" Knowing that it was for the bus fare, I'd pull out a $20 bill! How could I forget that even during his school years he gifted me $20 bills from his tutoring income?

It was our internal struggles that no one else was privy to!

But the irony was that some people believed in false rumors that he and I had millions stashed away elsewhere! An even bigger irony was that in my retirement years, I had to support two highly qualified individuals—A PhD husband and a gold medalist Doctor of Optometry, suffering through a financial tsunami. I had to caution myself not to let it get to my head, and thank the 'higher power' that enabled me. Thanks to the golden handshake, one year's worth of salary from WMB from 1998 … the rainy-day savings had become a *Tsunami Day Reservoir*. Nonetheless large sums were spent on 'recovery' measures. There was a big hole in our sack!

Kashif's loyal patients tracked us down. "We'll never forget what your son did for us, so we are praying for him and your family." Old friends like *Ishrat Ahmad and family*, *Rebecca* and Brian Hull, who knew and trusted us, came forward to offer much appreciated moral support.

As for Mujeeb, I admitted him to the 'Senior Life Enhancement Centre' once a week. I had primed them about his peculiar needs. So the first day we entered, the hall echoed with "Hello, Dr. Zoberi; Hi Dr. Zoberi; Welcome Dr. Zoberi." They even made a name tag for him! Other patients thought he was a medical doctor. Still, he often resisted going there.

....

Friends in Deed
(Personal Support Workers –PSW)

42 To understand the disease, I watched a documentary by **David Suzuki**. He warns:

"Alzheimer dementia is a Tsunami heading our way, but we are not prepared." *The statistics indicate an 83% rise in the past ten years. As well, 45% of Care Providers experience near or full-fledged breakdowns. One in every eight Canadians over sixty-five will become victims. In this age of research and technology, a cure has yet to be found!*

Suzuki's touching and raw personal experience of dementia resonated. A few of his family members had suffered the disease.

Heather from the Alzheimer Society and *Roshni Romero* from our provincial health system now called LHIN (Local Health Integration Networks) assisted me to get help from PSWs (personal support workers).

Young women from various religious and ethnic backgrounds made daily visits.

Upon their arrival I requested them, "Please call him Professor or Dr. Zoberi **not Mr.** and just agree with him...even if he is dead wrong." Resorting to humor at times I teased him,

"If you aggravate me, don't expect any *vestal virgins* or **Hoor* in Heaven. Better enjoy them in this life, a new one comes for you every day." (*no such entity, it's just a myth)

I chose to view this situation as a learning opportunity for me.

Each PSW shared stories of sacrifices they made to become Canadians; some even formed friendships. Once a Filipino named Divina was visiting when Mujeeb fell asleep. I recited to her my published poem "*Smiling Maids.*"

She burst into tears. "How do you know about us Filipinos?" She shared stories of her struggles and said, "Now *you* are our PSW."

They enjoyed when I shared little tricks such as how to keep bananas fresh for ten days. From them, I learned how to fold fitted bed sheets perfectly. They chuckled with my analogy:

"*Folding a fitted sheet is a nuisance...like Marriage...but once it's on the bed, it fits really well.*"

Once I was perusing our latest anthology by Writers and Editors, PSW *Jennifer Javier* was on duty that day. She became interested, so I gifted a copy to her and she had a joyous outburst, "Oh my God, it's the first time anyone has ever gifted me a Book!" I captured it.

The Victorian order of Nurses also provided us a volunteer, *Mr. Bahadur Ali,* a humble-looking petite gentleman in his seventies. Chatting in Urdu with strong Ismaili accent, he easily befriended Mujeeb. Bahadur was a widower who also needed company, so it was a win-win.

What a blessing that in the absence of family or close friends, total strangers were extending helping hands! I sent my thank you poem "*Friends in Deed*" to their Coordinator.

She appreciated it very much. "These women definitely deserve applause."

That's so true, but...who will applaud me for finding humor while dealing with crisis?

Advised to log any behavioral changes I had already created a D Diary in which I recorded numerous bizarre or humorous incidences (which could possibly be helpful in future research). Here's an interesting anecdote:

Wink of an Eye!

On a Sunday morning, a strange noise woke me up at seven. Mujeeb still snoring, I rushed downstairs, when looking out the windows I saw over a dozen petite Vietnamese men with bright yellow jackets and helmets. It reminded me of the squirrel attack we once had at our Hallstone home, when early morning we had found baby squirrels peeking through each window. Mommy, nestled snugly in our attic had been over-productive.

But these little guys with yellow helmets were suddenly ripping shingles off our roof and ruthlessly throwing them onto our lawn. Both our front and back entrances were blocked with wooden planks, even I was overwhelmed…let alone a dementia patient.

As expected, it triggered the worst ever anxiety attack and Mujeeb started shaking with fear and anger, screaming, *"It's **my house** who gave these idiots permission to destroy it?"* Loud drilling started, but then it suddenly stopped and I heard an angry exchange instead.

Our gorgeous landlady Jenny, dressed like a bridesmaid, and hubby Eric arrived, both looking extra tall in comparison to those workers. Mujeeb suddenly unplugged the power cord, now holding onto it defiantly, the work halted. The couple requested Mujeeb to let go of the cord. No such luck!

Jenny was begging, pleading at first, soon the situation escalated to a dangerous level. Mujeeb's dementia symptoms triggered, he told her to shut up and get lost. By the time I stepped in, seeing Jenny's pale face, I feared she may have a heart attack. Eric, like her tail following behind her, seemed flustered. The little Asian men looked extremely harassed . . . it was like a scary scene out of a funny movie. I suppressed my humorous side with difficulty.

The situation escalated to serious threats being hurled at each other. Another Chinese neighbor emerged as a captivated spectator. A thought flashed: During a support session the Alzheimer Society recommended, dealing with dementia patients, sometimes you may resort to 'Therapeutic Lies'. So...I invoked an innovative Therapeutic Lie:

Standing left of Mujeeb, he could only see my right eye. Jenny to my left would surely notice if I wink my left eye. I winked, she didn't catch on...pushing my face forward I winked harder, so the second time Jennie got the hint, I spoke with authority; loud and clear,

"My husband is right. **How dare you** change our roof?" I then turned around and gently whispered, "Okay, Zooby. I'm going inside to call the police right now."

I stepped inside and closed the front door... gained control of myself. Never before I felt like laughing and crying simultaneously, whilst they waited outside in suspense. A funny/scary drama was now being staged. Two minutes later, I stepped outside and blatantly declared:

"I just called the police. They've advised that for now we should let the work continue. On Monday, they will send over the city officials. That'll teach them a lesson, darling."

To everyone's surprise, Mujeeb loosened the grip, let go of the power cord ... just like that! Tension eased, spectators disbursed, the Korean/Chinese team were back into action.

Later that morning, as I treated him to a lavish Sunday brunch, he was all smiles and said, "At least we now have a new roof, but don't pay them anything, okay?"

"Are you kidding…of course I won't pay a penny." This time it was the truth.

By Monday morning, he had forgotten the entire incident.

……

Our Home Lit Up Again!

"Ammi, Abu, Good news! I'm finally going to meet my children but…you have to wait. You've been patient for almost a year, what's another week or two." We both sat in the dark.

Barely twenty minutes had passed when the front door opened and there they were, all the lights were switched on. The laughter, the jokes, that playful teasing—just like before! A miracle had occurred, and it was as if the children had never left. All five of us cuddled on our

'Love-seat' Kashif captured those moments of ecstasy on his cell camera.

I took pictures of the girls gleefully climbing over their dad's shoulders. Marzia, younger than Elina made a joke. "You saw us after a year, how come you didn't even faint?"

Eventually, regular visits were scheduled. The best way to integrate them back into our lives turned out to be those videos I had retained; dancercising in the basement, planting flowers in the patio, playing *Andha bhainsa* (blind folded buffalo). As the children adjusted to the changes in Mujeeb, his animated stories resurfaced, which had positive impact on him, and us.

Now that the digital gadgets had taken over, we couldn't revive our Club 23 Diary writing. We now introduced group readings. Everyone took turns to read from a book by my author friend *Jennifer Maruno*, one of her Cherry Blossoms series. Learning to read with intonations, little Daania even mimicked the Japanese accents. The games like Carom Board and Charades became our **Four Generation Family's** favorite. During those highlight moments, even the walls echoed with laughter.

So, the Bankside house too became our *Happy Home*.

Another family union was to further illuminate our spirits.

......

Marriage on a Rooftop...

The Radisson Plaza Hotel livened up on August 26, 2016 when two of my favorite people in love, Kashif and Shireen, celebrated their union. They had officially gotten married earlier; however, Kashif insisted that this was to be a small ceremony of fifty intimate guests. They may have a big wedding later, inclusive of their children.

Dressed in a pale gray lace and silk gown, Shireen looked stunning, and Kashif in matching pale gray suit, looked as handsome as she dreamed of. The weather was perfect for an *Outdoor Patio Event* and the fancy gazebo was great for wedding pictures. The guests were mostly physicians and a few friends. From our family we only had Sadaf and Junaid and our niece Dr. Lubna and Aslam who came from Philadelphia, staying with us, of course.

Everyone loved the Arabic touches...their unique style of *ululating* (a high-pitched rhythmical sound used to express immense joy). The most enjoyable moment was when the entire crowd started dancing around the bride and groom.

Once I found that they had booked Tariq Hameed for entertainment, I was certain that the party would be a blast. Multitalented Tariq, who had previously acted in two of my plays, knows exactly how to captivate any crowd. His live performance included not just old Indian and Pakistani songs, but he even prepared English as well as

Arabic numbers. His extempore selection geared to suit the diverse guests invoked a romantic mood, as all couples were entranced, and danced.

Since Kashif insisted it was more like an engagement party, there was to be no cake. However, at the last minute, he called to say Shireen's sisters are surprised as to why we don't have a cake. Who do I call when in panic mode? Fatima Jalil, she reassured me, "Leave it to me." A beautiful cake-cutting ceremony was held outside on the patio, under the gazebo, creating a magical ambience that evening.

People plan their weddings for months and months but…that relatively 'rushed' engagement party became a super exclusive wedding event. *Even Mujeeb livened up with music, and he danced as though nothing was wrong with him!*

But after the cake-cutting ceremony, he suddenly had an anxiety attack. "Let's go home, I can't stand being here." One of my friends whispered to me, "Just move away, we'll take care of him." Being the host I couldn't leave earlier, so Lubna and Aslam decided to take him home.

Upon my return, they told me he was livid as to why they forcefully brought him home.

They had a heart-to-heart talk with me and forewarned me, "We witnessed his anger, with his dementia progressing you have a rough road ahead."

Regardless, it was one of the happiest days of my life. As the newlywed couple danced entranced, Tariq's romantic rendition, rang in my ears for days:

"Jub koi baat bigar jaye, jub koi mushkil per jaye
Tum deyna saath mera, oh humnava"

(Love song...similar lyrics like the marriage vows: for better, for worse, in sickness and...)

I happen to be living the challenge of that very theme, I mused. Music revealed so much to me, as my unfolding experiences deepened my understanding of once familiar lyrics.

CARE PROVIDING CREATIVE STYLE

43 The Alzheimer Society facilitated workshops. The information they provided as well as Suzuki's warning that 43 percent care providers experience burnout, I realized that:

'Zohra actually needs to provide care for two people—Mujeeb and Shadan.'

I decided to recite stories and poetry to him, so I may catch up with my reading backlog as well. That experiment proved to be a win-win. Thanks to our author friend *Rubina Faisal*, reading her candid short stories in Urdu became our favorite pastime. When I attended her book launch I felt tempted to translate her book as 'Stories Wrapped in Dreams'. Maybe one day?

From 8:00 a.m. to noon, I'd sit glued to hubby, watching and interpreting the news or reciting poetry to him. Even when a PSW arrived, he wanted me to remain within his sight.

CD Epiphany…

Selecting music for him one morning, I didn't like the top CD so it dawned on me:

'Life is like a stack of these disks, the 'Problem CD' at the top is fully visible. However, underneath it there's much more music to play.' By now I was used to compartmentalizing issues at hand. To remain engaged in social activities became a necessity for both of us.

After all, don't people with special needs children try to lead a normal life? So, I too resolved to continue life as usual. Mujeeb often accompanied me as a silent spectator. We even enjoyed hosting some meetings with Courtney Park authors in our home. Everyone relished sizzling Pakistani *Samosas* with tea. Sharing our life stories bonded us and more importantly, they genuinely respected and cared for my hubby too (he became calm in their presence).

Rain or snow, I ventured out to brunch meetings of the Writers and Editors Network (WEN). Driving on Bloor Street all the way to Kipling took me back to 1977—my familiar route to Shaw College. Once I reached the Canadiana Restaurant at Six Points Plaza, I entered another world. Reva and John always saved me a seat on their table. Renowned guest speakers like Leonard Rosmarin sharing their personal journeys toward literary success motivated me.

……

I was also drawn to 'The Moonshine Café' on Kerr Street in Oakville. It was owned by a jovial couple, John and Jane. This quaint café had a country-like ambience, a bar, BBQ facility, and the walls were pasted with photos of hundreds of musicians' and poets. Jane delightfully addressed my curiosity: "We have collected these woolen hand-woven blankets on the couches over a decade." Even their Ladies' Room was decorated like a mini art gallery. Such a variety of artwork—oil paintings, sculptures, ceramics, and antique gems were on display that are preserved in my cherished videos.

John and Jane generously offered their cozy venue to us authors and poets for once a month. I was pleased that Ivy Reiss, once part of my book launch, was now the event coordinator of the Oakville Lit Café. Most authors were outside my *Desi* (South Asian) community, so I felt more liberated to write and recite whatever I felt like.

Ivy later launched *The Artis* coffee table art and literature magazine. As a regular reader at the Lit Café, I was excited when she included my story, '*A Culinary Adventure*' about bat hunting in Nigeria, in the inaugural issue of her magazine.

In 2015, the Lit Café was moved to another unique location: Joshua Creek Heritage Centre, run by famous artist Sybil Rampen. A renowned poet and a dear friend *Josie Di Sciascio-Andrews* became the Lit Café coordinator. One of Josie's books is titled '*When the Italians Created Canada*'. I used to jokingly say, "I'd love to write 'When the Indo-Pakistanis Created Mississauga!' This is where I met a genius author Dr. Ed Hamer –he too has great admiration for Sybil like I do. The delightful Josie competently runs the Lit Café to this day.

Since Mujeeb could not be left unsupervised, I always took him along. One of the authors usually helped him settle down on a comfortable couch, offering him coffee and cookies. Feeling relaxed, he usually dozed off. I was deeply touched as to how those authors respected and cared for my husband!

......

Food for Our Souls:
I wanted to join a music group once again.

As though my passion was revived by my own yearning! To my utmost joy, a music group **Sur Sangam** was established jointly by my relative Junaid Zuberi and my close friend Fatima Jalil. The Gala concerts they arranged with such enthusiasm that we could hardly wait for the next one. Their circle expanded leaps and bounds. Sensing my zesty enthusiasm, the young music connoisseurs warmly welcomed me into the fold.

Once they took me by utter surprise when seventy music lovers, including *Shaila Shahid, Shabana Kamran, Dr. Arshi,* and Fatima sang my birthday wish in chorus. Luckily, my challenges and my blessings seemed to be playing the game of *Yin and Yang* with my life.

*Junaid Zuberi, being an enthusiast of music and art, was instrumental in promoting Emerging and Established South Asian artists in large-scale concerts. The *silent force* behind him, his partner *Sadaf,* diligently preserved it all in her professional camera. I wondered if it was a passion inherited from her close relative—Mujeeb!?

When they asked if I would Emcee a concert, A Tribute to late Habib Wali Muhammad, I was super excited. The Vocalist happened to be his son Rizwan Wali Muhammad from USA. Thirty-five years ago I had organized his father's premier show. What a coincidence, it was to be held in the same location too—Burnhamthorpe Community Centre! A million fond memories cropped up: Rizwan's parents from a wealthy background were down-to-earth humble. They had stayed at my place for two weeks.

Rizwan's performance was superb, and our co-emcee Rajaz Abbas was a multitalented young man. We both opted for *lighthearted humor* on stage. Rajaz took full liberty with extempore 'leg pulling' this elderly lady on stage, in public! The response from the sprightly audience encouraged us to keep up the tempo. The overall scenario was bound to put me in my element as I got to share decades-old personal stories of the artist's parents.

Kashif and Shireen stayed with Mujeeb—so it was one special evening off for me.

(*Junaid is now Chief Executive Officer at NAPA (National Academy of Performing Arts in Pakistan)

......

Baithak was another music group that emerged under the leadership of fearless Fatima Jalil. Slim and smart like a model, this highly ambitious young lady, in mysterious ways had become my younger sister, like Chameli! To the envy of Pakistani women, she married a white guy, Bryan Gillis. Perceived as an ideal husband, he enjoyed his status and gladly tuned in.

Singing along familiar lyrics with that lively group was a joyous experience for me. In Mississauga the talents of established as well as emerging singers and musicians were phenomenal. Led by an amazing soloist Sahar Raza, *Bollywood, Lollywood* and even *Hollywood* songs were professionally rendered by local Pakistani artists. Such talent I could have tapped into, for my 'unfulfilled' dream to produce a musical play. Maybe one day?

Those made to measure activities not only refueled my emotional energy, these had the <u>healing effect on my husband</u> (Agitated at home, at those events he became calm!) I shared this information with the Alzheimer Society in Peel. However, the events posted on Facebook created a false impression. Mujeeb's friend from England made a hurtful comment, *"Lady, it's time you pay attention to your husband too."* Little did he know about the minute-to-minute attention Mujeeb received all day long, and he was still accompanying me everywhere—quietly enjoying the most comfortable seat offered to him, plus food on platter!

......

After further research into the 'Mind Body Healing', I learned to find humor in bizarre anecdotes that filled up my daily diaries. But I wanted to revive my abandoned practice—Meditation. Just then, a historical incident of great interest to me occurred in our cosmic world:

November 11, 2016 (a significant date in my life) brought good news –that the Super Moon would be closer to Earth than it has been in sixty-eight years! I relate my experience:

A Golden Opportunity

Mesmerized by the moon's charisma
  Gazing intently
      beside my bedroom window
          I stood... Stunned!
Uphill, from the window
I could almost reach out and touch
a Celestial body so enlarged
With intense gaze, I remained in a daze
On that historical day
the great moon descended . . .
closest to planet Earth in sixty-eight years!

  Imagination mused:
  As though my Celestial Neighbour
      was reaching out for me

When it last descended
I was only a little baby
Next such proximity predicted
is after I've exited this planet
    Absorbing the intensity
    of such a fleeting moment
    An opportunity of a lifetime, I seized.

                  … …zz

That image preserved in the hard drive of my mind somehow enhanced my meditation.

I practiced how to enter from *Beta* to *Alpha* state, at times I could even reach *Theta* state.

During meditation sometimes I visualize the galaxy, and the planets revolving in their orbits. Thereby I'm able to block all other noises and tune in to Music of the Universe.

Life sometimes brought me least expected surprises.

Client Loyalty…

On my birthday in 2017, an old client from WMB, Tom, called to invite me for lunch.

"My wife wants **you** to choose the restaurant."

"Mondello '*Creative Italian Cuisine*' in Streetsville, you'll like it." I knew they were fond of Italian cuisine. We met after almost ten years—an exciting reunion. They hadn't aged much. Tom, a tall blonde Scotsman with golden brown hair and thick moustache, resembled a younger, slender version of *Magnum PI's* Tom Selleck. His wife, a petite Guyanese woman, had flawless wheat complexion, a kind face, and a musical accent.

Over the years a few other clients also kept in touch. Tom and Teresa phoned me twice a year, once on my birthday, then to wish me *Eid Mubarak* at the end of Ramadan. However, since I left WMB, this was our first lunch.

Once we settled down in the intimate warm ambience, Teresa complimented me.

"You haven't changed much."

"Of course I have. A little help from Lancôme may be misleading," I humored.

"So how is everything, your son and the daughter-in-law you so adored? How is your garden at Whitchurch Mews?"

I replied, "To cut a long story short, **nothing is the same.**"

The waitress arrived to take our orders.

"*Shrimp Diavolo* for appetizer, am I right?" Tom remembered how I relished hot Italian devilled shrimps. "Followed by Fillet of Sole and mashed potatoes?" Teresa added.

I felt flattered that they remembered my favorite dishes so I too tried to jog my memory:

"Veal Parmesan…and…baked potatoes?" As we reminisced, they had more questions.

They were my loyal clients who had followed me branch to branch for years and often expressed, "*We are in good hands as long as you are our banker.*" They took every tidbit of banking advice from me: where to invest, what property to purchase, when to sell and how much to contribute to their RRSP, etc.

"Remember you guys treated me to exotic restaurants—first in Mississauga *La-Castile, Barber Town* and *Rogues* to name a few. Never let me utilize my expense account."

"But you treated us to fancy Portuguese restaurants around Bloor and Ossington in Toronto."

"Oh yes, good old days." I breathed a wistful sigh.

I wondered, 'maybe they've heard about my financial meltdown from a colleague?' I was sure Lucy Nogueira my friend Account Manager would never share confidential information.

After we got through the basics "How are the children? When did I last go on vacation?" they asked more questions.

"Well, it's a long story, where should I begin?" I started rambling on, as they listened attentively, their facial expressions became sullen.

After we ordered the dessert, Tom excused himself for a few minutes. May be smoking?

"It's wonderful seeing you in person." Teresa and I were immersed in conversation when Tom returned and settled down to fill his glass with Molson Light. After a brief silence, Teresa said, "We have a request to make, but promise you won't say no."

"How can I promise when I don't know the nature of your request?" I was skeptical.

"You know we wouldn't ask anything unreasonable." Tom asked, "So...it's a yes?"

"If you insist but..." Tom placed a sealed envelope on the table. "What's this for?"

Teresa explained. "It's a thank you gift from both of us."

"Thank you for what? No, no I can't accept this." I noticed it was Scotia bank envelope.

"You promised that you won't refuse."

"But why would you give me money just like that?" I continued, "Things aren't that bad. I worked at WMB for twenty years, they pay me pension, plus I'm a senior now."

"We are where we are... because of you. Maybe you don't remember what you did for us, but we do." I told them they were making stories but Tom went on to remind me:

"We were once on vacation with Teresa's family in Miami. Our flight was delayed, and you covered our mortgage payment until we returned." With mixed emotions I listened on.

"Remember you helped us close a rush deal on two townhouses during the peak market, which we flipped just when you suggested, and we made a huge profit."

"Oh yes, I was tempted to do the same for myself but…? My hubby was never a risk taker. Marrying me was the only risk he took." They cast a smile and went on,

"There's more, should I go on?" Teresa asked. I resisted, they persisted so I caved in but conditionally: "Only if it's a <u>loan,</u> to be repaid as soon as possible."

"Agreed," Teresa gently forwarded the envelope to me as if *I* was doing *them* a favor!

Have I come to this; people are taking pity on me? I swiftly shunned that thought.

Teresa cast an emotional smile and I observed Tom's eyes, even his face changed colors. It's interesting how emotions are more visible on people with white complexion.

"Offering financial advice was a part of my job, but thank you."

On the way back I opened the envelope and counted crisp $100 bills—fifteen of them! I didn't know if I should be excited or not. *I will pay them back, at my first opportunity.*

With that decision I headed to the bank machine. Strangely, those crisp bills sliding in the slot suddenly felt so good!

Soon after that I decided to cash the remaining RSP and closed the account.

…………………………………………

Our Public Health
(Benefits and Challenges)

---

44 After a comprehensive assessment by two geriatricians at Halton Peel Region, the Department of Seniors Mental Health, I was advised that my husband's dementia had reached stage four. "Deal with any aggression as a temper tantrum of a toddler." They also forewarned me about the rapid decline, the Eventual!

As soon as a PSW arrived and I wanted one hour to myself, he panicked,

"Where's my wife? **Where is my wife?**" He only felt safe in my presence.

One thing he repeated over and over was heart touching, "God is punishing me because I got in his way by preventing us from having another child."

I asked him why he didn't want even one child to begin with. He replied, "What if something happened to you? I didn't want our child to go through what I did."

So after all those years I finally found out what his reasoning was when he said, "*You and me, no third life.*" How deeply entrenched was the childhood trauma of his mother's loss!

During an emergency he was admitted to Free Care Hospital when the doctors said,

"It was a close call. His thyroid level could have resulted in a coma."

But within three weeks, I started receiving calls that he was ready to be discharged. Eventually, I was invited to meet a team of health professionals, a Geriatric Specialist, a Senior Nurse, as well as staff from LHIN, all determined to discharge him. I told them that, "Five out of twelve senior homes I've visited have a four to six years waiting list." The bottom line was there was a <u>shortage of beds</u> in that hospital.

The Alzheimer Society recommended he should be admitted to the Behavioral Control Unit…in vain!

......

Listening to the harrowing stories from other care providers, I had written a poem and shared it with the Alzheimer Society. Day by day, I was losing my life partner and now the poem I had written for *others…*resonated with *me.*

Mind Battle

Each morning
the angel of my **subconscious** *conscience*
whispers to my **conscious** *conscience:*
"Summon your patience:
perseverance; empathy; tolerance and…
forgiveness"

The list of demands goes on but….
as the day's events unfold
the story changes, dilemmas multiply:
How to deal with
        the 'Toddler-tantrums' of an adult

neurons faltering
flickering lights in the mind, dimming

Must I learn to lose each argument
agree that salt is black
the black pepper is white?

The cliché "Do unto others..." loudly echoes
throughout the day
But each angry bout tightens the noose
on my creative aspirations.

By the evening, the human in me
is tested beyond capacity
Inner voice invokes the angel within
to no avail
I fall asleep, with an awakening:
> *What if I were the victim?*
> *Aren't I?*

......zz

Sun Downing...

For many dementia patients, the transition from day into night can become quite difficult, it's known as Sun downing Syndrome. A sudden change of behavior is characterized by *confusion, agitation,* and *anxiety.* Even the doctors aren't clear as to why. Sadly, our health system does not authorize help during late hours.

Once I caught a nasty flu bug. I lay lethargic, suffering with high fever trying to explain to Mujeeb that I was sick, but he was experiencing sundown syndrome. He kept repeating, "No, you are not sick, I am sick." His agitation rose to a peak, failing to button up his coat, he blurted, "Help me dress up I want to go and kill myself."

It was about time I followed his Case Coordinator's repeated advice:

"Protect your own sanity. Summon the courage to take him back to the hospital."

This time I had called Urgent Care Hospital at Queensway, as his geriatrician was connected to that location. I handed them his medications and his Specialist's Reports. Mujeeb was finally admitted and I took a sigh of relief.

So our medical system does work. From then on he received excellent patient care. In Pakistan it would cost me millions of Rupees. I realized the blessing of our public health system.

......

A Surprise Treat…

The week after Mujeeb was admitted happened to be my birthday. Shireen and Kashif gave me a pleasant surprise—**Shen Yun**, a Chinese musical at the Living Arts Centre I had been craving for. 'Ancient legend… tells of Divine beings... who came down from the heavens to bestow a glorious civilization upon humankind.'

I missed Mujeeb's presence beside me. But I was soon captivated by the spectacular precision with which the dainty artists performed colorful ancient Chinese dances, depicting stories of its cultural heritage. After the grand finale, from the semi-lit Orchestra area as the crowd ascended the stairs, something caught my shoe and I fell forward. It was a nasty fall but luckily no fractures! "You haven't staged any plays lately, so you created your own drama!"

Jokes aside, it brought awareness that *Mujeeb could live to be a hundred despite his condition and I could have gone just like that —the strongest of us are always vulnerable*. In reality, it was a **wake-up fall**. Moreover, that dark cloud also had a silver lining:

Apart from my medical tests being clear, I discovered something I may never have known otherwise. From the Receptionist at the main desk, to the lab technicians and the Cardiologist's assistant and the Cardiologist herself, they all had words of praise for Kashif.

"Your son is the most amazing person we've met. You must be such a proud mom."

Those were familiar words I frequently heard in the past, before his financial tsunami.

I was happy to learn that the multidisciplinary clinic in Central Mississauga that Kashif recreated was now well established, even though not in his own name but...

Positive feedback about him at this time was **reward enough** for me.

......

Sweet Memories in the Hospital...

I visited the hospital every day from noon to midnight. I knew that helping Alzheimer patients recall the distant past is therapeutic. Once I mentioned to Mujeeb, our honeymoon song,

"Joh vada kiya voh nibhana pareyga
Rokay zamana chahay rokay khudai"

(Fulfill your promises, despite any hurdles)

His brain lit up and he started singing with me, recalling lyrics from fifty-four years back! Our granddaughters were stunned and captured our duet on video. In turn, I recorded them reciting six *Kalimah* (standard prayers) a credit to their maternal grandma for teaching them.

One day, after reading stories to Mujeeb, I tried to invoke more memories.

"Zooby, can you recall one special moment in our lives together—a year, a month or even one day that brightens your spirit?" He signaled to pull my chair closer, then asked to place my feet on his lap. I took off my shoes and complied. He signaled me to remove my socks; I did. In a languid voice, with difficulty he uttered, "Ask … me… again." I repeated my question.

Placing his freezing cold hands on my feet, he replied, *"This moment."*

As usual, I cracked a joke. "You manipulator, always know how to flatter me."

Deeply touched by his gesture, on my way back, I asked myself: *Have I been able to love him as much as he has loved me?* I admitted, *I love him dearly,* but I couldn't recall when last I was 'in love' with him…but he still is, or is he? Is there a difference? But what is the difference?

He often repeated, "Can we go together?" I'd ask where, he'd raise his forefinger upward.

I felt the jitters but made a joke, "Darling that usually happens in an air crash."

Then with sharp decline, each day became a living hell. To watch him wither away minute by minute, I wondered if *sudden death is better than prolonged illness*es. That's what I pray for myself. However I could not pray the same for him…but why?

The dementia patient's brain is like a ship going through a storm. Every now and then it stops at an island. I derived comfort from the fact that before admitting him to the hospital, on a bright sunny morning, I once seized a window of opportunity when his mind was 'anchored.' I opened our bedroom curtains, sunshine filling our room as I requested him:

"In the past fifty years plus, if I have ever hurt you, please forgive me."

"Oh no, no, no, never once did you hurt me!" he said emphatically.

"Really ... but you flare up so often." I still insisted, so he said, *"I forgive you."*

......

Mujeeb took his last breath on May 12, I assumed I was prepared for it but ...is anyone ever prepared when it really happens? The burial took place on Sunday, Mother's Day!

Apart from our own community, friends of various faiths—Hindus, Christians, Jewish—all came to the mosque for funeral prayer. Some accompanied us to the Meadowvale Cemetery! Strangely even after death, you remain divided ... Christian section, Muslim section, the thought of it bothered me, but I justified it in my mind.

As I poured the last fistful of soil over the coffin, his words rang in my ears, "Can we go together?" So I whispered, *"Zooby, I've accompanied you as far as I possibly could."*

On the way back I pondered if cremation is a better option?

......

There was a steady stream of visitors, overflowing from living room to the family room, dining room to the kitchen. What a huge circle of friends and acquaintances we had acquired over the years! Guests paid tribute, "Dr. Mujeeb Zoberi was *most respected* by our community."

In the Eastern tradition, our friends usually bring cooked meals to the home of the grieving family. My fridge and freezer were over-filled with biryani, qorma, and other dishes, Paul and Kerry, our co-tenants downstairs, were happy to receive ready meals after work.

Once my friends heard me rave over colorful bouquets, they confessed:

"We also wanted to bring flowers but wondered if you'd be offended."

"Offended, why?" I clarified, "What can better express the beauty of life:

'Birth, prime of youth, then demise— flowers eventually wither-away.'

Strangely, it 'liberated' our friends from a cultural inhibition! Soon our home was filled with dozens of bouquets to create a memorial, with a framed picture of Mujeeb center-front giving me that killer look of love, Bollywood-hero style.

....

A Muslim Widow in Canada

45 A friend texted me: "Just cautioning you, you'll be expected to observe **Iddath**." (Refrain from meeting any men other than immediate family for four months and ten days).

I texted back: "Surely none of *my* friends would expect a woman over seventy to observe iddat," but I was wrong! An old acquaintance, out of touch for years, now called me.

"My sisterly advice –You must observe iddat." I replied with disdain, "Do you know how old I am, it's only applicable to women of childbearing age."

However, within a few weeks I found that *Iddat imposers* were outnumbered by *Match Makers.* What a contrasting behavior by people of the same faith. A friend made scholarly advice: "At your age, Iddath is **Biddath.*" (It's a sin to preach the wrong version of faith).

"Didn't you write a play about the widows once?"

"Yes I did. 'From a Widow's Closet' it was staged at Celebration Square in 2009."

Even the thought of becoming a widow hadn't entered my mind then, but now I wondered, what did I write back then?

Out of curiosity I pulled out the anthology published in the USA. I had forgotten about the review of my play by a Professor of English Literature, from William Patterson University:

'From a Widow's Closet" dramatizes the refreshingly comic and ironic story of a middle-aged widow discovering a half-buried, romantic, and vibrant self beyond the dutiful role of the long-suffering mother and the grieving wife. It is a discovery facilitated by the Canadian Locale. The Play does a masterful and humorous job of exploring the mother's slowly dawning realization that her life is not over with the death of her husband and that she can indeed form a meaningful romantic relationship at her age.'

'A relationship that allows her to express her own individuality as a woman rather than just a mother and wife she has been all her life. In that sense the Widow's Closet transforms from one that contains relics of her previous self to one that now showcases objects that embody her slow discovery of self and independence. The diasporic location allows an expansion of self that perhaps might not have been available in the Subcontinent of India/Pakistan.'

I read the review twice, searching for take-away lessons for myself.

Back then, the standing ovation was rewarding, but now I sadly recalled Mujeeb crossing the stage. 'Why did we not catch his unusual behavior as early signs of dementia?'

I was forewarned: "Once you become a widow, most couples will stop inviting you."

It was true to a few who retreated, but I still had friends like *Nasreen Jamil, Parveen Arshad*, and *Yasmeen Jamil* who kept me in their caring circle. No doubt *Fouzia & Muzaffar* went the extra mile for me. Our Hallstone neighbors *Farida Mehrban* included me in all their family gatherings. Fatima and Reva's presence was always comforting.

I took to heart Mujeeb's advice: *"Don't ever be a Bechaari"* (Someone people pity). So, I attended social gatherings as usual, grieving on my own or even with total strangers.

The Rock Guard

It was a glorious summer morning when I decided to relish the memories of our adventurous life together. Cruising along slowly I spotted a park entrance and pulled in.

The serene surrounding captivated me. But it turned out to be the Streetsville Cemetery! Unfortunately, the bench was occupied. 'What's this young man doing here, maybe his loved one is buried here' I wondered. He signaled me toward another bench. Peace and tranquility surrounded by shady trees and flower beds! As I approached the bench, the young man and I exchanged greetings.

Once I took out my lunch, he got up and said, "I'm leaving, please come over here, this bench is facing the fountain, you'll enjoy the sound of water, very peaceful."

I picked up my sandwich and eagerly moved over, as he headed toward his car. We said goodbye, but something prompted him to call out from the car, "Do you need to talk?"

I gave a meek reply, "No thanks." He either didn't hear me or decided to ignore me.

Still, he returned and stood near my bench. Handing me his business card, he lit up a cigarette. "I think you do need to chat."

"This cemetery is so close to where I live. I wish we had chosen this location for my husband to rest in peace," I said but the young man replied, "I'm sorry for your loss. But things happen for a reason," his presence so warm and welcoming I thought he is right...after missing so many spots on the way, I was meant to find this spot we never knew about.

Looking at his card I asked, "Mitch Gouveia, are you Portuguese?"

"How do you know?" he asked with a spirited smile.

"I worked at a WMB branch downtown with mostly Portuguese staff who I called The Young and the Restless." He seemed pleased and invited my attention to the Rock.

"See how it stands firm and upright, the solid rock called Biffy, but I've named it The Bodyguard." He pointed toward the tall rock, approximately nine feet, upright with waving streaks in various brown and earth tones.

"Tune in to the music of water, it's so relaxing." Birds were chirping, so was Mitch, a young man in his late thirties? Yes, now even people in their forties seemed *young*!

I was curious as to what brings him to a cemetery for solace? We ended up sharing our stories. He told me about the trauma he had survived, his humble background, and the days of struggle. The rugged neighborhood he grew up in, how his father worked his way up from delivering a newspaper to becoming the Vice President of that company. Once their family moved toward having a more luxurious lifestyle, old friends became jealous. One day Mitch was caught off guard and was attacked by two gunmen in disguise. He shared what it took for him to survive that ordeal. In turn, I briefly shared my joys and my trials, but concluded,

"Mine is interesting but a bizarre story which I hope to write someday."

Mitch struck me as a strong, brave, young man who had weathered much, but now exuded confidence and stood sturdy like that *Biffy, a*s though helping others was his mission.

"This beautiful cemetery close to home would be a perfect place for me to reflect upon my life and mortality," I concluded.

Accepting his warm invitation to take a stroll through the park, we exchanged our philosophies of life and recipes for survival. Mitch attempted to comfort me.

"I believe that our loved ones revisit us through signs. Usually subtle signs we must recognize." Just then I spotted a large mushroom growing on the trunk of a tall tree.

"Oh my God…there is a sign right behind you, something my hubby would've been enthralled to see."

"Didn't I tell you they revisit you through signs?"

I asked Mitch if I could take a picture to show my son. He gladly posed in front of that tree with the mushroom. "As far as I remember, I think this bracket like fungus is called *Trametes hirsuta*, usually grows on dead trunk but sometimes on live trees as parasites, like this one," Mitch was surprised, "I'm impressed. How do you know so much about mushrooms?"

"My hubby was originally a Mycologist, they study fungi." I went on. "He even had a caption on his study room door: ***Mycologist is a Fungi***. Get it, fun guy?"

"Was he a fun guy?"

I replied, "Most of his life he was, except for the last few years."

"I must run along." Mitch suddenly looked at his watch.

On his way out he said, "This rock is my bodyguard, but now *I* want to be *your* bodyguard. Make sure I'm in your book and at the book launch, I will arrive in a suit and stand at the door to protect you from any evil eye."

By the time I reached home, there was a Facebook friend request from Mitch, along with an inspirational quotation. Kashif, Shireen, and my granddaughters were highly amused with my *Bodyguard* story. Mitch periodically sent me messages of reassurance to my inbox:

"If or when you need someone, just know your bodyguard is here."

I did have a serious concern, but it wasn't something Mitch could help me with—The Survivor Benefit. How losing a partner impacts the wallet.

......

The Survivor Benefits...

Whether the deceased leaves behind five dollars or five million, the paperwork seems to be the same. After fifty-four years of marriage and having filed joint tax returns, what a hassle it was to prove that I really was married to Dr. Mujeeb Zoberi. My *Nikah* papers were in Urdu, so I ended up requiring a lawyer.

Back in 2015 when I got a Power of Attorney document in my name finalized, I had the shocking discovery that,

*The **Nigerian University had not paid his pension for twenty years!***

Since I knew MP Dr. Qadri, I initially approached him. He advised me, "Let's worry about that later, there is a deadline for Senate appointments, and you should apply." I didn't think I'd qualify for that, lacking French but I knew two other languages. I learned that out of the three requirements, I was quite strong in two. The third condition—Legislative Knowledge, I could study. After all, I had entered every job as a rookie, including my teenage marriage to a Professor. So I met the four-day deadline, obtaining three strong recommendations, including one from the Wealth Management Bank.

Before mailing my application, I found out that under the Real Assets, they would only accept real estate (owning property in Canada). Even pledging Canada Savings Bonds would not be acceptable.

The Nigerian University was still not responding, and eventually my case was shunted over to the Ministry of Global Affairs. My high hopes soon deflated when they said,

"We only help Canadians in distress, Abroad."

Even the Canadian reciprocal pension arrangement with seventy countries did not include Nigeria, despite being part of Commonwealth. **I gave up**.

Now that I had reported hubby's demise, Service Canada instantly pressed the 'Delete button' for his Old Age pension. By now, all my financial assets had diminished, yet...

The survival instinct remained defiantly intact!

....

The United Nations International Women's Day
Conference (SW59)... inside the UN Building

Lilly Tadin and Eveline Steward from the
Women's Federation for World Peace (WFWP)

Five of us stayed in one room with only two beds!
With a young Japanese, Miho & Christina Tadin

With Rajni Iqbal, 'Peel Committee Against Women Abuse'--
Missing & Murdered Indigenous Women! Annual Vigil
City Hall

Inter-racial marriage (Shazia Zuberi/Henderson Leacock) Hena ceremony, feeding the bride and groom with our own hands, signifies total acceptance' into each others' family

'True Colours' My poetry book launch. Classical dances composed by Anwar Khurshid & Jenevieve Beaulieu

Traditional Poetry recital with
the Rap Band 'Vibonics'
At the Celebration Square (2012)

Annie Alam Baig read
my entire poetry book
'True Colours' during
her wedding festivities!

Moderated Open Mic event—Cyberbullying at the Amphitheatre
Coordinated by Heather Christine (Vocalist)
Picture with Shannon Claire

Meena Chopra is a renowned Visual Artist/Poet. At her exclusive book launch 'She'...*the Restless Streak*

Also bonded with well-known Visual Artist/Poet Eva Kolacz The launch of The Artis Nineofive magazine (Founder Ivy Reiss)

With Junaid Zuberi –Founder of 'Sur Sangam' a vibrant music group He promoted Amateur and Professional Artists

Sur Sangam event hosted
by Dr. Arshi Kizilbash

Nadeem Shah a Tabla
Master & Anwar Khurshid
A Sitar Maestro (I
served as Emcee)

A Tribute to late Habib Wali Muhammad by Junaid
Zuberi (L) Chief Guest Ashfaq Husain, Vocalist
Rizwan Ali, myself as one of two Emcees!

At the Celebration Square, to support Ian Khan
Scheduled to perform next (Sur Sangam & Baithak)

'The King of Ghazal' late Mehndi Hasan Vocalist/ Composer
One of the Sub-continent's icons in music (Taking notes as Emcee)

Bridging the Gap's 10th Anniversary
Honorable Consul General of India
Akilesh Mishra was a special guest

10th Annual
International Peace
Poetry by BTG
and WFWP
2nd Row L Guest
Mike Douglas (Exec
Director Arts Council)

Max Layton, Poet
and Composer (one of
our special guests)

Fatima Jalil.
Founder
of *Baithak*
Music Group

469

The Baithak Group of highly talented singers (Lollywood, <u>Bollywood</u> and even Hollywood songs) – led by Sahar Raza

Dr. Fawzia Afzal Khan (Prof English Lit Mont Claire University) Her book 'Siren Songs' is about Pakistani Women singers!

Dancing around the Bride and Groom, Shireen's sisters and other guests (Photo by Sadaf Zuberi 'Rangoli Moments)

Kashif and Shireen's
Engagement/wedding

Jennifer Javier-Valladolid.
a 'Friends in Deed
(One of our Frontline heroes)

Fifty-five years'
partnership until (2018)
Memory lives on!

Saima, Yojna, Billo and Zehra, my Streetsville neighbors
A God-sent support group to pamper me

Immigrant Stories
on Canvas by
Thaniath Siddiqui
Exhibition at the
Great Hall Toronto

We were asked to pick
a stone at the Memorial
Service Elina hand-painted
a mushroom on it

Literary Festival at the Living Arts Centre, with Fatmatta Kanu
We both belong to Writers and Editors Network

Celebrating 'Things
that Matter'
Anthology

My niece Dr. Lubna and husband Dr. Aslam
Came from Philadelphia for Kashif's wedding
Aslam wants to dance but she's playing hard to get!

The launch of another Immigrant
Story – Ujjal Dosanjh - Premier of British Columbia
once (Also a partition-child like me)

A surprise birthday organized by my children
I freaked out when my nephew Saad showed up with the cake!

PART FIVE

Sunset…and…Sunrise

Survival

Amidst a grove of green
one tree stood unique
half its barren branches burnt black
the other half bursting with vitality
the contrast enhances its beauty
the trunk firm, roots strong

What caused such trauma?
What feeds this thriving?

Of the entire forest, that one tree
an unforgettable impression
stirs emotions

Somehow it resonates
in our reality
… …zz

A Possibilitarian*

46 No longer interested in banking or optometry clinics, I wanted to explore other job possibilities, so I polished up my resume.

Getting ready for bed that night, at 11:30 p.m., I received a surprise text message:

"It's your neighbor *Saima*. Are you up, can we talk?"

I said a sleepy yes.

"Would you be interested in a part-time job?" Suddenly wide awake I waited…

"Our older son Asim is autistic and the younger son also needs help in his social skills. Actually, we already hired someone to watch my two sons, starting Monday. But on our way back from a dinner party, our younger son Usher has surprised us by suggesting why don't we ask Zohra Auntie first?"

Having no experience with Special Needs or Autistic children, I told her I'll get back to her the next day. In Canada Autism Spectrum Disorder (ASD) cases are alarmingly common, one child in 66 overall will be born autistic, but this frequency increases to one in 42 amongst males.

Interestingly, in recent years I had attended several exhibitions showcasing artwork created by the autistic children. It was in one such event I had met *Saima* and *Yojna*. A lady from our musical group, *Asfia Imran* once invited me to an exhibition at T. L. Kennedy School in Mississauga. Fascinated by these children with extra ordinary abilities in certain areas, like a Reporter I interviewed their parents as well as teachers, such as *Tony Cabral*. He passionately shared his devotion to this noble cause. I had posted such events on my Facebook page, including some of the artwork and video clips of the interviews. One posting was titled:

Our Autistic are exceptionally Artistic

What a rewarding opportunity I now found! The next morning without hesitation I accepted my fresh challenge. I ignored friends' warnings: "Your emotions are still fragile, don't take such a risk when you have no previous experience with special needs children."

A lady with a loving heart, Maryanne Funny from our writers' club gifted me a self-help book titled 'Autism Breakthrough' I brought it to work. For me it was on the job training.

Twenty-year-old Asim, being non-verbal, hardly spoke more than two words. The twelve-year-old Usher needed to fill gaps in his social skills, but his genius photographic memory retained numbers and dates with brilliant precision for months! We became good friends.

One after the other I had to answer a barrage of questions from Usher, nonstop. Once I said, "Hey, hey, slow down let me take a breath, I can't keep pace with your speed you curious cat." He said, "Call me *Curious Lamborghini*. It's a lot faster than a cat."

"Usher na ker mera *husher," (*Don't drive me crazy)

He would smile and say, "I love you *Soni* Zeezee."

Once he caught me off guard and said, "Your granddaughter turned sixteen, if her parents marry her to a stranger, would she agree?"

"Of course not," I replied.

"Would she go if they decide to send her to another country?"

"What kind of a question is that, why would they?"

"But your parents sent you…and you said yes,"

"Usher! Please don't ask me such questions again, okay?"

He obeyed. "OK, I love you Zee Zee."

One afternoon we were working on 'storytelling' while munching on cheese ringlets. Usher suddenly got up, asked for my hand, and kneeling down on one knee he gently slid the ringlet on to my finger and innocently proposed: "Will you marry me, *Soni* zee zee?" I laughed and while chewing the *ring*, I said, "Look, our marriage is already over."

Saima had a hearty laugh and 'insisted' that I must include that episode in my book.

She had just turned forty, filled with such positive energy Saima became a great source of inspiration. When she returned from work, I observed her outpouring of affection, the daily drills of changing gears for her *Second Shift*.

She would often stop me for dinner with freshly cooked *chapatis*. Through her I met other friends. Yojna, runs 'Ausum Charity;, a nonprofit organization for the autistic, she jogged my memory, "I remember you attended my event at the Living Arts Centre." Her autistic son Avnish is a brilliant artist. Another fun-loving friend Bilquees (Billo) even knows my family in Bahrain and Karachi! Zehra Naqvi, also part of that group proclaimed, "I also met you at the Ausum Charity event. In fact I even videotaped you dancing with an eleven-year-old blonde girl dressed as Rapunzel." It turned out that Zehra is related to my cousin in-law in Montreal, wow!

"What a small world!" we proclaimed in chorus.

Saima's house thus became our Grand Central Station for weekly gatherings. Who knew I'd find a support group of genuine friends, on the next street over? Much younger than me, when they became too wild, I teased them, "Go ahead you crazy bunch, I'm mostly here for my dopamine and serotonin."

*"Become a *possibilitarian no matter how dark things seem to be or actually are, raise your sights and see possibilities—for they're always there." Norman Vincent Peale*

......

The Queen of Ultrasound...

For condolence Mujeeb's nephew *Khawar* made a visit from Seattle. My cousins Dr. Musheer and Ishrat visited from USA. Together with them we relived and relished the old memories of 'Mango Mania' when we enjoyed the magic of Pakistani mangoes *Chaunsa* (most popular variety of mango). After their visit I wrote a therapeutic diary *'Mango Condolence'*.

But now, Tanveer was coming all the way from Pakistan! Her smiling round baby face pleased everyone. I teased her, "Maybe even the fetuses that you examine fall in love with you."

The day after her arrival at a Sur Sangam concert, we ran into one of her trainee doctor, and the news became viral. Dr. Tanveer being a pioneer in Ultrasound in Karachi had trained many doctors who now resided in Mississauga/Toronto. Unable to acquire the Canadian medical license, some of them work as lab technicians. They were thrilled to reunite with their 'Mentor.' I too was invited to dinners where I received free lessons on Pediatric Ultrasound.

Canada's fall foliage was at its peak, so each morning I drove Tanveer to enjoy the stunning sights such as Bell Fountain and High Park. Super fascinated Tanveer was forever taking pictures. However, in the afternoons I had to rush to my job at Saima's place.

Tanveer was like a God Mother to the group of doctors, with her I also got treated to several lavish dinners. Having published three academic books, one titled 'Atlas of Pediatric Ultrasound'. She gave a seminar at the Canadian Ultrasound and Research Centre, who honored her with an award:

Recognizing your Outstanding Dedication and Service In the Field of Radiology

I felt happy that *my country* Canada appreciated my sister. Time flew by, but memories lingered. Her visit encouraged me to move on. I was now ready to enter Mujeeb's study room.

The Mystery Room...

Since the onset of his dementia he prohibited others from entering that room.

It was his 'sanctuary' where all the memories of his once shining career were meticulously stored. A floor-to-ceiling, cherry-wood multi-functional wall unit, matching office desk, custom ordered from a Greek company Neoset with lifelong guarantee, still looked new. Now in 2018 I found even B Sc. and M Sc. dissertations of his Nigerian students from 1963! So we had been shipping all these from Nigeria to Canada, then from house to house?

Flipping through 'Mycologia' and other scientific journals from 1976, I found some included his publications or referenced his research contributions. How devastated he was when the libraries refused to accept scientific journals! *How does a brilliant mind experience cognitive impairment?* I was disturbed to also find a huge collection of tools he had never used! When and where did he get them from?

What to discard, and what to retain and cherish?

Diaries and Love Letters…

Buried behind a huge pile of files I found two hard cover diaries, yellowed out pages, both with following caption: *'Do not read, this is my private diary'*…Invitation enough.

I planted myself on a chair and went on a reading rampage—the stories of his youth.

So in 1947, he was writing about his crushes on young girls, now old ladies I met. What an interesting read: emotions of love, loneliness, isolation; as well as deeply entrenched fears and ambitions. Brilliantly written in polished Urdu, Mujeeb could have become a prolific author. Only when my stomach gurgled, I realized I had forgotten all about lunch.

Apart from the pile of neatly labeled cardboard boxes, I noticed one titled 'Love Letters'. So this is where I might also find that *unsent letter*, which I first found thirty-plus years after our marriage, when we moved to our Hallstone home. I opened the box and started flipping through that gem collection which became my bedtime companion. Reading those 'aero-grams' I felt tickled at our own sappy romantic letters to each other…especially during my first year in Canada alone, when Mujeeb had returned to his job in Nigeria.

I even found the missing box with my parents' letters to each other! Abbaji had once brought out a black leather portfolio with my mom's name engraved in calligraphy. He said, "These are fifty years of letters your mother and I wrote to one another. Should I burn these?"

"No way, I'm the rightful owner of these gems." I got lost in that memory:

That evening in Pindi I was permitted to read our parents' romantic letters when all of us children and grandchildren surrounded them.

Shahid's son Umair made an audio tape as everyone was cracking up with laughter. Our parents' sparkling faces shining with sheer delight. "See how romantic you once were," Dad teased my mom. That portfolio swiftly made its way into my suitcase.

And now, here it was to perk up my spirit!

How letter writing has evolved—Mujeeb and I used pale blue lightweight aero-grams, but in my parents' times, they used lined paper and square little canary envelopes. Handwritten letters nowadays are almost extinct, even email letters are being replaced by short messages on WhatsApp, Facebook, and Instagram. Fifty years of handwritten romantic letters, so invaluable! Filled with curiosity, I skimmed through some, set aside others to read again but wistfully I reminded myself, hubby may have even discarded the letter I was hoping to find.

Because Mujeeb pursued his research with zest, even represented the University of Toronto in International conferences all those years, it saddened me that he did not receive due recognition in Canada. ***Eventually my inner voice was heard.***

....

47 I was surprised to receive an invitation, A Service of Remembrance, to be held at the Urgent Care Hospital in Mississauga where Mujeeb had passed away. I had mixed feelings about inviting anyone else, so I went alone.

Approximately fifty family members of the deceased attended the somber ceremony. Upon three large television screens were displayed the image of piles of little rocks in various sizes. Scrolling down were the names of the deceased, one after the other. What a wonderful feeling to see <u>Mujeeb H. Zoberi</u> appear on all three screens. I took a shot and wiped my tears. The lady next to me, her eyes bloodshot from weeping, put her hand on my shoulder and whispered, "All of us in this room are in the same boat."

That non denominational ceremony was breathtaking.

Each of us was handed a program brochure. Everyone had to repeat after each verse, the tag line, 'We Will Remember Them.'

"At the rising of the sun and it's going down,"

> *"We Will Remember Them." (Chanted in chorus)*

"At the blowing wind and chill of winter,"

> *"We Will Remember Them." (Chanted in chorus)*

The sound of sobbing increased, the recital finally ending with:

"For as long as we live, they too shall live, for they are part of us."

This was followed by musical reflection from Hebrew Scripture:

"For everything there is a season and a time under heaven

A time to be born and a time to die

A time to plant and a time to pluck

A time to wound and a time to heal" – the reflection continued.

I was curious about the significance of a large bowl of water, surrounded by a pile of smooth pebbles/rocks of various shapes and shades.

'The Act of Remembrance' was a heart-wrenching speech which also explained the image of the small rocks—that life is like climbing a mountain. You continue until there is no more vegetation, and it gets harder to carry on…you continue to ascend…as long as you can. They asked each of us to choose one rock for safekeeping as a memory of our loved one.

My hand automatically reached out for one that was mushroom-shaped; Mujeeb was dedicated to his fungi. Even holding that little rock comforted me, I couldn't explain why.

Soon I found myself surrounded by a number of people. As we exchanged our experiences, sorrow seemed to dissipate in that moment. They wanted to know why I chose the mushroom-shaped rock. Explanation led to conversation about our research excursions in African forests. I related a funny story about when we ended up in a remote village, starving!

"We were looking for eggs, but the villagers didn't understand English. So I sat in the squat position, placed one hand under my behind and *quacked!* The villagers brought out eggs." The group burst out laughing. The event organizers came close, smiled as they probably felt gratified that their event had a positive impact on the loved ones of the Deceased.

I later requested Elina to add her artistic touches to that stone so she skilfully painted and transformed it to look like the mushroom

Amanita Muscaria. I shared the picture with my family via a Facebook post. After that Memorial I rejoiced that:

Canada bid my husband a respectful farewell.

......

Things that Matter...

On the following November 11, I woke up feeling exceptionally down as my friends had tantalized my hope again –that this year Chameli would definitely call on our friendship day. But once I checked the calendar, my spirits picked up. It was the launch of 'Things that Matter'–an Anthology of Literature and Art.

Avoiding the highway due to vertigo, I took the long rout to the Oakville Art Centre. Amidst a colorful display of visual arts, various authors including my favorites Sheila Tucker, Eva Kolacz, and Derik Hawley had gathered.

My poem "*A Quiet Revolutionary*" about a Canadian icon Viola Desmond was published. It was a historical recollection of how a black woman was dragged out of a movie theater for sitting in the 'Whites only' section. Almost six decades later, out of 26,000 names submitted, she was selected to grace our $10 bill. What a coincidence that I got to recite that poem on the first day that special $10 bill with Viola's picture was circulated! A sad morning thus ended with an evening of celebration. What 'mattered' to me also was that my small contribution to the Canadian literary scene was acknowledged on the back cover. Memories of lost friendships must be put to rest. Wisdom of the heart whispered,

'Do not regret if anyone leaves, they in fact create room for others.'

The Revolving Door of an Open Heart!

Friends who exited my life were outnumbered by those entering… or…re-entering my *Library of Friends.* While some were like new novels, others felt like the *Revised Editions.*

My first connection in 1963 in Nigeria, Shehnaz Khan who had taken me under her wing, now resides in a posh home by the waterfront in Mississauga. This 'Reigning Queen' is a highly respected mother to four sons, two daughters, and thirteen loving grandchildren. Her charming bubbly daughter, *Sabeeha Shaikh* and the soft-spoken niece *Sheeba Aslam* also connected with me. So I've won a wonderful family as my lottery! Shehnaz relishes in relating a highly exaggerated and animated versions of our first encounter in Nigeria. When she brought her 5 yr old son Moony to see a Pakistani bride, but found me wearing a mini dress instead. Each time she invokes laughter as the length of that dress keeps getting shorter and shorter.

Incidentally, in 1993 I met the same toddler but by then he was a 'Thirty-year-old Business Tycoon!' He took me out for a drive downtown Ottawa in his Lamborghini (I think)? Being a proactive banker, I acquired a sizeable complex real estate deal from him— the properties were in Vancouver but the investors in Ottawa! Oh those days of fax machines and carbon copies. Just to sign those documents, I had to pick him up from the airport and drive him to Harbour Castle Hotel. Good luck greeted me for I was duly rewarded by the bank.

Incidentally, Shehnaz and her family now run a charity named 'ASK Foundation.' They distribute hundreds of free meals every week to the Homeless in Toronto and other neighborhoods. I feel proud to be part of that family.

Then, one lucky day while browsing around the gift shop at the Tea Room in Streetsville, someone caught my attention: "Oh…my…God…Zohra, is that you?"

"Is that Sandy, my long-lost buddy?" My first friend in Canada since 1976, Sandy had been trying to trace me but she had forgotten my last name. Reunited after forty years, we shared with each other decades of our fascinating journeys.

Last but not least, who showed up at our WEN writers' club, Tyaba and Hussain, who also lived in the same Riverspray Crescent building back in the seventies! Hussain the scientist is now an award winning poet. Behind his success is Tyaba to inspire him. Her hospitality and mouth-watering *Hyderabadi* gourmet dishes are to die for.

The empty seats of the friends I lost have been occupied by wonderful people. Although they say '*You only need three or four close friends*,' considering my personal experience as well as the Pandemic environment, I am willing to **bend that rule**. Many lonely people in the city are in need of even a friendly chat and moral support. So my door continues to revolve.

A Free Vacation in Philadelphia…

My niece Lubna and Aslam sent me a return ticket. I asked her, "Did you know it was your mom who was my 'Emissary' in 1963? She accompanied me the bride, on my train journey to Karachi!" Lubna became emotional as her mom *Haseena* had recently passed away.

Now, fifty-five years later, imagine waking up in her daughter's home, I felt overwhelmed with the daughterly care Lubna provided me. She gave me a tour of Philadelphia—the iconic Art Museum and other historic sites. Our dinners were never ending marathons.

"Aslam, you are distracting me with your fun-filled conversation. We have been eating non-stop for two hours!" He wanted me to try all sorts of exotic food items.

Both medical *doctors, simple and humble, their home is tastefully yet moderately decorated. Their older son *Hammad* was away, younger *Omeir* was now twenty, handsome and a brilliant student. "Let's go shopping as I haven't brought a gift for you." We bonded and became ***Socks Buddies*** as we opted for identical pairs with aqua theme… octopus and swimming turtles. Omeir later sent me a picture of his feet with those socks. "You beat me to it, Omeir," I said.

I feel proud to claim that I have a near-perfect family living in this hemisphere as well.

*Incidentally, Pakistan is the 3rd largest source of Foreign Doctors in the USA.

Immigrants' Life Stories on Canvas

48 No credit to me that opportunities abound, be it a speaking engagement at the Women's Federation, or moderating a community concert. But to become a 'subject upon canvas' was a novel opportunity. The Founder of *Canvas Stories*, Thaniath Siddiqui and other artists planned an exhibition at the Great Hall in Toronto:

"Through My *Gulabi Tinted Chashma" (*pink tinted glasses)

"It is meant to explore immigration through different artists' frames of reference, amalgamation of East and West in a struggle to bring balance, comfort and understanding amidst the chaos that inevitably occurs when trying to find a place for oneself in a new world. The emotional need to hold on to a tested way of life yet meet the expectations to acclimatize to a different lifestyle can be overwhelming."

This innovative idea resonated and my curiosity peaked. A writer tells stories through words, but how would an artist paint personality traits, struggles, achievements, or failures of specific individuals?

I had initially met the visual artist *Thaniath* at Joshua Creek Heritage Centre. Charming, soft-spoken, and a skillful interviewer put me at ease to share my intimate story in the comfort of my own home.

The Great Hall, a heritage iconic landmark in Toronto was a great choice. Its illuminated hallways buzzed with activity—patrons and artists' murmurs, interpreting an array of immigrants' life stories on the walls. What a variety of art mediums, stories of struggles and disappointments, or achievements, were masterfully depicted. I recognized one from afar. Surprisingly, Thaniath painted an ancient Mosque in Pakistan, more like a *Spiritual Centre,* as a few of my poems were meticulously handwritten on various doors of the mosque, what a novel idea. To complete my personal story, she even included newspaper clippings from Nigeria, wow! The painting was titled '*Standing Strong.'*

I lingered as a fly on the wall to listen to visitors' remarks. 'Maybe I can use this painting as the cover for my memoir' I thought, but… the excitement soon transformed into doubt. Discussing this idea with my friend Meena Chopra (a renowned visual artist in Mississauga), I shared, "My friends get stereotyped, so they are often reluctant to reveal their faith. It's hard to be a Muslim these days." Meena agreed that this painting as my book cover could be misleading.

"Well, 'Perception is in the heart and mind of the Beholder'— some would mainly notice the mosque, while others might reflect that *modern poetry* is inscribed, not ancient scriptures!

Regardless, my story told through Thaniath's brush in her thousand strokes, deserves much applause. How Art thrived in our city. On such occasions I missed my artsy sister Arifa.

……

Sybil Rampen, my Role Model …

Thanks for a wedding in her husband Salman's family that he and Arifa visited Canada the second time. After attending multiple events, we sisters got a chance to meet one-on-one.

"I've been dying to introduce you to a legendary Artist, in our community." Arifa got ready bright and early in her fusion outfit, even borrowed my hat, and didn't she look dapper!

Introducing an 'Aspiring Artist' to an Inspiring Artist Sybil Rampen was a pleasure.

On a sunny afternoon we headed to Joshua Creek Heritage Art Centre, only to find Sybil outdoors, spreading her laundry on the clothes line. Arifa was surprised, as women of that stature in Pakistan would never be found doing their own laundry. I shared information with her:

"For fifty years Sybil's lifelong goal has been to establish a cultural legacy on her family farm to inspire the future generations. The barn is renovated as an art gallery and the 1827 house and studio are situated on 20,000-year-old valley" I continued, "It's a sanctuary for art and nature lovers like you and me. I've been a member and have attended ongoing innovative events, promoting art by 'Special Needs children and adults.' This lady is so versatile she has mastered not only the visual arts, but also quilting, photography, and gardening."

Arifa acknowledged, "I've seen videos you posted on Facebook. It seems Mujeeb's passion for photography has rubbed off on you,"

"By the way, Sybil was born in the same year as him, 1929."

She gave us a grand tour of not only the art gallery, but also took us inside her personal home. Once she pointed to her father's painting, I enquired, "Did he inspire you?"

She proclaimed, "Oh no, *I* inspired *him,* and he made his first painting at age sixty-five."

So I turned to Arifa. "Be happy, in your fifties only, you are not a late bloomer."

The combined passion of two artists ignited a spark in me. Arifa had many questions, Sybil had all the answers. She even gifted her one or two products not available in Pakistan.

We then took a tour of the open hilly space outdoors, admired Sybil's gardening talent.

What a saleswoman…both Arifa and I splurged to buy her creative cards with powerful messages inscribed within. I told Arifa,

"During one of my visits I asked Sybil, 'What would be your one advice for me?'

"She readily replied with a smile, '***Keep on keeping on***.'"

Incidentally, Sybil's son Ed was born with severe Down-syndrome and lives with her. She was advised not to take him home but she did. He became her main source of inspiration—her mission is to teach special needs children and adults. At ninety-two, she still has eight families under her wing who learn artwork, displayed at the Barn Gallery.

While their trip was short-lived, Arifa and Salman remained seriously concerned about me living alone. I raised their curiosity by declaring, "I've gained a nephew in Canada."

"Co-tenant, a male?" they were surprised but I said, "Wait till you meet him."

Once they met *Adnan,* they felt comforted. I needed to substitute the loss of half my income—Mujeeb's old-age pensions. Initially, I was apprehensive to keep a male tenant, but he turned out to be a likeable young professional. Interested in politics and a chatterbox like me, so we hit it off well. His polite mannerisms spelled a respectable upbringing. When he drank water in a traditional manner, he reminded me of my grandma Ammajan's teaching:

"Water is a blessing, drink it respectfully." She always sat down, held the glass in her right hand, placed the left hand over her head then took gentle sips. Our Canadian youngsters would laugh it off, but Adnan followed the drill. More than one foot taller than me, I

jokingly complained. "It's not fair that there 'is' more of you in this world than me."

"Who is this young man, attending musical concerts with her?" A few people in our community became curious. Likewise, Adnan's friends asked him how he ended up living with an elderly lady! My obsessive compulsive cleaning habit sometimes bothered him, but overall we remained happy campers. It delighted me that Adnan relished my *chappli kebab*.

....

Downsizing

49 Our landlady's retired parents were coming from China, perfect time for me to downsize. While selling household items, fed up with price haggling, I signed up with an auction company which became a disaster. This was the first time I learned about the Auction Hawks—they keep an eye on unsold items and bid a dollar or so minutes before the bidding closes. It hurt me when Mujeeb's custom-made office furniture was picked up for $1 only!

Attachment to a Rosewood Screen...

Luckily I had taken off from the list my cherished, two sided hand-carved screen.

Since 1980 it had found a cozy corner in every home I lived in, against the dim light creating a beautiful ambience—whenever I listened to classical music or meditated. If only the artist knew how it provided me decades of pleasure. I often wondered, *Did my countryman who carved such intricate maple leaves, get duly compensated?*

My friends made fun of my peculiar attachment and predicted, "No one would pay your asking price."

After weeks of offers and counteroffers, I decided to take it with me, "It's my shrine."

Eventually, a haggler not only agreed to pay my asking price, but also picked it up the same day. "We need it for our Spiritual Sufi Centre in Ottawa, opening tomorrow."

He later shared a video clip showing that screen displayed in a cozy corner, lights seeping through the filigree to create my familiar ambience. Crazy as it may sound, I felt as though my child got adopted by caring parents.

Wrapping up one's entire household is emotionally draining...
You only realize later, how liberating it really is!

I ended up with stomach flu, so my Streetsville clan meticulously packed my dinnerware and I lay on my couch, cracking jokes! Privy to my 'disarray' Fatima and Bryan mobilized the Baithak group, who diligently packed my stuff. Fait accompli, everyone enjoyed the *Biryani* and *Dahi Bara* lunch on paper plates…in my empty house.

My life had been packed into two suitcases and fifty cardboard boxes.

A Day etched in my memory...
The elements were against us, driving anxiously through a heavy downpour, I said to my granddaughters, "I told your daddy just a take-out would do. But he decided to punish me on my birthday instead." We finally reached our destination and I parked in the *only* remaining spot, stepping out straight into a puddle! What a dark depressing locale, I thought but…when we entered, the hall suddenly lit up with a loud "Surprise!" He had booked a Middle Eastern restaurant Mezgouf. Now I knew why his daughters joked, "Daddy is such a wannabe Arab."

Over sixty guests greeted me, as I stood stunned: "Oh Ashy is here, the guests from Baithak, Nabeel from the Optometric Dispensary; Nisa my old neighbor from Ralwalpindi!" I looked around and saw my author friends Reva, Brian, and Maria the President of WEN, even Rena who played lead roles in two of my plays. I remained stunned as everyone greeted me.

"By the way, who planned all this and when?" I asked.

I felt fortunate to have so many friends, although many more were missing.

It was a sit-down dinner, full program with music and DJ. After many flattering tributes to me, Kashif announced my favorite song: '*Laut kay ajaa meray meeth*' which instantly transported me to Rawalpindi in 1963. I was overwhelmed. Zaheer's rendition of Mukesh song was superb. His wife *Ummia* told me, "He stayed up to practice until 2:00 a.m. said its zeezee's favorite song." Then my favorite soloist Sahar Raza sang legendary vocalist Reshma's song, she announced, "I've chosen this song for Zohra's spiritual side."

Reva as well as Dr. Sohail rendered generous compliments about my literary endeavours. By then I realized that all aspects of my interests were kept in mind, wow! With Fatima and Shireen's help, my son had gone to such great lengths. And there I was…irritated with the long drive?

Oh, but there was more to come—wide-eyed I SCREAMED with delight and disbelief when I saw my nephew *Saad* bringing the cake tray! Our friend Moby captured the moment on his candid camera. Recently immigrated to Canada, Saad had come all the way from Winnipeg.

The last but most delightful item was an elaborate dance performance by Club 23 (my granddaughters). But how did everyone, especially the kids, keep this event such a secret?

On our way back, the stress of winding up suddenly gripped me. Saad was our neglected guest as he even had to share a bed with Adnan. However, the girls got a kick out of it.

……

Family Is Family

On board the Turkish airlines flight I breathed a sigh of relief and reclined to reflect upon my boxed-up life. We had pre-booked a small apartment for when I return.

Now I was looking forward to six weeks of sheer fun with the family, then fly back on March 20th to my 'New Beginning.' Fatigue accumulated, I dozed off.

We must've hit an air pocket as I woke up suddenly. A meal was being served by gorgeous hostesses. What a good-looking race the Turks are, I noted.

For the first time in decades, my fear of flying had mysteriously dissipated. Did the recent events make me fearless, or was it the repetition of *Ayat-al-kursi* (verse of the throne), when you leave your destiny to the 'Higher Power'? Or maybe a placebo effect! Regardless, I celebrated the miracle.

Nine hours had passed I was surprised when the landing was announced.

The five-hour transit at the Turkish Havalimani airport was great. I walked around and experienced a sample of rich Turkish culture reflected in their gift shops and fancy tea stalls.

......

It was the first time in fifty-five years that there wasn't a single soul from Mujeeb's family at the airport. I had a sinking feeling at first but...?

Received by my family as a celebrity, I arrived to a full house. My sister Nigma had come from Lahore for her knee surgery. During her convalescence her children, siblings and cousins had flocked to her apartment. Every meal was a feast, sometimes potlucks. How her family had multiplied, her children and their offsprings...what a difference five years had made! With ongoing intermarriages, the Zuberi Tree had sprouted many new branches.

My cousins commented that I had aged; in Pakistan, they don't hold back their honesty. But I guess it's because I'm not used to the family environment anymore. They had also aged but, surrounded by bubbly children and grandchildren, they were thriving. Again the respect reserved for the elderly in Pakistan was noticeable right away. I secretly thought 'would my husband have been better off over here?'

I was relieved when my in-laws visited, bringing along generous presents for me, pleading guilty alongside their explanations about driving at night. Our love bond with Farida and Fowzia instantly reignited. Nasreen arranged a lunch reception, so I got to meet everyone, their families had multiplied too. Around a huge dining table, more chairs were added, after a lavish lunch I had to relate my action-packed trip to Islamabad.

"By the way, we watched your TV interview on Rising Pakistan, and were amused that you were introduced as *four women*," "Well, the credit goes to the polished host Tauseeq. But I know that you all would love to hear about my unique return flight. They were all ears so I relished in relating that episode:

Praying in the Skies...

"It was a small plane and I was given a lone seat in a row, but once I said hello to the children peeking from above the head-rest to my front, soon a flock of them from age six to twelve surrounded me. A family of thirty was returning from a wedding. The children were super bright and curious, some stood up on the seat behind me, two sat down beside me...and more children arrived. Their parents cast worried looks, but I signalled them that I was happy. A barrage of questions followed: 'Why are you travelling alone, where are you from?' I asked them to guess…after naming several countries they finally identified Canada. Two children, age ten and twelve, were taking classes for **Hifz** (Memorize the entire Quran). I asked them, "Will you skip regular school then?" "Only one year, but we'll catch up." So confident!

My in-laws anxiously waited for the punch line, I continued: "Once I told the children I'm travelling alone because my husband has passed away, a boy named *Jamal* spontaneously reacted, 'So let's pray for uncle'. Can you believe all those children raised their little hands and recited ***Surah Fatiha,*** a universal prayer Mujeeb recited over and over during the early stage of dementia." They were ecstatic, "So many innocent children prayed for our **Ammu."** By the end of my visit, I had accepted multiple dinner invitations before returning to Nigma.

*Al-Fatiha is the first chapter in the Quran, praying to the God of the 'Universes'.

Our New Generation back home…

Eager to make the best of my trip, likely my last, I wanted to connect with the new generation, understand their lifestyles, dreams, and aspirations. "This time I'd interview my extended grandkids." I was pleasantly surprised at how bright Nigma's grandchildren are. Most of them opened up to me easily, surprised mothers were curious, but I had vowed confidentiality.

I asked, "How does your generation differ from the previous one?"

Thirteen-year-old Noor Fatima, sweet as a fragrant flower, softly replied,

"They had more grace than us."

Some children expressed challenges they faced… *how to strike a balance between the rising western influence and their traditional upbringing at home*. Our playful Hareem, bursting with vitality, introduced herself while emulating an English accent. "I am eighteen years old, and I've won a gold medal at Beaconhouse International Student Convention in Malaysia playing *Futsal*." I sensed a rebellious streak in her. I was impressed that Ayesha Faisal had made sacrifices to put her through private school.

I noticed with amusement how the kids gravitated to the dining table at the sound of spaghetti or pizza. In one of my plays I dubbed them as the 'Pasta Generation'. They listened with fascination as I shared my first sloppy attempt to eat spaghetti at Rome airport in 1963.

An afternoon of gift exchange later turned into a 'secret chat session' with my beautiful nieces Ayesha, Afsheen, and Maheen. They were comfortable sharing intimate details of their **Me-too** experiences while growing up. I shared mine, as though we were the same age. Such a heavenly feeling watching them cast loving smiles my way, while massaging my feet.

After some mathematical calculations, our family attempted to persuade me. "With your Canadian pensions, at the current exchange rate, you can live a luxurious life here."

Would I like to, would I even fit in? I wondered.

Luckily, I had already made a quick trip to Islamabad, to meet Arifa, all my cousins and the last surviving aunt Rasheeda. Each hug was precious and emotional as I kept reminding myself that '*this may likely be the last time I'm meeting them all.*' My eldest cousin Shahida I grew up with, my aunt Rashida and Farhana—my last experience of their warm and loving hospitality is etched in memory forever.

Arifa also took me to my first ever 'All Afghani' garden party. An elderly woman sat quietly aside as she didn't speak English. Strangely, my childhood memory ignited and I spontaneously recited to her the Afghani National Anthem—in *Pushto!* She instantly brightened up and invited others to join in. I did repeat the lyrics at their request but I had to admit, "I don't even know the meanings." Yet my sister took pride on my behalf.

Arifa and Salman surpassed their previous records of hospitality. One full year's worth of fancy dining out was sandwiched into two weeks. A fond memory was when Salman insisted we should try out his favourite fish dish. I accepted the invitation on the condition that he would have to share his success story. I always thought he was 'reserved' and hardly said much, especially about himself. But...that evening it was as though I turned on a tap. Ever flowing details of his story, how he overcame challenges, his gradual progression to becoming an Award winning Architect! I love hearing about how others overcome their challenges. And now my sister was plugging along passionately, being morphed into a recognized artist.

Abdullah, a professional Architect by now, even arranged my interview on TV at **Rising Pakistan.** It was interesting how brilliantly the host Tauseeq Haider introduced me as Four Women; covering all four aspects of my life's endeavors. That show was aired in March, and I was already back, in Karachi.

*Pushto: Official language of Afghanistan

......

A Country of Contrasts...

My usual sleepover at the Tanveers' came with unexpected perks. "I'm taking you to a special place for a barbeque."

Past their posh neighborhood, on our way I witnessed slums upon a hill. Poverty trickling down through filthy drains, open sewers, raggedy clothes hanging on the lines, trash scattered. I felt sad for our nations' deprived ones. We again entered an affluent locale in drastic contrast, roads paved with tree trunks painted white near the roots. Unique bungalows, architectural masterpieces were different from the uniform, rows of most homes in Mississauga. Unlike the slanting roofs of our Canadian houses, flat roofs afforded fancy upper decks. Everything was so different!

As we approached our host's mansion, about a dozen Valet Parking attendants were ready to take over the parking responsibility. We entered through a second gate, and then...a **Surprise**!

It was a brightly illuminated garden of a huge mansion. "It's Karachi city's best garden of the year." Professionally manicured flower beds with a wide variety of colorful blooms, trees decorated with ornaments—I was enamored. We didn't expect a crowd of approximately one hundred fifty guests socializing cocktail style, with fresh fruit juice (no alcohol). Smoke rising from the BBQ area, a whiff of breeze brought us the tempting aroma of mouth-watering kebabs.

I wondered how many horticulturalists must be involved in such an ornate floral display. There was a peacock, an ostrich, and other birds. A huge cage with colorful budgies happily chirping, reminded me of my father's collection (once we had sixty of them!)

For Canadians, it's hard to imagine a crowd of teetotallers having such fun.

The next day, I was invited by my niece Maheen's family to another BBQ at Karachi's *massive* Creek Club. What a vast, brightly illuminated lawn by the seashore, over a thousand people chatting around tables of tens and twenties, enjoying gentle sea breeze! A cricket match was being broadcast on a huge outdoor screen. Smoke and the aroma rising from the BBQ hut. It was a privileged crowd, 'what about our poverty-stricken masses?' The contrast always bothered me, but they were used to it. Poverty in Canada is not visible.

......

Dozens of my Cousins gathered...

On the following day, Shahid had arranged my Reception to meet our battalion of first cousins. But I caught a chill at the seaside... despite that I had no choice but to accept lunch at Ayesha's place. What a wide variety of gourmet dishes they made for me. By the time everyone gathered at Shahid's place, I had lost my voice completely!

"Oh no, we were all looking forward to the chirping of our *'Bulbul-e-Hazaar Dastaan'* (the nightingale with a thousand stories). But for once she can't utter a single word?" someone joked and I cast a friendly frown.

Our Moon Auntie, ninety plus, arrived and proclaimed, "It's your love that gave me the energy to climb two flights of stairs." I signaled gratitude.

She proudly presented me with a copy of her husband, our late uncle Majeed's Memoir which Shahid had compiled. His memory remained intact at **Ninety-nine**, he even wrote his own obituary. I concealed my sad thoughts of Mujeeb's memory loss. Through sign language, I requested if each of them could read excerpts from uncle's memoir. As they read his wisdom-packed messages, Moon Auntie's famous eyes like green marbles. were beaming with delight.

"*Shabaash Shadan!* (Kudos) All these youngsters have had their copies, but today you actually made them read it," she said with passion. As their cameras went on clicking rampage I said, "It's obvious that cell phone companies are thriving in Pakistan," Shahid replied, "With inefficient landlines, our massive population embraced this digital revolution long ago." Even the street sweepers have now been empowered with what they call 'mobiles.' Someone added, "Even our maids are now able to have flings." But Huma swiftly changed the subject:

"You bunch of paparazzi, acting as though this is our last opportunity to get together."

Sameen replied, "You never know. *The future is not ours to see.*"

……

Only two days prior to my departure, all international flights from Pakistan got cancelled!

The invisible enemy Covid-19 spreading indiscriminately saw no borders. Families glued to TV, multiple channels reporting the sensational news of rising death tolls, especially in Italy. With images of spiky round green balls floating on large screens, fears mounted. The terms *Lock down* and *Social Distancing* became a part of the Urdu language. What on earth is Corona virus? Dr. Saman explained in simple words, but others read out loud:

Corona is a zoonotic disease – a virus that jumps from animals to humans. The first case of this new virus emerged in November. Only in December did the Chinese officials realize they had a new virus on their hands COVID-19— first contracted by a 55-year-old man from the province of Hubei, China. The identity of 'Patient Zero' was still unconfirmed.

Stranded in Karachi...

Saman was visiting from Hong Kong, Nigma from Lahore, and I from Canada. '**We...** the Stranded' decided to move in with my sister-in-law Durdana.

I barely spent a day at Shahid's place but now when he came to visit me our usual warm hugs were replaced with 'elbow touches'. From a distance we cast helpless looks at each other. Conversation revolved around the memories of his trip to Canada.

"Remember how our Canadian girls were attracted to you, tanned complexion and green eyes combo is rare." He joked,

"It was like working in the Bank, all that money I see but it's not mine."

"You resemble like Abbaji, you've also inherited his sense of humor."

Even my sister Rubeena and her children I could only meet for two hours. Travel restrictions implemented as 'Smart Lockdowns', each minute was so precious—I felt like a prisoner who was granted limited time.

COVID really affected that trip I had intended to be my last. Each time I hinted that, they got upset. "Don't scare us like that." Saman and Durdana went out of their way to cater to me. Three meals of my choice, plus refreshments twice a day added five kg on the wrong spots.

Once I dared to vocalize my observation:

"Why have our women started wearing the Abaya to look like Arabs?" I went on, "Pakistan is a South Asian country, not the Middle East." Over the years, they had been under Saudi influence. I felt irritated, "Culturally, we have nothing in common with them."

When Saman and Yousaf had come to Canada as landed immigrants, we bonded really well. We had great discussions related to her subject, she being a gold medalist in Psychiatry from Agha Khan Hospital. But now, Saman and other family members were becoming much more religious, so our debates sometimes got overheated. We eventually decided:

"No more religious discussions."

I recommended that we watch ***Dumpukht***—a Pakistani drama serial that depicts how even the educated can be brainwashed by self-appointed religious/spiritual leaders. Everyone watched with deep interest, but I wasn't sure if it resonated? In any case they showered me with love and periodic visits by my cousin Shahana and Rukhsana helped us cope with COVID.

One thing I was impressed by was that nearly every day our relatives were calling Dr. Saman for urgent medical advice (free). She diligently played the role of a Physician on site 24/7, connecting people to the right hospitals, arranging chemo therapy sessions, you name it.

Five Decades in Five Months...

Ever since I left Pakistan in 1963, I never had a chance to have such quality time with my sister Nigma—an epitome of love and sacrifice. During innumerable annual visits, Mujeeb and I had too many social engagements. Covid lockdowns provided us sisters with a golden opportunity to rekindle our childhood memories.

She whispered, "You were sixteen when you left Pakistan, and I became the eldest at fourteen." It triggered guilt so I explained, "But I landed in Nigeria like an alien on a different planet." She cast a gentle smile of forgiveness, "There was no one to steal my school uniforms."

I reminded her, "As a kid you used to joke, I'm Nig Ma...sub ki Ma (everyone's mother) so you've become Mother Teresa, but now I'll call you Enigma," she looked at me innocently.

I extended my arm, "Give me your ***Dast-e-shafqat*** (elderly, caring hand)" she complied.

Nigma spoke with pride about her son Haris, how he has become a celebrity as one of the top fashion photographers. "His non traditional views of life are quite similar to yours," she said. "Yes, once he shared with me his creative aspirations and the initial hurdles he had to face. At five in the morning he lovingly made sloppy but a delicious omelette for me, the memory of which still lingers." Nigma affectionately tightened her grip so I added, "Tell him how anxious I was to meet him and all the show biz icons he is privileged to work with."

I'll never forget that loving smile emanating from her green eyes. Hour-long chats while holding hands became our routine goodnights.

What a *payback from being stranded! I was to realize its true value later on.

By April the temperatures soared to 40 degrees Celsius. Once you leave the air-conditioned room at 26, you get slapped with another 14 degrees, as if you've opened an oven.

My own clothes were useless. In that sweltering heat only the finest pure cotton fabric called *lawn* was tolerable. So Nigma's brand-new outfits made way into my closet. "The tap water is so hot one can almost make tea from it." I grumbled. "But you must let the tap run for a while first" that advice was a bit late. One day I nearly burned myself using the bidet.

One night a tiny lizard entered the washroom through a plumbing hole. I panicked and screamed as if it was a monster. "You've become such a foreigner!" someone teased me so I boasted: "Would you believe that once we confronted an eight-foot long wild lizard in Nigeria!"

When Ramadan approached I was amazed at their resilience— despite the heat (38-40 C) everyone fasted, but I took the **Fidyah* option. The value of thirty days' worth of meals was calculated in Rupees, and I felt happy that a poor person had a feast. *Wouldn't it* *be a win/win if most elderly folks took that option?* (* Fidya: those unable to fast may donate to the poor instead)

I had read a BBC article in a newspaper that—'Charity is in Pakistani nations' DNA.' Now I witnessed it with my own eyes—the generosity with which everyone donated money and food, I remained in *awe*. The affluent were always surrounded and outnumbered by the needy.

However, waking up with everyone for **Sehri** (pre-dawn breakfast), invoked childhood memories. **Iftar** at sunset to break the fast used to be such fun. Thirty days flew by enjoying customary delicacies of *pakoray, chaat* and zesty fruit salad with juicy, aromatic guavas added.

On Eid day everyone ignored Covid protocols. The dining table remained occupied with shift after shift. I counted, altogether seventy-one immediate and extended family dropped in for Eid Greetings. I felt paranoid as my Travel Medical Insurance from Canada had been cancelled using Covid excuse. Messages from my Canadian friends confused me:

"Try to get back with the first possible flight," but others suggested,

"Stay there we are bored with lockdowns, plus there's shortage of toilet roles." They cracked jokes. "Imagine you carrying a suitcase full of toilet roles from Pakistan to Canada."

The flights resumed in June, I purchased a new ticket but it got cancelled again. 'Would I EVER reach Canada and see my children?' Stranded for five months, I reached my breaking point. "Please don't say you are stranded."

Thankfully I had already spent a dream evening with Afsheen's family when they took me to a fancy Italian restaurant Aylanto, the outdoor temperature was perfect. I remarked, "In this part of the city (Clifton) I feel as if I'm in a posh locale of a European town." Relishing the ambience and Karachi's intoxicating sea breeze, they planned many more exotic culinary adventures for me. But suddenly ... all plans were *'Thupp'* (busted).

Now Afsheen ran around to find a fancy briefcase for my laptop, get a lawn outfit stitched urgently. Saman ordered gifts online, plus overstocked me with a wide variety of Masks. Their last-minute gestures of love earned me ample cash.

On the day of my departure my brother-in-law *Mustufa* surprised me with yet another envelope that added to my pile of 1000 Rs bills. I generously distributed those to the Airport staff; the Cleaners, Porters and the Waiters in the departure lounge. At first they looked stunned then bowed with gentle smiles to thank me. I still had a pile left.

The Act of Giving is so intoxicating... I craved for our good old days to return soon.

*A few months after my return my beloved sister bid farewell. I was hit with grief and gratitude simultaneously.

Travelling Under Covid Scare...

On June 15, 2020, I boarded Emirates airline headed to Dubai. The empty rows facilitated social distancing and everyone was masked, so I breathed a sigh of relief but...?

The connecting flight to Toronto was jam-packed. I could hardly make it to the washroom without brushing against someone's shoulder or elbow. The slightest sneeze or cough from the cabin raised alarms. You could see the 'paranoid skulls' simultaneously popping up.

Once I relinquished my better seat to accommodate a family with three children, they befriended me—a Lebanese couple migrating to Canada. I shared with them, "My husband and I once spent two weeks in the *Brummana Mountains.*"

"Oh that's where we are from."

An instant connection was formed as we exchanged notes. But on a somber note I added,

"Back then Lebanon was dubbed the *Heavenly Gateway to Asia.*"

Instead of the Emirates' usual gourmet meals, boxed lunches felt like charitable handouts. Fourteen hours seemed an eternity.

The Covid effect was reflected at all three deserted airports. The ground crew were disorganized and irritable. Nonetheless, landing back on Canadian soil was even more exciting than our first arrival forty-four years back, but...<u>no one to receive me at the airport?</u>

Kashif called, "If I receive you, I'll have to quarantine for fourteen days." He sent an Uber. The apartment I had booked was already taken. Anxiety mounted...where would I stay? Would my friends still be willing to rent me basement apartments they had offered? My curiosity peaked as the driver took an unexpected turn.

....

Thinker's Paradise
(*Quarantine Retreat*)

---

50 The Uber driver parked at The Arc—an iconic sky-rise building I had been fascinated by. From a distance it looked like a cruise ship. My son informed me,

"The Concierge named Jason will take your suitcases up; the entrance door is open."

Seventeenth floor! I felt a pang of excitement as I entered the apartment. The TV was on, Jagjit Singh was singing:

"Tere aanay ki jab khabar pohnchay
Teri khushboo se, sara ghar mehkay"

(When I hear the news of your arrival)
(The entire room is filled with the aroma of your presence)

Apparently our son has also inherited my parents' love of poetry and good music.

In any case, this was to be my temporary retreat only, until I could find a perfect location. Shireen had filled my fridge with groceries, and Kashif delivered ready meals. So, my fourteen-day quarantine seemed a welcome treat. The Government of Canada kept tabs, they asked me trick questions: "So where do you go for your walks?"

I joyfully replied, "I walk in my 36 ft balcony."

The entire city of Mississauga east of Erin Mills was spread before my eyes, past the Mississauga skyline, all the way up to the flickering CN Tower downtown Toronto!

The last day of quarantine was July 1, 2020, Canada Day. The annual fireworks at Square One got cancelled, I expected a somber evening. Surprisingly, a spectacular display of thirty or forty fireworks simultaneously lit up the sky mesmerizing me—my best Canada Day ever. But the next day was our *true* celebration…**a reunion with my children after six months**!

The extra spacious slightly curved balcony created a visual illusion, akin to standing at the edge of Planet Earth! I'd rise early to view the Morning Star…captivated with the changing moods of the sky.

Once during a weather alert, I *planned* to stay in the balcony in order to witness how those fluffy clouds gradually evolve into a full-fledged thunderstorm. That's when I realized that ***Sunrise; sunset; rainfall; thunderstorm and then… calm! All weathers are reflected in our inner beings as well.*** A poem was brewing. I called my concerned family abroad, "Don't worry about my isolation, I've been gifted the sky, and I've entered a *Thinkers Paradise.*"

Hindsight told me that being stranded with my family in Pakistan was the best thing for me. After my return, Aunt Rashida as well as my youngest surviving Uncle Waheed passed away. Luckily, I had met most of my relatives before Covid-19 struck, received a lifetime's worth of warm embraces. Moreover, it provided me a chance to compare the two lifestyles.

Descending into the evening of my life, nearing platinum landmark, a sea of questions and answers arose like surging waves: Am I afraid of death? No, all I fear is disability, especially

Dementia! The statistics of recent Covid deaths in senior homes were alarming. The topic of senior care and apprehensions of old age is on the minds of many. This universal dilemma is best expressed in the 'The Book of Mirdad' a spiritual masterpiece by Mikhail Naimy, I quote:

"The very young and the very old are equally helpless. But the helplessness of the young conscripts the loving, sacrificial help of all, while the helplessness of the old is able to command but the grudging help of few."

Our society has advanced in terms of increased longevity but to maintain a healthy and happy lifestyle is yet a challenge. Many ageing South Asian immigrants wonder if they would be better taken care of in their countries of origin, or here in Canada?! Our middle class and up are able to hire private help at a reasonable cost. Our family values emphasize *Filial Piety*. It's obligatory for children to cater to their ageing parents living ***at home***—in fact it's considered as a 'gateway to heaven.'

I pondered about my own *what if.* My family had asked if I would move there but based on my experience I replied, "I would probably be a misfit."

Living alone for the first time and under pandemic, I realized my top priority was to maintain my own mental and physical health. It required strategic planning.

As they say, "Silence is a true friend who never betrays." I implemented the silent hour that allowed me to revisit my inner self. It helped me identify my flaws, and serious knowledge gaps...

'How little have I tapped from the well' bothered me, but I received a timely advice.

Thanks to Kamran Siddiqui the literary member of Baithak, for recommending to me *Genius of the Ancient World* documentaries by Bettany Hughes, about scholars such as Buddha, Aristotle, Nietzsche, and Confucius. Bettany passionately takes you to the actual ancient sites. One by one I watched them all. The concepts such as 'Eudaimonia' and 'Amor Fati' enabled me to test myself: The values I practice, those also taught through my faith—what is *similar* and what *differs*? I realized that often it's 'the same message, only delivered in drastically different formats!'

As for learning about re-directing my 'mental chatter' I concluded that my Vertigo Philosophy is all about that.

The extended lockdowns also pulled me into the sad political drama unfolding in US politics that often impacts the world. The Committee hearings of possible impeachment of the President took me back to the Nixon era, when in Nigeria I had become a major news source about the Watergate Scandal and the Senate Committee hearings. However, watching the January 6 Insurrection at the Capitol Building eroded my confidence in Democracy.

Life continues to gift me the unexpected:

One morning my bank colleague/friend Saira Shaikh called, "Where are you living now, I'd like to drop by." I hadn't seen her in years, so I texted my address to her. That afternoon she showed up at my door: "Surprise, surprise." Delicious aromas instantly tantalized my taste buds. "What's this?" "Someone like you…living alone at this stage? I must do something for you." It was a grand gesture for three months, but we had to end it as she refused to accept any payment.

The downside of my unique balcony was the blaring traffic noise. It faced the Free Care Hospital which reminded me of my cousin Rani's recent demise. I felt the urge to at least start working on my priorities. From my diary I pulled out the plan I made before I travelled:

'I'll convert my handwritten Urdu stories onto the computer; digitize selected photos from thirty-eight large-size albums; read Mujeeb's diaries and letters; Publish the indigenous stories I have translated. My Priority Boxes with all those items have been marked -- to be stored in Kashif's basement.'

Reviewing that list my interest perked up, I asked Kashif to bring those boxes. Just then--

A head-spinning '**life-quake**' occurred! As he brought the boxes, I was shocked to find that those were the Donation Boxes I had left for pick up by the Diabetic Association. Instead, my Priority Boxes were inadvertently donated. So, all my items of sentimental value were lost!

Kashif had assigned the task to the Mover we knew well. But now that nearly half a year had elapsed, it was impossible to trace anything.

Devastated with such a loss, tossing and turning in bed, I hardly slept that night.

At sunrise, during my meditation, I tried to invoke my own philosophy of Panoramic Perception—***People have lost lives to Covid, what's my loss in comparison?*** I then wrote a heart wrenching but philosophical email to Reva who replied, "I wept for your loss, but let me tell you this is by far the best piece of your writing I've seen."

But what about Mujeeb's book *'Tropical Macro Fungi?'* It was our joint project we called Science and Art in perfect harmony.'

Kashif dropped in with the good news, "Amazon still has six of Abu's books available in Italy and two used ones in the USA, published in 1972!" Finding a lost treasure is such a pleasure. The book seemed to have doubled in its value. We immediately ordered two.

Then from an LCBO box emerged my precious collection—seventy-five artsy ducks that quarantined for five years in our garage. "Why such obsession with ducks?" someone asked, so I explained. "Ducks are inspirational, they can swim, walk on water, and the fastest duck species can fly between 100–160 miles an hour." As though my patience was now being rewarded.

Discovering a Treasure Trove!

When I was about to discard the old cassettes, I noticed one was marked 'Radio Interview UAE,' so I played it, old memories of Sikandar instantly rekindled. The flipside hard to decipher, was marked 'Talent party under the Stars—recording of our Family Gathering in 1967!' Under the starlit sky, on our rooftop in Pindi, everyone shared their talents including my father's popular '*Cat fight*' and Ammi's songs. Even my grandma's poetic rendition of the 'Ninety-nine attributes of God' she used to sing early morning. I was thrilled beyond words.

Half a century old treasures preserved in a cassette I nearly discarded? Finding these gems compensated for my recent losses. I recorded them on WhatsApp to share with my family.

Larger than life, our grandmother Ammajan named *Nayab* (rare) was a great source of inspiration. Who can forget that after the sudden demise of her daughter-in-law leaving behind nine children, she embraced the challenge of raising them! Now hearing her sing, everyone got super excited, my cousin Sarah established a WhatsApp group and named it **Durr-e-Nayab** (Rare Pearls). They also compiled a list of her children, grand and great-grandchildren. We are *One Hundred and Seventeen* strong! Now she is with us, forever singing the song of life.

Literary rendezvous didn't work out in my noisy balcony, and indoor gatherings were restricted. Instead, we enjoyed gourmet BBQs in Zehra's backyard. To address the Covid situation, she created an environment of comfort and ambience with music and lighting, so it became 'our little haven.' Their impromptu attempts to match-make me and our uncensored conversations were a great escape from the somber news of fluctuating Covid statistics.

Summer flew by fast...fall didn't last long, winter set in, and then suddenly...we found a perfect location for me to move. **But...I had to make an overnight decision!**

Who showed up to extend a helping hand? Surprisingly, it was Mitch, my Rock Guard.

....

The Celebration Square, 'Mosaic' is the largest South Asian Festival of Mississauga (Founders Asma and Arshad Mahmood) my apartment is right across the Clock Tower!

From my Living Room Window Celebration Square Skating rink in the winter splash-pad in the summer

From my bedroom ...The iconic Munro Towers usually identical but sometimes one becomes charcoal gray—an architectural masterpiece!

At the City Hall, Pakistani Artists, musicians & poets paid tribute to Hon Mayor Hazel McCallion (Mayor for 36 years, retired in 2014) The unveiling of the Portrait by Artist Shahid Rassam

Marty's Awards Gala (2018). The Honorable Mayor of Mississauga Bonnie Crombie, an avid supporter of the Arts

Sybil Rampen (our role model) established Joshua Creek Heritage Centre Arifa's memorable private tour of the Centre

An ambitious youth group 'Encore' that I'm connected to

My grand-daughters now
grown up—my Students
as well Teachers!

My nieces Ayesha,
Afsheen and Maheen

Mahnoor, Noor Fatima and the
Gold medalist Hareem (R)
My sister Nigma's
grand-daughters

Umair, Sameen and
Mahad (Shahids kids)

Saad Munazza family (Shahid's younger son)

Once in a lifetime memory of meeting Irfan my only cousin
living in New Delhi (I celebrate his success from a distance!

Shahid and Rubina were toddlers when I left for good
The day of my Rukhsati (The bride's send off)

Shahid a grandfather, now! We relish
the memories of bygone days

The fleeting moments, when Arifa visited Canada

The proud father Salman   Abdulla & Maryam's wedding

Zainab and cousin Rabiya Mansoor
…adventurous in the Rockies!

Our last picture with Mujeeb
(Kashif, Shireen and I)

Image (L) Nigma & her entire family,
Yousuf (R) 3rd row in sunglasses
The younger son Haris (R) is the artsy nephew of mine
He is an award winning fashion photographer based in Lahore

Shehnaz Khan's ever welcoming kitchen.

My Creative/supportive Family-- Courtney Park Authors
At the countryside residence of Trevor Trow our hero
Still publishing at age 95+

Mom & I -- this is worth more than a thousand words

With my Grandma who gifted me her mother's meaningful name

Surprise birthday by my sister-in-law Durdana (R) Kashif got to meet my entire family and became everyone's favorite

The last time I barged in my parents' bedroom before Dad passed away

Nigma passed away (after
I completed my memoir).
Grief for such a loss,
Gratitude for five months
together while stranded!

Sikandar still resides
in my memory

Rani, my closest
relative in Canada,
also lost her battle
to cancer!

My sister Dr. Tanveer
survived serious Covid,
but her husband Dr.
Khalid couldn't make it!

What a gift from Mujeeb's
family— a Great-grandson
Moosa! (Nazia and
Usman now in Toronto)

A Private Musical
at the 'Sky Lounge'
of our f irst abode
(1976). The moment I'll
always cherish…that
evening how we were
immersed in spiritual
music…*Together!*

Back to Square One
(February 2021)

---

51 "From seventeenth floor to the twenty-fourth, I feel as though I'm being promoted," I mused. Don't they say there are seven levels of paradise? There could be no better location in isolation, right across from the City Hall, Celebration Square. Again, a vast view of the sky plus an impressive skyline, I marveled at how Mississauga has miraculously transformed in four decades, from a small town to a bustling city.

What a hold this city has on me! Compelled to take a tour of the Celebration Square across the street, my memory reel started rolling as I walked near the amphitheater where I once shared the stage with Wali Shah to address Cyberbullying. Sprightly Heather Christine (a vocalist) had coordinated the event in 2012. A youth group YTGA (Founder Zehra Abbas) and I presented a skit based on Amanda Todd's story, a teenage victim of bullying who eventually committed suicide. To deliver our positive message, we utilized the verses from my poem *"Sparkling Space".*

I then approached the main stage where I stood still, reliving the 30th Anniversary of Mississauga Arts Council in 2012. Memories filed away in the hard drive of my mind resurfaced: The Vibonics Rap Band and I had presented 'The Internal Flame' with our core message:

"Keep your Internal flame Eternal"

This is where we also witnessed the TD Mosaic Festival, one of the largest South Asian annual festivals. Credit goes to the Founder/Directors Asma and Arshad Mahmood, a dynamic Pakistani couple. Over the past seventeen years, they have invited hundreds of renowned artists and musicians from India, Pakistan, and other countries.

I then walked toward the City Hall, where on December 6, I was one of the guest speakers at the annual events by PCAWA—Peel Committee against Women Abuse. The annual candlelight vigils held to honor the missing and murdered indigenous women, and the victims of the 1989 Montreal massacre. Those were supported by our dynamic Mayor Bonnie Crombie who replaced the intrepid Hazel McCallion. At the art gallery too we attended novel art exhibitions.

My sports spirit rejuvenated with the thought of *Toronto Raptors' historical win* of the 2019 NBA championship. Shireen, Kashif, the kids and I were part of a crowd when thousands of us at this Square were shoulder-to-shoulder cheering the Raptors. I then strolled toward the Mississauga Library—closed?! But my disappointment soon turned into excitement, renamed as Hazel McCallion Central Library, it was under major renovation. To top it all—

It happened to be the 10th Anniversary of the Celebration Square!

I woke up to view from my bedroom a fascinating sunrise, the iconic Munroe Towers romancing in golden glory. Suddenly I noticed that the *only* missing building from the entire skyline is the one in which Kashif's Optometry Clinic once thrived! It's just as well; otherwise my view of the towers would be partially blocked. So now I questioned my old conviction that 'the Universe has a language,'... aren't *we* the ones who give it meanings as life unfolds?

One day, I was caught off guard when suddenly, there was a fire alarm blaring out loudly. Fortunately, it turned out to be a false one. Considering that I am all the way up on the twenty-fourth floor, initially I felt a little paranoid. However a vast sky, a canvas of changing hues morning, noon, and night, for my delight…to reconcile was worth my while.

Thankfully, the pandemic isolation has not depressed me, as it has so many others.

Coping with Covid

We humans are blessed with such an innovative spirit (virtual ingenuity), that most of us readily 'Covidified' our lifestyles. I had already joined the Seniors Forum Canada. Under the dedicated leadership of Shaukat Rizvi, we were provided regular exercise programs on zoom. Who knew that each Saturday morning a charming young professional lady Faryal Zahir would help us with virtual exercises in the comfort of our homes?

I also signed up as a Seniors Lifestyle Coach/volunteer Counselor. Ironically, one of the first families who approached me turned out to be a victim of dementia! The pandemic protocol prevented me to make indoor visits. However, 'Necessity' the mother of invention whispered:

'In the absence of a comfy couch, the amateur therapist may utilize the Red Bench in front of the City Hall'. We did so, and it worked.

Living alone, one needs to be proactive. As for me, connecting with various age groups and artists was important. Isn't life really a Relay game? We inherit values from the previous generation, and pass these on to the next?

A Virtual Prom...

I reconnected with **Encore,** a group of Grade 12 students who were introduced to me before Covid by their dynamic teacher Jasmine Jackman (also a board member of Bridging the Gap) I asked them, "How has the pandemic impacted you all?"

Their soft-spoken leader Sureya replied, "We regret having to cancel the socio-drama we planned with you and... we also missed our high school Prom. But now we are in our first year."

"How about a Virtual Prom, would you like that?" That idea really appealed to them.

Soon they celebrated a Zoom Prom with me, the theme 'Style and Substance' appealed to everyone. I had flashbacks of my first dinner reception in Nigeria in 1963! How the elderly couples had been fascinated with me as a teenager, and now... nearly six decades later, I found it so heart warming to watch those young girls modelling. They each shared their aspirations and the lessons learned from the pandemic, even wrote articles I suggested. I also introduced them to a Japanese concept 'Ikigai' (the reason for being). We requested them to text their individual votes to me. The winner *Aryanna Daddio*, in her exotic white dress, had beautifully expressed the importance of family values enhanced by Covid-19. Initially reluctant, but later she humbly accepted a small cash prize from me. I reassured the Prom attendees,

"Once the pandemic is under control, we will plan a meaningful activity."

My own granddaughters (Club 23) are my best in-home youth connection. Together we enjoy choreographing fusion dance exercises to Urdu lyrics, and the art of storytelling by reading excerpts from my memoir alongside their input. Now that 'in-person schooling' is often replaced by online learning, we've recognized there's a dire need to fill that gap.

Since the 'Virtual Revolution' has taken place. despite being challenged in my digital skills, I'm dubbed as a *Silver Surfer.* I belong to four different authors' clubs, as well as the International Association of Top Professionals and two other organizations that hold regular meetings on zoom. Together, a fleet of us are virtually zooming along.

My author friends and I got our keyboards clicking. February 14th of 2021 was our iconic Mayor McCallion's 100th birthday! My tribute to her titled *"The Hazel Inspiration"* was published in Canadian Asian News. I also reconnected with the Director/President of Mississauga Writers Group, Elizabeth Banfalvi, dedicated to compiling yet another anthology. She published my story and a poem titled *"Sacred Heart"*—about the iconic young hockey player Logan Boulet. Incidentally his organs saved six lives. Subsequently, the 'Green Shirt Day' movement prompted over 150,000 signatures for organ donations!

The Vaccine Day...After being locked-in for months, I treated it as my fun outing. Many seniors were skeptical or curious about the vaccines, so I posted the 'adventure' on Facebook. They found entertainment and felt encouraged by reading my diary of that event.

Once most of us felt safer after our two doses, and the restrictions were eased, *people came out of their cocoons and morphed into social butterflies,* to celebrate whatever they could, be it theme parties or birthdays.

One of the highlights was a Golden Birthday of a special friend *Ashy Habib.* The theme being '**Bridgerton**' (a popular British TV drama), some fifty of us Pakistani women, dressed in eighteenth-century Regency era aristocratic attire. There was music and dancing.

All our fanciful hats, corsages, and over-the-top looks gave us respite from the doldrums of pandemic dressing down. I was privileged to ride with my long lost friend Farhat Abid, on our way we rekindled our memories of Kehkashan Club—how well we gelled during our tenure to form a lasting bond.

Our Baithak music group coordinated a few events. The party champion *Samina Mehar* hosted a Halloween get together at her lovely home turned into a Haunted House. We all dressed as the wicked witches, the wildest one, Sahar, role-played a *Fortune Teller*. Her hilarious predictions turned us into rowdy teenagers—a stress release from the prolonged lockdowns.

Our Courtney Park authors readily planned 'in-person' literary gatherings. We celebrated our revered author Trevor Trow's book *'Phyllis the Donkey Girl'*. Incidentally Trevor shares the same birthday as Queen Elizabeth. Yet another literary meet up was hosted by Konrad Brinks at his exquisite patio surrounded by tall trees. We captured those memories, knowing the 'uncertainties' life had in store. The threat of Delta and other possible variations lingered.

The Saigon Girl…

Greeting people_in the elevators, sometimes even passers-by especially if we exchange a glance, has been a habit which I tried to *nurture* during the pandemic isolation as a win-win. One warm greeting brought me a gift I really NEEDED (a walking partner).

One day she called. "It's Cathy…remember we met in the elevator, would you like to go for a walk?" Our one-hour walk was followed by another hour as we sat up on the green hill, off Prince of Wales Drive, and chatted away! Her features typical of her Vietnamese heritage, Cathy is agile, but not fragile, and a super confident woman who has her life totally under control… despite being ten years my junior.

When discussing the recent and hasty ***American departure from Afghanistan***, she related her own story, "In 1975, I was a young girl in school, when our mom called me and my siblings:

"Don't utter a single word to anyone, just come home, we are leaving tonight." On that night, they boarded a US Military aircraft and flew to Montreal. That was the historic end of the prolonged Vietnam War! "History repeats itself," she said. I made my lighthearted conclusion:

"Well, had your mother not taken that action, you and I would have never met."

I returned home and wrote a diary 'The Saigon girl' about the way we immediately clicked. Our initial walks have been more like having read the *synopsis* of each other's lives, but this story has the potential of becoming a novel in my Library of Friends. We probed into how we immigrants define ourselves?

Our Identity…

We are so different, yet so similar. Our diversity is to be celebrated. Each immigrant brings a unique story. Either we assimilate, integrate or feel isolated. A poet friend described us as being transplanted in a pot. Our conversation on that subject sent me into further reflection:

I imported precious values taught by my loving parents and grand- parents but…

My mentors have been from various racial and cultural backgrounds: Dr. Oyewusi from Nigeria; George Clark from Saskatchewan, Canada; Wim Faasen from Denmark; Terry Campbell from Jamaica; Mr. Schuler from Jewish background; and... Zamir Ahmad a Literary Scholar from Pakistan! The list goes on and on, not to mention my own Resident Professor. Neither of them ever wondered or asked about my ethnicity.

All of them have helped me become what I am today. I have therefore concluded that I can never be *just* Canadian, nor am I *just* a Pakistani anymore—maybe a 'Happily hyphenated' Canadian? My niece Madeeha once lovingly complimented:

"Shadan Phuppo, if anyone deserves to live twice, it's you." Well, living in two cultures simultaneously, I have enjoyed the double pleasures of life: language; music; drama; foods; customs; costumes; and much more! Those of us who have integrated may perceive ourselves as an emerging Hybrid Generation?

The Eastern in me I'll always cherish, but the Western in me feels like a breath of fresh air. I sometimes joke "East is best in the West," Mississauga city being a living example. Over the past four decades even the cultural landscape of our city has been drastically altered. I tell my family that "Over here it feels like I'm living in a new and improved Bombay or Karachi."

......

Our Connection with a Genius
'Oladokun'

For my new office, Kashif gifted me a filing cabinet from Ikea. While setting up the shelves, I found a book in Urdu about 'The impact of European settlements upon the Indigenous Culture', written by my author friend Nasim Syed! What a significant contribution to Urdu literature. It also reminded me of my own translations of the indigenous stories which I had lost. Before I could dwell in that, an excitement awaited. I found a scientific book by Professor Halstead! The eccentric professor from Reading University in UK once invited us for a ***Bat Hunting*** party in Nigeria, followed by dinner when bat meat was served as the main dish.

Curiosity now led me to Google Search Professor Halstead. I even found an article by him about the 'Palm Wine Drinkers Club' in The International Field Studies Journal of West Africa! The article was titled "A House Divided" which included the following famous quotation: "*A House Divided against itself... Shall Stand—Unity in Diversity*" (my pet subject).

Little did we realize that behind the façade of him wearing a Mexican hat and tie-dyed shorts, riding his tricycle to work, there was a genius lurking! Tarlo Lambert Beverly Halstead was a British Paleontologist and professor of Geology, Zoology and a 'popularizer' of science, noted for his theories of dinosaurs' sexual habits. A larger than life scholar, it's no wonder that the Nigerians honored him with a title ***Oladokun*** (Yoruba meaning: wealth as large as an ocean).

Reliving the scenario of bat hunting, his image came alive; so I tried to contact Halstead, but unfortunately he had passed away in 2019—one year after Mujeeb.

Flipping the pages of Halstead's book, LO AND BEHOLD there it was—Mujeeb's letter that I had completely given up on! My heart quickened its rhythm...I took a deep breath, plunked myself on the couch and began to read:

'*Dear Shadan: When I first met you, I was taken aback, I had no idea you were so young! Even though for me it was love at first sight, I came home disturbed, I felt guilty...like plucking a rare flower bud before it has fully bloomed. After much debate I decided to withdraw my proposal...in your best interest. I wrote you a letter to explain it all.*

But once I heard that you have said yes, I felt it was the happiest day of my life! Dear Shadan I promise I will do everything to make you happy. Will let my flower bloom, also will relish its fragrance for the rest of my life.'

Reading it over and over evoked intense emotions and triggered a chain of thoughts that circled my mind for several days. The truth of Rumi's words resonated:

"Anything you lose comes around in another form."

......

But how did all this happen to me? While many are feeling Covid isolation, I arrived back to Square One, the Hub of Art and Culture— beckoned to finally complete my story.

"This world is but a canvas to our imagination." *(*Henry Thoreau)

Years ago when dealing with complex situations, to minimize the problem, I'd close my eyes and imagine myself in Space. Looking down upon our planet Earth from above, I used to recite Ghalib's famous verse:

"Bazeecha-e-Atfal hai Dunya Mere Aagay
Hota hai shab-o-roze tamasha mere aagay"

(The world is but a children's playground. Day and night this drama unfolds before my eyes)

But now, a Replica of that Image is ***real***...but manifests in such a 'positive' way:

High up from the twenty-fourth floor, looking down upon the Celebration Square gives me immense pleasure. In summer it's a splash-pad but in the winter a skating rink where children and adults (of various races) go round and round in Circles, yet their shadows magically from geometrical patterns! Day in and day out, I watch a drama unfold:

Isn't our world one human chain, holding hands playing Ring-a-ring o' Roses?

While the beauty of life is in the mystery of predictable and the unpredictable, the Clock Tower of the City Hall right across my living room window, looks me in the eye and spells consistency and endlessness of time. In the evening it lights up so its beauty is enhanced, changing hues from orange, green, purple and pink, depicting colors of sunrise and sunset that I continue to capture.

Each day is a new beginning, time we've been gifted on this planet.

Smothered with the beauty of the sky I appreciate the gift of my 'zesty retina' which is instrumental in enjoying a 'hundred pleasures a day'—a philosophy passed on by Zamir. Sometimes I turn around to glance at our portrait on the wall, Mujeeb holding hands with me, under a golden tree at the High Park in Toronto, as though expressing joy watching me follow his passion for photography.

The Integrated 'I'

52 By undertaking *The Second Journey* (writing my memoir),
I have relived my fascinating life and realized that the tough times
were only a fraction!

Challenges were mostly overcome through escape into the
Literary Arts. I have not shied away from celebrating my successes,
but I attribute those to many individuals who ignited my passion.
Blunders I made were due to naivety and selfless love, not malice.

Having forgiven everyone, I feel lighthearted and liberated.
Fortunately, *regret* is one word deleted from my dictionary. I have
therefore reconciled with my financial losses. As my son says, "The
clinics we lost are operating well, and thousands of patients are being
looked after. Just take comfort knowing that your son created them,"
in response I humor him:

"In a way, our wealth is scattered on the streets of Mississauga—
this was also one of the three wishes of Alexander the Great." I
reminded him of the last verse of my poem:

Choreographing my Breakthrough
In reality I haven't lost anything
All that is in nature will forever belong to me

He cast an intriguing smile of approval so I added: "Money isn't
everything but it certainly is empowering." He nodded and I caught

him off guard: "By the way Kashif, are you really writing a book? What is it about, what's the title?"

"21 DAYS TO *Forever"* he said with a mysterious smirk.

"Great, we should always have something to look forward to." We remained engaged in a philosophical discussion.

Seeking the Meaning of Life…

Our ultimate purpose is to have love and peace. Love I've received in abundance but how can a sensitive writer have 'complete peace' knowing that the climate disaster is at our doorstep; 20 million children in our world are starving; genocides are taking place; and 215 indigenous children have been found in a mass grave? More are expected. So, my personal challenge is to control 'over-sensitivity'. Realizing that our blessings abound is so important.

To me, every living being is a miracle of life. Reflecting on the magic of our own body and mind is enough to be grateful. I'm reminded of my grandmother's words:

"Touch your jugular vein and feel the magic."

Each morning I marvel that even in a state of being half dead, my blood has been circulating, the digestive system is functioning, and I wake up 'intact.' We humans take so much for granted.

Gratitude is one of the best gifts I've received. I experience it with intensity like never before! I do have rare vulnerable moments, but my Vertigo Philosophy readily comes to rescue.

The feeling of independence when living alone, is new and surprisingly a rewarding experience. Had I not played my roles to the best of my ability and made necessary sacrifices, I wouldn't feel such gratification.

……

I'm grateful to my father for naming me Shadan—that is my *Internal Flame* (the pilot light). Thankfully, my dancing spirit and the music of the soul is very much alive.

Besides my faith, I've delved into diverse spiritual teachings. From the 'Living Presence' by Kabir Edmund Helminski, I quote:

"Egotism is the very devil itself, a limitless source of envy resentment and pride. A healthy passion for life is a gift but we need not let this passion become fixated on the desires of the limited self" We can transform this egotism by substituting more of 'We-ness'."

Our ultimate objective is to achieve the **Integrated 'I'**—in a way much in line with Plato's philosophy of 'Conquer Yourself' which I too strive for.

At one point, *Shadan* in me felt neglected, while Zohra continued to propel me along. It wasn't until they reconciled with each other, that the integrated 'I' inclusive of others (the human chain) was able to develop the third eye—that is, *'The Other I'* in this story.

I hope that the experiences I've shared from the life I've lived would inspire debate and be helpful to others.

......

The happiest person to see my book completed would have been Mujeeb, my life partner for over half a century. I will never forget a special moment at the hospital, when I asked him, "What was your most pleasurable moment with me that could spark your spirit?" He signaled me to pull my chair closer and put my feet on his lap. Barely able to speak, he again signaled me to remove my socks. Touching my bare feet gently, with difficulty he uttered, **"This moment."**

Dedicating my book to him can never match his grand gestures of love and gratitude that overwhelms me to this day.

....

THE END

There's a Room for You

In the replica of our global village
there's a special room
where East meets West
North greets South and . . .
light dispels darkness

> *Through the mysterious corridor*
> *you spiral down the dark stairway*
> *to descend in order to . . . 'Ascend'*

With the theme—East meets West
This 'exclusive' venue is inclusive
of all races
ordinary people come to perform
extraordinary deeds
A symbol of harmony
no stereotyping, true bonding
Creativity in common
people from all walks of life converge
Theatrical performances of
socio-dramas, or stage shows are rehearsed

> *Seeking common Canadian Values*
> *commonalities discovered*
> *diversity celebrated as . . .*
> *'Enlightenment through Entertainment'*

The magic of our multicultural mosaic
truly sparked when;
Eyal of Israel and Gada of Palestine

held hands and bonded
Indian Reena played Pakistani Zarina

   People in sarees, sarongs, and kimonos
   mingled with those in skirts and blue jeans
   United Nations truly 'united'

How we relished those lunches
of shami kebab, Italian pizza, Szechwan noodles
sushi, perogies and falafal
a potluck of food and folks

   This 'Replica' differs from
   the outside world:
   Complete harmony exists!
   This is a room
   where you bring your basket full
   empty it and refill till it overflows

No matter what colour you are
tears are all the same
laughter alike
The 'I' less significant`
'We' and 'Us' matter, and . . .
there is room for you

   Just think
   this grand, global gathering
   started in my home basement!

                 . . . .

Zohra Zoberi
'True Colours...*from the Universe to the Inner Mind'*

About the Author

(By common definition, a Canadian of Indo Pakistani origin)

Zohra is a global citizen. Her poetry, short stories, and plays have been published in over twenty anthologies in Canada and the USA. Two books to her credit are 'True Colours' (poetry collection) 'Questionably Ever After' (prose). This bilingual author has appeared in radio & TV interviews, locally and abroad. Founder and Artistic Director of Bridging the Gap Productions with a mission of *'Enlightenment through Entertainment'*

Winner of: 2 Performing Arts group Awards – 2007 and 2008
From Mississauga Arts Council (Live plays staged in Mississauga)
Best Emerging Literary Arts Award –2011 (Mississauga Arts Council)
Ambassador of Peace Award -- Universal Peace Federation 2012
Woman of Courage Award - Endless Possibilities 2013
Nominated for other awards including Hazel McCallion Volunteer Award

Top Artistic Director of a non profit organization by IAOTP 2018   (USA)
(International Association of Top Professionals) see Press Release   IAOTP

Other Awards:

Top National Sales Award as #1 in all of Canada CIBC   (Canada)
All Nigeria Open Badminton Championship – 2 Gold Medals   (Nigeria)
All Round Best Student "Tamgha-e-Seerat"   (Pakistan)

You tube: btg/org (website under review & update as: Btg4u)

Face book: 'Bridging the Gap Productions', and 'Zohra Zoberi's True Colours'

zohraz123@hotmail.com
416 433 5607